New Developments in Geometric Function Theory

New Developments in Geometric Function Theory

Editor

Georgia Irina Oros

MDPI • Basel • Beijing • Wuhan • Barcelona • Belgrade • Manchester • Tokyo • Cluj • Tianjin

Editor
Georgia Irina Oros
Department of Mathematics
and Computer Science
University of Oradea
Oradea
Romania

Editorial Office
MDPI
St. Alban-Anlage 66
4052 Basel, Switzerland

This is a reprint of articles from the Special Issue published online in the open access journal *Axioms* (ISSN 2075-1680) (available at: www.mdpi.com/journal/axioms/special_issues/Geometric_Function_Theory).

For citation purposes, cite each article independently as indicated on the article page online and as indicated below:

LastName, A.A.; LastName, B.B.; LastName, C.C. Article Title. *Journal Name* **Year**, *Volume Number*, Page Range.

ISBN 978-3-0365-6345-9 (Hbk)
ISBN 978-3-0365-6344-2 (PDF)

© 2023 by the authors. Articles in this book are Open Access and distributed under the Creative Commons Attribution (CC BY) license, which allows users to download, copy and build upon published articles, as long as the author and publisher are properly credited, which ensures maximum dissemination and a wider impact of our publications.

The book as a whole is distributed by MDPI under the terms and conditions of the Creative Commons license CC BY-NC-ND.

Contents

About the Editor vii

Georgia Irina Oros
New Developments in Geometric Function Theory
Reprinted from: *Axioms* 2023, 12, 59, doi:10.3390/axioms12010059 1

Richard D. Carmichael
Generalized Vector-Valued Hardy Functions
Reprinted from: *Axioms* 2022, 11, 39, doi:10.3390/axioms11020039 5

Hatun Özlem Güney, Georgia Irina Oros and Shigeyoshi Owa
An Application of Sălăgean Operator Concerning Starlike Functions
Reprinted from: *Axioms* 2022, 11, 50, doi:10.3390/axioms11020050 29

Gangadharan Murugusundaramoorthy and Teodor Bulboacă
Subclasses of Yamakawa-Type Bi-Starlike Functions Associated with Gegenbauer Polynomials
Reprinted from: *Axioms* 2022, 11, 92, doi:10.3390/axioms11030092 39

Alaa H. El-Qadeem and Ibrahim S. Elshazly
Hadamard Product Properties for Certain Subclasses of p-Valent Meromorphic Functions
Reprinted from: *Axioms* 2022, 11, 172, doi:10.3390/axioms11040172 53

Georgia Irina Oros, Gheorghe Oros and Ancuţa Maria Rus
Applications of Confluent Hypergeometric Function in Strong Superordination Theory
Reprinted from: *Axioms* 2022, 11, 209, doi:10.3390/axioms11050209 65

Alhanouf Alburaikan, Gangadharan Murugusundaramoorthy and Sheza M. El-Deeb
Certain Subclasses of Bi-Starlike Function of Complex Order Defined by Erdély–Kober-Type Integral Operator
Reprinted from: *Axioms* 2022, 11, 237, doi:10.3390/axioms11050237 79

Feras Yousef, Ala Amourah, Basem Aref Frasin and Teodor Bulboacă
An Avant-Garde Construction for Subclasses of Analytic Bi-Univalent Functions
Reprinted from: *Axioms* 2022, 11, 267, doi:10.3390/axioms11060267 93

Sevtap Sümer Eker, Bilal Şeker, Bilal Çekiç and Mugur Acu
Sharp Bounds for the Second Hankel Determinant of Logarithmic Coefficients for Strongly Starlike and Strongly Convex Functions
Reprinted from: *Axioms* 2022, 11, 369, doi:10.3390/axioms11080369 101

Luminiţa-Ioana Cotîrlă, Pál Aurel Kupán and Róbert Szász
New Results about Radius of Convexity and Uniform Convexity of Bessel Functions
Reprinted from: *Axioms* 2022, 11, 380, doi:10.3390/axioms11080380 115

Richard D. Carmichael
Cauchy Integral and Boundary Value for Vector-Valued Tempered Distributions
Reprinted from: *Axioms* 2022, 11, 392, doi:10.3390/axioms11080392 125

Alina Alb Lupaş
On Special Fuzzy Differential Subordinations Obtained for Riemann–Liouville Fractional Integral of Ruscheweyh and Sălă
Reprinted from: *Axioms* 2022, 11, 428, doi:10.3390/axioms11090428 139

Isra Al-Shbeil, Abbas Kareem Wanas, Afis Saliu and Adriana Cătaş
Applications of Beta Negative Binomial Distribution and Laguerre Polynomials on Ozaki Bi-Close-to-Convex Functions
Reprinted from: *Axioms* **2022**, *11*, 451, doi:10.3390/axioms11090451 . . . . **153**

Samir B. Hadid and Rabha W. Ibrahim
Geometric Study of 2D-Wave Equations in View of K-Symbol Airy Functions
Reprinted from: *Axioms* **2022**, *11*, 590, doi:10.3390/axioms11110590 . . . . **161**

Mohammad Faisal Khan, Shahid Khan, Saqib Hussain, Maslina Darus and Khaled Matarneh
Certain New Class of Analytic Functions Defined by Using a Fractional Derivative and Mittag-Leffler Functions
Reprinted from: *Axioms* **2022**, *11*, 655, doi:10.3390/axioms11110655 . . . . **173**

About the Editor

Georgia Irina Oros

Georgia Irina Oros teaches at University of Oradea, Romania, since 2004. She is Associate Professor at Faculty of Informatics and Sciences, Department of Mathematics and Computer Science since 2013. She obtained her Ph.D. in 2006 in Geometric Function Theory at Babeș-Bolyai University, Cluj-Napoca, Romania under the supervision of Prof. dr. Grigore Ștefan Sălăgean. Habilitation Thesis defended in 2018 at Babeș-Bolyai University, Cluj-Napoca, Romania. She has over 100 papers published in the field of Complex Analysis and Geometric Function Theory.

Editorial

New Developments in Geometric Function Theory

Georgia Irina Oros

Department of Mathematics and Computer Science, Faculty of Informatics and Sciences, University of Oradea, RO-410087 Oradea, Romania; georgia_oros_ro@yahoo.co.uk

1. Introduction

This Special Issue aims to highlight the latest developments in the research concerning complex-valued functions from the perspective of geometric function theory. Contributions were sought regarding any aspect of subordination and superordination, different types of operators specific to the research in this field, and special functions involved in univalent function theory with the hope that new approaches would emerge regarding the introduction and study of special classes of univalent functions using operators and the classical theories of differential subordination and superordination, as well as the newer adapted theories of strong differential subordination and superordination and fuzzy differential subordination and superordination. Authors were invited to submit their latest results related to analytic functions in all their variety and also related to their applications in other fields of research. Quantum calculus and its applications related to geometric function theory were also expected to provide interesting outcomes. The presentation of the results obtained by using any other technique that can be applied in the field of complex analysis and its applications was also encouraged.

This Special Issue is devoted especially to complex analysis and was proposed as a means to find new approaches using geometric function theory, to inspire further development in this field.

2. Overview of the Published Papers

The present Special Issue contains 14 papers accepted for publication after a rigorous reviewing process.

In the study [1], Richard D. Carmichael considers vector-valued analytic functions and distributions with values in Banach or Hilbert space. It is proved that certain vector-valued measurable functions generate the analytic functions using the Fourier–Laplace transform, and conversely, measurable functions are generated from the analytic functions, and it is shown that the analytic functions are representable through the generated measurable functions. Certain specific properties are obtained for the analytic functions and measurable functions, and it is proved that, under specified conditions, the analytic functions considered are in fact vector-valued Hardy functions, which immediately result in Cauchy and Poisson integral representations. The existence of boundary values of the analytic functions on the topological boundary is investigated, and problems to consider in future research are suggested. Notably, the author is convinced that future studies can focus on the integral representation, boundary values, and applications of the functions defined in this paper.

In another study [2], Hatun Özlem Güney, Georgia Irina Oros, and Shigeyoshi Owa provide an application of the well-known Sălăgean differential operator for defining a new operator, through which a new class of functions is defined, which has the classes of starlike and convex functions of order α as special cases. The renowned Jack–Miller–Mocanu lemma is applied for obtaining interesting properties for the newly defined class of functions. The new operator defined in this paper can be used to introduce other specific

Citation: Oros, G.I. New Developments in Geometric Function Theory. *Axioms* **2023**, *12*, 59. https://doi.org/10.3390/axioms12010059

Received: 28 December 2022
Accepted: 1 January 2023
Published: 4 January 2023

Copyright: © 2023 by the author. Licensee MDPI, Basel, Switzerland. This article is an open access article distributed under the terms and conditions of the Creative Commons Attribution (CC BY) license (https://creativecommons.org/licenses/by/4.0/).

subclasses of analytic functions, and quantum calculus can be also investigated in future studies.

The research of Gangadharan Murugusundaramoorthy and Teodor Bulboacă presented in reference [3] involves the new subclasses of bi-univalent functions defined in the open-unit disk, which are associated with the Gegenbauer polynomials and satisfy subordination conditions. Coefficient estimates are established for the defined classes, and the remarkable Fekete–Szegő problem is also considered. For particular values of the parameters involved in the definition of the classes, the results obtained in this paper provide new insights into the Yamakawa family of bi-starlike functions associated with the Chebyshev and Legendre polynomials, which are left as an exercise to interested readers.

The authors of reference [4], Alaa H. El-Qadeem and Ibrahim S. Elshazly, study the Hadamard product features of certain subclasses of p-valent meromorphic functions defined in the punctured open-unit disc using the q-difference operator. Convolution properties and coefficient estimates are also established regarding the new subclasses defined in this study. The authors suggest that future researchers focus on the use of these subclasses in studies involving the theories of differential subordination and superordination and also the investigation of the Fekete–Szegő problem.

In the research presented in reference [5], Georgia Irina Oros, Gheorghe Oros, and Ancuța Maria Rus use the confluent hypergeometric function embedded in the theory of strong differential superordinations. The form of the confluent hypergeometric function and that of the previously defined Kummer–Bernardi and Kummer–Libera operators are adopted by considering certain classes of analytic functions depending on an extra parameter previously introduced related to the theory of strong differential subordination and superordination. Strong differential superordinations are investigated, and the best subordinates are given. The applications of the established theoretical results are illustrated through two examples. As potential future studies, the authors suggest the use of the dual notion of strong differential subordination for investigations concerning the confluent hypergeometric function and the two operators used in the present study, which could yield sandwich-type results if combined with the results contained in this paper.

The topic of introducing new subclasses of bi-starlike and bi-convex functions of a complex order associated with the Erdély–Kober-type integral operator in the open-unit disc is considered by Alhanouf Alburaikan, Gangadharan Murugusundaramoorthy, and Sheza M. El-Deeb [6]. The estimates of initial coefficients are given, and Fekete–Szegő inequalities are investigated for the functions in those classes. Several consequences of the results are also highlighted as examples.

For the study presented in reference [7], Feras Yousef, Ala Amourah, Basem Aref Frasin, and Teodor Bulboacă again consider certain new subclasses of bi-univalent functions by exploiting the zero-truncated Poisson distribution probabilities and involving Gegenbauer polynomials and the concept of subordination. Coefficient-related problems are investigated, and the Fekete–Szegő functional problem is solved for those classes. The authors suggest that the results offered in this paper would lead to other different new results involving Legendre and Chebyshev polynomials.

Considering the importance of the logarithmic coefficients, in reference [8], Sevtap Sümer Eker, Bilal Şeker, Bilal Çekiç, and Mugur Acu obtain the sharp bounds for the second Hankel determinant concerning the logarithmic coefficients of strongly starlike functions and strongly convex functions. The results presented here could inspire further studies that focus on other subclasses of univalent functions and obtain the boundaries for higher-order Hankel determinants.

New results on the radius of uniform convexity of two kinds of normalization of the Bessel function J_ν in the case of $\nu \in (-2, -1)$ are presented by Luminița-Ioana Cotîrlă, Pál Aurel Kupán, and Róbert Szász in reference [9]. This study provides alternative proof regarding the radius of convexity of order alpha. The authors also provide alternative proof regarding the radius of convexity of order alpha and derive an interesting correlation between convexity and uniform convexity.

The research presented by Richard D. Carmichael in reference [10] is connected to the results obtained in reference [1]. A boundary value result concerning vector-valued tempered distributions as the boundary values of vector-valued analytic functions is given under the general norm growth on the analytic function, which is equivalent to the growth of Tillmann. The second goal of this paper was to obtain a Cauchy integral representation of the analytic functions by using the generally known structure of the spectral function and the structure of the tempered distributional boundary value. The analytic function used to obtain the boundary value was equated to the product of a polynomial and the constructed Cauchy integral. This paper concerns theoretical mathematics; however, the considered topics find applications in mathematical physics and the field of mathematics involving physical problems.

New results are obtained concerning fuzzy differential subordination theory and are highlighted by Alina Alb Lupaş [11]. A previously introduced operator defined by applying the Riemann–Liouville fractional integral to the convex combination of well-known Ruscheweyh and Sălăgean differential operators is used for defining a new fuzzy subclass. The convex property of this class is proved, and certain fuzzy differential subordinations involving the functions from this class and the operator mentioned earlier are obtained. The best fuzzy dominants are given for the considered fuzzy differential subordinations in theorems, and interesting corollaries emerge when specific functions with remarkable geometric properties are used as the best fuzzy dominants. Inspired by the research presented here, researchers can apply the operator used in this paper in future studies for the introduction of other subclasses of analytic functions. The dual theory of fuzzy differential superordination can also be used for obtaining similar results involving the operator and the class defined in this paper.

Using beta-negative binomial distribution series and Laguerre polynomials, Isra Al-Shbeil, Abbas Kareem Wanas, Afis Saliu, and Adriana Cătaş [12] investigate a new family of normalized holomorphic and bi-univalent functions associated with Ozaki close-to-convex functions. They provide estimates on the initial Taylor–Maclaurin coefficients and discuss Fekete–Szegő type inequality for the functions in this family in the special case of generalized Laguerre polynomials.

A symmetric–convex differential formula of normalized Airy functions in the open-unit disk is developed by Samir B. Hadid and Rabha W. Ibrahim in reference [13]. The equation is taken into account as a differential operator in the development of a class of normalized analytic functions. Two-dimensional wave propagation in the earth–ionosphere wave path using k-symbol Airy functions is used for the investigation. It is shown that the standard wave-mode working formula may be determined by orthogonality considerations without the use of intricate justifications of the complex plane.

The applications of fractional differential operators in the field of geometric function theory are obtained by Mohammad Faisal Khan, Shahid Khan, Saqib Hussain, Maslina Darus, and Khaled Matarneh in reference [14]. The fractional differential operator and the Mittag–Leffler functions are combined to formulate and arrange a new operator of fractional calculus. A new class of normalized analytic functions is introduced using the newly defined fractional operator, and some of its interesting geometric properties are discussed in the open-unit disk. The authors suggest that the operator introduced here can be utilized to define other classes of analytic functions or to generalize other types of differential operators.

3. Conclusions

The 14 papers published as part of this Special Issue entitled "New Developments in Geometric Function Theory" concern a broad range of subjects. Researchers interested in different aspects of geometric function theory and its related topics would find interesting insights and inspiring results, leading to increased reference to these contributions and the propagation of this Special Issue to a large audience.

Acknowledgments: The guest editor of this Special Issue would like to thank all the authors who decided to submit their works and have contributed to the success of this Special Issue, as well as all the reviewers for their time, constructive remarks, and help in maintaining high standards for the published materials. Special thanks are also given to the editors of *Axioms* and especially to the Managing Editor of this Special Issue, Alex Zhang.

Conflicts of Interest: The author declares no conflict of interest.

References

1. Carmichael, R.D. Generalized Vector-Valued Hardy Functions. *Axioms* **2022**, *11*, 39. [CrossRef]
2. Güney, H.Ö.; Oros, G.I.; Owa, S. An Application of Sălăgean Operator Concerning Starlike Functions. *Axioms* **2022**, *11*, 50. [CrossRef]
3. Murugusundaramoorthy, G.; Bulboacă, T. Subclasses of Yamakawa-Type Bi-Starlike Functions Associated with Gegenbauer Polynomials. *Axioms* **2022**, *11*, 92. [CrossRef]
4. El-Qadeem, A.H.; Elshazly, I.S. Hadamard Product Properties for Certain Subclasses of *p*-Valent Meromorphic Functions. *Axioms* **2022**, *11*, 172. [CrossRef]
5. Oros, G.I.; Oros, G.; Rus, A.M. Applications of Confluent Hypergeometric Function in Strong Superordination Theory. *Axioms* **2022**, *11*, 209. [CrossRef]
6. Alburaikan, A.; Murugusundaramoorthy, G.; El-Deeb, S.M. Certain Subclasses of Bi-Starlike Function of Complex Order Defined by Erdély–Kober-Type Integral Operator. *Axioms* **2022**, *11*, 237. [CrossRef]
7. Yousef, F.; Amourah, A.; Frasin, B.A.; Bulboacă, T. An Avant-Garde Construction for Subclasses of Analytic Bi-Univalent Functions. *Axioms* **2022**, *11*, 267. [CrossRef]
8. Sümer Eker, S.; Şeker, B.; Çekiç, B.; Acu, M. Sharp Bounds for the Second Hankel Determinant of Logarithmic Coefficients for Strongly Starlike and Strongly Convex Functions. *Axioms* **2022**, *11*, 369. [CrossRef]
9. Cotîrlă, L.-I.; Kupán, P.A.; Szász, R. New Results about Radius of Convexity and Uniform Convexity of Bessel Functions. *Axioms* **2022**, *11*, 380. [CrossRef]
10. Carmichael, R.D. Cauchy Integral and Boundary Value for Vector-Valued Tempered Distributions. *Axioms* **2022**, *11*, 392. [CrossRef]
11. Alb Lupaş, A. On Special Fuzzy Differential Subordinations Obtained for Riemann–Liouville Fractional Integral of Ruscheweyh and Sălăgean Operators. *Axioms* **2022**, *11*, 428. [CrossRef]
12. Al-Shbeil, I.; Wanas, A.K.; Saliu, A.; Cătaş, A. Applications of Beta Negative Binomial Distribution and Laguerre Polynomials on Ozaki Bi-Close-to-Convex Functions. *Axioms* **2022**, *11*, 451. [CrossRef]
13. Hadid, S.B.; Ibrahim, R.W. Geometric Study of 2D-Wave Equations in View of K-Symbol Airy Functions. *Axioms* **2022**, *11*, 590. [CrossRef]
14. Khan, M.F.; Khan, S.; Hussain, S.; Darus, M.; Matarneh, K. Certain New Class of Analytic Functions Defined by Using a Fractional Derivative and Mittag-Leffler Functions. *Axioms* **2022**, *11*, 655. [CrossRef]

Disclaimer/Publisher's Note: The statements, opinions and data contained in all publications are solely those of the individual author(s) and contributor(s) and not of MDPI and/or the editor(s). MDPI and/or the editor(s) disclaim responsibility for any injury to people or property resulting from any ideas, methods, instructions or products referred to in the content.

Article

Generalized Vector-Valued Hardy Functions

Richard D. Carmichael

Department of Mathematics and Statistics, Wake Forest University, Winston-Salem, NC 27109, USA; carmicha@wfu.edu

Abstract: We consider analytic functions in tubes $\mathbb{R}^n + iB \subset \mathbb{C}^n$ with values in Banach space or Hilbert space. The base of the tube B will be a proper open connected subset of $\mathbb{R}^n$, an open connected cone in $\mathbb{R}^n$, an open convex cone in $\mathbb{R}^n$, and a regular cone in $\mathbb{R}^n$, with this latter cone being an open convex cone which does not contain any entire straight lines. The analytic functions satisfy several different growth conditions in L^p norm, and all of the resulting spaces of analytic functions generalize the vector valued Hardy space H^p in $\mathbb{C}^n$. The analytic functions are represented as the Fourier–Laplace transform of certain vector valued L^p functions which are characterized in the analysis. We give a characterization of the spaces of analytic functions in which the spaces are in fact subsets of the Hardy functions H^p. We obtain boundary value results on the distinguished boundary $\mathbb{R}^n + i\{\overline{0}\}$ and on the topological boundary $\mathbb{R}^n + i\partial B$ of the tube for the analytic functions in the L^p and vector valued tempered distribution topologies. Suggestions for associated future research are given.

Keywords: analytic functions; vector valued Hardy functions; boundary values

MSC: 32A26; 32A35; 32A40; 42B30

Citation: Carmichael, R.D. Generalized Vector-Valued Hardy Functions. *Axioms* **2022**, *11*, 39. https://doi.org/10.3390/axioms11020039

Academic Editor: Georgia Irina Oros

Received: 18 December 2021
Accepted: 17 January 2022
Published: 20 January 2022

Publisher's Note: MDPI stays neutral with regard to jurisdictional claims in published maps and institutional affiliations.

Copyright: © 2022 by the authors. Licensee MDPI, Basel, Switzerland. This article is an open access article distributed under the terms and conditions of the Creative Commons Attribution (CC BY) license (https://creativecommons.org/licenses/by/4.0/).

1. Introduction

In [1] and related work, we defined and analyzed vector-valued Hardy $H^p(T^B, \mathcal{X})$ functions on tubes $T^B = \mathbb{R}^n + iB \subset \mathbb{C}^n$ with values in Banach space $\mathcal{X}$. We showed that any Banach space $\mathcal{X}$ vector-valued analytic function on T^B which obtained a $\mathcal{X}$ vector-valued distributional boundary value was a $H^p(T^B, \mathcal{X})$, $1 \leq p \leq \infty$, function with values in Banach space $\mathcal{X}$ if the $\mathcal{X}$ vector-valued boundary value was a $L^p(\mathbb{R}^n, \mathcal{X})$, $1 \leq p \leq \infty$, function. We showed that the $H^p(T^B, \mathcal{X})$, $1 \leq p \leq \infty$, functions admitted a representation by the Poisson integral of $L^p(\mathbb{R}^n, \mathcal{X})$, $1 \leq p \leq \infty$, functions if the values of the analytic functions were in a certain type of Banach space and then obtained a pointwise growth estimate for the $H^p(T^B, \mathcal{X})$ functions for this Banach space. In additional analysis, we have obtained many general results concerning $H^p(T^B, \mathcal{X})$ functions with values in Banach space including representations as Fourier–Laplace, Cauchy, and Poisson integrals and the existence of boundary values.

Previously, we defined generalizations of $H^p(T^B)$ functions in the scalar-valued case by using several more general growth conditions on the L^p norm of the analytic functions. Some of these scalar-valued results are contained in [2] (Chapter 5); other such results in the scalar-valued case are contained in papers listed under the author's name in the references in [1,2]. In this paper, we build upon these scalar-valued generalizations of $H^p(T^B)$ functions by considering the vector-valued case of functions and distributions with values in Banach or Hilbert space. The generalizations of the vector-valued analytic functions in $H^p(T^B, \mathcal{X})$, $\mathcal{X}$ being a Banach space, which we consider here are defined in Section 4 of this paper. Our results are obtained for the base B of the tube T^B successively being a proper open connected subset of $\mathbb{R}^n$, an open connected cone in $\mathbb{R}^n$, an open convex cone in $\mathbb{R}^n$, and a regular cone in $\mathbb{R}^n$, with this latter cone being an open convex cone which does not contain any entire straight lines; as the base B of the tube T^B is specialized, increasingly precise results are obtained in the analysis. For B being a proper open connected subset of $\mathbb{R}^n$ we show, for example, that the growth condition that defines the functions which generalize the Hardy functions can, in certain circumstances, be extended to the boundary of the base B of the tube T^B. At the open convex cone stage in our analysis we are able to show the equivalence of two types of vector-valued functions which generate $H^p(T^B, \mathcal{X})$ functions. In the cone setting for base B we show that certain elements of the defined analytic functions are in fact $H^p(T^B)$ functions which leads to the representation of these functions as Fourier–Laplace, Cauchy, and Poisson integrals. In the case that B is a regular cone we study the boundary values on the topological boundary of the tube defined by the cone as points in B approach a point on its boundary through circular bands within B. In general, our goal in this paper is to obtain results for the functions defined in Section 4 treated as generalizations of $H^p(T^B, \mathcal{X})$ functions and as generalizations of the scalar-valued functions noted in [2] (Chapter 5) and in some of our papers referenced in [2] and hence to generalize results concerning $H^p(T^B, \mathcal{X})$ spaces and concerning the scalar-valued functions noted in [2] (Chapter 5) and in certain references of [2] to these new spaces of analytic functions. Additionally, our goal is to obtain additional new results for the analytic functions of Section 4 which we accomplish.

As noted above, the vector-valued analytic functions considered in this paper are defined in Section 4. In Section 5, we show that certain vector-valued measurable functions generate the analytic functions by the Fourier–Laplace transform; conversely, in Section 6, we generate the measurable functions from the analytic functions and show that the analytic functions are representable through the generated measurable functions. As the base B of the tube T^B is made more specific the analytic functions and measurable functions obtain more specific properties. In Section 7, we show that under specified conditions the analytic functions considered are in fact vector-valued Hardy H^2 functions which immediately results in Cauchy and Poisson integral representations. Section 8 concerns the existence of boundary values of the analytic functions in vector-valued L^p and in vector-valued $\mathcal{S}'$ topologies on both the distinguished boundary and the topological boundary of the tube. Problems for future research are considered in Section 9, and conclusions are provided in Section 10.

2. Definitions and Notation

Throughout, $\mathcal{X}$ will denote a Banach space, $\mathcal{H}$ will denote a Hilbert space, $\mathcal{N}$ will denote the norm of the specified Banach or Hilbert space, and Θ will denote the zero vector of the specified Banach or Hilbert space. We reference Dunford and Schwartz [3] for integration of vector-valued functions and for vector-valued analytic functions. For foundational information concerning vector-valued distributions we refer to Schwartz ([4,5]).

The n-dimensional notation used in this paper will be the same as that in [1,2]. The information concerning cones in $\mathbb{R}^n$ needed here is contained in [2] (Chapter 1). We recall some very important notation and concepts of cones here that are necessary for this paper. $C \subset \mathbb{R}^n$ is a cone (with vertex at $\bar{0} = (0,0,...,0) \in \mathbb{R}^n$) if $y \in C$ implies $\lambda y \in C$ for all positive scalars λ. The intersection of C with the unit sphere $|y| = 1$ is called the projection of C and is denoted $pr(C)$. A cone C' such that $pr(\overline{C'}) \subset pr(C)$ is a compact subcone of C which we will denote as $C' \subset\subset C$. The function

$$u_C(t) = \sup_{y \in pr(C)} (-\langle t, y \rangle), \ t \in \mathbb{R}^n,$$

is the indicatrix of C. The dual cone C^* of C is defined as

$$C^* = \{t \in \mathbb{R}^n : \langle t, y \rangle \geq 0 \text{ for all } y \in C\}$$

and satisfies $C^* = \{t \in \mathbb{R}^n : u_C(t) \leq 0\}$. An open convex cone which does not contain any entire straight lines will be called a regular cone. See [2] (Section 1.2) for examples of cones in $\mathbb{R}^n$. In this paper, we will be concerned with the distance from a point in a cone to the boundary of the cone; for C being an open connected cone in $\mathbb{R}^n$, the distance from $y \in C$ to the topological boundary ∂C of C is

$$d(y) = \inf\{|y - y_1| : y_1 \in \partial C\}.$$

For an open connected cone $C \subset \mathbb{R}^n$, we know from [2] (p. 6, (1.14)) that

$$d(y) = \inf_{t \in pr(C^*)} \langle t, y \rangle, \ y \in C,$$

and $0 < d(y) \leq |y|$, $y \in C$. Additionally, $d(\lambda y) = \lambda d(y), \lambda > 0$.

The $L^p(\mathbb{R}^n, \mathcal{X})$ functions, $1 \leq p \leq \infty$, with values in $\mathcal{X}$ and their norm $|\mathbf{h}|_p$ are noted in [3] (Chapter III). The Fourier transform on $L^1(\mathbb{R}^n)$ or $L^1(\mathbb{R}^n, \mathcal{X})$ is given in [2] (p. 3). All Fourier (inverse Fourier) transforms on scalar or vector-valued functions will be denoted $\hat{\phi} = \mathcal{F}[\phi(t); x]$ ($\mathcal{F}^{-1}[\phi(t); x]$). As stated in [6] the Plancherel theory is not true for vector-valued functions except when $\mathcal{X} = \mathcal{H}$, a Hilbert space. The Plancherel theory is complete in the $L^2(\mathbb{R}^n, \mathcal{H})$ setting in that the inverse Fourier transform is the inverse mapping of the Fourier transform with $\mathcal{F}^{-1}\mathcal{F} = I = \mathcal{F}\mathcal{F}^{-1}$ with I being the identity mapping.

As usual, we denote $\mathcal{S}(\mathbb{R}^n)$ as the tempered functions with associated distributions being $\mathcal{S}'(\mathbb{R}^n)$ or associated vector-valued distributions being $\mathcal{S}'(\mathbb{R}^n, \mathcal{X})$. The Fourier transform on $\mathcal{S}'(\mathbb{R}^n)$ and on $\mathcal{S}'(\mathbb{R}^n, \mathcal{X})$ is the usual such definition and is given in [4] (p. 73).

Let B be an open subset of $\mathbb{R}^n$ and $\mathcal{X}$ be a Banach space. The Hardy space $H^p(T^B, \mathcal{X})$, $0 < p < \infty$, consists of those analytic functions $\mathbf{f}(z)$ on the tube $T^B = \mathbb{R}^n + iB \subset \mathbb{C}^n$ with values in the Banach space $\mathcal{X}$ such that for some constant $M > 0$ and every $y \in B$

$$\int_{\mathbb{R}^n} (\mathcal{N}(\mathbf{f}(x + iy)))^p dx \leq M;$$

the usual modification is made for the case $p = \infty$.

3. Cauchy and Poisson Kernels and Integrals

Let C be a regular cone in $\mathbb{R}^n$. C^* is the dual cone of C. The Cauchy kernel corresponding to $T^C = \mathbb{R}^n + iC$ is

$$K(z - t) = \int_{C^*} e^{2\pi i \langle z - t, \eta \rangle} d\eta, \ t \in \mathbb{R}^n, \ z \in T^C.$$

The Poisson kernel corresponding to T^C is

$$Q(z; t) = \frac{K(z - t)\overline{K(z - t)}}{K(2iy)} = \frac{|K(z - t)|^2}{K(2iy)}, \ t \in \mathbb{R}^n, \ z \in T^C.$$

Referring to [2] (Chapters 1 and 4) for details, we know for $z \in T^C$ that $K(z - \cdot) \in \mathcal{D}(*, L^p) \subset \mathcal{D}_{L^p}$, $1 < p \leq \infty$; and $Q(z; \cdot) \in \mathcal{D}(*, L^p) \subset \mathcal{D}_{L^p}$, $1 \leq p \leq \infty$, where $*$ is Beurling (M_p) or Roumieu $\{M_p\}$. These ultradifferentiable functions are contained in the Schwartz space $\mathcal{D}_{L^p} = \mathcal{D}(L^p, \mathbb{R}^n)$. Because of the combined properties of the Cauchy and Poisson kernels from [2], we know that the Cauchy and Poisson integrals

$$\int_{\mathbb{R}^n} \mathbf{h}(t) K(z - t) dt, \ z \in T^C,$$

and

$$\int_{\mathbb{R}^n} \mathbf{h}(t) Q(z; t) dt, \ z \in T^C,$$

are well defined for $\mathbf{h} \in L^p(\mathbb{R}^n, \mathcal{X})$, $1 \leq p < \infty$, and $\mathbf{h} \in L^p(\mathbb{R}^n, \mathcal{X})$, $1 \leq p \leq \infty$, respectively, for $\mathcal{X}$ being a Banach space.

We conclude this section with a boundary value calculation concerning the integral which defines the Cauchy kernel. Our calculations here provide motivation and guidance for boundary value results concerning the analytic functions considered in this paper which we obtain subsequently. Let C be a regular cone and put

$$K(z) = \int_{C^*} e^{2\pi i \langle z, t \rangle} dt, \ z \in T^C.$$

We know that $K(z)$ is analytic in T^C and is a bounded function of $x \in \mathbb{R}^n$ for $y \in C$. Thus, $K(x+iy) \in \mathcal{S}'(\mathbb{R}^n)$ as a function of $x \in \mathbb{R}^n$ for $y \in C$. Let $I_{C^*}(t)$ denote the characteristic function of C^*. We have the following result concerning points on the boundary of C, ∂C.

Theorem 1. *Let $y_o \in \partial C$. We have*

$$\lim_{y \to y_o, y \in C} K(x+iy) = \mathcal{F}[I_{C^*}(t) e^{-2\pi \langle y_o, t \rangle}]$$

in the strong topology of $\mathcal{S}'(\mathbb{R}^n)$.

Proof. For $y_o \in \partial C$, choose a sequence of points $\{y_m\}$, $m = 1, 2, ...,$ in C which converges to y_o. We have

$$\langle y_o, t \rangle = \lim_{y_m \to y_o} \langle y_m, t \rangle \geq 0, \ t \in C^*.$$

Thus, $e^{-2\pi \langle y_o, t \rangle} I_{C^*}(t) \in \mathcal{S}'(\mathbb{R}^n)$ and $\mathcal{F}[e^{-2\pi \langle y_o, t \rangle} I_{C^*}(t)] \in \mathcal{S}'(\mathbb{R}^n)$. Let $\phi \in \mathcal{S}(\mathbb{R}^n)$ and $y \in C$.

$$\langle K(x+iy) - \mathcal{F}[e^{-2\pi \langle y_o, t \rangle} I_{C^*}(t)], \phi(x) \rangle$$
$$= \langle \mathcal{F}[(e^{-2\pi \langle y, t \rangle} - e^{-2\pi \langle y_o, t \rangle}) I_{C^*}(t)], \phi(x) \rangle$$
$$= \langle (e^{-2\pi \langle y, t \rangle} - e^{-2\pi \langle y_o, t \rangle}) I_{C^*}(t), \widehat{\phi}(t) \rangle.$$

Now

$$|(e^{-2\pi \langle y, t \rangle} - e^{-2\pi \langle y_o, t \rangle}) I_{C^*}(t) \widehat{\phi}(t)| \leq (e^{-2\pi \langle y, t \rangle} + e^{-2\pi \langle y_o, t \rangle}) I_{C^*}(t) |\widehat{\phi}(t)| \leq 2|\widehat{\phi}(t)|.$$

By the Lebesgue dominated convergence theorem, we have

$$\lim_{y \to y_o, y \in C} K(x+iy) = \mathcal{F}[I_{C^*}(t) e^{-2\pi \langle y_o, t \rangle}]$$

in the weak topology of $\mathcal{S}'(\mathbb{R}^n)$. Since $\mathcal{S}(\mathbb{R}^n)$ is a Montel space we have this convergence in the strong topology of $\mathcal{S}'(\mathbb{R}^n)$ also. □

In Theorem 1, notice that $\overline{0}$ is on the boundary of C. Thus, for $y_o = \overline{0}$,

$$\lim_{y \to \overline{0}, y \in C} K(x+iy) = \mathcal{F}[I_{C^*}(t)]$$

in the strong topology of $\mathcal{S}'(\mathbb{R}^n)$ in the conclusion of Theorem 1.

4. The Analytic Functions

As previously noted, we have studied vector-valued Hardy spaces in [1]; previous to this analysis we had generalized scalar-valued Hardy spaces by placing a more general bound on the L^p norm of the scalar-valued analytic function. These main scalar-valued generalizations are contained in [2] with other related work referenced in [2]. In the scalar-valued generalizations, we obtained Fourier–Laplace transform representation of the analytic functions and characterized the measurable function which generated this representation along with related results.

Given our recent work in studying vector-valued Hardy spaces, we now desire to study vector-valued generalizations of vector-valued Hardy spaces.

In this section, we introduce and define the vector-valued analytic functions that we study here. Throughout this section, B will denote a proper open connected subset of $\mathbb{R}^n$ unless stated otherwise; and, as previously stated, $\mathcal{X}$ will denote a Banach space with norm $\mathcal{N}$.

Definition 1. $H_A^p(T^B, \mathcal{X})$, $1 \leq p < \infty$, is the set of analytic functions $f(z)$ on T^B with values in $\mathcal{X}$ such that

$$|f(x+iy)|_p = \left(\int_{\mathbb{R}^n} (\mathcal{N}(f(x+iy)))^p dx\right)^{1/p} \leq M(1+(d(y))^{-r})^s e^{2\pi A|y|}, \quad y \in B,$$

where $r \geq 0, s \geq 0, A \geq 0$, and $M = M(f, p, A, r, s) > 0$.

Definition 2. $R_A^p(T^B, \mathcal{X})$, $1 \leq p < \infty$, is the set of analytic functions $f(z)$ on T^B with values in $\mathcal{X}$ such that

$$|f(x+iy)|_p \leq M(1+|y|^{-r})^s e^{2\pi A|y|}, \quad y \in B,$$

where $r \geq 0, s \geq 0, A \geq 0$, and $M = M(f, p, A, r, s) > 0$.

Definition 3. $V_A^p(T^B, \mathcal{X})$, $1 \leq p < \infty$, is the set of analytic functions $f(z)$ on T^B with values in $\mathcal{X}$ such that

$$|f(x+iy)|_p \leq M e^{2\pi A|y|}, \quad y \in B,$$

were $A \geq 0$ and $M = M(f, p, A) > 0$.

We consider situations and examples which help emphasize containment of these spaces although the definitions of these sets of functions show the containment in many cases. If B is an open connected cone we know from Section 2 that $d(y) \leq |y|$, $y \in B$; thus, $R_A^p(T^B, \mathcal{X}) \subseteq H_A^p(T^B, \mathcal{X})$ in general in this case. For specific examples which help show proper containment let us just consider scalar-valued analytic functions in half planes in $\mathbb{C}^1$. Let $B = (0, \infty)$; thus, $T^{(0,\infty)} = \mathbb{R}^1 + i(0, \infty)$. We have

$$f(z) = \frac{e^{-2\pi i z}}{z(i+z)} \in R_1^2(T^{(0,\infty)}, \mathbb{C}^1) \cap H_1^2(T^{(0,\infty)}, \mathbb{C}^1), \quad y = \mathrm{Im}(z) \in (0, \infty),$$

as

$$\|f(x+iy)\|_{L^2(\mathbb{R}^1)} \leq \pi^{1/2}(1+y^{-1})e^{2\pi y}, \quad y = \mathrm{Im}(z) > 0;$$

but this $f(z)$ is not in $V_1^2(T^{(0,\infty)}, \mathbb{C}^1)$. We have

$$f(z) = \frac{e^{-2\pi i z}}{i+z} \in V_1^2(T^{(0,\infty)}, \mathbb{C}^1)$$

but is not in $H^2(T^{(0,\infty)}, \mathbb{C}^1)$. Of course $f(z) = 1/(i+z) \in H^2(T^{(0,\infty)}, \mathbb{C}^1)$ and hence is in all of $V_1^2(T^{(0,\infty)}, \mathbb{C}^1), R_1^2(T^{(0,\infty)}, \mathbb{C}^1)$, and $H_1^2(T^{(0,\infty)}, \mathbb{C}^1)$. These examples help to see the containment of the defined spaces and the Hardy functions for most of the specified conditions on the base B of the tube T^B in our analysis in this paper.

For our next set of analytic functions, we must remember properties of sequences M_p, $p = 0, 1, 2, \ldots$, with which ultradifferentiable functions and ultradistributions are defined. These sequences and properties are discussed in [2] (Section 2.1). In this paper, we are principally concerned with the properties $(M.1)$ and $(M.3')$ and with the associated function

$$M^*(\rho) = \sup_p \log(\rho^p p! M_0/M_p), \; 0 < \rho < \infty.$$

With these facts in mind we define additional vector-valued analytic functions.

Definition 4. *For B, being a proper open connected subset of $\mathbb{R}^n$ which does not contain $\bar{0}$, $H^p_*(T^B, \mathcal{X})$, $1 \leq p < \infty$, is the set of analytic functions $f(z)$ on T^B with values in $\mathcal{X}$ such that*

$$|f(x+iy)|_p \leq K(1 + (d(y))^{-r})^s e^{M^*(w/|y|)}, \; y \in B,$$

where $r \geq 0, s \geq 0, w > 0$, and $K = K(f, p, r, s, w) > 0$.

With Definition 4 in place, we can now state definitions for $R^p_*(T^B, \mathcal{X})$ and $V^p_*(T^B, \mathcal{X})$ from Definition 4 similarly as we did for $R^p_A(T^B, \mathcal{X})$ and $V^p_A(T^B, \mathcal{X})$ from Definition 1. In the scalar-valued case, we have proved that the Cauchy integral of ultradistributions $U \in \mathcal{D}'(*, L^p)$, where $*$ is Beurling (M_p) or Roumieu $\{M_p\}$, is analytic in T^C and satisfies the growth of Definition 4 where C is a regular cone in $\mathbb{R}^n$; see [2] (Section 4.2). Additionally, we have obtained boundary value results for scalar-valued functions of the type in Definition 4 in [2] (Chapter 5).

Throughout this paper, results concerning $H^p_*(T^B, \mathcal{X})$ and its subsets and associated norm growth bounds are obtained under the assumption that the sequence of positive numbers M_p, $p = 0, 1, 2, ...$, from which the associated function $M^*(\rho)$ is defined, will always be assumed to satisfy properties $(M.1)$ and $(M.3')$ in [2] (p. 13).

5. Measurable Functions Generating Analytic Functions

The results which we will prove in this paper are obtained for functions in $H^p_A(T^B, \mathcal{X})$ of Definition 1 and for functions in $H^p_*(T^B, \mathcal{X})$ of Definition 4 by very similar methods. The results corresponding to $H^p_A(T^B, \mathcal{X})$ however are somewhat more general in nature than the corresponding ones for $H^p_*(T^B, \mathcal{X})$. Thus, we will concentrate our proofs on the results corresponding to $H^p_A(T^B, \mathcal{X})$ and subsequently state the corresponding results for $H^p_*(T^B, \mathcal{X})$ which will be denoted by a * next to the result number.

We begin by obtaining properties on measurable functions which we will use to generate analytic functions in $H^p_A(T^B, \mathcal{X})$. Let B be a proper open connected subset of $\mathbb{R}^n$ and let $\mathcal{X}$ be a Banach space. Let $1 \leq p < \infty$ and $\mathbf{g}(t)$ be a $\mathcal{X}$ valued measurable function on $\mathbb{R}^n$ such that

$$|e^{-2\pi \langle y, t \rangle} \mathbf{g}(t)|_p \leq M(1 + (d(y))^{-r})^s e^{2\pi A|y|}, \; y \in B, \quad (1)$$

where $r \geq 0, s \geq 0, A \geq 0$, and $M = M(\mathbf{g}, p, A, r, s) > 0$ do not depend on $y \in B$.

Theorem 2. *For B, being a proper open connected subset of $\mathbb{R}^n$ and $\mathcal{X}$ being a Banach space let $g(t)$ be a $\mathcal{X}$ valued measurable function on $\mathbb{R}^n$ such that (1) holds for $y \in B$ and for $1 \leq p < \infty$. We have*

$$f(z) = \int_{\mathbb{R}^n} g(t) e^{2\pi i \langle z, t \rangle} dt, \; z = x + iy \in T^B, \quad (2)$$

is a $\mathcal{X}$ valued analytic function of $z \in T^B$.

Proof. Let $y_o \in B$. Choose an open neighborhood $N(y_o; r)$, $r > 0$, and a compact subset $S \subset B$ such that $y_o \in N(y_o; r) \subset S \subset B$. Decompose $\mathbb{R}^n$ into a union of a finite number of non-overlapping cones $C_1, C_2, ..., C_k$ each having vertex at $\bar{0}$ and such that whenever two points y_1 and y_2 belong to one of these cones the angle between the rays from $\bar{0}$ to y_1 and from $\bar{0}$ to y_2 is less than $\pi/4$ radians; and hence $\langle y_1, y_2 \rangle = |y_1||y_2|\cos(\theta) > |y_1||y_2|2^{1/2}/2$ where θ is the angle between the two rays. There is a $\delta > 0$ such that $0 < \delta < r$ and $\{y : |y - y_o| = \delta\} \subset N(y_o; r)$. Put $\epsilon = 2\pi p \delta / 2^{1/2} > 0$. For each $j = 1, 2, ..., k$ choose a fixed y_j such that $y_o - y_j \in C_j$ and $|y_j - y_o| = \delta$. For each $j = 1, 2, ..., k$ let $t \in C_j$; we have

$$\langle y_o - y_j, t\rangle \geq |y_o - y_j||t|/2^{1/2}, \ t \in C_j, \ j = 1, 2, \ldots, k.$$

Thus, for $t \in C_j$, $j = 1, 2, \ldots, k$,,

$$\epsilon|t| = (2\pi p\delta/2^{1/2})|t| = 2\pi p|y_o - y_j||t|/2^{1/2} \leq 2\pi p\langle y_o - y_j, t\rangle = -2\pi p\langle y_j - y_o, t\rangle.$$

Hence, for each $j = 1, 2, \ldots, k$, using (1) we have

$$\int_{C_j} e^{-2\pi p\langle y_o, t\rangle} e^{\epsilon|t|} (\mathcal{N}(\mathbf{g}(t)))^p dt$$
$$\leq \int_{C_j} e^{-2\pi p\langle y_o, t\rangle} e^{-2\pi p\langle y_j - y_o, t\rangle} (\mathcal{N}(\mathbf{g}(t)))^p dt = \int_{C_j} e^{-2\pi p\langle y_j, t\rangle} (\mathcal{N}(\mathbf{g}(t)))^p dt$$
$$\leq \int_{\mathbb{R}^n} (\mathcal{N}(e^{-2\pi\langle y_j, t\rangle} \mathbf{g}(t)))^p dt \leq M^p (1 + (d(y_j))^{-r})^{sp} e^{2\pi pA|y_j|}$$

and

$$\int_{\mathbb{R}^n} e^{-2\pi p\langle y_o, t\rangle} e^{\epsilon|t|} (\mathcal{N}(\mathbf{g}(t)))^p dt = \sum_{j=1}^{k} \int_{C_j} e^{-2\pi p\langle y_o, t\rangle} e^{\epsilon|t|} (\mathcal{N}(\mathbf{g}(t)))^p dt$$
$$\leq M^p \sum_{j=1}^{k} (1 + (d(y_j))^{-r})^{sp} e^{2\pi pA|y_j|} \tag{3}$$

for arbitrary $y_o \in B$. For $p = 1$ and the fact that $(\epsilon|t|/2) \leq \epsilon|t|$, $t \in \mathbb{R}^n$, we have from (3) that

$$\int_{\mathbb{R}^n} e^{-2\pi\langle y_o, t\rangle} e^{\epsilon|t|/2} \mathcal{N}(\mathbf{g}(t)) dt \leq M \sum_{j=1}^{k} (1 + (d(y_j))^{-r})^{s} e^{2\pi A|y_j|}. \tag{4}$$

For $1 < p < \infty$, Hölder's inequality, the identity $e^{\epsilon|t|/2p} = e^{\epsilon|t|/p} e^{-\epsilon|t|/2p}$ and (3) yield

$$\int_{\mathbb{R}^n} e^{-2\pi\langle y_o, t\rangle} e^{\epsilon|t|/2p} \mathcal{N}(\mathbf{g}(t)) dt \leq ||e^{-\epsilon|t|/2p}||_{L^q(\mathbb{R}^n)} |e^{-2\pi\langle y_o, t\rangle} e^{\epsilon|t|/p} \mathbf{g}(t)|_p$$
$$\leq M ||e^{-\epsilon|t|/2p}||_{L^q(\mathbb{R}^n)} \left(\sum_{j=1}^{k} (1 + (d(y_j))^{-r})^{sp} e^{2\pi pA|y_j|} \right)^{1/p} \tag{5}$$

where $1/p + 1/q = 1$. If $|y - y_o| < \epsilon/4\pi p$, $y = \text{Im}(z)$, $1 \leq p < \infty$, then for $z = x + iy$

$$\mathcal{N}(\mathbf{g}(t) e^{2\pi i\langle z, t\rangle}) = e^{-2\pi\langle y, t\rangle} \mathcal{N}(\mathbf{g}(t)) = e^{-2\pi\langle y - y_o, t\rangle} e^{-2\pi\langle y_o, t\rangle} \mathcal{N}(\mathbf{g}(t))$$
$$\leq e^{2\pi|y - y_o||t|} e^{-2\pi\langle y_o, t\rangle} \mathcal{N}(\mathbf{g}(t)) \leq e^{-2\pi\langle y_o, t\rangle} e^{\epsilon|t|/2p} \mathcal{N}(\mathbf{g}(t)) \tag{6}$$

for all $t \in \mathbb{R}^n$. (4) and (5) now show that the right side of (6) is a $L^1(\mathbb{R}^n)$ function which is independent of $y = \text{Im}(z)$ such that $|y - y_o| < \epsilon/4\pi p$ for all cases $1 \leq p < \infty$. Since $y_o \in B$ is arbitrary we conclude from (6) that $f(z)$ defined by (2) is a $\mathcal{X}$ valued analytic function of $z \in T^B$. Further, (6) proves that $e^{-2\pi\langle y, t\rangle} \mathbf{g}(t) \in L^1(\mathbb{R}^n, \mathcal{X})$, $y \in B$, for all cases $1 \leq p < \infty$ in addition to the fact that $e^{-2\pi\langle y, t\rangle} \mathbf{g}(t) \in L^p(\mathbb{R}^n, \mathcal{X})$, $y \in B$, for each of the specific cases for p, $1 \leq p < \infty$, because of the assumption (1). The proof is complete. □

The exact same method of proof used for Theorem 2 yields the following result corresponding to the growth for $H_*^p(T^B, \mathcal{X})$.

Theorem 3. *Let B be a proper open connected subset of $\mathbb{R}^n$ which does not contain $\overline{0} \in \mathbb{R}^n$, and let $\mathcal{X}$ be a Banach space. Let $1 \leq p < \infty$ and $\mathbf{g}(t)$ be a $\mathcal{X}$ valued measurable function on $\mathbb{R}^n$ such that*

$$|e^{-2\pi\langle y, t\rangle} \mathbf{g}(t)|_p \leq M(1 + (d(y))^{-r})^s e^{M^*(w/|y|)}, \ y \in B,$$

where $r \geq 0, s \geq 0, w > 0$, and $M = M(g, p, r, s, w) > 0$ are independent of $y \in B$. We have

$$f(z) = \int_{\mathbb{R}^n} g(t) e^{2\pi i \langle z, t \rangle} dt, \; z \in T^B,$$

is a $\mathcal{X}$ valued analytic function of $z \in T^B$.

The Fourier transform of vector-valued functions $L^p(\mathbb{R}^n, \mathcal{X})$ with the Plancherel theory and Parseval identity holding occurs only if $p = 2$ and $\mathcal{X} = \mathcal{H}$, a Hilbert space. For $p = 2$ in order to have an isomorphism of the Fourier transform of $L^2(\mathbb{R}^n, \mathcal{X})$ onto itself with the Parseval identity holding it is necessary and sufficient that $\mathcal{X} = \mathcal{H}$, a Hilbert space [6] (pp. 45, 61). We use the Fourier transform considerably in this paper, and its use is the reason we sometimes restrict the result to $p = 2$ and $\mathcal{X} = \mathcal{H}$. We obtain a corollary to Theorem 2.

Corollary 1. *Let B be a proper open connected subset of $\mathbb{R}^n$ and $\mathcal{H}$ be a Hilbert space. Let $g(t)$ be a $\mathcal{H}$ valued measurable function on $\mathbb{R}^n$ such that (1) holds for $p = 2$. We have $f(z) \in H_A^2(T^B, \mathcal{H})$ for $f(z)$ defined in (2).*

Proof. $f(z)$ is analytic in T^B by Theorem 2. By the assumption (1) for $p = 2$ and the proof of Theorem 2, $e^{-2\pi \langle y, t \rangle} g(t) \in L^1(\mathbb{R}^n, \mathcal{H}) \cap L^2(\mathbb{R}^n, \mathcal{H})$ for $y \in B$. Thus, $\mathbf{f}(x + iy) = \mathcal{F}[e^{-2\pi \langle y, t \rangle} \mathbf{g}(t); x]$, $y \in B$, with the Fourier transform being in the $L^1(\mathbb{R}^n, \mathcal{H})$ and the $L^2(\mathbb{R}^n, \mathcal{H})$ cases. By the Parseval equality $|\mathbf{f}(x + iy)|_2 = |e^{-2\pi \langle y, t \rangle} \mathbf{g}(t)|_2$ for $y \in B$. From (1) the desired growth on $\mathbf{f}(x + iy)$ of Definition 1 is obtained, and $f(z) \in H_A^2(T^B, \mathcal{H})$. □

Under certain circumstances, the growth on the $L^2(\mathbb{R}^n, \mathcal{H})$ function $e^{-2\pi \langle y, t \rangle} \mathbf{g}(t), y \in B$, in Corollary 1 can be extended to hold for $y \in \overline{B}$.

Corollary 2. *Assume the hypotheses of Corollary 1 with the addition that (1) holds for $p = 2$ with $r = 0$ or $s = 0$. We have $f(z) \in V_A^2(T^B, \mathcal{H})$ for $f(z)$ defined in (2) and*

$$|e^{-2\pi \langle y, t \rangle} \mathbf{g}(t)|_2 \leq M e^{2\pi A |y|}, \; y \in \overline{B}.$$

Further if $\overline{0} \in \partial B$ then $\mathbf{g} \in L^2(\mathbb{R}^n, \mathcal{H})$.

Proof. From the proof of Corollary 1 and Definition 3, we have $\mathbf{f}(z) \in V_A^2(T^B, \mathcal{H})$ for $r = 0$ or $s = 0$ in (1). Let $y_o \in \partial B$ and let $\{y_m\}$ be a sequence of points in B which converges to y_o. By Fatou's lemma we have

$$\int_{\mathbb{R}^n} e^{-4\pi \langle y_o, t \rangle} (\mathcal{N}(\mathbf{g}(t)))^2 dt \leq \limsup_{m \to \infty} \int_{\mathbb{R}^n} e^{-4\pi \langle y_m, t \rangle} (\mathcal{N}(\mathbf{g}(t)))^2 dt$$

$$\leq \limsup_{m \to \infty} M^2 e^{4\pi A |y_m|} = M^2 e^{4\pi A |y_o|}$$

and

$$|e^{-2\pi \langle y_o, t \rangle} \mathbf{g}(t)|_2 \leq M e^{2\pi A |y_o|}.$$

Thus, (1) holds with $r = 0$ or $s = 0$ for $y \in \overline{B}$. If $\overline{0} \in \partial B$ then $\mathbf{g}(t) \in L^2(\mathbb{R}^n, \mathcal{H})$ from the above inequality for $y_o = \overline{0}$. □

For B being a proper open connected subset of $\mathbb{R}^n$ and $\mathcal{X}$ being a Banach space, assume (1) holds for $1 \leq p < \infty$ with $r = 0$ or $s = 0$ and for $\mathbf{g}$ having values in $\mathcal{X}$. The proof of Corollary 2 shows that (1) will hold for $y \in \overline{B}$ in this situation.

We study the extension of $\mathbf{f}(z)$ or $e^{-2\pi \langle y, t \rangle} \mathbf{g}(t)$, $y \in B$, in norm to the ∂B in greater detail later in this paper in section 8.

The proof of the following result is the same as that of Corollary 1 using Theorem 3.

Corollary 3. Let B be a proper open connected subset of $\mathbb{R}^n$ which does not contain $\overline{0} \in \mathbb{R}^n$, and let $\mathcal{H}$ be a Hilbert space such that the growth of Theorem 3 holds for $p = 2$. We have $f(z) \in H^2_*(T^B, \mathcal{H})$ for $f(z)$ defined in (2).

In several following results, we restrict the base B of the tube T^B to cones and obtain additional properties of the function $\mathbf{g}(t)$ in the results. Throughout supp$(\mathbf{g})$ denotes the support of $\mathbf{g}$.

Theorem 4. Let C be an open connected cone in $\mathbb{R}^n$ and $1 \leq p < \infty$. Let $\mathbf{g}(t)$ be a Banach space $\mathcal{X}$ valued measurable function on $\mathbb{R}^n$ such that (1) holds for $y \in C$. We have supp$(\mathbf{g}) \subseteq \{t \in \mathbb{R}^n : u_C(t) \leq A\}$ almost everywhere (a.e.).

Proof. Assume $\mathbf{g}(t) \neq \Theta$ on a set of positive measure in $\{t \in \mathbb{R}^n : u_C(t) > A\}$; there is a point $t_o \in \{t \in \mathbb{R}^n : u_C(t) > A\}$ such that $\mathbf{g}(t) \neq \Theta$ on a set of positive measure in the neighborhoods $N(t_o, \eta) = \{t \in \mathbb{R}^n : |t - t_o| < \eta\}$ for arbitrary $\eta > 0$. Since $t_o \in \{t \in \mathbb{R}^n : u_C(t) > A\}$ there is a point $y_o \in pr(C) \subset C$ such that $(-\langle t_o, y_o \rangle) > A \geq 0$. Using the continuity of $(-\langle t, y_o \rangle)$ at t_o as a function of t, there is a fixed $\sigma > 0$ and a fixed neighborhood $N(t_o; \eta')$ such that $-\langle t, y_o \rangle) > A + \sigma > 0$ for all $t \in N(t_o; \eta')$. Choose η above to be η'. For any $\lambda > 0$ we have

$$-\langle \lambda y_o, t \rangle = -\lambda \langle y_o, t \rangle > \lambda A + \lambda \sigma > 0, \ t \in N(t_o; \eta'), \ \lambda > 0. \tag{7}$$

$y_o \in pr(C) \subset C$ and C being a cone imply $\lambda y_o \in C, \lambda > 0$. From (7) and (1) with $y = \lambda y_o$ we have for all $\lambda > 0$ that

$$e^{2\pi p(\lambda A + \lambda \sigma)} \int_{N(t_o; \eta')} (\mathcal{N}(\mathbf{g}(t)))^p dt \leq \int_{N(t_o; \eta')} e^{-2\pi \langle \lambda y_o, t \rangle} (\mathcal{N}(\mathbf{g}(t)))^p dt$$

$$\leq \int_{\mathbb{R}^n} e^{-2\pi p \langle \lambda y_o, t \rangle} (\mathcal{N}(\mathbf{g}(t)))^p dt \leq M^p (1 + (d(\lambda y_o))^{-r})^{sp} e^{2\pi p A |\lambda y_o|}$$

$$= M^p (1 + \lambda^{-r} (d(y_o))^{-r})^{sp} e^{2\pi p \lambda A} \tag{8}$$

since $y_o \in pr(C)$ and $d(\lambda y_o) = \lambda d(y_o)$. The integral on the left of (8) is finite. From (8) we have

$$(1 + \lambda^{-r} (d(y_o))^{-r})^{-sp} e^{2\pi p \lambda \sigma} \int_{N(t_o; \eta')} (\mathcal{N}(\mathbf{g}(t)))^p dt \leq M^p \tag{9}$$

for all $\lambda > 0$ with $\sigma > 0$ being fixed and independent of λ. Recall that y_o depends only on t_o. The constants $d(y_o), r, s, p, \sigma, \eta'$, and M are all independent of $\lambda > 0$. We have $(1 + \lambda^{-r}(d(y_o))^{-r})^{-sp} = 1$ if $r = 0$ or $s = 0$, and $(1 + \lambda^{-r}(d(y_o))^{-r})^{-sp} \to 1$ as $\lambda \to \infty$ if $r > 0$ and $s > 0$. We let $\lambda \to \infty$ in (9) and conclude that $\mathbf{g}(t) = \Theta$ almost everywhere in $N(t_o; \eta')$ which contradicts the fact that $\mathbf{g}(t) \neq \Theta$ on a set of positive measure in $N(t_o, \eta')$. Thus, $\mathbf{g}(t) = \Theta$ a.e. in $\{t \in \mathbb{R}^n : u_C(t) > A\}$, and supp$(\mathbf{g}) \subseteq \{t \in \mathbb{R}^n : u_C(t) \leq A\}$ a.e. since $\{t \in \mathbb{R}^n : u_C(t) \leq A\}$ is a closed set in $\mathbb{R}^n$. □

The proof of the corresponding result for the growth of Theorem 3 can be obtained by similar techniques as in Theorem 4.

Theorem 5. Let C be an open connected cone in $\mathbb{R}^n$ and $1 \leq p < \infty$. Let $\mathbf{g}(t)$ be a Banach space $\mathcal{X}$ valued measurable function on $\mathbb{R}^n$ such that the growth of Theorem 3 holds for $y \in C$. We have supp$(\mathbf{g}) \subseteq C^*$ a.e.

In [7,8], Vladimirov introduced a space of measurable functions on $\mathbb{R}^n$, denoted $\mathcal{S}'_0$, which when multiplied by a polynomial raised to a suitable negative power become $L^2(\mathbb{R}^n)$ functions. Analysis concerning the space $\mathcal{S}'_0$ can also be found in [9,10]. We now extend this space to the vector-valued case and for p such that $1 \leq p < \infty$. We then show that these new spaces of functions become equivalent to the measurable functions $\mathbf{g}$ of the preceding results in this section for each p and for the base of the tube being open convex cones in $\mathbb{R}^n$.

Definition 5. Let $\mathcal{X}$ be a Banach space. $\mathcal{S}'_p(\mathbb{R}^n, \mathcal{X})$, $1 \le p < \infty$, is the set of all measurable functions $g(t)$, $t \in \mathbb{R}^n$, with values in $\mathcal{X}$ such that there exists a real number $m \ge 0$ for which $(1 + |t|^p)^{-m} g(t) \in L^p(\mathbb{R}^n, \mathcal{X})$.

First note that $\mathcal{S}'_p(\mathbb{R}^n, \mathcal{X}) \subset \mathcal{S}'(\mathbb{R}^n, \mathcal{X})$, $1 \le p < \infty$. In our first result concerning the spaces $\mathcal{S}'_p(\mathbb{R}^n, \mathcal{X})$ the base of the tube T^C will be an open connected cone.

Theorem 6. Let C be an open connected cone in $\mathbb{R}^n$ and $1 \le p < \infty$. Let $g(t)$ be a measurable function on $\mathbb{R}^n$ with values in a Banach space $\mathcal{X}$ such that (1) holds for $y \in C$. We have $g \in \mathcal{S}'_p(\mathbb{R}^n, \mathcal{X})$ and $\operatorname{supp}(g) \subseteq \{t \in \mathbb{R}^n : u_C(t) \le A\}$ a.e.

Proof. The support property of $\mathbf{g}$ has been proved in Theorem 4. We now prove that $\mathbf{g} \in \mathcal{S}'_p(\mathbb{R}^n, \mathcal{X})$. Choose a fixed point $y_o \in pr(C)$ and put $Y = \{y : y = \lambda y_o, 0 < \lambda \le 1\} \subset C$; choose a fixed compact subcone $C' \subset\subset C$ such that $y_o \in C'$. We have $Y \subset C' \subset\subset C$. Let $y \in Y$ be arbitrary; using (1) we have

$$\int_{\mathbb{R}^n} e^{-2\pi p \langle y, t \rangle} (\mathcal{N}(\mathbf{g}(t)))^p dt \le M^p (1 + (d(y))^r)^{sp} e^{2\pi p A |y|}, \ y \in C,$$

and hence

$$(d(y))^{rsp} \int_{\mathbb{R}^n} e^{-2\pi p \langle y, t \rangle} (\mathcal{N}(\mathbf{g}(t)))^p dt \le M^p (1 + (d(y))^r)^{sp} e^{2\pi p A |y|}, \ y \in C. \quad (10)$$

(10) holds in particular for $y \in Y$ for which $|y| = \lambda |y_o| = \lambda$, $0 < \lambda \le 1$, since $y_o \in pr(C)$; and $\langle y, t \rangle \le |y| |t|$, $t \in \mathbb{R}^n$, implies $(-|y| |t|) \le -\langle y, t \rangle$, $t \in \mathbb{R}^n$. Corresponding to $C' \subset\subset C$ we use [7] (p. 6, (1.14)) and obtain $\delta = \delta(C') > 0$ depending only on C' and not on $y \in C'$ such that

$$0 < \delta |y| \le d(y) \le |y|, \ y \in C' \subset\subset C. \quad (11)$$

Using (11) and (10), we have

$$(\delta \lambda)^{rsp} \int_{\mathbb{R}^n} e^{-2\pi p \lambda |t|} (\mathcal{N}(\mathbf{g}(t)))^p dt \le (d(y))^{rsp} \int_{\mathbb{R}^n} e^{-2\pi p \langle y, t \rangle} (\mathcal{N}(\mathbf{g}(t)))^p dt$$
$$\le M^p (1 + (d(y))^r)^{sp} e^{2\pi p A |y|} \le M^p (1 + \lambda^r)^{sp} e^{2\pi p \lambda A} \quad (12)$$

for $y = \lambda y_o \in Y \subset C' \subset\subset C$, $0 < \lambda \le 1$, with δ being independent of C' and hence independent of $y \in Y$ and independent of λ, $0 < \lambda \le 1$. Let $\epsilon > 1$ be fixed. Multiply both sides of (12) by $\lambda^{-1+\epsilon}$ and integrate the result from (12) over $0 < \lambda \le 1$ with respect to λ to obtain

$$\int_0^1 \lambda^{-1+\epsilon} (\delta \lambda)^{rsp} \int_{\mathbb{R}^n} e^{-2\pi p \lambda |t|} (\mathcal{N}(\mathbf{g}(t)))^p dt d\lambda \le M^p \int_0^1 \lambda^{-1+\epsilon} (1 + \lambda^r)^{sp} e^{2\pi p \lambda A} d\lambda.$$

Now multiply this inequality by δ^{-rsp} and use Fubini's theorem on the left to obtain

$$\int_{\mathbb{R}^n} (\mathcal{N}(\mathbf{g}(t)))^p \int_0^1 \lambda^{rsp-1+\epsilon} e^{-2\pi p \lambda |t|} d\lambda dt \le M^p \delta^{-rsp} \int_0^1 \lambda^{-1+\epsilon} (1 + \lambda^r)^{ps} e^{2\pi p \lambda A} d\lambda. \quad (13)$$

We note that all constants $M, \delta, r, s, p, \epsilon$, and A are independent of $y = \lambda y_o \in Y$ and hence independent of λ, $0 < \lambda \le 1$. Using the change of variable $u = 2\pi p \lambda |t|$ in the inner integral on the left of (13) and considering the cases $0 < |t| \le 1/2\pi p$ and $|t| > 1/2\pi p$ we obtain

$$\int_0^1 \lambda^{rsp-1+\epsilon} e^{-2\pi p \lambda |t|} d\lambda = (2\pi p |t|)^{-rsp-\epsilon} \int_0^{2\pi p |t|} u^{rsp-1+\epsilon} e^{-u} du \ge \quad (14)$$

$$\left\{\begin{array}{ll}(ersp+\epsilon\epsilon)^{-1}(1+|t|^p)^{-rs-\epsilon/p} & \text{for } 0<|t|\leq 1/2\pi p \\ (2\pi p)^{-rsp-\epsilon}\int_0^1 u^{rsp-1+\epsilon}e^{-u}du(1+|t|^p)^{-rs-\epsilon/p} & \text{for } |t|>1/2\pi p\end{array}\right\}.$$

Put

$$K = \min\left\{(ersp+\epsilon\epsilon)^{-1}, (2\pi p)^{-rsp-\epsilon}\int_0^1 u^{rsp-1+\epsilon}e^{-u}du\right\} > 0.$$

From (14), we have

$$\int_0^1 \lambda^{rsp-1+\epsilon}e^{-2\pi p\lambda|t|}d\lambda \geq K(1+|t|^p)^{-rs-\epsilon/p}, \ |t|>0, \tag{15}$$

with this inequality holding also at $t=\bar{0}$ by adjusting the constant K if needed. Putting (15), which holds for all $t\in\mathbb{R}^n$ now, into (13) and recalling $\epsilon>1$, we have

$$K\int_{\mathbb{R}^n}(1+|t|^p)^{-rs-\epsilon/p}(\mathcal{N}(\mathbf{g}(t)))^p dt \leq M^p\delta^{-rsp}\int_0^1 \lambda^{-1+\epsilon}(1+\lambda^r)^{ps}e^{2\pi p\lambda A}d\lambda$$
$$\leq M^p\delta^{-rsp}2^{ps}e^{2\pi pA}$$

with the right side being a fixed constant. Thus, $(1+|t|^p)^{-rs/p-\epsilon/p^2}\mathbf{g}(t)\in L^p(\mathbb{R}^n,\mathcal{X})$, and $\mathbf{g}\in\mathcal{S}_p'(\mathbb{R}^n,\mathcal{X})$ since $(rs/p+\epsilon/p^2)\geq 0$. □

We similarly obtain the following result from Theorem 5.

Theorem 7. *Let C be an open connected cone in $\mathbb{R}^n$ and $1\leq p<\infty$. Let $\mathbf{g}(t)$ be a Banach space $\mathcal{X}$ valued measurable function on $\mathbb{R}^n$ such that the growth of Theorem 3 holds for $y\in C$. We have $\mathbf{g}\in\mathcal{S}_p'(\mathbb{R}^n,\mathcal{X})$ and $\mathrm{supp}(\mathbf{g})\subseteq C^*$ a.e.*

In order for the converse implication of Theorem 6 to hold we need the cone C to be convex as well as open.

Theorem 8. *Let C be an open convex cone in $\mathbb{R}^n$, $1\leq p<\infty$, and $A\geq 0$. Let $\mathbf{g}\in\mathcal{S}_p'(\mathbb{R}^n,\mathcal{X})$ with $\mathrm{supp}(\mathbf{g})\subseteq\{t\in\mathbb{R}^n:u_C(t)\leq A\}$ a.e. where $\mathcal{X}$ is a Banach space. We have $\mathbf{g}$ is a measurable function with values in $\mathcal{X}$ such that (1) holds for all $y\in C$.*

Proof. From [9] (p. 74, Lemma 3), $\{t\in\mathbb{R}^n:u_C(t)\leq A\}=C^*+\overline{N(\bar{0};A)}, N(\bar{0};A)=\{t\in\mathbb{R}^n:|t|<A\}$, since the cone C is open and convex here. Thus, $t\in\{t\in\mathbb{R}^n:u_C(t)\leq A\}$ yields $t=t_1+t_2$, $t_1\in C^*$, $t_2\in\overline{N(\bar{0};A)}$. Since $\mathbf{g}\in\mathcal{S}_p'(\mathbb{R}^n,\mathcal{X})$, $\mathbf{g}$ is measurable on $\mathbb{R}^n$ and $(1+|t|^p)^{-m}\mathbf{g}(t)\in L^p(\mathbb{R}^n,\mathcal{X})$ for some $m\geq 0$; thus

$$\int_{\mathbb{R}^n}(1+|t|^p)^{-mp}(\mathcal{N}(\mathbf{g}(t)))^p dt \leq K < \infty$$

for a constant $K>0$. Let $y\in C$ be arbitrary. We have

$$\int_{\mathbb{R}^n}e^{-2\pi p\langle y,t\rangle}(\mathcal{N}(\mathbf{g}(t)))^p dt$$
$$=\int_{C^*+\overline{N(\bar{0};A)}}e^{-2\pi p\langle y,t\rangle}(1+|t|^p)^{mp}(1+|t|^p)^{-mp}(\mathcal{N}(\mathbf{g}(t))))^p dt$$
$$\leq \sup_{t\in C^*+\overline{N(\bar{0};A)}}((1+|t|^p)^{mp}e^{-2\pi p\langle y,t\rangle})\int_{\mathbb{R}^n}(1+|t|^p)^{-mp}(\mathcal{N}(\mathbf{g}(t)))^p dt$$
$$\leq K\sup_{t\in C^*+\overline{N(\bar{0};A)}}(1+|t|^p)^{mp}e^{-2\pi p\langle y,t\rangle} \tag{16}$$
$$\leq K\sup_{t_1\in C^*,t_2\in\overline{N(\bar{0};A)}}(1+(|t_1|+|t_2|)^p)^{mp}e^{-2\pi p\langle y,t_1+t_2\rangle}.$$

For $t_2 \in \overline{N(\vec{0}; A)}$, we have $|t_2| \leq A$ and

$$e^{-2\pi p \langle y, t_2 \rangle} \leq e^{2\pi p |t_2| |y|} \leq e^{2\pi p A |y|}, \quad t_2 \in \overline{N(\vec{0}; A)}, \ y \in C. \tag{17}$$

For $t_1 \in C^*$, we have $t_1 = \lambda_1 t_1^*$ where $\lambda_1 \geq 0$ and $t_1^* \in pr(C^*)$. From Section 2 we have

$$d(y) = \inf_{u \in pr(C^*)} \langle u, y \rangle = - \sup_{u \in pr(C^*)} (-\langle u, y \rangle), \ y \in C. \tag{18}$$

For $y \in C$, using (17) and (18) we continue (16) as

$$\int_{\mathbb{R}^n} e^{-2\pi p \langle y, t \rangle} (\mathcal{N}(\mathbf{g}(t)))^p dt$$

$$\leq K e^{2\pi p A |y|} \sup_{\lambda_1 \geq 0, t_1^* \in pr(C^*)} ((1 + (\lambda_1 + A)^p)^{mp} e^{-2\pi p \lambda_1 \langle t_1^*, y \rangle})$$

$$\leq K e^{2\pi p A |y|} \sup_{\lambda_1 \geq 0} ((1 + (\lambda_1 + A)^p)^{mp} e^{-2\pi p \lambda_1 d(y)}) \tag{19}$$

$$\leq K (1 + (1+A)^p)^{mp} e^{2\pi p A |y|} \sup_{\lambda_1 \geq 0} ((1 + \lambda_1^p)^{mp} e^{-2\pi p \lambda_1 d(y)})$$

$$\leq K (1 + (1+A)^p)^{mp} e^{2\pi p A |y|} \sup_{\lambda_1 \geq 0} ((1 + \lambda_1)^{mp^2} e^{-2\pi p \lambda_1 d(y)}).$$

The supremum in the last line of (19) is a maximum which can be obtained using the first derivative test. If $(mp^2 - 2\pi p d(y)) > 0$ then $m > 0$ and the supremum occurs at $\lambda_1 = (mp^2 - 2\pi p d(y))/2\pi p d(y)$, and in this case

$$\sup_{\lambda_1 \geq 0} ((1 + \lambda_1)^{mp^2} e^{-2\pi p \lambda_1 d(y)}) \leq \left(1 + \frac{mp^2 - 2\pi p d(y)}{2\pi p d(y)}\right)^{mp^2}$$

$$\leq \left(1 + \frac{mp^2}{2\pi p d(y)}\right)^{mp^2} = \left(\frac{mp}{2\pi}\right)^{mp^2} \left(\frac{2\pi}{mp} + \frac{1}{d(y)}\right)^{mp^2}$$

$$\leq max\{1, \left(\frac{mp}{2\pi}\right)^{mp^2}\} (1 + (d(y))^{-1})^{mp^2}.$$

If $(mp^2 - 2\pi p d(y)) \leq 0$, the supremum in the last line of (19) occurs at $\lambda_1 = 0$ and

$$\sup_{\lambda_1 \geq 0} ((1 + \lambda_1)^{mp^2} e^{-2\pi p \lambda_1 d(y)}) = 1 \leq (1 + (d(y))^{-1})^{mp^2}.$$

Combining (19) with the above two estimates on the supremum over $\lambda_1 \geq 0$ we have for $y \in C$

$$\int_{\mathbb{R}^n} e^{-2\pi p \langle y, t \rangle} (\mathcal{N}(\mathbf{g}(t)))^p dt$$

$$\leq K(1 + (1+A)^p)^{mp} max\{1, \left(\frac{mp}{2\pi}\right)^{mp^2}\} (1 + (d(y))^{-1})^{mp^2} e^{2\pi p A |y|}.$$

Taking the pth root of this inequality, we obtain (1) holding for all $y \in C$ with $r = 1$ and $s = mp$. □

For C being an open convex cone in $\mathbb{R}^n$ Theorems 6 and 8 show that $\mathbf{g}$ being a Banach space $\mathcal{X}$ valued measurable function with (1) holding for $y \in C$, $A \geq 0$, and $1 \leq p < \infty$ is an equivalent statement to $\mathbf{g} \in \mathcal{S}'_p(\mathbb{R}^n, \mathcal{X})$ with $supp(\mathbf{g}) \subseteq \{t \in \mathbb{R}^n : u_C(t) \leq A\}$ a.e. for $A \geq 0$ and $1 \leq p < \infty$. Thus, for any future result concerning open convex cones C, these two statements are interchangeable in hypotheses.

If $A = 0$, $\{t \in \mathbb{R}^n : u_C(t) \leq 0\} = C^*$. In this case we have the following corollary to Theorem 8.

Corollary 4. *Let C be an open convex cone in $\mathbb{R}^n$ and $1 \leq p < \infty$. Let $g \in S'_p(\mathbb{R}^n, \mathcal{X})$ for $\mathcal{X}$ being a Banach space and $\text{supp}(\hat{g}) \subset C^*$ a.e. We have*

$$|e^{-2\pi\langle y,t\rangle}g(t)|_p \leq M(1 + (d(y))^{-1})^{mp}, \; y \in C,$$

for constants $M > 0$ and $m \geq 0$.

6. Analytic Functions Generating Measurable Functions

In this section, we consider generalized vector-valued Hardy functions and construct measurable functions which yield Fourier–Laplace transform representations. This material is followed in Section 7 by representing the analytic functions, in particular cases, by Cauchy and Poisson integrals.

We use the Fourier transform on $L^2(\mathbb{R}^n, \mathcal{H})$ considerably in this section and in Section 7. This causes us to restrict the results to $p = 2$ and functions having values in Hilbert space $\mathcal{H}$ as previously discussed in Section 2 in relation to the function Fourier transform.

To prove the Fourier–Laplace representation of functions in $H^2_A(T^B, \mathcal{H})$ in terms of a constructed measurable function we first need the following lemma.

Lemma 1. *Let B be a proper open connected subset of $\mathbb{R}^n$. Let $\mathbf{f}(z) \in H^2_A(T^B, \mathcal{H}))$, where $\mathcal{H}$ is Hilbert space, and be bounded for $x = \text{Re}(z) \in \mathbb{R}^n$ and $y = \text{Im}(z)$ in any compact subset of B. Let $\epsilon > 0$. Put*

$$\mathbf{g}_{\epsilon,y}(t) = \int_{\mathbb{R}^n} e^{-\epsilon \sum_{j=1}^n z_j^2} \mathbf{f}(x+iy) e^{-2\pi i\langle x+iy,t\rangle} dx, \; y \in B, \tag{20}$$

and

$$\mathbf{g}_y(t) = \mathcal{F}^{-1}[e^{2\pi\langle y,t\rangle} \mathbf{f}(x+iy); t], \; y \in B, \; t \in \mathbb{R}^n, \tag{21}$$

in $L^2(\mathbb{R}^n, \mathcal{H})$. We have $\mathbf{g}_{\epsilon,y}(t)$ is independent of $y \in B$ for any $\epsilon > 0$;

$$\lim_{\epsilon \to 0+} |\mathbf{g}_{\epsilon,y}(t) - \mathbf{g}_y(t)|_2 = 0, \; y \in B; \tag{22}$$

and $\mathbf{g}_y(t)$ is independent of $y \in B$.

Proof. For $y \in B$ and $t \in \mathbb{R}^n$, $\mathbf{f}(x+iy) \in L^2(\mathbb{R}^n, \mathcal{H})$ and $e^{2\pi\langle y,t\rangle} \mathbf{f}(x+iy) \in L^2(\mathbb{R}^n, \mathcal{H})$ as functions of $x \in \mathbb{R}^n$. Further, $(e^{2\pi\langle y,t\rangle} e^{-\epsilon \sum_{j=1}^n z_j^2} \mathbf{f}(x+iy)) \in L^1(\mathbb{R}^n, \mathcal{H}) \cap L^2(\mathbb{R}^n, \mathcal{H})$ for $y \in B$ and $t \in \mathbb{R}^n$. Thus, both $\mathbf{g}_{\epsilon,y}(t)$ and $\mathbf{g}_y(t)$ are well defined for $y \in B$ and both are in $L^2(\mathbb{R}^n, \mathcal{H})$. We assume here that $0 < \epsilon \leq 1$ since we are letting $\epsilon \to 0+$ in (22). We have for $y \in B$

$$|\mathbf{g}_{\epsilon,y}(t) - \mathbf{g}_y(t)|_2 = |\mathcal{F}^{-1}[e^{2\pi\langle y,t\rangle}(e^{-\epsilon \sum_{j=1}^n z_j^2} - 1)\mathbf{f}(x+iy); t]|_2$$

$$= |e^{2\pi\langle y,t\rangle}(e^{-\epsilon \sum_{j=1}^n z_j^2} - 1)\mathbf{f}(x+iy)|_2. \tag{23}$$

For $0 < \epsilon \leq 1$

$$(\mathcal{N}(e^{2\pi\langle y,t\rangle}(e^{-\epsilon \sum_{j=1}^n z_j^2} - 1)\mathbf{f}(x+iy)))^2$$
$$= |e^{-\epsilon \sum_{j=1}^n z_j^2} - 1|^2 e^{4\pi\langle y,t\rangle}(\mathcal{N}(\mathbf{f}(x+iy)))^2$$
$$\leq (|e^{-\epsilon z_1^2}|...|e^{-\epsilon z_n^2}| + 1)^2 e^{4\pi\langle y,t\rangle}(\mathcal{N}(\mathbf{f}(x+iy)))^2$$
$$\leq (e^{|y|^2} + 1)^2 e^{4\pi\langle y,t\rangle}(\mathcal{N}(\mathbf{f}(x+iy)))^2,$$

and the right side of this inequality is independent of $0 < \epsilon \le 1$ and is integrable as a function of $x \in \mathbb{R}^n$. By the Lebesgue dominated convergence theorem (22) follows from (23).

To show that $\mathbf{g}_{\epsilon,y}(t)$ is independent of $y \in B$ let S be any compact subset of B, and let $y \in S \subset B$. We have

$$|e^{-\epsilon \sum_{j=1}^n z_j^2}| \le e^{\epsilon n a^2} e^{-\epsilon |x|^2}, \ x \in \mathbb{R}^n, \ y \in S,$$

where $a = \max_{y \in S}\{|y_1|, |y_2|, ..., |y_n|\}$. For $y \in S \subset B$ and $t \in \mathbb{R}^n$

$$\int_S \mathcal{N}(e^{-\epsilon \sum_{j=1}^n z_j^2} \mathbf{f}(x+iy) e^{-2\pi i \langle x+iy, t\rangle} dy$$
$$= \int_S |e^{-\epsilon \sum_{j=1}^n z_j^2}| |e^{-2\pi i \langle x+iy,t\rangle}| \mathcal{N}(\mathbf{f}(x+iy)) dy$$
$$\le A_S e^{\epsilon n a^2} e^{-\epsilon |x|^2} \int_S e^{2\pi |y||t|} dy \tag{24}$$

where A_S is a bound on $\mathcal{N}(\mathbf{f}(x+iy))$ for $x \in \mathbb{R}^n$ and $y \in S$; and the right side of (24) approaches 0 as $|x| \to \infty$. An application of the Caucyh-Poincare theorem yields $\mathbf{g}_{\epsilon,y}$ is independent of $y \in S$ for any $\epsilon > 0$ and hence independent of $y \in B$ for any $\epsilon > 0$ since S is any arbitrary compact subset of B. In the future we refer to $\mathbf{g}_{\epsilon,y}, y \in B$, as $\mathbf{g}_\epsilon$ since this function is independent of $y \in B$ for any $\epsilon > 0$.

Now to prove that $\mathbf{g}_y(t) \in L^2(\mathbb{R}^n, \mathcal{H})$ is independent of $y \in B$ let y_1 and y_2 both be points of B. Since $\mathbf{g}_\epsilon = \mathbf{g}_{\epsilon,y}$ is independent of $y \in B$, for any $\epsilon > 0$ we have

$$|\mathbf{g}_{y_1}(t) - \mathbf{g}_{y_2}(t)|_2 = |\mathbf{g}_{y_1}(t) - \mathbf{g}_{\epsilon,y_1}(t) + \mathbf{g}_{\epsilon,y_2}(t) - \mathbf{g}_{y_2}(t)|_2$$
$$\le |\mathbf{g}_{y_1}(t) - \mathbf{g}_{\epsilon,y_1}(t)|_2 + |\mathbf{g}_{y_2}(t) - \mathbf{g}_{\epsilon,y_2}(t)|_2. \tag{25}$$

Letting $\epsilon \to 0+$ in (25) and using (22), the right side of (25) approaches 0 while the left side is independent of $\epsilon > 0$. Thus, $\mathbf{g}_{y_1}(t) = \mathbf{g}_{y_2}(t)$ a.e., $t \in \mathbb{R}^n$, and $\mathbf{g}_y(t)$ defined in (21) is independent of $y \in B$. We write $\mathbf{g}_y(t)$ defined in (21) as $\mathbf{g}(t)$, $y \in B$, $t \in \mathbb{R}^n$, in the future; and recall that $\mathbf{g}(t) \in L^2(\mathbb{R}^n, \mathcal{H})$. □

We obtain a Fourier–Laplace representation of elements in $H_A^2(T^B, \mathcal{H})$ now.

Theorem 9. *Let B be a proper open connected subset of $\mathbb{R}^n$. Let $\mathbf{f}(z) \in H_A^2(T^B, \mathcal{H})$, where $\mathcal{H}$ is Hilbert space, and be bounded for $x = \text{Re}(z) \in \mathbb{R}^n$ and $y = \text{Im}(z)$ in any compact subset of B. There is a measurable function $\mathbf{g}(t) \in L^2(\mathbb{R}^n, \mathcal{H})$ for which*

$$|e^{-2\pi \langle y, t\rangle} \mathbf{g}(t)|_2 \le M(1 + (d(y))^{-r})^s e^{2\pi A |y|}, \ y \in B, \tag{26}$$

where $r \ge 0$, $s \ge 0$, $A \ge 0$, and $M = M(g, r, s, A) > 0$ are independent of $y \in B$; and

$$\mathbf{f}(z) = \int_{\mathbb{R}^n} \mathbf{g}(t) e^{2\pi i \langle z, t\rangle} dt, \ z \in T^B. \tag{27}$$

Proof. From Lemma 1 the function $\mathbf{g}(t) = \mathbf{g}_y(t)$ defined in (21) is independent of $y \in B$ and is in $L^2(\mathbb{R}^n, \mathcal{H})$. From (21)

$$e^{-2\pi \langle y, t\rangle} \mathbf{g}(t) = \mathcal{F}^{-1}[\mathbf{f}(x+iy); t], \ y \in B, \tag{28}$$

and by the Parseval equality

$$|e^{-2\pi \langle y, t\rangle} \mathbf{g}(t)|_2 = |\mathbf{f}(x+iy)|_2, \ y \in B,$$

where $e^{-2\pi\langle y,t\rangle}\mathbf{g}(t) \in L^2(\mathbb{R}^n, \mathcal{H})$, $y \in B$. Thus, (26) holds from the norm growth on $\mathbf{f}(z) \in H_A^2(T^B, \mathcal{H})$. Using the now obtained Equation (26), by the proof of Theorem 2 for $p = 2$ we have $e^{-2\pi\langle y,t\rangle}\mathbf{g}(t) \in L^1(\mathbb{R}^n, \mathcal{H}) \cap L^2(\mathbb{R}^n, \mathcal{H})$, $y \in B$, and

$$\int_{\mathbb{R}^n} \mathbf{g}(t)e^{2\pi i\langle z,t\rangle} dt = \mathcal{F}[e^{-2\pi\langle y,t\rangle}\mathbf{g}(t); x], \ z = x + iy \in T^B,$$

is analytic in T^B with the Fourier transform being the $L^1(\mathbb{R}^n, \mathcal{H})$ transform. Thus, from (28),

$$\mathbf{f}(z) = \mathcal{F}[e^{-2\pi\langle y,t\rangle}\mathbf{g}(t); x] = \int_{\mathbb{R}^n} \mathbf{g}(t)e^{2\pi i\langle z,t\rangle} dt, \ z = x + iy \in T^B,$$

with the Fourier transform being in both the $L^1(\mathbb{R}^n, \mathcal{H})$ and $L^2(\mathbb{R}^n, \mathcal{H})$ sense, and (27) is obtained. □

The structure of the proofs of Lemma 1 and Theorem 9 can be used to prove a result like Theorem 9 for functions in $H_*^2(T^B, \mathcal{H})$; we state this result now.

Theorem 10. Let B be an open connected subset of $\mathbb{R}^n$ which does not contain $\overline{0} \in \mathbb{R}^n$. Let $\mathbf{f}(z) \in H_*^2(T^B, \mathcal{H})$, where $\mathcal{H}$ is Hilbert space, and be bounded for $x = Re(z) \in \mathbb{R}^n$ and $y = Im(z)$ in any compact subset of B. There is a measurable function $\mathbf{g}(t) \in L^2(\mathbb{R}^n, \mathcal{H})$ for which

$$|e^{-2\pi\langle y,t\rangle}\mathbf{g}(t)|_2 \leq M(1 + (d(y))^{-r})^s e^{M^*(w/|y|)}, \ y \in B,$$

where $r \geq 0, s \geq 0, w > 0$, and $M = M(g, r, s, w) > 0$ are independent of $y \in B$; and

$$\mathbf{f}(z) = \int_{\mathbb{R}^n} \mathbf{g}(t)e^{2\pi i\langle z,t\rangle} dt, \ z \in T^B.$$

By restricting the base B in Theorem 9, further information is obtained.

Corollary 5. Let C be an open connected cone in $\mathbb{R}^n$. Let $\mathbf{f}(z) \in H_A^2(T^C, \mathcal{H})$, where $\mathcal{H}$ is Hilbert space, and be bounded for $x = Re(z) \in \mathbb{R}^n$ and $y = Im(z)$ in any compact subset of C. There is a measurable function $\mathbf{g} \in L^2(\mathbb{R}^n, \mathcal{H}) \cap \mathcal{S}_2'(\mathbb{R}^n, \mathcal{H})$ with $\text{supp}(\mathbf{g}) \subseteq \{t \in \mathbb{R}^n : u_C(t) \leq A\}$ a.e. such that (26) and (27) hold. Further, if C is an open convex cone in $\mathbb{R}^n$ we have

$$\lim_{y \to \overline{0}, y \in C} |\mathbf{f}(x + iy) - \mathcal{F}[\mathbf{g}(t); x]|_2 = 0, \tag{29}$$

and

$$\lim_{y \to \overline{0}, y \in C} \mathbf{f}(x + iy) = \mathcal{F}[\mathbf{g}(t); x] \tag{30}$$

in the strong topology of $\mathcal{S}'(\mathbb{R}^n, \mathcal{H})$.

Proof. The existence of $\mathbf{g} \in L^2(\mathbb{R}^n, \mathcal{H})$ such that (26) and (27) hold follow from Theorem 9. The facts that $\mathbf{g} \in \mathcal{S}_2'(\mathbb{R}^n, \mathcal{H})$ with $\text{supp}(\mathbf{g}) \subseteq \{t \in \mathbb{R}^n : u_C(t) \leq A\}$ a.e. now follow by Theorem 6. Let us further assume that the cone C is open and convex. From the proof of Theorem 8 we know that $\{t \in \mathbb{R}^n : u_C(t) \leq A\} = C^* + \overline{N(\overline{0}; A)}$ where C^* is the dual cone of C and $N(\overline{0}; A) = \{t \in \mathbb{R}^n : |t| < A\}$ since C is assumed to be convex now. Thus, $t \in \{t \in \mathbb{R}^n : u_C(t) \leq A\}$ yields $t = t_1 + t_2$, $t_1 \in C^*$, $t_2 \in \overline{N(\overline{0}; A)}$ as in the proof of Theorem 8. Returning to the proof of Theorem 9 we have for $y \in C$

$$|\mathbf{f}(x + iy) - \mathcal{F}[\mathbf{g}(t); x]|_2 = |\mathcal{F}[e^{-2\pi\langle y,t\rangle}\mathbf{g}(t); x] - \mathcal{F}[\mathbf{g}(t); x]|_2$$
$$= |\mathcal{F}[(e^{-2\pi\langle y,t\rangle} - 1)\mathbf{g}(t); x]|_2 = |(e^{-2\pi\langle y,t\rangle} - 1)\mathbf{g}(t)|_2. \tag{31}$$

In (29) and (30), we prove limit properties as $y \to \bar{0}$, $y \in C$; so we assume that $|y| \leq 1$, $y \in C$, in the remainder of this proof. For $t = t_1 + t_2 \in C^* + \overline{N(\bar{0}; A)}$ we have

$$\begin{aligned}(\mathcal{N}((e^{-2\pi\langle y,t\rangle} - 1)\mathbf{g}(t)))^2 &= |e^{-2\pi\langle y,t\rangle} - 1|^2(\mathcal{N}(\mathbf{g}(t)))^2 \\ &\leq (e^{-2\pi\langle y,t\rangle} + 1)^2(\mathcal{N}(\mathbf{g}(t)))^2 = (e^{-2\pi\langle y,t_1\rangle}e^{-2\pi\langle y,t_2\rangle} + 1)^2(\mathcal{N}(\mathbf{g}(t)))^2 \\ &\leq (1 + e^{2\pi A})^2(\mathcal{N}(\mathbf{g}(t)))^2\end{aligned} \quad (32)$$

for $|y| \leq 1, y \in C$, where $\langle y, t_1 \rangle \geq 0$, $y \in C$ and $t_1 \in C^*$, and $|t_2| \leq A$ for $t_2 \in \overline{N(\bar{0}; A)}$. Since $\mathbf{g} \in L^2(\mathbb{R}^n, \mathcal{H})$ and $\mathrm{supp}(\mathbf{g}) \subseteq C^* + \overline{N(\bar{0}; A)}$, (32) and the Lebesgue dominated convergence theorem combined with (31) prove (29). For (30), let $\phi \in \mathcal{S}(\mathbb{R}^n)$. Using the Hölder inequality we have

$$\begin{aligned}&\mathcal{N}(\langle \mathbf{f}(x+iy), \phi(x)\rangle - \langle \mathcal{F}[\mathbf{g}(t); x], \phi(x)\rangle \\ &\leq \int_{\mathbb{R}^n} \mathcal{N}((\mathbf{f}(x+iy) - \mathcal{F}[\mathbf{g}(t); x])\phi(x))dx \\ &\leq |\mathbf{f}(x+iy) - \mathcal{F}[\mathbf{g}(t); x]|_2 \|\phi\|_{L^2(\mathbb{R}^n)},\end{aligned}$$

and the use of (29) now shows (30) in the weak topology of $\mathcal{S}'(\mathbb{R}^n, \mathcal{H})$. But $\mathcal{S}(\mathbb{R}^n)$ is a Montel space; thus, (30) also holds in the strong topology of $\mathcal{S}'(\mathbb{R}^n, \mathcal{H})$. □

We now desire a converse result to Corollary 5 in the setting of tubes T^C where C is an open connected cone in $\mathbb{R}^n$.

Corollary 6. *Let C be an open connected cone in $\mathbb{R}^n$ and $\mathcal{H}$ be a Hilbert space. Let $\mathbf{g}(t)$ be a $\mathcal{H}$ valued measurable function on $\mathbb{R}^n$ such that (26) holds. We have $\mathbf{g} \in \mathcal{S}'_2(\mathbb{R}^n, \mathcal{H})$ with $\mathrm{supp}(\mathbf{g}) \subseteq \{t \in \mathbb{R}^n : u_C(t) \leq A\}$ a.e., and $\mathbf{f}(z) \in H^2_A(T^C, \mathcal{H})$ for $\mathbf{f}(z)$ defined as in (27) for $z \in T^C$. Further, if C is an open convex cone in $\mathbb{R}^n$ we have (30) holding in the strong topology of $\mathcal{S}'(\mathbb{R}^n, \mathcal{H})$.*

Proof. We apply Theorem 6 and Corollary 1 to obtain $\mathbf{g} \in \mathcal{S}'_2(\mathbb{R}^n, \mathcal{H})$ with $\mathrm{supp}(\mathbf{g}) \subseteq \{t \in \mathbb{R}^n : u_C(t) \leq A\}$ a.e. and to obtain that $\mathbf{f}(z)$ defined as in (27) for $z \in T^C$ is an element of $H^2_A(T^C, \mathcal{H})$. Now assume that C is an open convex cone in the remainder of this proof to obtain (30) here. Since $\mathbf{g} \in \mathcal{S}'_2(\mathbb{R}^n, \mathcal{H}) \subset \mathcal{S}'(\mathbb{R}^n, \mathcal{H})$, the Fourier transform $\mathcal{F}[\mathbf{g}]$ is well defined in $\mathcal{S}'(\mathbb{R}^n, \mathcal{H})$. From the proof of Corollary 1 we have $e^{-2\pi\langle y,t\rangle}\mathbf{g}(t) \in L^1(\mathbb{R}^n, \mathcal{H}) \cap L^2(\mathbb{R}^n, \mathcal{H})$ for $y \in C$. Thus, $\mathbf{f}(x+iy) = \mathcal{F}[e^{-2\pi\langle y,t\rangle}\mathbf{g}(t); x]$, $y \in C$, with the Fourier transform being in the $L^1(\mathbb{R}^n, \mathcal{H})$, the $L^2(\mathbb{R}^n, \mathcal{H})$, and the $\mathcal{S}'(\mathbb{R}^n, \mathcal{H})$ cases. Recalling that $\mathrm{supp}(\mathbf{g}) \subseteq \{t \in \mathbb{R}^n : u_C(t) \leq A\}$ a.e. and referring to [9] (p. 119), we choose a function $\lambda(t) \in C^\infty$, $t \in \mathbb{R}^n$, such that for any n-tuple α of nonnegative integers $|D^\alpha \lambda(t)| \leq M_\alpha$, $t \in \mathbb{R}^n$, where M_α is a constant which depends only on α; and for $\epsilon > 0$, $\lambda(t) = 1$ for t on an ϵ neighborhood of $\{t \in \mathbb{R}^n : u_C(t) \leq A\}$, and $\lambda(t) = 0$ for $t \in \mathbb{R}^n$ but not on a 2ϵ neighborhood of $\{t \in \mathbb{R}^n : u_C(t) \leq A\}$. For $\phi \in \mathcal{S}(\mathbb{R}^n)$ we have for $y \in C$

$$\langle \mathbf{f}(x+iy), \phi(x)\rangle = \langle \mathcal{F}[e^{-2\pi\langle y,t\rangle}\mathbf{g}(t); x], \phi(x)\rangle = \langle \lambda(t)e^{-2\pi\langle y,t\rangle}\mathbf{g}(t), \mathcal{F}[\phi(x); t]\rangle.$$

For C being convex we apply [9] (p. 74, Lemma 3) as in our proof of Theorem 8 to obtain $\{t \in \mathbb{R}^n : u_C(t) \leq A\} = C^* + \overline{N(\bar{0}; A)}$. The result (30) in this corollary now follows from the above equality, $\phi \in \mathcal{S}(\mathbb{R}^n)$, by the same analysis in [9] (p. 119, lines 2–22) in the weak topology of $\mathcal{S}'(\mathbb{R}^n, \mathcal{H})$ as $y \to \bar{0}, y \in C$; and the weak topology implies the strong topology of $\mathcal{S}'(\mathbb{R}^n, \mathcal{H})$ as in the proof of (30) in Corollary 5. The proof is complete. □

Note that we can not say that $\mathbf{g} \in L^2(\mathbb{R}^n, \mathcal{H})$ in Corollary 6 and hence can not obtain the convergence (29) in this converse of Corollary 5.

For B being a proper open connected subset of $\mathbb{R}^n$ and $\mathcal{X}$ being a Banach space, the spaces $V^p_A(T^B, \mathcal{X})$ follow as subspaces of $H^p_A(T^B, \mathcal{X})$ (or appropriately of $R^p_A(T^B, \mathcal{X})$)

by letting either $r = 0$ or $s = 0$ in the norm growth defining these other spaces. Thus, Theorem 9 holds for $\mathbf{f}(z) \in V_A^2(T^B, \mathcal{H})$; and by the proof of Theorem 9, (26) will hold for the obtained function $\mathbf{g}$ in the form

$$|e^{-2\pi\langle y,t\rangle}\mathbf{g}(t)|_2 \leq e^{2\pi A|y|}, \ y \in B.$$

Using the same proof as in Corollary 2 we then can extend the norm growth on $e^{-2\pi\langle y,t\rangle}\mathbf{g}(t)$ to hold for $y \in \overline{B}$. This is stated in the following corollary to Theorem 9.

Corollary 7. *Let B be a proper open connected subset of $\mathbb{R}^n$. Let $\mathbf{f}(z) \in V_A^2(T^B, \mathcal{H})$, where $\mathcal{H}$ is Hilbert space, and be bounded for $x = Re(z) \in \mathbb{R}^n$ and $y = Im(z)$ in any compact subset of B. There is a measurable function $\mathbf{g}(t) \in L^2(\mathbb{R}^n, \mathcal{H})$ for which*

$$|e^{-2\pi\langle y,t\rangle}\mathbf{g}(t)|_2 \leq Me^{2\pi A|y|}, \ y \in \overline{B},$$

where $A \geq 0$ and $M = M(\mathbf{g}, A) > 0$ are independent of $y \in \overline{B}$; and

$$\mathbf{f}(z) = \int_{\mathbb{R}^n} \mathbf{g}(t) e^{2\pi i \langle z,t\rangle} dt, \ z \in T^B.$$

For the base of the tube being an open connected cone in $\mathbb{R}^n$ we have the following corollary of Theorem 10 by combining Theorems 7 and 10. The limit properties in the following corollary will hold for C being an open connected cone in $\mathbb{R}^n$ by similar techniques as in the proof of Corollary 5; C does not need to be convex here for these limit properties to hold because the support of $\mathbf{g}$ is in C^*.

Corollary 8. *Let C be an open connected cone in $\mathbb{R}^n$. Let $\mathbf{f}(z) \in H_*^2(T^C, \mathcal{H})$, where $\mathcal{H}$ is Hilbert space, and be bounded for $x = Re(z) \in \mathbb{R}^n$ and $y = Im(z)$ in any compact subset of C. There is a measurable function $\mathbf{g}(t) \in L^2(\mathbb{R}^n, \mathcal{H}) \cap S_2'(\mathbb{R}^n, \mathcal{H})$ with $supp(\mathbf{g}) \subseteq C^*$ a.e. such that the norm inequality for $e^{-2\pi\langle y,t\rangle}\mathbf{g}(t)$ and the representation of $\mathbf{f}(z)$ hold as in the conclusions of Theorem 10. Further we have*

$$\lim_{y \to \overline{0}, y \in C} |\mathbf{f}(x + iy) - \mathcal{F}[\mathbf{g}(t); x]|_2 = 0$$

and

$$\lim_{y \to \overline{0}, y \in C} \mathbf{f}(x + iy) = \mathcal{F}[\mathbf{g}(t); x]$$

in the strong topology of $S'(\mathbb{R}^n, \mathcal{H})$.

7. Subsets of $H^2(T^C, \mathcal{H})$

Let C be an open connected cone in $\mathbb{R}^n$, and $1 \leq p < \infty$. Let $\mathbf{g}(t)$ be a measurable function on $\mathbb{R}^n$ with values in a Banach space $\mathcal{X}$ such that

$$|e^{-2\pi\langle y,t\rangle}\mathbf{g}(t)|_p \leq M(1 + (d(y))^{-r})^s e^{2\pi A|y|}, \ y \in C, \tag{33}$$

where $A \geq 0$, $r \geq 0$, $s \geq 0$, and $M = M(\mathbf{g}, p, r, s, A) > 0$, or

$$|e^{-2\pi\langle y,t\rangle}\mathbf{g}(t)|_p \leq M(1 + (d(y))^{-r})^s e^{M^*(w/|y|)}, \ y \in C, \tag{34}$$

where $w > 0$, $r \geq 0$, $s \geq 0$, and $M = M(\mathbf{g}, p, w, r, s) > 0$ with all constants being independent of $y \in C$. We have from Theorems 4 and 5 that $supp(\mathbf{g}) \subseteq \{t \in \mathbb{R}^n : u_C(t) \leq A\}$ a.e. and $supp(\mathbf{g}) \subseteq C^*$ a.e. respectively. Restricting to $p = 2$ and letting $\mathcal{X} = \mathcal{H}$, a Hilbert space, now we have from Corollarys 1 and 3 that the function

$$\mathbf{f}(z) = \int_{\mathbb{R}^n} \mathbf{g}(t) e^{2\pi i \langle z,t\rangle} dt, \ z \in T^C,$$

is an element of $H^2_A(T^C, \mathcal{H})$ or $H^2_*(T^C, \mathcal{H})$, respectively. Conversely, we have proved in Corollary 5 or Corollary 8 that if $\mathbf{f}(z) \in H^2_A(T^C, \mathcal{H})$ or $\mathbf{f}(z) \in H^2_*(T^C, \mathcal{H})$ and in each case $\mathbf{f}(z)$ is bounded for $x = \mathrm{Re}(z)$ and $y = \mathrm{Im}(z)$ in any compact subset of C then in each case there exists a measurable function $\mathbf{g} \in L^2(\mathbb{R}^n, \mathcal{H}) \cap S'_2(\mathbb{R}^n, \mathcal{H})$ with $\mathrm{supp}(\mathbf{g}) \subseteq \{t \in \mathbb{R}^n : u_C(t) \leq A\}$ a.e. and (33) holds for $p = 2$ or $\mathrm{supp}(\mathbf{g}) \subseteq C^*$ a.e. and (34) holds for $p = 2$ with

$$\mathbf{f}(z) = \int_{\mathbb{R}^n} \mathbf{g}(t) e^{2\pi i \langle z, t \rangle} dt, \ z \in T^C,$$

in each case.

We will now show from these results that both spaces $H^2_0(T^C, \mathcal{H})$, $A = 0$, and $H^2_*(T^C, \mathcal{H})$ are subsets of the Hardy space $H^2(T^C, \mathcal{H})$ and obtain immediate results from these subset properties.

Theorem 11. *Let C be an open connected cone in $\mathbb{R}^n$ and $\mathcal{H}$ be a Hilbert space. Let $\mathbf{f}(z) \in H^2_0(T^C, \mathcal{H})$ or $\mathbf{f}(z) \in H^2_*(T^C, \mathcal{H})$ and in either case be bounded for $x = \mathrm{Re}(z) \in \mathbb{R}^n$ and $y = \mathrm{Im}(z)$ in any compact subset of C. In either case there is a measurable function $\mathbf{g}(t) \in L^2(\mathbb{R}^n, \mathcal{H}) \cap S'_2(\mathbb{R}^n, \mathcal{H})$ with $\mathrm{supp}(\mathbf{g}) \subseteq C^*$ a.e. such that*

$$\mathbf{f}(z) = \int_{\mathbb{R}^n} \mathbf{g}(t) e^{2\pi i \langle z, t \rangle} dt, \ z \in T^C;$$

$$\sup_{y \in C} |\mathbf{f}(x + iy)|_2 = \sup_{y \in C} |e^{-2\pi \langle y, t \rangle} \mathbf{g}(t)|_2 = |\mathbf{g}|_2;$$

and $\mathbf{f}(z) \in H^2(T^C, \mathcal{H})$.

Proof. As noted previously in this section a function $\mathbf{g} \in L^2(\mathbb{R}^n, \mathcal{H}) \cap S'_2(\mathbb{R}^n, \mathcal{H})$ is obtained from previous results such that

$$\mathbf{f}(z) = \int_{\mathbb{R}^n} \mathbf{g}(t) e^{2\pi i \langle z, t \rangle} dt, \ z \in T^C.$$

Further from the analysis leading to Corollarys 5 and 8 we know $e^{-2\pi \langle y, t \rangle} \mathbf{g}(t) \in L^1(\mathbb{R}^n, \mathcal{H}) \cap L^2(\mathbb{R}^n, \mathcal{H})$, $y \in C$, in both cases. If $A = 0$, $\{t \in \mathbb{R}^n : u_C(t) \leq 0\} = C^*$; thus, in both cases $\mathrm{supp}(\mathbf{g}) \subseteq C^*$ a.e. In both cases we have

$$|\mathbf{f}(x + iy)|_2 = |e^{-2\pi \langle y, t \rangle} \mathbf{g}(t)|_2, \ y \in C.$$

In both cases

$$\int_{\mathbb{R}^n} (\mathcal{N}(e^{-2\pi \langle y, t \rangle} \mathbf{g}(t)))^2 dt = \int_{C^*} (e^{-4\pi \langle y, t \rangle} (\mathcal{N}(\mathbf{g}(t)))^2 dt \leq \int_{C^*} (\mathcal{N}(\mathbf{g}(t)))^2 dt = |\mathbf{g}|_2^2$$

for all $y \in C$. We thus have for all $y \in C$

$$|\mathbf{f}(x + iy)|_2 = |e^{-2\pi \langle y, t \rangle} \mathbf{g}(t)|_2 \leq |\mathbf{g}|_2, \ y \in C,$$

which yields $\mathbf{f}(x + iy) \in H^2(T^C, \mathcal{H})$. Further,

$$\sup_{y \in C} |\mathbf{f}(x + iy)|_2 = \sup_{y \in C} |e^{-2\pi \langle y, t \rangle} \mathbf{g}(t)|_2 \leq (\int_{C^*} (\mathcal{N}(\mathbf{g}(t)))^2 dt)^{1/2} = |\mathbf{g}|_2. \tag{35}$$

But $\overline{0} \in C^* = \{t \in \mathbb{R}^n : \langle t, y \rangle \geq 0 \text{ for all } y \in C\}$. Hence, the inequality in (35) is an equality. □

Because of this result we have immediate consequences for $\mathbf{f}(x + iy)$ in either space in Theorem 11 from previously proven results. If C is an open convex cone in $\mathbb{R}^n$ which contains an entire straight line then $\mathbf{f}(z) = \Theta$, $z \in T^C$, for both cases of $\mathbf{f}(z)$ in Theorem 11. If C is a regular cone in $\mathbb{R}^n$ then

$$\mathbf{f}(z) = \int_{\mathbb{R}^n} \mathcal{F}[\mathbf{g}(u); t] K(z-t) dt = \int_{\mathbb{R}^n} \mathcal{F}[\mathbf{g}(u); t] Q(z; t) dt, \ z \in T^C,$$

for the function $\mathbf{g}(t)$ in Theorem 11 and for both cases of $\mathbf{f}(z)$ in Theorem 11. Further, we note that Vindas has proved using functional analysis techniques in [1] that for C being a regular cone in $\mathbb{R}^n$ and $\mathcal{X}$ being a dual Banach space having the Radon-Nikodým property, any $\mathbf{f}(z) \in H^p(T^C, \mathcal{X})$, $1 \leq p \leq \infty$, is the Poisson integral of some $\mathbf{h} \in L^p(\mathbb{R}^n, \mathcal{X})$, $1 \leq p \leq \infty$. We say more about the use of functional analysis techniques in obtaining results corresponding to those of this paper and those of [1] in Section 9 below.

8. Boundary Values on the Topological Boundary

In Corollary 5 we obtained boundary value properties of $H_A^2(T^C, \mathcal{H})$ functions on the distinguished boundary of the tube T^C where C is an open convex cone in $\mathbb{R}^n$. The boundary values were obtained in the $L^2(\mathbb{R}^n, \mathcal{H})$ and $\mathcal{S}'(\mathbb{R}^n, \mathcal{H})$ topologies. We now investigate boundary value properties of a subset of $H_A^2(T^C, \mathcal{H})$ on the topological boundary of the tube.

Our basic result in this section depends on the cone C being regular. We consider the subset $R_A^2(T^C, \mathcal{H})$ of $H_A^2(T^C, \mathcal{H})$ consisting of analytic functions $\mathbf{f}(z)$ in T^C with values in $\mathcal{H}$ such that

$$|\mathbf{f}(x+iy)|_2 \leq M(1+|y|^{-r})^s e^{2\pi A|y|}, \ y \in C, \quad (36)$$

where $A \geq 0$, $r \geq 0$, $s \geq 0$, and $M = M(\mathbf{f}, A, r, s) > 0$ are all independent of $y \in C$. We prove that $R_A^2(T^C, \mathcal{H})$ functions have boundary values on the topological boundary of T^C again in the $L^2(\mathbb{R}^n, \mathcal{H})$ and $\mathcal{S}'(\mathbb{R}^n, \mathcal{H})$ topologies. We have $R_A^2(T^C, \mathcal{H}) \subseteq H_A^2(T^C, \mathcal{H})$ since $0 < d(y) \leq |y|$ for y in any open connected cone in $\mathbb{R}^n$ from [2] (p. 6, (1.14)); recall Section 2 above.

Before proving our main result in this section we focus on the growth bound as in (36). If we had used this growth bound of (36) in the inequality (1) for $e^{-2\pi \langle y, t \rangle} \mathbf{g}(t)$ and in the inequality for $|\mathbf{f}(x+iy)|_p$ which defines $H_A^p(T^B, \mathcal{X})$, that is if we replace $d(y)$ by $|y|$ in the growth bound, then the results, proofs, and conclusions from Theorem 2 through Theorem 11 in Sections 5–7 will all hold as before. In any conclusion in these results that contains the growth bound, the growth bound in the conclusion will be that of (36). We state this to emphasize the content of our proofs in this section which deal with $R_A^2(T^C, \mathcal{H})$ instead of $H_A^2(T^C, \mathcal{H})$.

Theorem 12. Let C be a regular cone in $\mathbb{R}^n$. Let $\mathbf{f}(z) \in R_A^2(T^C, \mathcal{H})$ and be bounded for $x = Re(z) \in \mathbb{R}^n$ and $y = Im(z)$ in any compact subset of C. Let $y_0 \in \partial C$, $y_0 \neq \bar{0}$. There exists a function $\mathbf{F}(x+iy_0) \in L^2(\mathbb{R}^n, \mathcal{H})$ such that

$$\lim_{y \to y_0} |\mathbf{f}(x+iy) - \mathbf{F}(x+iy_0)|_2 = 0 \quad (37)$$

for $y \in \{y \in C : 0 < a < |y| < b\}$ where a and b are any constants such that $0 < a < |y_0| < b$; and

$$\lim_{y \to y_0} \mathbf{f}(x+iy) = \mathbf{F}(x+iy_0) \quad (38)$$

in the strong topology of $\mathcal{S}'(\mathbb{R}^n, \mathcal{H})$ with $y \in \{y \in C : 0 < a < |y| < b\}$ again where a and b are any constants such that $0 < a < |y_0| < b$.

Proof. As noted previously the growth (36) for $R_A^2(T^C, \mathcal{H})$ functions is a special case of the growth for $H_A^2(T^C, \mathcal{H})$ functions since $0 < d(y) \leq |y|$, $y \in C$. Thus, $\mathbf{f}(z)$, $z \in T^C$, in this theorem satisfies the hypotheses of Corollary 5; and the conclusions of Corollary 5 follow for the $\mathbf{f}(z)$, $z \in T^C$, here. In fact the construction of proofs above leading to Corollary 5 for the growth bound of type

$$M(1 + (d(y))^{-r})^s e^{2\pi A|y|}, \quad y \in C,$$

would be the same for the growth of type (36) with $d(y)$ replaced by $|y|$ in the analysis of the proofs as noted before. Thus, there is a measurable function $\mathbf{g} \in L^2(\mathbb{R}^n, \mathcal{H}) \cap S'_2(\mathbb{R}^n, \mathcal{H})$ with $\mathrm{supp}(\mathbf{g}) \subseteq \{t \in \mathbb{R}^n : u_C(t) \leq A\}$ a.e. such that (26) and (27) hold with $d(y)$ replaced by $|y|$ in (26), and $z = x + iy \in T^C$. From the construction of $\mathbf{g}$ in Lemma 1 and the proof of Theorem 2, $e^{-2\pi \langle y,t \rangle} \mathbf{g}(t) \in L^1(\mathbb{R}^n, \mathcal{H}) \cap L^2(\mathbb{R}^n, \mathcal{H})$, $y \in C$. Let $y_o \in \partial C$, the boundary of C, $y_o \neq \bar{0}$. Since $|y_o| > 0$ choose constants a and b such that $0 < a < |y_o| < b$ and consider the band $\{y \in C : 0 < a < |y| < b\} \subset C$. Let $\{y_m\}$, $m = 1, 2, \ldots$, be a sequence of points in this band which converges to y_o. For each y_m, $m = 1, 2, \ldots$, in this band

$$\int_{\mathbb{R}^n} (\mathcal{N}(e^{-2\pi \langle y_m,t \rangle} \mathbf{g}(t)))^2 dt \leq M^2 (1 + |y_m|^{-r})^{2s} e^{4\pi A|y_m|} \leq M^2 (1 + a^{-r})^{2s} e^{4\pi bA}.$$

Using Fatou's lemma we have

$$\int_{\mathbb{R}^n} (\mathcal{N}(e^{-2\pi \langle y_o,t \rangle} \mathbf{g}(t)))^2 dt \leq \limsup_{y_m \to y_o} \int_{\mathbb{R}^n} (\mathcal{N}(e^{-2\pi \langle y_m,t \rangle} \mathbf{g}(t)))^2 dt$$
$$\leq M^2 (1 + a^{-r})^{2s} e^{4\pi bA};$$

and $e^{-2\pi \langle y_o,t \rangle} \mathbf{g}(t) \in L^2(\mathbb{R}^n, \mathcal{H})$ for $y_o \in \partial C$; further $e^{-2\pi \langle y_o,t \rangle} \mathbf{g}(t) \in L^2(\mathbb{R}^n, \mathcal{H})$ even if $y_o = \bar{0}$ since $\mathbf{g} \in L^2(\mathbb{R}^n, \mathcal{H})$. Recall $\mathbf{g} \in L^2(\mathbb{R}^n, \mathcal{H}) \cap S'_2(\mathbb{R}^n, \mathcal{H})$ and $e^{-2\pi \langle y,t \rangle} \mathbf{g}(t) \in L^1(\mathbb{R}^n, \mathcal{H}) \cap L^2(\mathbb{R}^n, \mathcal{H})$, $y \in C$. Form

$$\mathbf{F}(x + iy_o) = \mathcal{F}[e^{-2\pi \langle y_o,t \rangle} \mathbf{g}(t); x], \quad y_o \in \partial C, \quad y_o \neq \bar{0};$$

thus, $\mathbf{F}(x + iy_o) \in L^2(\mathbb{R}^n, \mathcal{H})$, $y_o \in \partial C$, $y_o \neq \bar{0}$. From the definition of $\mathbf{F}(x + iy_o)$ and Corollary 5 we have

$$|\mathbf{f}(x + iy) - \mathbf{F}(x + iy_o)|_2 = |\mathcal{F}[(e^{-2\pi \langle y,t \rangle} - e^{-2\pi \langle y_o,t \rangle}) \mathbf{g}(t); x]|_2$$
$$= |(e^{-2\pi \langle y,t \rangle} - e^{-2\pi \langle y_o,t \rangle}) \mathbf{g}(t)|_2, \qquad (39)$$

for $y \in C$ and $y_o \in \partial C$, $y_o \neq \bar{0}$. We consider

$$\int_{\mathbb{R}^n} (\mathcal{N}((e^{-2\pi \langle y,t \rangle} - e^{-2\pi \langle y_o,t \rangle}) \mathbf{g}(t)))^2 dt$$

and want to show that this integral approaches 0 as $y \to y_o$, $y \in \{y \in C : 0 < a < |y| < b\}$. We have $\mathrm{supp}(\mathbf{g}) \subseteq \{t \in \mathbb{R}^n : u_C(t) \leq A\} = C^* + N(\bar{0}; A)$ since C is open and convex as noted before in the proof of Theorem 8; thus, $t \in \{t \in \mathbb{R}^n : u_C(t) \leq A\}$ implies $t = t_1 + t_2$ where $t_1 \in C^*$ and $t_2 \in \overline{N(\bar{0}, A)}$. For $y \in \{y \in C : 0 < a < |y| < b\}$ with $0 < a < |y_o| < b$ by definition of a and b we have for almost all $t \in \mathbb{R}^n$

$$(\mathcal{N}((e^{-2\pi \langle y,t \rangle} - e^{-2\pi \langle y_o,t \rangle}) \mathbf{g}(t)))^2 = |e^{-2\pi \langle y, t_1+t_2 \rangle} - e^{-2\pi \langle y_o, t_1+t_2 \rangle}|^2 (\mathcal{N}(\mathbf{g}(t)))^2.$$

Since $t_1 \in C^*$, $\langle y, t_1 \rangle \geq 0$ for all $y \in C$ which implies $\langle y_o, t_1 \rangle \geq 0$ also. Continuing the preceding inequality we have for $t_1 \in C^*$, $t_2 \in \overline{N(\bar{0}, A)}$, and all $y \in \{y \in C : 0 < a < |y| < b\}$

$$(\mathcal{N}((e^{-2\pi \langle y,t \rangle} - e^{-2\pi \langle y_o,t \rangle}) \mathbf{g}(t)))^2 \leq (e^{-2\pi \langle y, t_2 \rangle} + e^{-2\pi \langle y_o, t_2 \rangle})^2 (\mathcal{N}(\mathbf{g}(t)))^2$$
$$\leq (e^{2\pi |y||t_2|} + e^{2\pi |y_o||t_2|})^2 (\mathcal{N}(\mathbf{g}(t)))^2 \leq 4 e^{4\pi bA} (\mathcal{N}(\mathbf{g}(t)))^2$$

with the bound being independent of $y \in \{y \in C : 0 < a < |y| < b\}$ and being in $L^1(\mathbb{R}^n)$ since $\mathbf{g} \in L^2(\mathbb{R}^n, \mathcal{H})$. Since $(e^{-2\pi \langle y,t \rangle} - e^{-2\pi \langle y_o,t \rangle}) \mathbf{g}(t) \to \Theta$ as $y \to y_o$, $y \in \{y \in C : 0 <$

$a < |y| < b$} with $0 < a < |y_o| < b$, the Lebesgue dominated convergence theorem and (39) yield (37).

To prove (38) let $\phi \in \mathcal{S}(\mathbb{R}^n)$ and $y_o \in \partial C$, $y_o \neq \bar{0}$. As before choose constants a and b such that $0 < a < |y_o| < b$. For $y \in \{y \in C : 0 < a < |y| < b\}$ we have

$$\mathcal{N}(\langle \mathbf{f}(x+iy), \phi(x) \rangle - \langle \mathbf{F}(x+iy_o), \phi(x) \rangle)$$
$$\leq \int_{\mathbb{R}^n} \mathcal{N}((\mathbf{f}(x+iy) - \mathbf{F}(x+iy_o))\phi(x))dx$$
$$\leq |\mathbf{f}(x+iy) - \mathbf{F}(x+iy_o)|_2 ||\phi||_{L^2(\mathbb{R}^n)}.$$

Using (37) we obtain (38) in the weak topology of $\mathcal{S}'(\mathbb{R}^n, \mathcal{H})$ as $y \to y_o$, $y \in \{y \in C : 0 < a < |y| < b\}$ with $0 < a < |y_o| < b$. Now (38) is obtained in the strong topology of $\mathcal{S}'(\mathbb{R}^n, \mathcal{H})$ since $\mathcal{S}(\mathbb{R}^n)$ is a Montel space. The proof is complete. □

Since both $R_A^2(T^C, \mathcal{H})$ and $V_A^2(T^C, \mathcal{H})$ are subsets of $H_A^2(T^C, \mathcal{H})$, functions in both of these subset spaces satisfy (29) and (30) on the distinguished boundary of T^C with C being a regular cone. Also $V_A^2(T^C, \mathcal{H})$ functions will have the results of Theorem 12 since $V_A^2(T^C, \mathcal{H}) \subseteq R_A^2(T^C, \mathcal{H})$.

Boundary value results for the analytic functions on the topological boundary of the tube may be able to be obtained for various types of base sets C of the tube T^C. For example one could consider C to be an open polyhedron in $\mathbb{R}^n$ as defined in [11] and [12] (p. 97). One could follow this situation by considering an open convex subset B of $\mathbb{R}^n$ with y_o being a point on its boundary; consideration could be given then to constructing an open polyhedron in B with y_o as boundary point and approaching y_o within the open polyhedron as Stein and Weiss have done in [12] (p. 98) for functions in $H^2(T^B)$. Clearly the types of boundary values available will depend on the specifics of the analytic functions and on the base of the tube if boundary values exist at all. More will be stated in Section 9 concerning boundary values.

We have previously obtained boundary value results on the distinguished boundary of the tube for functions of type $V_*^p(T^C)$, $1 < p \leq 2$, in the scalar-valued ultradistribution sense where C is a regular cone in $\mathbb{R}^n$. That is, the norm growth on the analytic functions on T^C is

$$||\mathbf{f}(x+iy)||_{L^p(\mathbb{R}^n)} \leq K e^{M^*(w/|y|)}, \; y \in C,$$

where $w > 0$ and $K = K(\mathbf{f}, p, w)$ are independent of $y \in C$. We have proved that such functions obtain a boundary value at $\bar{0}$ in the ultradistribution space $\mathcal{D}'((M_p), L^1(\mathbb{R}^n))$. We refer to [2] (p. 106, Theorem 5.2.1) and the preceding analysis in [2] (Section 5.2).

9. Suggested Research

In this section, we suggest problems to consider in future research which are associated with the analysis of this paper.

Let B be an open connected subset of $\mathbb{R}^n$. Stein and Weiss use a bound condition on $H^p(T^B)$ obtained in [12] (p. 99, Lemma 2.12) to prove [12] (p. 93, Theorem 2.3), the representation theorem for functions in $H^2(T^B)$. The bound condition holds for z in a tube whose base is restricted uniformly away from the complement of B. We have used a similarly needed growth condition, obtained in [2] (p. 87, Lemma 5.1.3), on the analytic functions studied in [2] (Chapter 5) in relation to boundary values in ultradistribution spaces.

Starting with Lemma 1 in Section 6 of this paper we have used the following assumption on $\mathbf{f}(z) \in H_A^2(T^B, \mathcal{H})$ to obtain several results; the assumption on $\mathbf{f}(z)$ is that it "be bounded for $x = \text{Re}(z) \in \mathbb{R}^n$ and $y = \text{Im}(z)$ in any compact subset of B". We conjecture that a bound condition like [12] (p. 99, Lemma 2.12) holds for $\mathbf{f}(z) \in H_A^p(T^B, \mathcal{X})$; such a result will allow us to delete the above quoted assumption used in Sections 6–8.

Additionally we suggest research to obtain a bound condition like [12] (p. 99, Lemma 2.12) for functions in $H^p(T^B, \mathcal{X})$.

Throughout this paper we have obtained boundary value results both on the distinguished boundary of the tube and on the topological boundary of the tube. In every case a question that had to be considered was the method to approach a point on the boundary by points in the base in order to obtain a desired result. Our results before Section 8 concerned tubes with base being a regular cone, an open connected cone in $\mathbb{R}^n$, or a proper open connected subset of $\mathbb{R}^n$. In these cases we could approach a considered boundary point y_0 on the boundary of the base by a sequence of points within the base. Because of the nature of the analytic functions considered in Section 8 we needed to approach any boundary point y_0, $y_0 \neq \bar{0}$, on the boundary of the base, a regular cone, by a sequence of points inside a band contained in the cone in order to obtain the desired result. Indications of other boundary point approaches for consideration were stated at the end of Section 8.

Stein and Weiss [12] (pp. 94–98) discuss situations in which boundary values on the boundary of tubes can not be obtained as points within the base arbitrarily approach the point y_0 on the boundary of the base. In the first case a specific type of analytic function was constructed in order to show the non-existence of a boundary value for arbitrary approach to a point on the boundary by points within the base. In the second case a $H^2(T^B)$ function was constructed for which no limit in the L^2 norm existed for arbitrary approach to $\bar{0}$ within B; but if the base B was suitably restricted, any function in $H^2(T^B)$ for the restricted base B was shown to have a boundary value at any point on ∂B. Considerations of the approach to the boundary by points within bases B of other types than those of this paper could be made concerning the types of analytic functions defined in this paper. Are there base sets B in which an analytic function will not have a boundary value at a specified point $y_0 \in \partial B$ or such that there could be a boundary value if the base B is specialized?

The basic results of Section 5, Theorems 2, 4, 6 and 8, have all been proved for the most general appropriate situation. B was an open connected subset of $\mathbb{R}^n$ or open (or convex) connected cone in $\mathbb{R}^n$; values were in Banach space $\mathcal{X}$; results held for all p, $1 \leq p < \infty$, in Section 5. In Sections 6–8, the base B of the tube remained an open connected subset of $\mathbb{R}^n$ or a cone in $\mathbb{R}^n$ as appropriate; but all of the main results of these sections were proved for values in Hilbert space $\mathcal{H}$ with $p = 2$.

Of course the reason for the restrictions in these sections to $p = 2$ and values in $\mathcal{H}$ is that the primary tool in our proofs was the Fourier transform which, as previously noted, is available in its desired completeness to the specific cases of $p = 2$ and values in $\mathcal{H}$. We desire to extend the results of Sections 6–8 to $1 \leq p < \infty$ and values in Banach space $\mathcal{X}$ as appropriate by using different techniques. This has been done by Vindas in [1] where functional analysis techniques have been used to extend the Poisson integral representation of functions in $H^p(T^C, \mathcal{H})$ from $p = 2$ with values in $\mathcal{H}$ to $1 \leq p \leq \infty$ with values in $\mathcal{X}$. See [1] (Theorem 2); similarly see also [1] (Theorem 1). Use of functional analysis techniques and accumulated knowledge related to vector-valued fuctions to obtain the desired extensions of the results noted in this paragraph should be considered. Extensions of results from $p = 2$ to $1 \leq p < \infty$ could possibly also be obtained here for Hilbert space $\mathcal{H}$ by applying limit processes using the $p = 2$ case. We believe that the basic results of Sections 6–8 can be extended to $1 \leq p < \infty$ and values in Banach space $\mathcal{X}$ as appropriate. We suggest consideration of this extension in future research.

For $p = 2$ we have proved in previous work that the $\mathcal{S}'(\mathbb{R}^n)$ Fourier transform maps the distribution space $\mathcal{D}'_{L^2(\mathbb{R}^n)}$ one-one and onto $\mathcal{S}'_2$; further we have proved that the $\mathcal{S}'(\mathbb{R}^n)$ Fourier transform maps $\mathcal{D}'_{L^p(\mathbb{R}^n)}$, $1 \leq p < 2$, one-one and into $\mathcal{S}'_q$, $(1/p) + (1/q) = 1$. The proofs are obtained using the characterization results for the form of elements in $\mathcal{D}'_{L^p(\mathbb{R}^n)}$, $1 \leq p \leq 2$. With knowledge of a characterization of elements in the vector-valued distribution space equivalent to $\mathcal{D}'_{L^2(\mathbb{R}^n)}$ we conjecture that the $\mathcal{S}'(\mathbb{R}^n, \mathcal{H})$ Fourier transform maps this vector-valued distribution space one-one and onto $\mathcal{S}'_2(\mathbb{R}^n, \mathcal{H})$. Of course the values of the vector-valued distributions would need to be in Hilbert space $\mathcal{H}$ because of the probable use of the function Fourier transform on $L^2(\mathbb{R}^n, \mathcal{H})$ functions.

Results similar to those of this paper may be in order concerning the functions defined as $H(C)$ in [7]. We leave this for future research.

10. Conclusions

As stated in Section 1 our goal in this paper was to obtain results for the analytic functions defined in Section 4 treated as generalizations of $H^p(T^B, \mathcal{X})$ functions and as generalizations of the scalar-valued functions noted in [2] (Chapter 5) and in some of our papers referenced in [2] and hence to generalize results concerning $H^p(T^B, \mathcal{X})$ spaces and concerning the functions of [2] (Chapter 5) to these new spaces of analytic functions. Additionally, we stated that our goal also was to obtain additional new results for the analytic fuctions of Section 4.

We were successful in our goals in Section 5 for all of the results there that had as assumption that $\mathbf{g}(t)$ was a $\mathcal{X}$ valued measurable function for which the growth (1) held and for all of the results that had as assumption that $\mathbf{g} \in \mathcal{S}'_p(\mathbb{R}^n, \mathcal{X})$; these results held for $\mathcal{X}$ being a Banach space and for all $p, 1 \leq p < \infty$.

We were partially successful in our goals in Section 6 where the results depended on hypotheses on the analytic function concerning $\mathcal{X}$ and p. Because our proofs of these results depended on the Fourier transform we had to restrict $\mathcal{X}$ to $\mathcal{H}$, a Hilbert space, and $p = 2$ as described previously. But under these restrictions in Section 6 we were able to obtain Fourier–Laplace integral representation and boundary value results on the distinguished boundary of the tube for the analytic functions. In Section 7, we were able to prove containment of certain analytic functions from Definitions 1–4 in the Hardy space $H^2(T^C, \mathcal{H})$. In Section 8, we were able to obtain boundary value results on the topological boundary of the tube domain for the functions considered there. We desire to have the results of Sections 6–8 holding as well for $\mathcal{X}$ being a Banach space and for $1 \leq p < \infty$.

In our previous work concerning scalar-valued generalizations of $H^p(T^B)$ functions we have been able to obtain results under the assumption on the analytic functions of the type in Sections 6–8 for all p, $1 \leq p < \infty$. That is we have obtained Fourier–Laplace integral representation and boundary value results for all p, $1 \leq p < \infty$, on the assumed scalar-valued analytic function. Additionally, we have obtained Cauchy and Poisson integral representations as appropriate. Because of the existence of these results for all p in the scalar-valued case we have emphasized in Section 9 our belief that the basic results of Sections 6–8 can be extended to $1 \leq p < \infty$ and to values in Banach space $\mathcal{X}$ under assumption on the analytic function in the results. We believe that new techniques apart from the Fourier transform will be used to obtained these desired results as described in Section 9. We pursue the analysis of these topics for the generalized setting in the future.

The author believes that there is considerable additional interesting analysis in the generalized format of the results in this paper that can be obtained in regards to integral representation, boundary values, and applications for the functions of Definitions 1–4.

Funding: This research received no external funding.

Conflicts of Interest: The author declares no conflict of interest.

References

1. Carmichael, R.D.; Pilipović, S.; Vindas, J. Note on vector valued Hardy spaces related to analytic functions having distributional boundary values. In Proceedings of the 12th ISAAC Congress, Aveiro, Portugal, 29 July–2 August 2019; Research Perspectives; Birkhäuser: Basel, Switzerland, 2019; in press.
2. Carmichael, R.D.; Kamiński, A.; Pilipović, S. *Boundary Values and Convolution in Ultradistribution Spaces*; World Scientific Publishing: Singapore, 2007.
3. Dunford, N.; Schwartz, J. *Linear Operators Part I*; Interscience Publishers Inc.: New York, NY, USA, 1966.
4. Schwartz, L. Théorie des Distributions a Valeurs Vectorielles I. *Ann. Inst. Fourier* **1957**, *7*, 1–149. [CrossRef]
5. Schwartz, L. Théorie des Distributions a Valeurs Vectorielles II. *Ann. Inst. Fourier* **1958**, *8*, 1–209. [CrossRef]
6. Arendt, W.; Batty, C.; Hieber, M.; Neubrander, F. *Vector-Valued Laplace Transforms and Cauchy Problems*, 2nd ed.; Birkhauser/Springer: Basel, Switzerland, 2011.
7. Vladimirov, V. S. Generalization of the Cauchy-Bochner integral representation. *Math. USSR-Izv.* **1969**, *3*, 87–104. [CrossRef]

8. Vladimirov, V. S. On Cauchy-Bochner representations. *Math. USSR-Izv.* **1972**, *6*, 529–535. [CrossRef]
9. Vladimirov, V. S. *Generalized Functions in Mathematical Physics*; Mir Publishers: Moscow, Russia, 1979.
10. Vladimirov, V. S. *Methods of the Theory of Functions of Many Complex Variables*; The M.I.T. Press: Cambridge, MA, USA, 1966.
11. Stein, E.; Weiss, G.; Weiss, M. H^p classes of holomorphic functions in tube domains. *Proc. Nat. Acad. Sci. USA* **1964**, *52*, 1035–1039. [CrossRef] [PubMed]
12. Stein, E.; Weiss, G. *Introduction to Fourier Analysis on Euclidean Spaces*; Princeton Univ. Press: Princeton, NJ, USA, 1971.

Article

An Application of Sălăgean Operator Concerning Starlike Functions [†]

Hatun Özlem Güney [1], Georgia Irina Oros [2] and Shigeyoshi Owa [3,*]

[1] Department of Mathematics, Faculty of Science Dicle University, Diyarbakır 21280, Turkey; ozlemg@dicle.edu.tr
[2] Department of Mathematics and Computer Sciences, Faculty of Informatics and Sciences, University of Oradea, 410087 Oradea, Romania; georgia_oros_ro@yahoo.co.uk
[3] "1 Decembrie 1918" University of Alba Iulia, 510009 Alba Iulia, Romania
* Correspondence: shige21@ican.zaq.ne.jp
[†] Dedicated to the memory of Professor Yaşar Polatoğlu.

Abstract: As an application of the well-known Sălăgean differential operator, a new operator is introduced and, using this, a new class of functions $S_n(\alpha)$ is defined, which has the classes of starlike and convex functions of order α as special cases. Original results related to the newly defined class are obtained using the renowned Jack–Miller–Mocanu lemma. A relevant example is given regarding the applications of a new proven result concerning interesting properties of class $S_n(\alpha)$.

Keywords: analytic function; starlike function of order α; convex function of order α; Sălăgean differential operator; Alexander integral operator

1. Introduction and Preliminaries

Many operators have been used since the beginning of the study of analytic functions. The most interesting of these are the differential and integral operators. Since the beginning of the 20th century, many mathematicians, especially J.W. Alexander [1], S.D. Bernardi [2] and R.J. Libera [3], have worked on integral operators. It has become easier to introduce new classes of univalent functions with the use of operators. In his article, published in 1983, Sălăgean introduced differential and integral operators, which bear his name. Those operators were very inspiring and many mathematicians have obtained new, interesting results using these operators. In particular, researchers have introduced many new operators, examined their properties, and further used the newly defined operators to introduce classes of univalent functions with remarkable properties. At the same time, some mathematicians obtained interesting results in different lines of research by combining differential and integral operators, where Sălăgean differential operator was involved, as is seen, for example, in very recent papers [4–6]. The topic of strong differential subordination was also approached recently using Sălăgean differential operator in [7], and new operators were introduced using a fractional integral of Sălăgean and Ruscheweyh operators in [8]. The operators introduced using the Sălăgean differential operator were also recently used to obtain results related to the celebrated Fekete–Szegö inequality [9].

In this work, we introduce a new class as an application of the Sălăgean operator and discuss some interesting problems with this class.

Let A be the class of functions f of the form

$$f(z) = z + \sum_{k=2}^{\infty} a_k z^k \tag{1}$$

which are analytic in the open unit disc $\mathbb{U} = \{z \in \mathbb{C} : |z| < 1\}$ and $\mathcal{S}$ be the subclass of A consisting of univalent functions. Also,

$$S^*(\alpha) = \left\{ f \in A : \operatorname{Re}\left(\frac{zf'(z)}{f(z)}\right) > \alpha, z \in \mathbb{U}, 0 \leq \alpha < 1 \right\}$$

is the class of starlike functions of order α and

$$K(\alpha) = \left\{ f \in A : \operatorname{Re}\left(1 + \frac{zf''(z)}{f'(z)}\right) > \alpha, z \in \mathbb{U}, 0 \leq \alpha < 1 \right\}$$

is the class of convex functions of order α.

Let us start by recalling the well-known definitions for the Sălăgean differential and integral operators.

Definition 1 (Sălăgean [10]). *For $f \in A$, the Sălăgean differential operator D^n is defined by $D^n : A \to A$,*

$$D^0 f(z) = f(z) = z + \sum_{k=2}^{\infty} a_k z^k, \tag{?}$$

$$D^1 f(z) = Df(z) = zf'(z) = z + \sum_{k=2}^{\infty} k a_k z^k, \tag{3}$$

$$D^n f(z) = D(D^{n-1} f(z)) = z + \sum_{k=2}^{\infty} k^n a_k z^k \quad (n = 1, 2, 3, \cdots), \tag{4}$$

and Sălăgean integral operator D^{-n} is defined by

$$D^{-1} f(z) = \int_0^z \frac{f(t)}{t} dt = z + \sum_{k=2}^{\infty} \frac{1}{k} a_k z^k \tag{5}$$

and

$$D^{-n} f(z) = D^{-1}(D^{-n+1} f(z)) = z + \sum_{k=2}^{\infty} \frac{1}{k^n} a_k z^k \quad (n = 1, 2, 3, \cdots). \tag{6}$$

In view of Definition 1, the following new operator is introduced:

Definition 2. *For $f \in A$*

$$D^j f(z) = z + \sum_{k=2}^{\infty} k^j a_k z^k \quad (j = \cdots, -2, -1, 0, 1, 2, \cdots). \tag{7}$$

With the above operator $D^j f$, we introduce the subclass $S_n(\alpha)$.

Definition 3. *The subclass $S_n(\alpha)$ of A consists of functions f, which satisfy*

$$\operatorname{Re}\left(\frac{D^{n+1} f(z)}{D^n f(z)}\right) > \alpha \quad (n = \cdots, -2, -1, 0, 1, 2, \cdots) \tag{8}$$

for $z \in \mathbb{U}$, where $0 \leq \alpha < 1$.

Remark 1. *Since $D^0 f(z) = f(z)$, $D^1 f(z) = zf'(z)$ and $D^2 f(z) = zf'(z) + z^2 f''(z)$, $f \in S_0(\alpha)$ satisfies*

$$\operatorname{Re}\left(\frac{zf'(z)}{f(z)}\right) > \alpha \quad (z \in \mathbb{U}), \tag{9}$$

and $f \in S_1(\alpha)$ satisfies
$$Re\left(1 + \frac{zf''(z)}{f'(z)}\right) > \alpha \quad (z \in \mathbb{U}). \tag{10}$$

Therefore, $f \in S_0(\alpha) = S^*(\alpha)$ is starlike of order α in $\mathbb{U}$, and $f \in S_1(\alpha) = K(\alpha)$ is convex of order α in $\mathbb{U}$ (cf. Robertson [11]). Since $D^{-1}f$ is Alexander integral operator, $D^{-n}f$ $(n = 1, 2, 3, \cdots)$ is the generalization for Alexander integral operator (cf. Alexander [1]).

For a function $f \in A$, we introduce
$$M_p(r, f) = \begin{cases} \left(\frac{1}{2\pi}\int_0^{2\pi}|f(re^{i\theta})|^p d\theta\right)^{\frac{1}{p}} & , \quad (0 < p < \infty) \\ max_{|z| \leq r}|f(z)| & , \quad (p = \infty). \end{cases} \tag{11}$$

For the above $M_p(r, f)$, we define
$$\mathcal{H}^p = \left\{f \in A : \|f\|_p = \lim_{r \to 1^-} M_p(r, f) < \infty\right\}. \tag{12}$$

To discuss our problems, we have to introduce the following lemmas.

Lemma 1 (Wilken and Feng [12]). *If $f \in S_1(\alpha)$, then $f \in S_0(\beta)$, where*
$$\beta = \beta(\alpha) = \begin{cases} \frac{2\alpha - 1}{2(1 - 2^{1-2\alpha})} & , \quad (\alpha \neq \frac{1}{2}) \\ \frac{1}{2log 2} = 0.7213\ldots & , \quad (\alpha = \frac{1}{2}). \end{cases} \tag{13}$$

The result is sharp.

Lemma 2 (Eenigenburg and Keogh [13]). *If $f \in S_0(\alpha)$ and*
$$f(z) \neq \frac{z}{(1 - ze^{i\theta})^2}, \tag{14}$$

then there exists $\delta = \delta(f) > 0$ such that $\frac{f(z)}{z} \in \mathcal{H}^{\delta + \frac{1}{2(1-\alpha)}}$.

Lemma 3 (Nunokawa [14]). *Let a function p be analytic in $\mathbb{U}$ with $p(0) = 1$. If p satisfies*
$$Re(p(z) + zp'(z)) > \frac{1 - 2log 2}{2(1 - log 2)} = -0.629\ldots \quad (z \in \mathbb{U}) \tag{15}$$

then $Re p(z) > 0$ $(z \in \mathbb{U})$.

Lemma 4 (Duren [15]). *If a function p is analytic in $\mathbb{U}$ and $Re p(z) > 0$ $(z \in \mathbb{U})$, then $p \in \mathcal{H}^p$ $(0 < p < 1)$.*

Lemma 5 (Kim, Lee and Srivastava [16]). *If $f \in A$ satisfies $z^\gamma f(z) \in \mathcal{H}^p$ $(0 < p < \infty)$ for some real γ, then $f \in \mathcal{H}^p$ $(0 < p < \infty)$.*

Lemma 6 (Duren [15]). *If $f \in A$ satisfies $f' \in \mathcal{H}^p$ $(0 < p < 1)$, then $f \in \mathcal{H}^{\frac{p}{1-p}}$.*

Discussing our problems for Sălăgean operator, we need to introduce the following lemma due to Miller and Mocanu [17,18] (also, by Jack [19]).

Lemma 7 (Miller and Mocanu [17,18]). *Let the function w given by*
$$w(z) = b_n z^n + b_{n+1} z^{n+1} + b_{n+2} z^{n+2} + \ldots, \quad n \in \mathbb{N} \tag{16}$$

be analytic in $\mathbb{U}$ with $w(0) = 0$. If $|w(z)|$ attains its maximum value on the circle $|z| = r$ at a point $z_0 \in \mathbb{U}$, then a real number $k \geq n$ exists, such that

$$\frac{z_0 w'(z_0)}{w(z_0)} = k \tag{17}$$

and

$$\operatorname{Re}\left(1 + \frac{z_0 w''(z_0)}{w'(z_0)}\right) \geq k. \tag{18}$$

The original results obtained by the authors and presented in this paper are contained in the next section. A new operator is introduced with Sălăgean differential operator as the inspiration. Using this newly introduced operator, a new class of functions denoted by $S_n(\alpha)$ is defined, with known classes as particular cases. Certain properties involving the applications of Sălăgean differential operator related to class $S_n(\alpha)$ are discussed in the theorems and corollaries. Examples are also included to prove the applications of the proved results.

2. Main Results

Now, we derive the following result.

Theorem 1. *If $f \in S_n(\alpha)$, then $f \in S_{n-j}(\alpha_j)$, where $n > j \geq 0$ and*

$$\alpha_j = \begin{cases} \frac{2\alpha_{j-1} - 1}{2(1 - 2^{1 - 2\alpha_{j-1}})} & , (\alpha_j \neq \frac{1}{2}) \\ \frac{1}{2\log 2} = 0.7213\ldots & , (\alpha_j = \frac{1}{2}). \end{cases} \tag{19}$$

Further, if

$$D^{n-j}f(z) \neq \frac{z}{(1 - z e^{i\theta})^{2(1-\alpha_j)}}, \tag{20}$$

then there exists $\delta > 0$, such that $D^{n-j}f \in \mathcal{H}^{\delta + \frac{1}{2(1-\alpha_j)}}$.

Proof. We note that if $f \in S_n(\alpha)$, then

$$\operatorname{Re}\left(\frac{D^{n+1}f(z)}{D^n f(z)}\right) > \alpha_0 \quad (z \in \mathbb{U}), \tag{21}$$

where $\alpha_0 = \alpha$. Since

$$D^{n+1}f(z) = z(D^n f(z))' = z(D^{n-1}f(z))' + z^2(D^{n-1}f(z))'' \tag{22}$$

and

$$D^n f(z) = z(D^{n-1}f(z))', \tag{23}$$

we see that

$$\operatorname{Re}\left(\frac{D^{n+1}f(z)}{D^n f(z)}\right) = \operatorname{Re}\left(1 + \frac{z(D^{n-1}f(z))''}{(D^{n-1}f(z))'}\right) > \alpha_0 \quad (z \in \mathbb{U}). \tag{24}$$

Applying Lemma 1, we say that

$$
\begin{aligned}
f \in S_n(\alpha_0) &\Leftrightarrow D^{n-1}f \in S_1(\alpha_0) \\
&\Rightarrow D^{n-1}f \in S_0(\alpha_1) \\
&\Leftrightarrow D^{n-2}f \in S_1(\alpha_1) \\
&\Rightarrow D^{n-2}f \in S_0(\alpha_2) \\
&\Leftrightarrow D^{n-3}f \in S_1(\alpha_2) \\
&\vdots \\
&\Leftrightarrow D^{n-j}f \in S_0(\alpha_{j-1}) \\
&\Rightarrow D^{n-j}f \in S_1(\alpha_j).
\end{aligned}
\tag{25}
$$

This implies that

$$
\operatorname{Re}\left(\frac{z(D^{n-j}f(z))'}{D^{n-j}f(z)}\right) = \operatorname{Re}\left(\frac{D^{n-j+1}f(z)}{D^{n-j}f(z)}\right) > \alpha_j \quad (z \in \mathbb{U}), \tag{26}
$$

that is, that $f \in S_{n-j}(\alpha_j)$. Further, applying Lemma 2, we see that if

$$
D^{n-j}f(z) \neq \frac{z}{(1 - ze^{i\theta})^{2(1-\alpha_j)}}, \tag{27}
$$

then there exists $\delta > 0$, such that $D^{n-j}f \in \mathcal{H}^{\delta + \frac{1}{2(1-\alpha_j)}}$. $\square$

Example 1. *Let us consider a function f belonging to the class $S_3(\alpha)$. Then $f \in S_2(\alpha_1)$ with (19), where*

$$
\alpha_1 = \begin{cases} \frac{2\alpha-1}{2(1-2^{1-2\alpha})}, & (\alpha \neq \frac{1}{2}) \\ \frac{1}{2\log 2} \doteq 0.7213\ldots, & (\alpha = \frac{1}{2}). \end{cases} \tag{28}
$$

Further, $f \in S_1(\alpha_2)$, where

$$
\alpha_2 = \begin{cases} \frac{2\alpha_1-1}{2(1-2^{1-2\alpha_1})}, & (\alpha_1 \neq \frac{1}{2}) \\ \frac{1}{2\log 2} \doteq 0.7213\ldots, & (\alpha_1 = \frac{1}{2}). \end{cases} \tag{29}
$$

Also, $f \in S_0(\alpha_3)$, where

$$
\alpha_3 = \begin{cases} \frac{2\alpha_2-1}{2(1-2^{1-2\alpha_2})}, & (\alpha_2 \neq \frac{1}{2}) \\ \frac{1}{2\log 2} \doteq 0.7213\ldots, & (\alpha_2 = \frac{1}{2}). \end{cases} \tag{30}
$$

If we consider the case of $\alpha = \frac{1}{4}$, then we have

$$
\alpha_1 = \frac{1}{4(\sqrt{2}-1)} \doteq 0.60355, \tag{31}
$$

$$
\alpha_2 = \frac{3 - 2\sqrt{2}}{4(\sqrt{2}-1)(1 - 2^{\frac{1-\sqrt{2}}{2}})} \doteq 0.77436, \tag{32}
$$

and

$$
\alpha_3 \doteq 0.8672. \tag{33}
$$

Further, if we consider the case of $\alpha = \frac{1}{8}$, then

$$\alpha_1 = \frac{3}{8(\sqrt[4]{8}-1)} \doteq 0.55002, \tag{34}$$

and

$$\alpha_2 = \frac{7 - 4\sqrt[4]{8}}{8(\sqrt[4]{8}-1)\left(1 - 2^{\frac{4\sqrt[4]{8}-7}{4(\sqrt[4]{8}-1)}}\right)} \doteq 0.60607. \tag{35}$$

Remark 2. *For some positive integer j, we know that*

$$\alpha_{j+1} = \frac{2\alpha_j - 1}{2(1 - 2^{1-2\alpha_j})} \quad , \quad (\alpha_j \neq \tfrac{1}{2}). \tag{36}$$

If we consider

$$g(\alpha_j) = \alpha_{j+1} - \alpha_j = \frac{2\alpha_j - 1}{2(1 - 2^{1-2\alpha_j})} - \alpha_j \quad , \quad (\alpha_j \neq \tfrac{1}{2}), \tag{37}$$

$g(0) = \frac{1}{2}$ and $g(1) = 0$. From this fact, we know that $\alpha_j < \alpha_{j+1}$ for $0 \le \alpha_j < 1$. This implies that

$$0 \le \alpha < \alpha_1 < \alpha_2 < \cdots < \alpha_j < \cdots < 1. \tag{38}$$

Letting $j = n$ in Theorem 1, we see

Corollary 1. *If $f \in S_j(\alpha)$, then $f \in S_0(\alpha_j)$. If*

$$f(z) \neq \frac{z}{(1 - ze^{i\theta})^{2(1-\alpha_j)}}, \tag{39}$$

then there exists $\delta > 0$, such that $f \in \mathcal{H}^{\delta + \frac{1}{2(1-\alpha_j)}}$.

Next we have

Theorem 2. *If $f \in A$ satisfies*

$$\operatorname{Re}\left(\frac{D^{n+1}f(z)}{z}\right) = \frac{1 - 2\log 2}{2(1 - \log 2)} = -0.629\ldots \quad (z \in \mathbb{U}) \tag{40}$$

for some $n \in \mathbb{N}$, then there exists p_j, such that $D^{n-j+1}f \in \mathcal{H}^{p_j}$, where

$$p_j > \frac{1}{j - k + 1} \quad (k = 1, 2, 3, \cdots, j) \tag{41}$$

and $j \le n + 1$.

Proof. If we define p by

$$p(z) = \frac{D^n f(z)}{z}, \tag{42}$$

then p is analytic in $\mathbb{U}$ with $p(0) = 1$. Since

$$p(z) + zp'(z) = \frac{D^{n+1}f(z)}{z}, \tag{43}$$

we see that

$$\operatorname{Re}\left(\frac{D^{n+1}f(z)}{z}\right) = \operatorname{Re}(p(z) + zp'(z)) > \frac{1 - 2\log 2}{2(1 - \log 2)} \quad (z \in \mathbb{U}). \tag{44}$$

Applying Lemma 3, we have that

$$\operatorname{Re} p(z) = \operatorname{Re}\left(\frac{D^n f(z)}{z}\right) > 0 \quad (z \in \mathbb{U}). \tag{45}$$

Using Lemma 4, we know that

$$\frac{D^n f(z)}{z} \in \mathcal{H}^{p_1} \quad (0 < p_1 < \frac{1}{j}), \tag{46}$$

that is, that $(D^{n-1}f(z))' \in \mathcal{H}^{p_1}$. By Lemma 6, we have that

$$D^{n-1}f \in \mathcal{H}^{p_2} \quad (0 < p_2 = \frac{p_1}{1-p_1} < \frac{1}{j-1}). \tag{47}$$

Noting that

$$D^{n-1}f(z) = z(D^{n-2}f(z))', \tag{48}$$

we obtain that

$$D^{n-2}f \in \mathcal{H}^{p_3} \quad (0 < p_3 = \frac{p_2}{1-p_2} < \frac{1}{j-2}). \tag{49}$$

Repeating the above, we have that

$$D^{n-j+2}f \in \mathcal{H}^{p_{j-1}} \quad (0 < p_{j-1} < \frac{1}{2}). \tag{50}$$

Finally, we get

$$D^{n-j+1}f \in \mathcal{H}^{p_j} \quad (0 < p_j < 1). \tag{51}$$

□

Making $j = n+1$ in Theorem 2, we have

Corollary 2. *If $f \in A$ satisfies*

$$\operatorname{Re}\left(\frac{D^{n+1}f(z)}{z}\right) > \frac{1 - 2\log 2}{2(1 - \log 2)} = -0.629\ldots \quad (z \in \mathbb{U}), \tag{52}$$

then, there exists p_{n+1} such that $f \in \mathcal{H}^{p_{n+1}}$ $(0 < p_{n+1} < 1)$.

Next, we derive

Theorem 3. *If $f \in A$ satisfies*

$$\left|\frac{D^{n+2}f(z)}{D^{n+1}f(z)} - 1\right| < \frac{5\alpha - 2\alpha^2 - 1}{2\alpha} \quad (z \in \mathbb{U}), (n \in \mathbb{N}) \tag{53}$$

for some real α ($\frac{1}{3} \leq \alpha \leq \frac{1}{2}$), or

$$\left|\frac{D^{n+2}f(z)}{D^{n+1}f(z)} - 1\right| < \frac{\alpha - 2\alpha^2 + 1}{2\alpha} \quad (z \in \mathbb{U}), (n \in \mathbb{N}) \tag{54}$$

for some real α ($\frac{1}{2} \leq \alpha < 1$), then $D^n f \in S_0(\alpha)$, that is, $D^n f$ is starlike of order α in $\mathbb{U}$. Further, if

$$D^{n-j}f(z) \neq \frac{z}{(1 - ze^{i\theta})^{2(1-\alpha_j)}}, \tag{55}$$

then, there exists $\delta > 0$ such that $D^{n-j}f \in \mathcal{H}^{\delta + \frac{1}{2(1-\alpha_j)}}$, where

$$\alpha_j = \begin{cases} \frac{2\alpha_{j-1}-1}{2(1-2^{1-2\alpha_{j-1}})} & , (\alpha_{j-1} \neq \frac{1}{2}) \\ \frac{1}{2\log 2} = 0.7213\ldots & , (\alpha_{j-1} = \frac{1}{2}) \end{cases} \quad (56)$$

and $j \leq n$.

Proof. Define a function w by

$$\frac{D^{n+1}f(z)}{D^n f(z)} = \frac{1 + (1-2\alpha)w(z)}{1 - w(z)} \quad (w(z) \neq 1). \quad (57)$$

It follows from the above that

$$\frac{D^{n+2}f(z)}{D^{n+1}f(z)} - \frac{D^{n+1}f(z)}{D^n f(z)} = \frac{(1-2\alpha)zw'(z)}{1+(1-2\alpha)w(z)} + \frac{zw'(z)}{1-w(z)}. \quad (58)$$

Therefore, we have that

$$\frac{D^{n+2}f(z)}{D^{n+1}f(z)} - 1 = \left(\frac{w(z)}{1-w(z)}\right)\left\{2(1-\alpha) + \frac{zw'(z)}{w(z)}\left(1 + \frac{(1-2\alpha)(1-w(z))}{1+(1-2\alpha)w(z)}\right)\right\}. \quad (59)$$

Suppose that there exists a point $z_0 \in \mathbb{U}$, such that

$$max_{|z| \leq |z_0|}|w(z)| = |w(z_0)| = 1 \quad (w(z_0) \neq 1). \quad (60)$$

Then, Lemma 7 say that $w(z_0) = e^{i\theta}$ and $z_0 w'(z_0) = kw(z_0)$ $(k \geq 1)$. This implies that

$$\left|\frac{D^{n+2}f(z_0)}{D^{n+1}f(z_0)} - 1\right| = \left|\frac{e^{i\theta}}{1-e^{i\theta}}\right|\left|2(1-\alpha) + k\left(1 + \frac{(1-2\alpha)(1-e^{i\theta})}{1+(1-2\alpha)e^{i\theta}}\right)\right|$$

$$\geq \frac{2(1-\alpha_0)+k}{|1-e^{i\theta}|} - \frac{k|1-2\alpha|}{|1+(1-2\alpha)e^{i\theta}|} \quad (61)$$

$$\geq \frac{2(1-\alpha_0)+k}{2} - \frac{k|1-2\alpha|}{2\alpha}.$$

If $\frac{1}{3} \leq \alpha < \frac{1}{2}$, then

$$\left|\frac{D^{n+2}f(z_0)}{D^{n+1}f(z_0)} - 1\right| \geq \frac{5\alpha - 2\alpha^2 - 1}{2\alpha} \quad (62)$$

and if $\frac{1}{2} \leq \alpha < 1$, then

$$\left|\frac{D^{n+2}f(z_0)}{D^{n+1}f(z_0)} - 1\right| \geq \frac{\alpha - 2\alpha^2 + 1}{2\alpha}. \quad (63)$$

This contradicts our condition of the theorem. Thus we say that $|w(z)| < 1$ for all $z \in \mathbb{U}$. From the definition (57) for w, we obtain that

$$\text{Re}\left(\frac{D^{n+1}f(z)}{D^n f(z)}\right) > \alpha \quad (z \in \mathbb{U}). \quad (64)$$

This means that $D^n f \in S_0(\alpha)$. Letting $\alpha = \alpha_0$ and using Lemma 1, we obtain $D^{n-j}f \in S_0(\alpha_j)$, where α_j is given by (56). Applying Lemma 2, we know that if

$$D^{n-j}f(z) \neq \frac{z}{(1-ze^{i\theta})^{2(1-\alpha_j)}}, \quad (65)$$

then, there exists $\delta > 0$ such that $D^{n-j}f \in \mathcal{H}^{\delta + \frac{1}{2(1-\alpha_j)}}$. □

Making $j = n$ in Theorem 3, we have

Corollary 3. *If $f \in A$ satisfies*

$$\left|\frac{D^{n+2}f(z)}{D^{n+1}f(z)} - 1\right| < \frac{5\alpha - 2\alpha^2 - 1}{2\alpha} \quad (z \in \mathbb{U}), \tag{66}$$

for some real α ($\frac{1}{3} \leq \alpha \leq \frac{1}{2}$), or

$$\left|\frac{D^{n+2}f(z)}{D^{n+1}f(z)} - 1\right| < \frac{\alpha - 2\alpha^2 + 1}{2\alpha} \quad (z \in \mathbb{U}), \tag{67}$$

for some real α ($\frac{1}{2} \leq \alpha < 1$), then $D^n f \in S_0(\alpha)$. If

$$f(z) \neq \frac{z}{(1 - ze^{i\theta})^{2(1-\alpha_n)}}, \tag{68}$$

then, there exists $\delta > 0$, such that $f \in \mathcal{H}^{\delta + \frac{1}{2(1-\alpha_n)}}$.

3. Conclusions

Inspired by the classic and well-known Sălăgean differential operator, a new operator is introduced in Definition 2. By applying this operator, a new class of functions is defined, denoted by $S_n(\alpha)$. It is shown that classes of starlike and convex functions of the order α are obtained for specific values of n. Some interesting problems concerning the class $S_n(\alpha)$ are discussed in the theorems and corollaries. One example is given as an application for special cases of n for the class $S_n(\alpha)$. The new operator defined in this paper can be used to introduce other certain subclasses of analytic functions. Quantum calculus can be also associated for future studies, as can be seen in paper [20] regarding the Sălăgean differential operator and involving symmetric Sălăgean differential operator in paper [21]. Symmetry properties can be investigated for this operator, taking the symmetric Sălăgean derivative investigated in [22] as inspiration.

Author Contributions: Conceptualization, S.O., H.Ö.G. and G.I.O.; Investigation, S.O., H.Ö.G. and G.I.O.; Methodology, S.O.; Writing—original draft, S.O.; Writing—review and editing, H.Ö.G. and G.I.O. All authors have read and agreed to the published version of the manuscript.

Funding: This research received no external funding.

Institutional Review Board Statement: Not applicable.

Informed Consent Statement: Not applicable.

Data Availability Statement: Not applicable.

Conflicts of Interest: The authors declare no conflict of interest.

References

1. Alexander, J.W. Functions which map the interior of the unit circle upon simple regions. *Ann. Math.* **1915**, *17*, 12–22. [CrossRef]
2. Bernardi, S.D. Convex and starlike univalent functions. *Trans. Am. Math. Soc.* **1969**, *135*, 429–446. [CrossRef]
3. Libera, R.J. Some classes of regular univalent functions. *Proc. Am. Math. Soc.* **1965**, *16*, 755–758. [CrossRef]
4. Acu, M.; Oros, G. Starlikeness condition for a new differential-integral operator. *Mathematics* **2020**, *8*, 694. [CrossRef]
5. Oros, G.I.; Alb Lupaş, A. Sufficient conditions for univalence obtained by using Briot-Bouquet differential subordination. *Math. Stat.* **2020**, *8*, 26–136. [CrossRef]
6. Páll-Szabó, Á.O.; Wanas, A.K. Coefficient estimates for some new classes of bi-Bazilevič functions of Ma-Minda type involving the Sălăgean integro-differential operator. *Quaest. Math.* **2021**, *44*, 495–502.
7. Alb Lupaş, A.; Oros, G.I. Strong differential superordination results involving extended Sălăgean and Ruscheweyh Operators. *Mathematics* **2021** *9*, 2487. [CrossRef]

8. Alb Lupaş, A.; Oros, G.I. On Special Differential Subordinations Using Fractional Integral of Sălăgean and Ruscheweyh Operators. *Symmetry* **2021** *13*, 1553. [CrossRef]
9. Aouf, M.K.; Mostafa, A.O.; Madian, S.M. Fekete–Szegö properties for quasi-subordination class of complex order defined by Sălăgean operator. *Afr. Mat.* **2020**, *31*, 483–492. [CrossRef]
10. Sălăgean, G.S. Subclasses of Univalent Functions. In *Complex Analysis—Fifth Romanian-Finnish Seminar, Part I Bucharest*; Lecture Notes in Mathematics 1013; Springer: Berlin/Heidelberg, Germany, 1981; pp. 362–372.
11. Robertson, M.I. On the theory of univalent functions. *Ann. Math.* **1936**, *37*, 374–408. [CrossRef]
12. Wilken, D.R.; Feng, J. A remark on convex and starlike functions. *J. Lond. Math. Soc.* **1980**, *2*, 287–290. [CrossRef]
13. Eenigenburg, P.J.; Keogh, F.R. The Hardy class of some univalent functions and their derivatives. *Mich. Math. J.* **1970**, *17*, 335–346. [CrossRef]
14. Nunokawa, M. On starlikeness of Libera transformation. *Complex Var. Elliptic Equs.* **1991**, *17*, 79–83. [CrossRef]
15. Duren P.L. *Univalent Functions*; Grundlehren der Mathematischen Wissenschaften, Band 259; Springer: New York, NY, USA; Berlin/Heidelberg, Germany; Tokyo, Japan, 1983.
16. Kim, Y.C.; Lee, K.S.; Srivastava, H.M. Certain classes of integral operators associated with the Hardy space of analytic functions. *Complex Var. Elliptic Equs.* **1992**, *20*, 1–12. [CrossRef]
17. Miller, S.S.; Mocanu, P.T. Second order differential inequalities in the complex plane. *J. Math. Anal. Appl.* **1978**, *65*, 289–305. [CrossRef]
18. Miller, S.S.; Mocanu, P.T. Differential Subordinations. In *Theory and Applications*; Marcel Dekker Inc.: New York, NY, USA, 2000.
19. Jack, I.S. Functions starlike and convex of order α. *J. Lond. Math. Soc.* **1971**, *2*, 469–474. [CrossRef]
20. Govindaraj, M.; Sivasubramanian, S. On a class of analytic functions related to conic domains involving q-calculus. *Anal. Math.* **2017**, *43*, 475–487. [CrossRef]
21. Ibrahim, R.W.; Elobaid, R.M.; Obaiys, S.J. Geometric Inequalities via a Symmetric Differential Operator Defined by Quantum Calculus in the Open Unit Disk. *J. Funct. Spaces* **2020**, *2020*, 6932739. [CrossRef]
22. Ibrahim, R.W.; Darus, M. Univalent functions formulated by the Sălăgean-difference operator. *Int. J. Anal. Appl.* **2019**, *17*, 652–658.

Article

Subclasses of Yamakawa-Type Bi-Starlike Functions Associated with Gegenbauer Polynomials

Gangadharan Murugusundaramoorthy [1,†] and Teodor Bulboacă [2,*,†]

1. Department of Mathematics, School of Advanced Sciences, Vellore Institute of Technology, Vellore 632014, TN, India; gms@vit.ac.in
2. Faculty of Mathematics and Computer Science, Babeș-Bolyai University, 400084 Cluj-Napoca, Romania
* Correspondence: bulboaca@math.ubbcluj.ro; Tel.: +40-729087153
† These authors contributed equally to this work.

Abstract: In this paper, we introduce and investigate new subclasses (Yamakawa-type bi-starlike functions and another class of Lashin, both mentioned in the reference list) of bi-univalent functions defined in the open unit disk, which are associated with the Gegenbauer polynomials and satisfy subordination conditions. Furthermore, we find estimates for the Taylor–Maclaurin coefficients $|a_2|$ and $|a_3|$ for functions in these new subclasses. Several known or new consequences of the results are also pointed out.

Keywords: starlike and convex functions; hadamard product; subordination; bi-univalent functions; Fekete–Szegő problem; Gegenbauer polynomials; Yamakawa-type bi-starlike functions

MSC: 30C45; 30C50

1. Introduction and Preliminaries

In geometric function theory, there have been numerous interesting and fruitful usages of a wide variety of special functions, q-calculus and special polynomials; for example, the Fibonacci polynomials, the Faber polynomials, the Lucas polynomials, the Pell polynomials, the Pell–Lucas polynomials, and the Chebyshev polynomials of the second kind. The Horadam polynomials are potentially important in a variety of disciplines in the mathematical, physical, statistical, and engineering sciences. Gegenbauer polynomials or ultra spherical polynomials $\mathfrak{G}_n^\lambda$ can be obtained using the Gram–Schmidt orthogonalization process for polynomials in the domain $(-1,1)$ with the weight factor $(1-\ell^2)^{\lambda-\frac{1}{2}}$, $\lambda > -\frac{1}{2}$. Also, $\mathfrak{G}_n^0(\ell)$ is defined as $\lim_{\lambda \to 0} \frac{\mathfrak{G}_n^\lambda(\ell)}{\lambda}$, and for $\lambda \neq 0$ the resulting polynomial $R_n(\ell)$ is multiplied by a number which makes the value at $\ell = 1$ equal to $(2\lambda)_n/n! = 2\lambda(2\lambda+1)(2\lambda+2)\ldots(2\lambda+n-1)/n!$. For $\lambda = 0$ and $n \neq 0$, the value at $\ell = 1$ is $\frac{2}{n}$, while $\mathfrak{G}_0^0(\ell) = 1$.

The Gegenbauer polynomials (for details, see Kim et al. [1] and references cited therein) are given in terms of the Jacobi polynomials $P_n^{(\nu,\nu)}$, with $\nu = \upsilon = \lambda - \frac{1}{2}$, $\left(\lambda > -\frac{1}{2}, \lambda \neq 0\right)$, defined by

$$\mathfrak{G}_n^\lambda(\ell) = \frac{\Gamma\left(\lambda+\frac{1}{2}\right)\Gamma(n+2\lambda)}{\Gamma(2\lambda)\Gamma\left(n+\lambda+\frac{1}{2}\right)} P_n^{\left(\lambda-\frac{1}{2},\lambda-\frac{1}{2}\right)}(\ell)$$

$$= \binom{n+2\lambda-1}{n}\sum_{k=0}^{n}\frac{\binom{n}{k}(2\lambda+n)_k}{\left(\lambda+\frac{1}{2}\right)_k}\left(\frac{\ell-1}{2}\right)^k, \quad (1)$$

where $(a)_n := a(a+1)(a+2)\ldots(a+n-1)$, and $(a)_0 := 1$.

From (1), it follows that $\mathfrak{G}_n^\lambda(\ell)$ is a polynomial of degree n with real coefficients, and $\mathfrak{G}_n^\lambda(1) = \binom{n+2\lambda-1}{n}$, while the leading coefficient of $\mathfrak{G}_n^\lambda(\ell)$ is $2^n \binom{n+\lambda-1}{n}$. By the theory of Jacobi polynomials, for $\mu = \nu = \lambda - \frac{1}{2}$, with $\lambda > -\frac{1}{2}$, and $\lambda \neq 0$, we get

$$\mathfrak{G}_n^\lambda(-\ell) = (-1)^n \mathfrak{G}_n^\lambda(\ell).$$

It is easy to show that $\mathfrak{G}_n^\lambda(\ell)$ is a solution of the Gegenbauer differential equation

$$(1-\ell^2)y'' - (2\lambda)\ell y' + n(n+2\lambda)y = 0,$$

with $\ell = 0$ an ordinary point; this means that we can express the solution in the form of a power series $y = \sum_{n=0}^{\infty} a_n \ell^n$, and the Rodrigues formula for the Gegenbauer polynomials is (see [2,3]) as follows:

$$\left(1-\ell^2\right)^{\lambda-\frac{1}{2}} \mathfrak{G}_n^\lambda(\ell) = \frac{(-2)^n (\lambda)_n}{n!(n+2\lambda)_n} \left(\frac{d}{d\ell}\right)^n \left(1-\ell^2\right)^{n+\lambda-\frac{1}{2}},$$

and the above relation can be easily derived from the properties of Jacobi polynomials.

The generating function of Gegenbauer polynomials is given by (see [1,4])

$$\frac{2^{\lambda-\frac{1}{2}}}{(1-2\ell t+t^2)^{\frac{1}{2}}\left(1-\ell t+\sqrt{1-2\ell t+t^2}\right)^{\lambda-\frac{1}{2}}} = \frac{\left(\lambda-\frac{1}{2}\right)_n}{(2\lambda)_n} \mathfrak{G}_n^\lambda(\ell) t^n, \qquad (2)$$

and this equality can be derived from the generating function of Jacobi polynomials.

From the above relation (2), we note that

$$\frac{1}{(1-2\ell t+t^2)^\lambda} = \sum_{n=0}^{\infty} \mathfrak{G}_n^\lambda(\ell) t^n, \ t \in \mathbb{C}, \ |t|<1, \ \ell \in [-1,1], \ \lambda \in \left(-\frac{1}{2}, +\infty\right) \setminus \{0\}, \qquad (3)$$

and the proof is given in [4] and Kim et al. [1] (also, see [5]) where the authors extensively studied many results from different perspectives. For $\lambda = 1$, the relation (3) gives the ordinary generating function for the Chebyshev polynomials, and for $\lambda = \frac{1}{2}$, we obtain the ordinary generating function for the Legendre polynomials (see also [6]).

In 1935, Robertson [7] proved an integral representation for the typically real-valued function class T_R having the form

$$f(z) = z + \sum_{n=2}^{\infty} a_n z^n, \ z \in \Delta := \{z \in \mathbb{C} : |z|<1\}, \qquad (4)$$

which is holomorphic in the open unit disc Δ, real for $z \in (-1,1)$, and satisfies the condition

$$\operatorname{Im} f(z) \operatorname{Im} z > 0, \ z \in \Delta \setminus (-1,1).$$

Namely, $f \in T_R$ if and only if it has the representation

$$f(z) = \int_{-1}^{1} \frac{z}{1-2\ell z+z^2} \, d\mu, \ z \in \Delta,$$

where μ is a probability measure on $[-1,1]$. The class T_R has been extended in [8] to the class $T_R(\lambda)$, $\lambda > 0$, which was defined by

$$f(z) = \int_{-1}^{1} \Phi_\ell^\lambda(z) \, d\mu(\ell), \quad z \in \Delta, \quad -1 \leq \ell \leq 1, \tag{5}$$

where

$$\Phi_\ell^\lambda(z) := \frac{z}{(1 - 2\ell z + z^2)^\lambda}, \quad z \in \Delta, \quad -1 \leq \ell \leq 1, \tag{6}$$

and μ is a probability measure on $[-1, 1]$. The function $\Phi_\ell^\lambda(z)$ has the following Taylor–Maclaurin series expansion:

$$\Phi_\ell^\lambda(z) = z + \mathfrak{G}_1^\lambda(\ell) z^2 + \mathfrak{G}_2^\lambda(\ell) z^3 + \mathfrak{G}_3^\lambda(\ell) z^4 + \cdots + \mathfrak{G}_{n-1}^\lambda(\ell) z^n + \ldots, \tag{7}$$

where $\mathfrak{G}_n^\lambda(\ell)$ denotes the Gegenbauer (or ultra spherical) polynomials of order λ and degree n in ℓ, which are generated by

$$\Phi_\ell^\lambda(z) = \sum_{n=0}^{\infty} \mathfrak{G}_n^\lambda(\ell) z^n = z\left(1 - 2\ell z + z^2\right)^{-\lambda}.$$

In particular,

$$\mathfrak{G}_0^\lambda(\ell) = 1, \quad \mathfrak{G}_1^\lambda(\ell) = 2\lambda\ell, \quad \mathfrak{G}_2^\lambda(\ell) = 2\lambda(\lambda+1)\ell^2 - \lambda = 2(\lambda)_2 \ell^2 - \lambda. \tag{8}$$

Of course, we have $T_R(1) \equiv T_R$, and if f given by (5) is written in the power expansion series (4), then we have

$$a_n = \int_{-1}^{1} \mathfrak{G}_{n-1}^\lambda(\ell) \, d\mu(\ell).$$

One can easily see that the class $T_R(\lambda)$, $\lambda > 0$, is a compact and convex set in the linear space of holomorphic functions $f(z) = z + \sum_{n=2}^{\infty} a_n z^n$ which are holomorphic in Δ, endowed with the topology of local uniform convergence on compact subsets of Δ. The importance of the class $T_R(\lambda)$, $\lambda > 0$, follows as well from the paper of Hallenbeck [9], who studied the extreme points of some families of univalent functions and proved that

$$\text{co } \mathcal{S}_R^*(1-\lambda) = T_R(\lambda), \quad \text{and} \quad \text{ext co } \mathcal{S}_R^*(1-\lambda) = \left\{ \frac{z}{(1 - 2\ell z + z^2)^\lambda} : \ell \in [-1; 1] \right\},$$

where "co A" denotes the closed convex hull of A, "ext A" represents the set of the extremal points of A, while $\mathcal{S}_R^*(\vartheta)$ denotes the class of holomorphic functions given by (5), which are univalent and starlike of order ϑ, $\vartheta \in [0, 1)$, in Δ, and have real coefficients.

Let $\mathcal{A}$ represents the class of functions whose members are of the form

$$f(z) = z + \sum_{n=2}^{\infty} a_n z^n, \quad z \in \Delta, \tag{9}$$

which are analytic in Δ, and let $\mathcal{S}$ be the subclass of $\mathcal{A}$ whose members are univalent in Δ. The Koebe one quarter theorem [10] ensures that the image of Δ under every univalent function $f \in \mathcal{A}$ contains a disk of radius $\frac{1}{4}$. Thus every univalent function f has an inverse f^{-1} satisfying

$$f^{-1}(f(z)) = z, \quad (z \in \Delta) \quad \text{and} \quad f\left(f^{-1}(w)\right) = w, \quad \left(|w| < r_0(f), \, r_0(f) \geq \frac{1}{4}\right).$$

A function $f \in \mathcal{A}$ is said to be bi-univalent in Δ if both f and f^{-1} are univalent in Δ, and let Σ denote the class of bi-univalent functions defined in the unit disk Δ. Since $f \in \Sigma$

has the Maclaurin series given by (9), a computation shows that its inverse $g = f^{-1}$ has the expansion

$$g(w) = f^{-1}(w) = w - a_2 w^2 + \left(2a_2^2 - a_3\right)w^3 + \ldots. \tag{10}$$

We notice that the class Σ is not empty. For instance, the functions

$$f_1(z) = \frac{z}{1-z}, \quad f_2(z) = \frac{1}{2}\log\frac{1+z}{1-z}, \quad f_3(z) = -\log(1-z)$$

with their corresponding inverses

$$f_1^{-1}(w) = \frac{w}{1+w}, \quad f_2^{-1}(w) = \frac{e^{2w}-1}{e^{2w}+1}, \quad f_3^{-1}(w) = \frac{e^w - 1}{e^w}$$

are elements of Σ. However, the Koebe function is not a member of Σ. Lately, Srivastava et al. [11] have essentially revived the study of analytic and bi-univalent functions; this was followed by such works as those of [12–17]. Several authors have introduced and examined subclasses of bi-univalent functions and obtained bounds for the initial coefficients (see [11–13,15]), bi-close-to-convex functions [18,19], and bi-prestarlike functions by Jahangiri and Hamidi [20].

Orthogonal polynomials have been broadly considered in recent years from various perceptions due to their importance in mathematical physics, mathematical statistics, engineering, and probability theory. Orthogonal polynomials that appear most often in applications are the classical orthogonal polynomials (Hermite polynomials, Laguerre polynomials, and Jacobi polynomials). The previously mentioned Fibonacci polynomials, Faber polynomials, the Lucas polynomials, the Pell polynomials, the Pell–Lucas polynomials, the Chebyshev polynomials of the second kind, and Horadam polynomials have been studied in several papers from a theoretical point of view and recently in the case of bi-univalent functions (see [21–28] also the references cited therein).

Here, in this article, we associate certain bi-univalent functions with Gegenbauer polynomials and then explore some properties of the class of bi-starlike functions based on earlier work of Srivastava et al. (also, see [11]). In addition, motivated by recent works by Murugusundaramoorthy et al. [29], Wannas [30] and Amourah et al. [31], we introduce a new subclass of the Yamakawa-type bi-starlike function class (see [32]) associated with Gegenbauer polynomials, obtain upper bounds of the initial Taylor coefficients $|a_2|$ and $|a_3|$ for the functions $f \in \mathcal{GY}_\Sigma(\Phi_\ell^\lambda)$ defined by subordination, and consider the remarkable Fekete–Szegő problem. We also provide relevant connections of our results with those of some earlier investigations.

First, we define a new subclass Yamakawa-type bi-starlike in the open unit disk, associated with Gegenbauer polynomials as below.

Unless otherwise stated, we let $0 \leq \vartheta \leq 1$, $\lambda > \frac{1}{2}$ and $\ell \in \left(\frac{1}{2}, 1\right]$.

Definition 1. *For $0 \leq \vartheta \leq 1$ and $\ell \in \left(\frac{1}{2}, 1\right]$, a function $f \in \Sigma$ of the form (9) is said to be in the class $\mathcal{GY}_\Sigma(\vartheta, \Phi_\ell^\lambda)$ if the following subordinations hold:*

$$\frac{f(z)}{(1-\vartheta)z + \vartheta z f'(z)} \prec \Phi_\ell^\lambda(z), \tag{11}$$

and

$$\frac{g(w)}{(1-\vartheta)w + \vartheta w g'(w)} \prec \Phi_\ell^\lambda(w), \tag{12}$$

where $z, w \in \Delta$, Φ_ℓ^λ is given by (6), and $g = f^{-1}$ is given by (10).

By specializing the parameter ϑ, we state a new subclass of Yamakawa-type bi-starlike in the open unit disk, associated with Gegenbauer polynomials as below:

Remark 1. *For $\vartheta = 1$, we get $\mathcal{YS}_\Sigma^*(\Phi_\ell^\lambda) := \mathcal{GY}_\Sigma(1, \Phi_\ell^\lambda)$, thus $f \in \mathcal{YS}_\Sigma^*(\Phi_\ell^\lambda)$ iff $f \in \Sigma$ and the following subordinations hold:*

$$\frac{f(z)}{zf'(z)} \prec \Phi_\ell^\lambda(z) \quad \text{and} \quad \frac{g(w)}{wg'(w)} \prec \Phi_\ell^\lambda(w)$$

where $z, w \in \Delta$, and $g = f^{-1}$ is given by (10).

Remark 2. *For $\vartheta = 0$, we get $\mathcal{N}_\Sigma(\Phi_\ell^\lambda) := \mathcal{GY}_\Sigma(0, \Phi_\ell^\lambda)$, thus $f \in \mathcal{N}_\Sigma(\Phi_\ell^\lambda)$ iff $f \in \Sigma$ and the following subordinations hold:*

$$\frac{f(z)}{z} \prec \Phi_\ell^\lambda(z) \quad \text{and} \quad \frac{g'(w)}{w} \prec \Phi_\ell^\lambda(w)$$

where $z, w \in \Delta$ and $g = f^{-1}$ is given by (10).

Note that if in the above Remarks 1 and 2, we choose $\lambda = 1$ or $\lambda = \frac{1}{2}$, then we can state the new subclasses of $\mathcal{YS}_\Sigma^*(\Phi_\ell^\lambda)$ and $\mathcal{N}_\Sigma(\Phi_\ell^\lambda)$ related with Chebyshev polynomials and Legendre polynomials, respectively.

2. Initial Taylor Coefficients Estimates for the Functions of $\mathcal{GY}_\Sigma\left(\vartheta, \Phi_\ell^\lambda\right)$

To obtain our first results, we need the following lemma:

Lemma 1 ([33], p. 172). *Assume that $\omega(z) = \sum\limits_{n=1}^\infty \omega_n z^n$, $z \in \mathbb{U}$, is an analytic function in $\mathbb{U}$ such that $|\omega(z)| < 1$ for all $z \in \mathbb{U}$. Then,*

$$|\omega_1| \leq 1, \quad |\omega_n| \leq 1 - |\omega_1|^2, \; n = 2, 3, \ldots.$$

In the next result, we obtain the upper bounds for the modules of the first two coefficients for the functions that belong to the class $\mathcal{GY}_\Sigma(\vartheta, \Phi_\ell^\lambda)$.

Theorem 1. *Let f given by (9) be in the class $\mathcal{GY}_\Sigma(\vartheta, \Phi_\ell^\lambda)$. Then,*

$$|a_2| \leq \frac{2\lambda\ell\sqrt{2\lambda\ell}}{\sqrt{|(1 - 6\vartheta + 6\vartheta^2)4\lambda^2\ell^2 - 2(2(\lambda)_2\ell^2 - \lambda)(1 - 2\vartheta)^2|}}, \tag{13}$$

and

$$|a_3| \leq \frac{2(\lambda\ell)^2(1 - 2\vartheta - 2\vartheta^2)}{|(1 - 3\vartheta)(1 - 2\vartheta)^2|} + \frac{2\lambda\ell}{|1 - 3\vartheta|}, \tag{14}$$

where $\vartheta \neq \frac{1}{3}$.

Proof. Let $f \in \mathcal{GY}_\Sigma(\vartheta, \Phi_\ell^\lambda)$ and $g = f^{-1}$. From the definition in Formulas (11) and (12), we have

$$\frac{f(z)}{(1 - \vartheta)z + \vartheta z f'(z)} = \Phi_\ell^\lambda(u(z)) \tag{15}$$

and

$$\frac{g(w)}{(1 - \vartheta)w + \vartheta w g'(w)} = \Phi_\ell^\lambda(v(w)), \tag{16}$$

43

where the functions u and v are of the form

$$u(z) = c_1 z + c_2 z^2 + \ldots, \tag{17}$$

and

$$v(w) = d_1 w + d_2 w^2 + \ldots, \tag{18}$$

are analytic in Δ with $u(0) = 0 = v(0)$, and $|u(z)| < 1$, $|v(w)| < 1$, for all $z, w \in \Delta$. From Lemma 1 it follows that

$$|c_j| \leq 1 \quad \text{and} \quad |d_j| \leq 1, \text{ for all } j \in \mathbb{N}. \tag{19}$$

Replacing (17) and (18) in (15) and (16), respectively, we have

$$\frac{f(z)}{(1-\vartheta)z + \vartheta z f'(z)} = 1 + \mathfrak{G}_1^\lambda(\ell) u(z) + \mathfrak{G}_2^\lambda(\ell) u^2(z) + \ldots, \tag{20}$$

and

$$\frac{g(w)}{(1-\vartheta)w + \vartheta w g'(w)} = 1 + \mathfrak{G}_1^\lambda(\ell) v(w) + \mathfrak{G}_2^\lambda(\ell) v^2(w) + \ldots. \tag{21}$$

In view of (9) and (10), from (20) and (21), we obtain

$$1 + (1 - 2\vartheta)a_2 z + \left[(1 - 3\vartheta)a_3 - 2\vartheta(1 - 2\vartheta)a_2^2\right]z^2 + \ldots$$
$$= 1 + \mathfrak{G}_1^\lambda(\ell) c_1 z + \left[\mathfrak{G}_1^\lambda(\ell) c_2 + \mathfrak{G}_2^\lambda(\ell) c_1^2\right]z^2 + \ldots,$$

and

$$1 - (1 - 2\vartheta)(\alpha)a_2 w + \left\{\left(1 - 4\vartheta + 2\vartheta^2\right)a_2^2 - (1 - 3\lambda)a_3\right\}w^2 + \ldots$$
$$= 1 + \mathfrak{G}_1^\lambda(\ell) d_1 w + \left[\mathfrak{G}_1^\lambda(\ell) d_2 + \mathfrak{G}_2^\lambda(\ell) d_1^2\right]w^2 + \ldots,$$

which yields the following relations:

$$(1 - 2\vartheta)a_2 = \mathfrak{G}_1^\lambda(\ell) c_1, \tag{22}$$
$$(1 - 3\vartheta)a_3 - 2\vartheta(1 - 2\vartheta)a_2^2 = \mathfrak{G}_1^\lambda(\ell) c_2 + \mathfrak{G}_2^\lambda(\ell) c_1^2, \tag{23}$$

and

$$-(1 - 2\vartheta)a_2 = \mathfrak{G}_1^\lambda(\ell) d_1, \tag{24}$$
$$-(1 - 3\vartheta)a_3 + \left(1 - 4\vartheta + 2\vartheta^2\right)a_2^2 = \mathfrak{G}_1^\lambda(\ell) d_2 + \mathfrak{G}_2^\lambda(\ell) d_1^2. \tag{25}$$

From (22) and (24), it follows that

$$c_1 = -d_1, \tag{26}$$

and

$$2(1 - 2\vartheta)^2 a_2^2 = [\mathfrak{G}_1^\lambda(\ell)]^2 (c_1^2 + d_1^2),$$
$$a_2^2 = \frac{[\mathfrak{G}_1^\lambda(\ell)]^2}{2(1 - 2\vartheta)^2}(c_1^2 + d_1^2) \tag{27}$$

Adding (23) and (25), using (27), we obtain

$$a_2^2 = \frac{[\mathfrak{G}_1^\lambda(\ell)]^3 (c_2 + d_2)}{(1 - 6\vartheta + 6\vartheta^2)[\mathfrak{G}_1^\lambda(\ell)]^2 - 2(1 - 2\vartheta)^2 \mathfrak{G}_2^\lambda(\ell)}. \tag{28}$$

Applying (19) for the coefficients c_2 and d_2 and using (8), we obtain the Inequality (13).

By subtracting (25) from (23), using (26) and (27), we get

$$a_3 = \frac{\mathfrak{G}_1^\lambda(\ell)(c_2-d_2)}{2(1-3\vartheta)} + \frac{(1-2\vartheta-2\vartheta^2)[\mathfrak{G}_1^\lambda(\ell)]^2}{2(1-3\vartheta)}a_2^2 \qquad (29)$$
$$= \frac{(1-2\vartheta-2\vartheta^2)[\mathfrak{G}_1^\lambda(\ell)]^2(c_1^2+d_1^2)}{4(1-3\vartheta)(1-2\vartheta)^2} + \frac{\mathfrak{G}_1^\lambda(\ell)(c_2-d_2)}{2(1-3\vartheta)}.$$

Using (8) and once again applying (19) for the coefficients c_1, c_2, d_1, and d_2, we deduce the required Inequality (14). □

By taking $\vartheta = 0$ or $\vartheta = 1$ and $\ell \in (0,1)$, one can easily state the upper bounds for $|a_2|$ and $|a_3|$ for the function classes $\mathcal{GY}_\Sigma(0,\Phi) =: \mathcal{N}_\Sigma(\Phi_\ell^\lambda)$ and $\mathcal{GY}_\Sigma(1,\Phi) =: \mathcal{YS}_\Sigma^*(\Phi_\ell^\lambda)$, respectively, as follows:

Remark 3. *Let f given by (9) be in the class $\mathcal{N}_\Sigma(\Phi_\ell^\lambda)$. Then,*

$$|a_2| \leq \frac{2\lambda\ell\sqrt{2\lambda\ell}}{\sqrt{|4\lambda^2\ell^2 - 2(2(\lambda)_2\ell^2 - \lambda)|}},$$

and

$$|a_3| \leq 2(\lambda\ell)^2 + 2\lambda\ell.$$

Remark 4. *Let f given by (9) be in the class $\mathcal{YS}_\Sigma^*(\Phi_\ell^\lambda)$. Then,*

$$|a_2| \leq \frac{2\lambda\ell\sqrt{2\lambda\ell}}{\sqrt{|4\lambda^2\ell^2 - 2(2(\lambda)_2\ell^2 - \lambda)|}},$$

and

$$|a_3| \leq 3(\lambda\ell)^2 + \lambda\ell.$$

Remark 5. *Let f given by (9) be in the class $\mathcal{GY}_\Sigma^*(\vartheta,\Phi_\ell^1)$. Then,*

$$|a_2| \leq \frac{2\ell\sqrt{2\ell}}{\sqrt{|(1-6\vartheta+6\vartheta^2)4\ell^2 - 2(4\ell^2-1)(1-2\vartheta)^2|}},$$

and

$$|a_3| \leq \frac{2\ell^2(1-2\vartheta-2\vartheta^2)}{|(1-3\vartheta)(1-2\vartheta)^2|} + \frac{2\ell}{|1-3\vartheta|},$$

where $\vartheta \neq \frac{1}{3}$.

Remark 6. *Let f given by (9) be in the class $\mathcal{GY}_\Sigma^*(\vartheta,\Phi_\ell^{1/2})$. Then, for $\ell \neq \frac{1}{\sqrt{2}}$,*

$$|a_2| \leq \frac{\ell\sqrt{\ell}}{\sqrt{|(1-6\vartheta+6\vartheta^2)\ell^2 - (3\ell^2-1)(1-2\vartheta)^2|}},$$

and

$$|a_3| \leq \frac{\ell^2(1-2\vartheta-2\vartheta^2)}{2|(1-3\vartheta)(1-2\vartheta)^2|} + \frac{\ell}{|1-3\vartheta|},$$

where $\vartheta \neq \dfrac{1}{3}$.

In the above Remarks 3 and 4, by fixing $\lambda = 1$ and $\lambda = \dfrac{1}{2}$, we obtain the new estimates of $|a_2|$ and $|a_3|$ for the function classes $\mathcal{YS}_\Sigma^*(\Phi_\ell^\lambda)$ and $\mathcal{N}_\Sigma(\Phi_\ell^\lambda)$ related with Chebyshev polynomials and Legendre polynomials, respectively.

3. Fekete–Szegő Inequality for the Function Class $\mathcal{GY}_\Sigma\left(\vartheta, \Phi_\ell^\lambda\right)$

Due to the result of Zaprawa [34], in this section, we obtain the Fekete–Szegő inequality for the function classes $\mathcal{GY}_\Sigma(\vartheta, \Phi_\ell^\lambda)$.

Theorem 2. *Let f given by (9) be in the class $\mathcal{GY}_\Sigma(\vartheta, \Phi_\ell^\lambda)$, and $\mu \in \mathbb{R}$. Then, we have*

$$|a_3 - \mu a_2^2| \leq \begin{cases} \dfrac{2\lambda\ell}{|1-3\vartheta|}, & \text{if } |h(\mu)| \leq \dfrac{1}{2|1-3\vartheta|}, \\ 4\lambda\ell|h(\mu)|, & \text{if } |h(\mu)| \geq \dfrac{1}{2|1-3\vartheta|}, \end{cases}$$

where

$$h(\mu) := \dfrac{2\lambda\ell^2[2\lambda^2\ell^2(1-2\vartheta-2\vartheta^2) - \mu(1-3\vartheta)]}{(1-3\vartheta)\{2\lambda\ell^2(1-6\vartheta+6\vartheta^2) - (1-2\vartheta)^2[2(\lambda+1)\ell^2-1]\}},$$

and $\vartheta \neq \dfrac{1}{3}$.

Proof. If $f \in \mathcal{GY}_\Sigma(\vartheta, \Phi_\ell^\lambda)$ is given by (9), from (28) and (29), we have

$$a_3 - \mu a_2^2 = \dfrac{\mathfrak{G}_1^\lambda(\ell)(c_2 - d_2)}{2(1-3\vartheta)} + \left(\dfrac{(1-2\vartheta-2\vartheta^2)[\mathfrak{G}_1^\lambda(\ell)]^2}{2(1-3\vartheta)} - \mu\right) a_2^2$$

$$= \dfrac{\mathfrak{G}_1^\lambda(\ell)(c_2 - d_2)}{2(1-3\vartheta)} + \left(\dfrac{(1-2\vartheta-2\vartheta^2)[\mathfrak{G}_1^\lambda(\ell)]^2}{2(1-3\vartheta)} - \mu\right)$$

$$\times \dfrac{[\mathfrak{G}_1^\lambda(\ell)]^3(c_2 + d_2)}{(1-6\vartheta+6\vartheta^2)[\mathfrak{G}_1^\lambda(\ell)]^2 - 2(1-2\vartheta)^2\mathfrak{G}_2^\lambda(\ell)}$$

$$= \mathfrak{G}_1^\lambda(\ell)\left[\left(h(\mu) + \dfrac{1}{2(1-3\vartheta)}\right) c_2 + \left(h(\mu) - \dfrac{1}{2(1-3\vartheta)}\right) d_2\right],$$

where

$$h(\mu) = \dfrac{((1-2\vartheta-2\vartheta^2)[\mathfrak{G}_1^\lambda(\ell)]^2 - 2\mu(1-3\vartheta))[\mathfrak{G}_1^\lambda(\ell)]^3}{2(1-3\vartheta)\{(1-6\vartheta+6\vartheta^2)[\mathfrak{G}_1^\lambda(\ell)]^2 - 2(1-2\vartheta)^2\mathfrak{G}_2^\lambda(\ell)\}}.$$

Now, by using (8)

$$a_3 - \mu a_2^2 = 2\lambda\ell\left[\left(h(\mu) + \dfrac{1}{2(1-3\vartheta)}\right) c_2 + \left(h(\mu) - \dfrac{1}{2(1-3\vartheta)}\right) d_2\right],$$

where

$$h(\mu) = \dfrac{2\lambda^2\ell^2[2\lambda^2\ell^2(1-2\vartheta-2\vartheta^2) - \mu(1-3\vartheta)]}{(1-3\vartheta)\{2\lambda^2\ell^2(1-2\vartheta+2\vartheta^2) - \lambda(1-2\vartheta)^2[2(\lambda+1)\ell^2-1]\}}$$

$$= \dfrac{2\lambda\ell^2[2\lambda^2\ell^2(1-2\vartheta-2\vartheta^2) - \mu(1-3\vartheta)]}{(1-3\vartheta)\{2\lambda\ell^2(1-6\vartheta+6\vartheta^2) - (1-2\vartheta)^2[2(\lambda+1)\ell^2-1]\}}.$$

Therefore, in view of (8) and (19), we conclude that the required inequality holds. □

4. The Subclass $\mathfrak{M}_\Sigma\left(\tau, \Phi_\ell^\lambda\right)$ of Bi-Univalent Functions

In [35] Obradović et al. gave some criteria for univalence expressed by $\operatorname{Re} f'(z) > 0$ for the linear combination

$$\tau\left(1 + \frac{zf''(z)}{f'(z)}\right) + (1-\tau)\frac{1}{f'(z)}, \quad \tau \geq 1, \ z \in \Delta.$$

Based on the above definitions, recently, Lashin [36] introduced and studied new subclasses of the bi-univalent function. In our further discussions, unless otherwise stated, we let $\tau \geq 1$, $\lambda > \frac{1}{2}$, and $\ell \in \left(\frac{1}{2}, 1\right]$.

Definition 2. *A function $f \in \Sigma$ given by (9) is said to be in the class $\mathfrak{M}_\Sigma(\tau, \Phi_\ell^\lambda)$ if it satisfies the conditions*

$$\tau\left(1 + \frac{zf''(z)}{f'(z)}\right) + (1-\tau)\frac{1}{f'(z)} \prec \Phi_\ell^\lambda(z) \tag{30}$$

and

$$\tau\left(1 + \frac{wg''(w)}{g'(w)}\right) + (1-\tau)\frac{1}{g'(w)} \prec \Phi_\ell^\lambda(w) \tag{31}$$

where $\tau \geq 1$, $z, w \in \Delta$, Φ_ℓ^λ is given by (6), and the function $g = f^{-1}$ is given by (10).

Remark 7. *For the particular case $\tau = 1$, a function $f \in \Sigma$ given by (9) is said to be in the class $\mathfrak{M}_\Sigma(\Phi_\ell^\lambda) =: \mathfrak{K}_\Sigma(\Phi_\ell^\lambda)$ if it satisfies the subordination relations*

$$1 + \frac{zf''(z)}{f'(z)} \prec \Phi_\ell^\lambda(z) \quad \text{and} \quad 1 + \frac{wg''(w)}{g'(w)} \prec \Phi_\ell^\lambda(w),$$

$z, w \in \Delta$, Φ_ℓ^λ is given by (6), and $g = f^{-1}$ is given by (10).

Theorem 3. *Let f be given by (9) and $f \in \mathfrak{M}_\Sigma(\tau, \Phi_\ell^\lambda)$, with $\tau \geq 1$. Then,*

$$|a_2| \leq \min\left\{\frac{\lambda\ell}{2(2\tau-1)}; \frac{\lambda\ell\sqrt{2\lambda\ell}}{2\sqrt{|(1+\tau)\lambda^2\ell^2 - 4(2\tau-1)^2[2\ell^2(\lambda)_2 - \lambda]|}}\right\}, \tag{32}$$

and

$$|a_3| \leq \min\left\{\frac{2\lambda\ell}{3(3\tau-1)} + \frac{\lambda^2\ell^2}{4(2\iota-1)^2};\right.$$

$$\left.\frac{2\lambda\ell}{3(3\tau-1)} + \frac{2\lambda^3\ell^3}{|(1+\tau)\lambda^2\ell)_1^2 - (2\tau-1)^2[2\ell^2(\lambda)_2 - \lambda]|}\right\}.$$

Proof. $f \in \mathfrak{M}_\Sigma(\tau, \Phi_\ell^\lambda)$, from (30) and (31) it follows that

$$\tau\left(1 + \frac{zf''(z)}{f'(z)}\right) + (1-\tau)\frac{1}{f'(z)} = \Phi_\ell^\lambda(u(z)), \tag{33}$$

and

$$\tau\left(1 + \frac{wg''(w)}{g'(w)}\right) + (1-\tau)\frac{1}{g'(w)} = \Phi_\ell^\lambda(v(w)), \tag{34}$$

where the functions u and v are analytic in Δ with $u(0) = 0 = v(0)$, such that $|u(z)| < 1$, $|v(w)| < 1$, for all $z, w \in \Delta$, and are of the form (17) and (18), respectively.

From (33) and (34), we have

$$1 + 2(2\tau - 1)a_2 z + \left[3(3\tau - 1)a_3 + 4(1 - 2\tau)_2 a_2^2\right] z^2 + \ldots$$
$$= 1 + \mathfrak{G}_1^\lambda(\ell) c_1 z + \left[\mathfrak{G}_1^\lambda(\ell) c_2 + \mathfrak{G}_2^\lambda(\ell) c_1^2\right] z^2 + \ldots,$$

and

$$1 - 2(2\tau - 1)a_2 w + \left[2(5\tau - 1)a_2^2 - 3(3\tau - 1)a_3\right] w^2 - \ldots$$
$$= 1 + \mathfrak{G}_1^\lambda(\ell) d_1 w + \left[\mathfrak{G}_1^\lambda(\ell) d_2 + \mathfrak{G}_2^\lambda(\ell) d_1^2\right] w^2 + \ldots,$$

and equating the coefficients of the above two relations, we get

$$2(2\tau - 1)a_2 = \mathfrak{G}_1^\lambda(\ell) c_1, \tag{35}$$
$$3(3\tau - 1)a_3 + 4(1 - 2\tau)a_2^2 = \mathfrak{G}_1^\lambda(\ell) c_2 + \mathfrak{G}_2^\lambda(\ell) c_1^2, \tag{36}$$

and

$$-2(2\tau - 1)a_2 = \mathfrak{G}_1^\lambda(\ell) d_1, \tag{37}$$
$$2(5\tau - 1)a_2^2 - 3(3\tau - 1)a_3 = \mathfrak{G}_1^\lambda(\ell) d_2 + \mathfrak{G}_2^\lambda(\ell) d_1^2. \tag{38}$$

From (35) and (37), we get

$$p_1 = -q_1 \tag{39}$$

From (35), by using the Inequality (19) for the coefficients c_j and d_j, from (8), we have

$$|a_2| \leq \frac{\mathfrak{G}_1^\lambda(\ell)}{2(2\tau - 1)} = \frac{\lambda \ell}{(2\tau - 1)}.$$

Furthermore,

$$8(2\tau - 1)^2 a_2^2 = \left(\mathfrak{G}_1^\lambda(\ell)\right)^2 \left(c_1^2 + d_1^2\right),$$

that is,

$$a_2^2 = \frac{\left(\mathfrak{G}_1^\lambda(\ell)\right)^2 \left(c_1^2 + d_1^2\right)}{8(2\tau - 1)^2}. \tag{40}$$

Thus, from the Inequality (19) and using (8), we obtain

$$|a_2| \leq \frac{\mathfrak{G}_1^\lambda(\ell)}{4(2\tau - 1)} = \frac{\lambda \ell}{2(2\tau - 1)}. \tag{41}$$

Now, from (36), (38) and using (40), we get

$$\left[2(1 + \tau)\left(\mathfrak{G}_1^\lambda(\ell)\right)^2 - 8(2\tau - 1)^2 \mathfrak{G}_2^\lambda(\ell)\right] a_2^2 = \left(\mathfrak{G}_1^\lambda(\ell)\right)^3 (c_2 + d_2). \tag{42}$$

Thus, according to (42), we obtain

$$a_2^2 = \frac{\left(\mathfrak{G}_1^\lambda(\ell)\right)^3 (c_2 + d_2)}{2(1 + \tau)\left(\mathfrak{G}_1^\lambda(\ell)\right)^2 - 8(2\tau - 1)^2 \mathfrak{G}_2^\lambda(\ell)},$$

hence,

$$|a_2| \leq \frac{\lambda \ell \sqrt{2 \lambda \ell}}{2\sqrt{|(1 + \tau)\lambda^2 \ell^2 - 4(2\tau - 1)^2 [2\ell^2(\lambda)_2 - \lambda]|}}, \tag{43}$$

and the Inequality (32) is proved.

From (36), (38) and using (39), we get

$$a_3 = \frac{\mathfrak{G}_1^\lambda(\ell)(c_2 - d_2)}{6(3\tau - 1)} + a_2^2, \tag{44}$$

which implies

$$|a_3| \leq \frac{2\lambda\ell}{3(3\tau - 1)} + |a_2^2|. \tag{45}$$

From this inequality, using (41), we obtain

$$|a_3| \leq \frac{2\lambda\ell}{3(3\tau - 1)} + \frac{\lambda^2\ell^2}{4(2\tau - 1)^2}.$$

Combining (45) and (43), it follows that

$$|a_3| \leq \frac{2\lambda\ell}{3(3\tau - 1)} + \frac{2\lambda^3\ell^3}{|(1+\tau)\lambda^2\ell|_1^2 - (2\tau - 1)^2[2\ell^2(\lambda)_2 - \lambda]|}.$$

□

Motivated by the result of Zaprawa [34], we discuss the Fekete–Szegő inequality [37] for the functions $f \in \mathfrak{M}_\Sigma(\tau, \Phi_\ell^\lambda)$.

Theorem 4. *For $v \in \mathbb{R}$, let $f \in \mathfrak{M}_\Sigma(\tau, \Phi_\ell^\lambda)$ be given by (9). Then,*

$$\left|a_3 - va_2^2\right| \leq \begin{cases} \dfrac{2\lambda\ell}{3(3\tau - 1)}, & \text{if } |h(v)| \leq \dfrac{1}{6(3\tau - 1)}, \\ 4|h(v)|, & \text{if } |h(v)| \geq \dfrac{1}{6(3\tau - 1)}, \end{cases}$$

where

$$h(v) = \frac{(1-v)\lambda\ell^2}{4\{(1+\tau)\lambda\ell^2 - (2\tau - 1)^2[2\ell^2(\lambda + 1) - 1]\}}. \tag{46}$$

Proof. If $f \in \mathfrak{M}_\Sigma(\tau, \Phi_\ell^\lambda)$ be given by (9), from (44) we have

$$a_3 - va_2^2 = \frac{\mathfrak{G}_1^\lambda(\ell)(c_2 - d_2)}{6(3\tau - 1)} + (1 - v)a_2^2. \tag{47}$$

By substituting (42) in (47), we obtain

$$a_3 - va_2^2 = \frac{\mathfrak{G}_1^\lambda(\ell)(c_2 - d_2)}{6(3\tau - 1)} + \frac{(1-v)\left(\mathfrak{G}_1^\lambda(\ell)\right)^3(c_2 + d_2)}{2(1+\tau)\left(\mathfrak{G}_1^\lambda(\ell)\right)^2 - 8(2\tau - 1)^2\mathfrak{G}_2^\lambda(\ell)}$$

$$= \mathfrak{G}_1^\lambda(\ell)\left[\left(h(v) + \frac{1}{6(3\tau - 1)}\right)c_2 + \left(h(v) - \frac{1}{6(3\tau - 1)}\right)d_2\right],$$

where

$$h(v) = \frac{(1-v)\left(\mathfrak{G}_1^\lambda(\ell)\right)^2}{2(1+\tau)\left(\mathfrak{G}_1^\lambda(\ell)\right)^2 - 8(2\tau - 1)^2\mathfrak{G}_2^\lambda(\ell)}.$$

From (8), it follows

$$a_3 - va_2^2 = 2\lambda\ell\left[\left(h(v) + \frac{1}{6(3\tau - 1)}\right)c_2 + \left(h(v) - \frac{1}{6(3\tau - 1)}\right)d_2\right], \tag{48}$$

where the function h is given by (46). Hence, by using the triangle inequality for the modulus of (48) together with (19), we get our result. □

For $\nu = 1$ the above theorem reduces to the following special case:

Remark 8. *If $f \in \mathfrak{M}_\Sigma(\tau, \Phi_\ell^\lambda)$ is given by (9), then*

$$\left|a_3 - a_2^2\right| \leq \frac{2\lambda\ell}{3(3\tau - 1)}.$$

5. Conclusions

Yamakawa-type bi-starlike functions related with the Gegenbauer polynomials are defined for the first time, and initial Taylor coefficients and Fekete–Szegő inequality are obtained. Further, by fixing $\lambda = 1$ or $\lambda = \frac{1}{2}$, the Gegenbauer polynomials lead to the Chebyshev polynomials and the Legendre polynomials, respectively. Hence, our results represent a new study of the Yamakawa family of bi-starlike functions associated with Chebyshev and Legendre polynomials, which are also not considered in the literature. We have left this as an exercise to interested readers.

Author Contributions: Conceptualization, T.B. and G.M.; methodology, T.B. and G.M.; validation, T.B. and G.M.; formal analysis, T.B. and G.M.; investigation, T.B. and G.M.; resources, T.B. and G.M.; writing—original draft preparation, T.B. and G.M.; writing—review and editing, T.B. and G.M.; supervision, T.B. and G.M.; project administration, T.B. and G.M. All authors have read and agreed to the published version of the manuscript.

Funding: This research received no external funding.

Institutional Review Board Statement: Not applicable.

Informed Consent Statement: Not applicable.

Data Availability Statement: Not applicable.

Acknowledgments: The authors are grateful to the reviewers of this article who gave valuable comments and advice that allowed us to revise and improve the content of the paper.

Conflicts of Interest: The authors declare no conflict of interest.

References

1. Kim, D.S.; Kim, T.; Rim, S.H. Some identities involving Gegenbauer polynomials. *Adv. Differ. Equ.* **2012**, *2012*, 219. [CrossRef]
2. Al-Salam, W.A.; Carlitz, L. The Gegenbauer addition theorem. *J. Math. Phys.* **1963**, *42*, 147–156. [CrossRef]
3. McFadden, J.A. A diagonal expansion in Gegenbauer polynomials for a class of second-order probability densities. *SIAM J. Appl. Math.* **1966**, *14*, 1433–1436. [CrossRef]
4. Stein, E.M.; Weiss, G. *Introduction to Fourier Analysis in Euclidean Space*; Princeton University Press: Princeton, NJ, USA, 1971.
5. Kiepiela, K.; Naraniecka, I.; Szynal, J. The Gegenbauer polynomials and typically real functions. *J. Comp. Appl. Math.* **2003**, *153*, 273–282. [CrossRef]
6. Arfken, G.B.; Weber, H.J. *Mathematical Methods for Physicists*, 6th ed.; Elsevier Academic Press: Amsterdam, The Netherlands, 2005.
7. Robertson, M.S. On the coefficients of typically-real functions. *Bull. Am. Math. Soc.* **1935**, *41*, 565–572. [CrossRef]
8. Szynal, J. An extension of typically-real functions. *Ann. Univ. Mariae Curie-Skłodowska Sect. A* **1994** *48*, 193–201.
9. Hallenbeck, D.J. Convex hulls and extreme points of families of starlike and close-to-convex mappings. *Pac. J. Math.* **1975**, *57*, 167–176. [CrossRef]
10. Duren, P.L. *Univalent Functions*; Grundlehren der Mathematischen Wissenschaften Series, 259; Springer: New York, NY, USA, 1983.
11. Srivastava, H.M.; Mishra, A.K.; Gochhayat, P. Certain subclasses of analytic and bi-univalent functions. *Appl. Math. Lett.* **2010**, *23*, 1188–1192. [CrossRef]
12. Brannan, D.A.; Clunie, J.; Kirwan, W.E. Coefficient estimates for a class of star-like functions. *Canad. J. Math.* **1970**, *22*, 476–485. [CrossRef]
13. Brannan, D.A.; Taha, T.S. On some classes of bi-univalent functions. *Stud. Univ. Babeş-Bolyai Math.* **1986**, *31*, 70–77.
14. Frasin, B.A.; Aouf, M.K. New subclasses of bi-univalent functions. *Appl. Math. Lett.* **2011**, *24*, 1569–1573. [CrossRef]
15. Lewin, M. On a coefficient problem for bi-univalent functions. *Proc. Am. Math. Soc.* **1967**, *18*, 63–68. [CrossRef]
16. Li, X.-F.; Wang, A.-P. Two new subclasses of bi-univalent functions. *Int. Math. Forum* **2012**, *7*, 1495–1504.
17. Netanyahu, E. The minimal distance of the image boundary from the origin and the second coefficient of a univalent function in $|z| < 1$. *Arch. Ration. Mech. Anal.* **1969**, *32*, 100–112.

18. Güney, H.Ö.; Murugusundaramoorthy, G.; Srivastava, H.M. The second Hankel determinant for a certain class of bi-close-to-convex functions. *Results Math.* **2019**, *74*, 93. [CrossRef]
19. Kowalczyk, B.; Lecko, A.; Srivastava, H.M. A note on the Fekete-Szegő problem for close-to-convex functions with respect to convex functions. *Publ. Inst. Math.* **2017**, *101*, 143–149. [CrossRef]
20. Jahangiri, J.M.; Hamidi, S.G. Advances on the coefficients of bi-prestarlike functions. *Comptes Rendus Acad. Sci. Paris* **2016**, *354*, 980–985. [CrossRef]
21. Murugusundaramoorthy, G.; Yalçin, S.; On λ pseudo bi-starlike functions related (p;q)-Lucas polynomial. *Lib. Math.* **2019**, *39*, 59–77.
22. Srivastava, H.M. Operators of basic (or q-) calculus and fractional q-calculus and their applications in geometric function theory of complex analysis. *Iran. J. Sci. Technol. Trans. A Sci.* **2020**, *44*, 327–344. [CrossRef]
23. Srivastava, H.M.; Altınkaya, S.; Yalçin, S. Certain subclasses of bi-univalent functions associated with the Horadam polynomials. *Iran. J. Sci. Technol. Trans. A Sci.* **2018**, *43*, 1873–1879. [CrossRef]
24. Srivastava, H.M.; Eker, S.S.; Hamidi, S.G.; Jahangiri, J.M. Faber polynomial coefficient estimates for bi-univalent functions defined by the Tremblay fractional derivative operator. *Bull. Iran. Math. Soc.* **2018**, *44*, 149–157. [CrossRef]
25. Srivastava, H.M.; Kamali, M.; Urdaletova, A. A study of the Fekete-Szegő functional and coefficient estimates for subclasses of analytic functions satisfying a certain subordination condition and associated with the Gegenbauer polynomials. *AIMS Math.* **2022**, *7*, 2568–2584. [CrossRef]
26. Srivastava, H.M.; Motamednezhad, A.; Adegani, E.A. Faber polynomial coefficient estimates for bi-univalent functions defined by using differential subordination and a certain fractional derivative operator. *Mathematics* **2020** *8*, 172. [CrossRef]
27. Srivastava, H.M.; Wanas, A.K.; Murugusundaramoorthy, G. A certain family of bi-univalent functions associated with the Pascal distribution series based upon the Horadam polynomials. *Surv. Math. Appl.* **2021**, *16*, 193–205.
28. Srivastava, H.M.; Wanas, A.K.; Srivastava, R. Applications of the q-Srivastava-Attiya operator involving a certain family of bi-univalent functions associated with the Horadam polynomials. *Symmetry* **2021**, *13*, 1230. [CrossRef]
29. Murugusundaramoorthy, G.; Güney, H.Ö.; Vijaya, K. Coefficient bounds for certain suclasses of bi-prestarlike functions associated with the Gegenbauer polynomial. *Adv. Stud. Contemp. Math.* **2022**, *32*, 5–15.
30. Wanas, A.K. New families of bi-univalent functions governed by Gegenbauer Polynomials. *Earthline J. Math. Sci.* **2021**, *7*, 403–427. [CrossRef]
31. Amourah, A.; Frasin, B.A.; Abdeljawad, T. Fekete-Szegő inequality for analytic and bi-univalent functions subordinate to Gegenbauer Polynomials. *J. Funct. Spaces* **2021**, *2021*, 5574673.
32. Yamakawa, R. Certain Subclasses of p-Valently Starlike Functions with negative coefficients. In *Current Topics in Analytic Function Theory*; Srivastava, H.M., Owa, S., Eds.; World Scientific Publishing Company: Singapore; Hackensack, NJ, USA; London, UK; Hong Kong, China, 1992; pp. 393–402.
33. Nehari, Z. *Conformal Mapping*; McGraw-Hill: New York, NY, USA, 1952.
34. Zaprawa, P. On the Fekete-Szegő problem for classes of bi-univalent functions. *Bull. Belg. Math. Soc. Simon Stevin* **2014**, *21*, 169–178. [CrossRef]
35. Obradović, M.; Yaguchi, T.; Saitoh, H. On some conditions for univalence and starlikeness in the unit disc. *Rend. Math. Ser. VII* **1992**, *12*, 869–877.
36. Lashin, A.Y. Coefficient estimates for two subclasses of analytic and bi-univalent functions. *Ukr. Math. J.* **2019**, *70*, 1484–1492. [CrossRef]
37. Fekete, M.; Szegő, G. Eine Bemerkung uber ungerade schlichte Funktionen. *J. Lond. Math. Soc.* **1933**, *8*, 85–89. [CrossRef]

Article

Hadamard Product Properties for Certain Subclasses of p-Valent Meromorphic Functions

Alaa H. El-Qadeem [1,*] and Ibrahim S. Elshazly [2]

[1] Department of Mathematics, Faculty of Science, Zagazig University, Zagazig 44519, Egypt
[2] Department of Basic Sciences, Common First Year, King Saud University, Alriyad 11451, Saudi Arabia; iali2.c@ksu.edu.sa
* Correspondence: ahhassan@science.zu.edu.eg

Abstract: We study the Hadamard product features of certain subclasses of p-valent meromorphic functions defined in the punctured open-unit disc using the q-difference operator. For functions belonging to these subclasses, we obtained certain coefficient estimates and inclusion characteristics. Furthermore, linkages between the results given here and those found in previous publications are highlighted.

Keywords: analytic function; univalent function; starlike function; convex function; meromorphic function; q-difference operator

MSC: 30C45; 30D30

1. Introduction

Let $\mathcal{M}_p$ stand for the class of functions of the form:

$$f(z) = z^{-p} + \sum_{k=-p+1}^{\infty} a_k z^k, \qquad (1)$$

which are analytic in the perforated unit disc $U^* = U\setminus\{0\} = \{z : z \in \mathbb{C} : 0 < |z| < 1\}$. The class $\mathcal{M}_p$ refers to the a class of p-valent meromorphic functions. It is worth noting that $\mathcal{M}_1 = \mathcal{M}$, which is the class of univalent meromorphic functions. If the function $g \in \mathcal{M}_p$ is given by

$$g(z) = z^{-p} + \sum_{k=-p+1}^{\infty} b_k z^k,$$

then the Hadamard product (or convolution) of f and g is provided by

$$(f * g)(z) = z^{-p} + \sum_{k=-p+1}^{\infty} a_k b_k z^k = (g * f)(z).$$

Interesting traits such as coefficient estimates, subordination relations and univalence features related some subclasses of p-valent functions were obtained in [1–3] (see also, [4]). With the help of the q-differential operator, a new subclass of meromorphic multivalent functions in the Janowski domain were introduced by Bakhtiar et al. in [5] (see also, [6]). Moreover, new subclasses of meromorphically p-valent functions were defined using q-derivative operator and investigations related to geometric properties of the class are conducted in [7–9].

If f and g are analytic in the open unit disc U, we say that f is subordinate to g, written as $f \prec g$ in U or $f(z) \prec g(z)(z \in U)$, if there exists a Schwarz function $w(z)$, which (by definition) is analytic in U with $w(0) = 0$ and $|w(z)| < 1, (z \in U)$ such that $f(z) = g(w(z))$ $(z \in U)$ [10].

For $0 < q < 1$, the q-difference operator, which was introduced by Jackson [11], is characterised with

$$\partial_q f(z) = \begin{cases} \frac{f(qz) - f(z)}{(q-1)z}, & z \neq 0, \\ f'(0), & z = 0. \end{cases}$$

The Jackson q-difference operator is another name for the q-difference operator. Additionally, for f given by (1), one can write

$$\partial_q f(z) = -q^{-p}[p]_q z^{-p-1} + \sum_{k=-p+1}^{\infty} [k]_q a_k z^{k-1} (z \in U^*), \quad (2)$$

where $[k]_q = (1 - q^k)/(1 - q)$ is the well-known q-bracket, $\lim_{q \to 1^-} [k]_q = k$ and $\lim_{q \to 1^-} \partial_q f(z) = f'(z)$.

Now, for $n \in \mathbb{N}_0 = \mathbb{N} \cup \{0\}$, we define the operator $\mathfrak{D}_{p,q}^n : \mathcal{M}_p \longrightarrow \mathcal{M}_p$ with the help of the q-difference operator, as follows:

$$\mathfrak{D}_{p,q}^0 f(z) = f(z),$$
$$\mathfrak{D}_{p,q}^1 f(z) = z^{-p} \partial_q \left(z^{p+1} f(z) \right),$$
$$\mathfrak{D}_{p,q}^n f(z) = z^{-p} \partial_q \left(z^{p+1} \mathfrak{D}_{p,q}^{n-1} f(z) \right) \ (n \in \mathbb{N}),$$

then

$$\mathfrak{D}_{p,q}^n f(z) = z^{-p} + \sum_{k=-p+1}^{\infty} [k + p + 1]_q^n a_k z^k \ (n \in \mathbb{N}_0), \quad (3)$$

which satisfies the following recurrence relation:

$$q^{p+1} z \partial_q \left(\mathfrak{D}_{p,q}^n f(z) \right) = \mathfrak{D}_{p,q}^{n+1} f(z) - [p+1]_q \mathfrak{D}_{p,q}^n f(z). \quad (4)$$

Definition 1. *Utilising the q-derivative $\partial_q f(z)$, the subclasses $\mathcal{MS}_{p,q}^*(A, B)$ and $\mathcal{MK}_{p,q}(A, B)$ are introduced as follows:*

$$\mathcal{MS}_{p,q}^*(A, B) = \left\{ f \in \mathcal{M}_p : \frac{-q^p z \partial_q f(z)}{[p]_q f(z)} \prec \frac{1 + Az}{1 + Bz} \right\}, \quad (5)$$

$$(0 < q < 1; -1 \leq B < A \leq 1; z \in U),$$

and

$$\mathcal{MK}_{p,q}(A, B) = \left\{ f \in \mathcal{M}_p : \frac{-q^p \partial_q (z \partial_q f(z))}{[p]_q \partial_q f(z)} \prec \frac{1 + Az}{1 + Bz}, z \in U \right\}, \quad (6)$$

$$(0 < q < 1; -1 \leq B < A \leq 1; z \in U).$$

Using (5) and (6), we have the following equivalence relation:

$$f(z) \in \mathcal{MK}_{p,q}(A, B) \iff -\frac{q^p z \partial_q f(z)}{[p]_q} \in \mathcal{MS}_{p,q}^*(A, B). \quad (7)$$

Remark 1. *We list the following subclasses by specialising the parameters p, q, A and B:*

(i) $\mathcal{MS}_{p,q}^*(1 - 2\alpha, -1) = \mathcal{MS}_{p,q}^*(\alpha) = \left\{ f \in \mathcal{M}_p : \text{Re}\left(-\frac{q^p z \partial_q f(z)}{[p]_q f(z)} \right) > \alpha; 0 \leq \alpha < 1, z \in U \right\}$ the subclass of p-valent meromorphic q-starlike functions, and $\mathcal{MK}_{p,q}(1 - 2\alpha, -1) = \mathcal{MK}_{p,q}(\alpha) =$

$\{f \in \mathcal{M}_p : \text{Re}\left(-\frac{q^p \partial_q(z\partial_q f(z))}{[p]_q \partial_q f(z)}\right) > \alpha; 0 \leq \alpha < 1, z \in U\}$ the subclass of p-valent meromorphic q-convex functions;

(ii) $\mathcal{MS}^*_{1,q}(1 - 2\alpha, -1) = \mathcal{MS}^*_q(\alpha) = \{f \in \mathcal{M}: \text{Re}\left(-\frac{qz\partial_q f(z)}{f(z)}\right) > \alpha; 0 \leq \alpha < 1, z \in U\}$ the subclass of meromorphic q-starlike functions, and $\mathcal{MK}_{1,q}(1 - 2\alpha, -1) = \mathcal{MK}_q(\alpha) = \{f \in \mathcal{M}: \text{Re}\left(-\frac{q\partial_q(z\partial_q f(z))}{\partial_q f(z)}\right) > \alpha; 0 \leq \alpha < 1, z \in U\}$ the subclass of meromorphic q-convex functions;

(iii) $\lim_{q \to 1^-} \mathcal{MS}^*_{p,q}(A, B) = \mathcal{MS}^*_p(A, B) = \{f \in \mathcal{M}_p: -\frac{zf'(z)}{pf(z)} \prec \frac{1+Az}{1+Bz}; -1 \leq B < A \leq 1, z \in U\}$, and $\lim_{q \to 1^-} \mathcal{MK}_{p,q}(A, B) = \mathcal{MK}_p(A, B) = \{f \in \mathcal{M}_p: -\frac{1}{p}\left(1 + \frac{zf''(z)}{f'(z)}\right) \prec \frac{1+Az}{1+Bz}; -1 \leq B < A \leq 1, z \in U\}$, were introduced and studied by Ali and Ravichandran [12];

(iv) $\lim_{q \to 1^-} \mathcal{MS}^*_{1,q}(1 - 2\alpha, -1) = \mathcal{MS}^*(\alpha) = \{f \in \mathcal{M}: \text{Re}\left(-\frac{zf'(z)}{f(z)}\right) > \alpha; 0 \leq \alpha < 1, z \in U\}$, and $\lim_{q \to 1^-} \mathcal{MK}_{p,q}(1 - 2\alpha, -1) = \mathcal{MK}(\alpha) = \{f \in \mathcal{M}: \text{Re}\left(-1 - \frac{zf''(z)}{f'(z)}\right) > \alpha; 0 \leq \alpha < 1, z \in U\}$, were introduced and studied by Kaczmarski [13];

(v) $\lim_{q \to 1^-} \mathcal{MS}^*_{1,q}(1, -1) = \mathcal{MS}^*$, and $\lim_{q \to 1^-} \mathcal{MK}_{1,q}(1, -1) = \mathcal{MK}$, which are well-known function classes of meromorphic starlike and meromorphic convex functions, respectively; see Pommerenke [14], Clunie [15] and Miller [16] for more details.

Definition 2. *For $n \in \mathbb{N}_0$ and $0 < q < 1$, we define the following subclasses:*

$$\mathcal{MS}^*_{p,q}(n; A, B) = \left\{f \in \mathcal{M}_p : \mathfrak{D}^n_{p,q} f(z) \in \mathcal{MS}^*_{p,q}(A, B)\right\}, \quad (8)$$

$$(n \in \mathbb{N}_0; 0 < q < 1; -1 \leq B < A \leq 1; z \in U),$$

and

$$\mathcal{MK}_{p,q}(n; A, B) = \left\{f \in \mathcal{M}_p : \mathfrak{D}^n_{p,q} f(z) \in \mathcal{MK}_{p,q}(A, B)\right\}, \quad (9)$$

$$(n \in \mathbb{N}_0; 0 < q < 1; -1 \leq B < A \leq 1; z \in U).$$

It is easy to show that

$$f(z) \in \mathcal{MK}_{p,q}(n; A, B) \iff -\frac{q^p z \partial_q f(z)}{[p]_q} \in \mathcal{MS}^*_{p,q}(n; A, B). \quad (10)$$

There is extensive literature dealing with convolution properties of different families of analytic and meromorphic functions; for details, see [17–23]. More recently, the quantum derivative was utilised by Seoudy and Aouf [24] (see also [25]) to introduce the convolution features for certain classes of analytic functions. Here, we use the quantum derivative to obtain some convolution properties of the meromorphic functions. For this purpose, we defined the new classes $\mathcal{MS}^*_{p,q}(A, B)$ and $\mathcal{MK}_{p,q}(A, B)$. The convolution results are followed by some consequences such as necessary and sufficient conditions, the estimates of coefficients and inclusion characteristics of the subclasses $\mathcal{MS}^*_{p,q}(n; A, B)$ and $\mathcal{MK}_{p,q}(n; A, B)$.

2. Convolution Properties

Theorem 1. *The function f given by (1) is in the class $\mathcal{MS}^*_{p,q}(A, B)$, if and only if*

$$z^p \left[f(z) * \frac{1 + (C - q)z}{z^p(1 - z)(1 - qz)} \right] \neq 0 \ (z \in U), \quad (11)$$

for all

$$C = \frac{B + e^{-i\theta}}{A - [p]_q B - q[p - 1]_q e^{-i\theta}}; \ \theta \in [0, 2\pi), \quad (12)$$

and also for $C = 0$.

Proof. It is simple to check the following two equalities

$$f(z) * \frac{1}{z^p(1-z)} = f(z) \tag{13}$$

and

$$f(z) * \left(\frac{1}{qz^p(1-z)(1-qz)} - \frac{[1+p]_q}{qz^p(1-z)} \right) = q^p z \partial_q f(z) \tag{14}$$

In view of (5), $f \in MS^*_{p,q}(A, B)$, if and only if (1.4) holds. Since the function $\frac{1+Az}{1+Bz}$ is analytic function on U, it follows that $f(z) \neq 0$, $z \in U^*$; that is $z^p f(z) \neq 0$, $z \in U$, and using the first identity of (13). That is the same as saying that the relation (11) is satisfied for $C = 0$. According to the concept of subordination of two functions in (14), there exists an analytic function $w(z)$ in U with $w(0) = 0$, $|w(z)| < 1$ in such a way that

$$\frac{-q^p z \partial_q f(z)}{[p]_q f(z)} = \frac{1 + Aw(z)}{1 + Bw(z)} \quad (z \in U),$$

which leads to

$$\frac{-q^p z \partial_q f(z)}{[p]_q f(z)} \neq \frac{1 + A e^{i\theta}}{1 + B e^{i\theta}} \quad (f(z) \neq 0, z \in U; 0 \leq \theta < 2\pi),$$

or

$$z^p \left[(q^p z \partial_q f(z))\left(1 + B e^{i\theta}\right) + [p]_q f(z)\left(1 + A e^{i\theta}\right) \right] \neq 0 \tag{15}$$

We may now deduce the following from (13)–(15):

$$z^p \left[\left(f(z) * \frac{1 - [1+p]_q(1-qz)}{qz^p(1-z)(1-qz)} \right)\left(1 + B e^{i\theta}\right) + \left(1 + A e^{i\theta}\right)\left(f(z) * \frac{1}{z^p(1-z)} \right) \right] \neq 0,$$

$$z^p \left[f(z) * \left(\frac{\left(1 - [1+p]_q + q[1+p]_q z\right)\left(1 + B e^{i\theta}\right) + q(1-qz)\left(1 + A e^{i\theta}\right)}{qz^p(1-z)(1-qz)} \right) \right] \neq 0,$$

but $1 - [1+p]_q = -q[p]_q$; then, the condition became

$$z^p \left[f(z) * \left(\frac{q\left([1+p]_q z - [p]_q\right)\left(1 + B e^{i\theta}\right) + q(1-qz)\left(1 + A e^{i\theta}\right)}{qz^p(1-z)(1-qz)} \right) \right] \neq 0,$$

or,

$$z^p \left[f(z) * \left(\frac{\left([1+p]_q z - [p]_q\right)\left(1 + B e^{i\theta}\right) + (1-qz)\left(1 + A e^{i\theta}\right)}{z^p(1-z)(1-qz)} \right) \right] \neq 0,$$

or, equivalent to

$$z^p \left[f(z) * \left(\frac{1 - [p]_q + \left(A - [p]_q B\right)e^{i\theta} + \left([1+p]_q - q + \left([1+p]_q B - qA\right)e^{i\theta}\right)z}{z^p(1-z)(1-qz)} \right) \right] \neq 0,$$

or,

$$z^p \left[f(z) * \left(\frac{-q[p-1]_q + \left(A - [p]_q B\right)e^{i\theta} + \left([1+p]_q - q + \left([1+p]_q B - qA\right)e^{i\theta}\right)z}{z^p(1-z)(1-qz)} \right) \right] \neq 0,$$

or,

$$z^p\left[f(z) * \left(1 + \frac{\left([1+p]_q - q + \left([1+p]_q B - qA\right)e^{i\theta}\right)z}{z^p(1-z)(1-qz)}\left(\left(A - [p]_q B\right)e^{i\theta} - q[p-1]_q\right)\right)\right] \neq 0,$$

by dividing both sides by the non-zero quantity $\left(A - [p]_q B\right)e^{i\theta} - q[p-1]_q$, then we have

$$z^p\left[f(z) * \left(1 + \frac{\left([1+p]_q - q + \left([1+p]_q B - qA\right)e^{i\theta}\right)z}{z^p(1-z)(1-qz)}\right)\right] \neq 0,$$

which is the same as

$$z^p\left[f(z) * \left(1 + \frac{\left(\frac{[1+p]_q - q + \left([1+p]_q B - qA\right)e^{i\theta} + q\left(-q[p-1]_q + \left(A - [p]_q B\right)e^{i\theta}\right)}{-q[p-1]_q + \left(A - [p]_q B\right)e^{i\theta}} - q\right)z}{z^p(1-z)(1-qz)}\right)\right] \neq 0,$$

or,

$$z^p\left[f(z) * \left(1 + \frac{\left(\frac{[1+p]_q - q - q^2[p-1]_q + \left([1+p]_q - q[p]_q\right)Be^{i\theta}}{-q[p-1]_q + \left(A - [p]_q B\right)e^{i\theta}} - q\right)z}{z^p(1-z)(1-qz)}\right)\right] \neq 0,$$

but $[1+p]_q - q - q^2[p-1]_q = [1+p]_q - q[p]_q = 1$, then the convolution condition became

$$z^p\left[f(z) * \left(1 + \frac{\left(\frac{e^{-i\theta} + B}{A - [p]_q B - q[p-1]_q e^{-i\theta}} - q\right)z}{z^p(1-z)(1-qz)}\right)\right] \neq 0,$$

This leads to (11), proving the first part of Theorem 1.

In contrast, because (11) holds for $C = 0$, it follows that $z^p f(z) \neq 0$ for all $z \in U$, and hence the function.

$$\varphi(z) = \frac{-q^p z \partial_q f(z)}{[p]_q f(z)},$$

is analytic in U (i.e., it is regular at $z_0 = 0$, with $\varphi(0) = 1$). We obtain that because the assumption (11) is equivalent to (15), as shown in the first section of the proof.

$$\frac{-q^p z \partial_q f(z)}{[p]_q f(z)} \neq \frac{1 + Ae^{i\theta}}{1 + Be^{i\theta}} \quad (\theta \in [0, 2\pi), f(z) \neq 0, z \in U), \tag{16}$$

if we denote

$$\psi(z) = \frac{1 + Az}{1 + Bz}, \tag{17}$$

therefore $\varphi(U) \cap \psi(\partial U) = \phi$, with the help of the relation (16). Thus, the simply connected domain $\varphi(U)$ is included in a connected component of $\mathbb{C}\setminus\psi(\partial U)$. As a result, a connected component of $\mathbb{C}\setminus\psi(\partial U)$ includes the simply connected domain $\varphi(U)$. The fact that $\varphi(0) = \psi(0)$ and the univalence of the function ψ lead to the conclusion that

$\varphi(z) \prec \psi(z)$. This completes the proof of the second item of Theorem 1 by representing the subordination (5), i.e., $f \in \mathcal{MS}^*_{p,q}(A,B)$. □

Remark 2. *(i) We obtain the results obtained in the paper of Aouf et al. in [17] (Theorem 4, with $\lambda = 0$ and $b = 1$) by putting $p = 1$ and $q \to 1^-$ in Theorem 1. See also, Bulboacă et al. [20] (Theorem 1, with $b = 1$) and El-Ashwah [21] (Theorem 1, with $p = 1$);*
(ii) Putting $p = 1$, $q \to 1^-$, $A = 1$ and $B = -1$ in Theorem 1, we obtain the result of Aouf et al. [18] (Theorem 1, with $b = m = 1$).

In Theorem 1, we have the following corollary if $A = 1 - 2\alpha$ and $B = -1$.

Corollary 1. *The function f defined by (1) is in the class $\mathcal{MS}^*_{p,q}(\alpha)$, if and only if*

$$z^p \left[f(z) * \frac{1 + \left(\frac{\left(1 + q^2[p-1]_q\right)e^{-i\theta} - q(1-2\alpha+[p]_q)}{1-2\alpha+[p]_q - q[p-1]_q e^{-i\theta}} \right) z}{z^p(1-z)(1-qz)} \right] \neq 0 \ (z \in U),$$

Taking $q \to 1^-$, $A = 1 - 2\alpha$ and $B = -1$ in Theorem 1, we obtain the following corollary.

Corollary 2. *The function f expressed in (1) belongs to $\mathcal{MS}^*_p(\alpha)$, if and only if*

$$z^p \left[f(z) * \frac{1 + \left[\frac{2(1-\alpha) + p(e^{-i\theta} - 1)}{1 - 2\alpha + p - (p-1)e^{-i\theta}} \right] z}{z^p(1-z)^2} \right] \neq 0 \ (z \in U),$$

Theorem 2. *The function f of the form (1) is a member of the class $\mathcal{MK}_{p,q}(A,B)$, if and only if*

$$z^p \left[f(z) * \frac{1 - \frac{(1-q^{p+2}) - q(1-q^{p-1})(C-q)}{1-q^p} z - \frac{q(1-q^{p+1})(C-q)}{1-q^p} z^2}{z^p(1-z)(1-qz)(1-q^2 z)} \right] \neq 0 \ (z \in U), \qquad (18)$$

for all C defined by (12), and also for $C = 0$.

Proof. If

$$g(z) = \frac{1 + (C-q)z}{z^p(1-z)(1-qz)}, \qquad (19)$$

then

$$-\frac{q^p z \partial_q g(z)}{[p]_q} = \frac{-q^p z}{[p]_q} \left[\frac{1}{(q-1)z}(g(qz) - g(z)) \right]$$

which leads to

$$-\frac{q^p z \partial_q g(z)}{[p]_q} = \frac{1 - \left(\frac{(1-q^{p+2}) - q(1-q^{p-1})(C-q)}{1-q^p} \right)z - \left(\frac{q(1-q^{p+1})(C-q)}{1-q^p} \right)z^2}{z^p(1-z)(1-qz)(1-q^2z)} \qquad (20)$$

The following identity remains true for two functions, f and g, which belong to $\mathcal{M}_p$.

$$\left(-\frac{q^p z \partial_q f(z)}{[p]_q} \right) * g(z) = f(z) * \left(-\frac{q^p z \partial_q g(z)}{[p]_q} \right). \qquad (21)$$

Now, by using equivalence relation (7) and Theorem 1, the proof can be achieved by applying (20) and (21). □

Remark 3. (i) Putting $p = 1$ and $q \to 1^-$ in Theorem 2, we arrive at the results of Aouf et al. [17] (Theorem 6, with $\lambda = 0$ and $b = 1$) and Bulboacă et al. [20] (Theorem 2, with $b = 1$), and El-Ashwah [21] (Theorem 2, with $p = 1$);
(ii) Putting $p = 1$, $q \to 1^-$, $A = 1$ and $B = -1$ in Theorem 2, we reach the conclusion of Aouf et al. [18] (Theorem 3, with $b = m = 1$).

As a result, we have the following corollary by taking $A = 1 - 2\alpha$ and $B = -1$ in Theorem 2.

Corollary 3. *The function* $f \in \mathcal{MK}_{p,q}(\alpha)$, *if and only if*

$$z^p \left[f(z) * \frac{1 - Dz - Ez^2}{z^p(1-z)(1-qz)(1-q^2z)} \right] \neq 0 \ (z \in U),$$

where

$$D = \frac{(1-q^{p+2}) - q(1-q^{p-1})\left(\frac{\left(1+q^2[p-1]_q\right)e^{-i\theta} - q\left(1-2\alpha+[p]_q\right)}{1-2\alpha+[p]_q - q[p-1]_q e^{-i\theta}}\right)}{1-q^p},$$

and

$$E = \frac{q(1-q^{p+1})\left(\left(1+q^2[p-1]_q\right)e^{-i\theta} - q(1-2\alpha+[p]_q)\right)}{(1-q^p)\left(1-2\alpha+[p]_q - q[p-1]_q e^{-i\theta}\right)}.$$

As a result, we have the following corollary by taking $q \to 1^-$, $A = 1 - 2\alpha$ and $B = -1$ in Theorem 2.

Corollary 4. *The function* $f \in \mathcal{MK}_p(\alpha)$, *if and only if*

$$z^p\left[f(z) * \frac{1 - \frac{2p(1-2\alpha+p) - (2p^2-p-1)e^{-i\theta}}{p(1-2\alpha+p) - p(p-1)e^{-i\theta}}z - \frac{(p+2)(pe^{-i\theta} - (1-2\alpha+p)) - 1}{p(1-2\alpha+p) - p(p-1)e^{-i\theta}}z^2}{z^p(1-z)^3}\right] \neq 0 \ (z \in U).$$

Theorem 3. *The following are necessary and sufficient requirements for the function $f \in \mathcal{M}_p$ to be in the class $\mathcal{MS}^*_{p,q}(n; A, B)$:*

$$1 + \sum_{k=-p+1}^{\infty} [k+p+1]_q^n a_k z^{k+p} \neq 0 \ (z \in U), \tag{22}$$

or

$$1 + \sum_{k=-p+1}^{\infty} \left([k+p]_q C + 1\right)[k+p+1]_q^n a_k z^{k+p} \neq 0 \ (z \in U), \tag{23}$$

where C is defined by (12).

Proof. Let $f \in \mathcal{M}_p$, then, by using Theorem 1 and (8) we have $f \in \mathcal{MS}^*_{p,q}(n; A, B)$, if and only if

$$z^p\left[\left(\mathfrak{D}_q^n f\right)(z) * \frac{1 + (C-q)z}{z^p(1-z)(1-qz)}\right] \neq 0 \ (z \in U), \tag{24}$$

for all $C = \frac{B + e^{-i\theta}}{A - [p]_q B - q[p-1]_q e^{-i\theta}}$; $\theta \in [0, 2\pi)$, and also for $C = 0$. Since

$$\frac{1 + (0-q)z}{z^p(1-z)(1-qz)} = z^{-p} + \sum_{k=-p+1}^{\infty} z^k, \tag{25}$$

by using (3) and (25) in (24) in case of $C = 0$, then we can obtain (22).

Similarly, it can be shown that

$$\frac{1+(C-q)z}{z^p(1-z)(1-qz)} = z^{-p} + \sum_{k=-p+1}^{\infty} \left([k+p]_q C + 1\right) z^k, \qquad (26)$$

then using (3) and (26) in (24), we can obtain (23). The proof is complete. $\square$

The next theorem can be established using the same method, and the proof is eliminated.

Theorem 4. *The following are necessary and sufficient requirements for the function $f \in \mathcal{M}_p$ to be in the class $\mathcal{MK}_{p,q}(n; A, B)$:*

$$1 - \sum_{k=-p+1}^{\infty} q[k]_q [k+p+1]_q^n a_k z^{k+p} \neq 0 \ (z \in U), \qquad (27)$$

or

$$1 - \sum_{k=-p+1}^{\infty} q[k]_q \left([k+p]_q C + 1\right) [k+p+1]_q^n a_k z^{k+p} \neq 0 \ (z \in U). \qquad (28)$$

3. Estimates of Coefficients and Inclusion Characteristics

In this section, as an application of Theorems 3 and 4, we introduce some estimates of the coefficients a_k ($k \geq -p+1$) of functions of the form (1) which belong to the two main classes $\mathcal{MS}^*_{p,q}(n; A, B)$ and $\mathcal{MK}_{p,q}(n; A, B)$, respectively. Moreover, we give the inclusion relationships of the two classes.

Theorem 5. *If the function $f \in \mathcal{M}_p$ fulfills the inequalities*

$$\sum_{k=-p+1}^{\infty} [k+p+1]_q^n |a_k| < 1, \qquad (29)$$

and

$$\sum_{k=-p+1}^{\infty} \left([k+p]_q |C| + 1\right) [k+p+1]_q^n |a_k| < 1, \qquad (30)$$

then $f \in \mathcal{MS}^*_{p,q}(n; A, B)$.

Proof. According to (29), a simple calculation shows that

$$\left| 1 + \sum_{k=-p+1}^{\infty} [k+p+1]_q^n a_k z^{k+p} \right| \geq 1 - \left| \sum_{k=-p+1}^{\infty} [k+p+1]_q^n a_k z^{k+p} \right|$$

$$\geq 1 - \sum_{k=-p+1}^{\infty} [k+p+1]_q^n |a_k| |z|^{k+p}$$

$$> 1 - \sum_{k=-p+1}^{\infty} [k+p+1]_q^n |a_k| > 0$$

which leads to satisfaction of (22), then $f \in \mathcal{MS}^*_{p,q}(n; A, B)$. Similarly, using the assumption (30), we conclude that

$$\left| 1 + \sum_{k=-p+1}^{\infty} \left([k+p]_q C + 1 \right) [k+p+1]_q^n a_k z^{k+p} \right|$$

$$\geq 1 - \left| \sum_{k=-p+1}^{\infty} \left([k+p]_q C + 1 \right) [k+p+1]_q^n a_k z^{k+p} \right|$$

$$\geq 1 - \sum_{k=-p+1}^{\infty} \left([k+p]_q |C| + 1 \right) [k+p+1]_q^n |a_k| |z|^{k+p}$$

$$> 1 - \sum_{k=-p+1}^{\infty} \left([k+p]_q |C| + 1 \right) [k+p+1]_q^n |a_k| > 0,$$

which shows that (23) holds true and $f \in \mathcal{MS}^*_{p,q}(n; A, B)$; the proof is finished. □

Similarly, results regarding $\mathcal{MK}_{p,q}(n; A, B)$ can be introduced as follows:

Theorem 6. *If the function* $f \in \mathcal{M}_p$ *fulfills the inequalities*

$$\sum_{k=-p+1}^{\infty} q[k]_q [k+p+1]_q^n |a_k| < 1, \tag{31}$$

and

$$\sum_{k=-p+1}^{\infty} q[k]_q \left([k+p]_q |C| + 1 \right) [k+p+1]_q^n |a_k| < 1, \tag{32}$$

then $f \in \mathcal{MK}_{p,q}(n; A, B)$.

Now, using the appropriate technique due to Ahuja [26], we introduce the inclusion relationships of $\mathcal{MS}^*_{p,q}(n; A, B)$ and $\mathcal{MK}_{p,q}(n; A, B)$, respectively.

Theorem 7. *If* $n \in \mathbb{N}_o$, *then*

$$\mathcal{MS}^*_{p,q}(n+1; A, B) \subset \mathcal{MS}^*_{p,q}(n; A, B). \tag{33}$$

Proof. If $f \in \mathcal{MS}^*_{p,q}(n+1; A, B)$, then using Theorem 3, we can write

$$1 + \sum_{k=-p+1}^{\infty} [k+p+1]_q^{n+1} a_k z^{k+p} \neq 0 \quad (z \in U), \tag{34}$$

or

$$1 + \sum_{k=-p+1}^{\infty} \left([k+p]_q C + 1 \right) [k+p+1]_q^{n+1} a_k z^{k+p} \neq 0 \quad (z \in U), \tag{35}$$

but (34) and (35) can be written as follows:

$$\left(1 + \sum_{k=-p+1}^{\infty} [k+p+1]_q z^{k+p} \right) * \left(1 + \sum_{k=-p+1}^{\infty} [k+p+1]_q^n a_k z^{k+p} \right) \neq 0, \tag{36}$$

and

$$\left(1 + \sum_{k=-p+1}^{\infty} [k+p+1]_q z^{k+p} \right) * \left(1 + \sum_{k=-p+1}^{\infty} \left([k+p]_q C + 1 \right) [k+p+1]_q^n a_k z^{k+p} \right) \neq 0. \tag{37}$$

Let us really define the function

$$h_1(z) = 1 + \sum_{k=-p+1}^{\infty} [k+p+1]_q z^{k+p}. \tag{38}$$

We note that the assumption that $h_1(z) = 0$ leads to $|z| > 1$, Thus, we deduce that $h_1(z) \neq 0$. Using the property that if $h_1 * g \neq 0$ and $h_1 \neq 0$, then $g \neq 0$. Thus from (36) and (37) and using the function $h_1(z) \neq 0$, we obtain

$$1 + \sum_{k=-p+1}^{\infty} [k+p+1]_q^n a_k z^{k+p} \neq 0, \tag{39}$$

and

$$1 + \sum_{k=-p+1}^{\infty} \left([k+p]_q C + 1\right)[k+p+1]_q^n a_k z^{k+p} \neq 0, \tag{40}$$

then Theorem 3 tells us that $f \in \mathcal{MS}_{p,q}^*(n; A, B)$. □

The following theorem gives the inclusion relationship regarding $\mathcal{MK}_{p,q}(n; A, B)$.

Theorem 8. *For $n \in \mathbb{N}_0$, we have*

$$\mathcal{MK}_{p,q}(n+1; A, B) \subset \mathcal{MK}_{p,q}(n; A, B). \tag{41}$$

Our results in Theorems 7 and 8 above can be utilised to introduce the following consequences.

Corollary 5. *Suppose that $m = n+1, n+2, \ldots (n \in \mathbb{N}_0)$. Then*

$$f \in \mathcal{MS}_{p,q}^*(m; A, B) \Longrightarrow f \in \mathcal{MS}_{p,q}^*(n; A, B).$$

Equivalently, if

$$\mathfrak{D}_q^m f(z) \in \mathcal{MS}_{p,q}^*(A, B),$$

then

$$f \in \mathcal{MS}_{p,q}^*(n; A, B).$$

Corollary 6. *Suppose that $m = n+1, n+2, \ldots (n \in \mathbb{N}_0)$. Then*

$$f \in \mathcal{MK}_{p,q}(m; A, B) \Longrightarrow f \in \mathcal{MK}_{p,q}(n; A, B).$$

Equivalently, if

$$\mathfrak{D}_q^m f(z) \in \mathcal{MK}_{p,q}(A, B),$$

then

$$f \in \mathcal{MK}_{p,q}(n; A, B).$$

4. Conclusions

We have defined a new operator on the set of meromorphically multivalent functions. With the help of this operator, we introduced the new subclasses $\mathcal{MK}_{p,q}(n; A, B)$ and $\mathcal{MS}_{p,q}^*(n; A, B)$. The study was concentrated on convolution conditions. Our suggestions for future studies on these subclasses is to use them in studies involving the theories of differential subordination and superordination. Additionally, one can define the results concerning the calculation of the bounds of coefficients of the bi-univalent functions, also obtaining the Fekete–Szegö functionals.

Author Contributions: Formal analysis and methodology, A.H.E.-Q.; resources, I.S.E. All authors have read and agreed to the published version of the manuscript.

Funding: The authors would like to thank the Common First Year Research Unit at King Saud University for giving us the funds for this article.

Institutional Review Board Statement: Not applicable.

Informed Consent Statement: Not applicable.

Data Availability Statement: Not applicable.

Acknowledgments: The authors would like to give thanks for the help of HM Abbas.

Conflicts of Interest: The authors confirm no competing interests.

References

1. Yousef, A.T.; Salleh, Z.; Al-Hawary, T. On a class of p-valent functions involving generalized differential operator. *Afr. Mat.* **2021**, *32*, 275–287. [CrossRef]
2. Al-Janaby, H.F.; Ghanim, F. A subclass of Noor-type harmonic p-valent functions based on hypergeometric functions. *Kragujev. J. Math.* **2021**, *45*, 499–519. [CrossRef]
3. Oros, G.I.; Oros, G.; Owa, S. Applications of Certain p-Valently Analytic Functions. *Mathematics* **2022**, *10*, 910. [CrossRef]
4. El-Ashwah, R.M.; Hassan, A.H. Properties of certain subclass of p-valent meromorphic functions associated with certain linear operator. *J. Egyptian Math. Soc.* **2016**, *24*, 226–232. [CrossRef]
5. Bakhtiar, A.; Mashwani, W.K.; Serkan, A.; Saima, M.; Khan, M.G.; Khan, B. A subclass of meromorphic Janowski-type multivalent q-starlike functions involving a q-differential operator. *Adv. Differ. Equ.* **2022**, *2022*, 5. [CrossRef]
6. El-Qadeem, A.H.; Mamon, M.A. Comprehensive subclasses of multivalent functions with negative coefficients defined by using a q-difference operator. *Trans. A Razmadze Math. Inst.* **2018**, *172*, 510–526. [CrossRef]
7. Golmohammadi, M.H.; Najafzadeh, S.; Forutan, M.R. On a Generalized Subclass of p-Valent Meromorphic Functions by Defined q-Derivative Operator. *Adv. Math. Finance Appl.* **2021**, *6*, 869–881.
8. Khan, B.; Srivastava, H.M.; Arjika, S.; Khan, S.; Khan, N.; Ahmad, Q.Z. A certain q-Ruscheweyh type derivative operator and its applications involving multivalent functions. *Adv. Differ. Equ.* **2021**, *2021*, 279. [CrossRef]
9. Aldawish, I.; Aouf, M.K.; Frasin, B.A.; Al-Hawary, T. New subclass of analytic functions defined by q-analogue of p-valent Noor integral operator. *AIMS Math.* **2021**, *6*, 10466–10484. [CrossRef]
10. Miller, S.S.; Mocanu, P.T. *Differenatial Subordinations: Theory and Applications*; Series on Monographs and Textbooks in Pure and Appl. Math. No. 255; Marcel Dekker, Inc.: New York, NY, USA, 2000.
11. Jackson, F.H. On q-functions and a certain difference operator. *Trans. Roy. Soc. Edinb* **1909**, *46*, 253–281. [CrossRef]
12. Ali, R.M.; Ravichandran, V. Classes of meromorphic alpha-convex functions. *Taiwan J. Math.* **2010**, *14*, 1479–1490. [CrossRef]
13. Kaczmarski, J. On the coefficients of some classes of starlike functions. *Bull. Acad. Polon. Sci. Ser. Sci. Math. Astronom. Phys.* **1969**, *17*, 495–501.
14. Pommerenke, C. On meromorphic starlike functions. *Pac. J. Math.* **1963**, *13*, 221–235. [CrossRef]
15. Clune, J. On meromorphic Schlicht functions. *J. Lond. Math. Soc.* **1959**, *34*, 215–216. [CrossRef]
16. Miller, J.E. Convex meromorphic mappings and related functions. *Proc. Am. Math. Soc.* **1970**, *25*, 220–228. [CrossRef]
17. Aouf, M.K.; Mostafa, A.O.; Zayed, H.M. Convolution properties for some subclasses of meromorphic functions of complex order. *Abstract Appl. Anal.* **2015**, *2015*, 973613. [CrossRef]
18. Aouf, M.K.; Mostafa, A.O.; Zayed, H.M. Convolution conditions for some subclasses of meromorphic bounded functions of complex order. *Thai J. Math.* **2016**, *14*, 249–258.
19. Aouf, M.K.; Seoudy, T.M. Classes of analytic functions related to the Dziok–Srivastava operator. *Integral Transforms Spec. Funct.* **2011**, *22*, 423–430. [CrossRef]
20. Bulboacă, T.; Aouf, M.K.; El-Ashwah, R.M. Convolution properties for subclasses of meromorphic univalent functions of complex order. *Filomat* **2012**, *26*, 153–163. [CrossRef]
21. El-Ashwah, R.M. Some convolution and inclusion properties for subclasses of meromorphic p-valent functions involving integral operator. *Acta Math. Sci.* **2013**, *33*, 1749–1758. [CrossRef]
22. Mostafa, A.O.; Aouf, M.K. On convolution properties for certain classes of p-valent meromorphic functions defined by linear operator. *Lematematiche* **2014**, *69*, 259–266.
23. Mostafa, A.O.; Aouf, M.K. On convolution properties for some classes of meromorphic functions associated with linear operator. *Bull. Iranian Math. Soc.* **2015**, *41*, 325–332.
24. Seoudy, T.M.; Aouf, M.K. Convolution properties for classes of bounded analytic functions with complex order defined by q-derivative operator. *RACSAM* **2019**, *113*, 1279–1288.
25. Seoudy, T.M.; Aouf, M.K. Convolution properties for certain classes of analytic functions defined by q-derivative operator. *Abstract Appl. Anal.* **2014**, *2014*, 846719. [CrossRef]
26. Ahuja, O.P. Families of analytic functions related to Ruscheweyh derivatives and subordinate to convex functions. *Yokohama Math. J.* **1993**, *41*, 39–50.

Article

Applications of Confluent Hypergeometric Function in Strong Superordination Theory

Georgia Irina Oros [1], Gheorghe Oros [1] and Ancuța Maria Rus [2,*]

[1] Department of Mathematics and Computer Science, Faculty of Informatics and Sciences, University of Oradea, 410087 Oradea, Romania; georgia_oros_ro@yahoo.co.uk (G.I.O.); gh_oros@yahoo.com (G.O.)

[2] Doctoral School of Engineering Sciences, University of Oradea, 410087 Oradea, Romania

* Correspondence: rusancuta4@gmail.com

Abstract: In the research presented in this paper, confluent hypergeometric function is embedded in the theory of strong differential superordinations. In order to proceed with the study, the form of the confluent hypergeometric function is adapted taking into consideration certain classes of analytic functions depending on an extra parameter previously introduced related to the theory of strong differential subordination and superordination. Operators previously defined using confluent hypergeometric function, namely Kummer–Bernardi and Kummer–Libera integral operators, are also adapted to those classes and strong differential superordinations are obtained for which they are the best subordinants. Similar results are obtained regarding the derivatives of the operators. The examples presented at the end of the study are proof of the applicability of the original results.

Keywords: analytic function; starlike function; convex function; strong differential superordination; best subordinant; confluent (Kummer) hypergeometric function

Citation: Oros, G.I.; Oros, G.; Rus, A.M. Applications of Confluent Hypergeometric Function in Strong Superordination Theory. *Axioms* **2022**, *11*, 209. https://doi.org/10.3390/axioms11050209

Academic Editor: Sidney A. Morris

Received: 18 April 2022
Accepted: 21 April 2022
Published: 29 April 2022

Publisher's Note: MDPI stays neutral with regard to jurisdictional claims in published maps and institutional affiliations.

Copyright: © 2022 by the authors. Licensee MDPI, Basel, Switzerland. This article is an open access article distributed under the terms and conditions of the Creative Commons Attribution (CC BY) license (https://creativecommons.org/licenses/by/4.0/).

1. Introduction

The theory of strong differential subordination was initiated by Antonino and Romaguera [1] as a generalization of the classical concept of differential subordination introduced by Miller and Mocanu [2,3]. The results obtained by Antonino and Romaguera for the case of strong Briot–Bouquet differential subordinations inspired the development of the general theory related to strong differential subordination as seen for the classical case of differential subordination which is synthetized in [4]. The main aspects of strong differential subordination theory were established in a paper published in 2009 [5] by stating the three problems on which the theory is based on and by defining the notions of solution of a strong differential subordination and dominant of the solutions of the strong differential subordination. The class of admissible functions, a basic tool in the study of strong differential subordinations, was also introduced in this paper. The theory developed rapidly especially through studies associated to different operators like Liu–Srivastava operator [6], a generalized operator [7], multiplier transformation [8,9], Komatu integral operator [10], Sălăgean operator and Ruscheweyh derivative [11] or a certain differential operator [12]. The topic is still interesting for researchers as it is obvious from the numerous publications in the last two years when multiplier transformation and Ruscheweyh derivative [13] or integral operators [14] were used for obtaining new strong subordination results. We can refer to [15,16] for applications of differential operators in the analyses of phenomena from mathematical biology.

The dual notion of strong differential superordination was introduced also in 2009 [17] following the pattern set by Miller and Mocanu for the classical notion of differential superordination [18]. The special case of first order strong differential superordinations was next investigated [19]. Strong differential superodinations were applied to a general equation [20] and they were also related to different operators such as generalized Sălăgean and Ruscheweyh operators [21], new generalized derivative operator [22], or certain general operators [23]. This notion is still popular as it can be proved by listing a few more papers than already shown, published recently [24–26].

In 2012 [27], some interesting new classes were introduced related to the theory of strong differential subordination and superordination. They are intensely used for obtaining new results ever since they were connected to the studies.

The study presented in this paper uses those classes which we list as follows:

For $U = \{z \in \mathbb{C} : |z| < 1\}$ the unit disc of the complex plane, there are some notations used: $\overline{U} = \{z \in \mathbb{C} : |z| \leq 1\}$ and $\partial U = \{z \in \mathbb{C} : |z| = 1\}$. $H(U)$ denotes the class of holomorphic functions in the unit disc.

Let $H(U \times \overline{U})$ denote the class of analytic functions in $U \times \overline{U}$.

The following subclasses of $H(U \times \overline{U})$ are defined in [27]:

$$H_\zeta[a, n] = \left\{ f \in H(U \times \overline{U}) : f(z, \zeta) = a + a_n(\zeta)z^n + a_{n+1}(\zeta)z^{n+1} + \ldots, z \in U, \zeta \in \overline{U} \right\}$$

with $a_k(\zeta)$ holomorphic functions in $\overline{U}$, $k \geq n$, $a \in \mathbb{C}$, $n \in \mathbb{N}$.

$$H\zeta_U(U) = \left\{ f \in H_\zeta[a, n] : f(\cdot, \zeta) \text{ univalent in } U \text{ for all } \zeta \in \overline{U} \right\}$$

$$A\zeta_n = \left\{ f \in H(U \times \overline{U}) : f(z, \zeta) = z + a_{n+1}(\zeta)z^{n+1} + \ldots, z \in U, \zeta \in \overline{U} \right\}, \text{ with } A\zeta_1 = A\zeta$$

and $a_k(\zeta)$ holomorphic functions in $\overline{U}$, $k \geq n+1$, $n \in \mathbb{N}$.

$$S^*\zeta = \left\{ f \in A\zeta : \operatorname{Re} \frac{z f'_z(z, \zeta)}{f(z, \zeta)} > 0, z \in U, \zeta \in \overline{U} \right\}$$

denotes the class of starlike functions in $U \times \overline{U}$.

$$K\zeta = \left\{ f \in A\zeta : \operatorname{Re} \left(\frac{z f''_{z^2}(z, \zeta)}{f'_z(z, \zeta)} + 1 \right) > 0, z \in U, \zeta \in \overline{U} \right\}$$

denotes the class of convex functions in $U \times \overline{U}$.

For obtaining the original results of this paper, the following definitions and notations introduced in [27] are necessary:

Definition 1 ([27]). *Let $h(z, \zeta)$ and $f(z, \zeta)$ be analytic functions in $U \times \overline{U}$. The function $f(z, \zeta)$ is said to be strongly subordinate to $h(z, \zeta)$, or $h(z, \zeta)$ is said to be strongly superordinate to $f(z, \zeta)$ if there exists a function w analytic in U with $w(0) = 0$, $|w(z)| < 1$ such that $f(z, \zeta) = h(w(z), \zeta)$, for all $\zeta \in \overline{U}$, $z \in U$. In such a case, we write*

$$f(z, \zeta) \prec\prec h(z, \zeta),\ z \in U,\ \zeta \in \overline{U}.$$

Remark 1 ([27]). *(a) If $f(z, \zeta)$ is analytic in $U \times \overline{U}$ and univalent in U for $\zeta \in \overline{U}$, then Definition 1 is equivalent to:*

$$f(0, \zeta) = h(0, \zeta), \text{for all } \zeta \in \overline{U} \text{ and } f(U \times \overline{U}) \subset h(U \times \overline{U}).$$

(b) If $f(z, \zeta) = f(z)$, $h(z, \zeta) = h(z)$, then the strong superordination becomes the usual superordination.

Definition 2 ([27]). *We denote by Q_ζ the set of functions $q(\cdot, \zeta)$ that are analytic and injective, as function of z, on $\overline{U} \setminus E(q(z, \zeta))$ where*

$$E(q(z, \zeta)) = \left\{ \xi \in \partial U : \lim_{z \to \xi} q(z, \zeta) = \infty \right\}$$

and are such that $q'_z(\xi, \zeta) \neq 0$ for $\xi \in \partial U \setminus E(q(z, \zeta))$, $\zeta \in \overline{U}$.

The subclass of Q_ζ for which $q(0,\zeta) = a$ is denoted by $Q_\zeta(a)$.

Definition 3 ([27]). *Let Ω_ζ be a set in $\mathbb{C}$, $q(\cdot,\zeta) \in \Omega_\zeta$, and n a positive integer. The class of admissible functions $\Phi_n[\Omega_\zeta, q(\cdot,\zeta)]$ consists of those functions $\varphi : \mathbb{C}^3 \times U \times \overline{U} \to \mathbb{C}$ that satisfy the admissibility condition*

$$\varphi(r,s,t;\xi,\zeta) \in \Omega_\zeta \tag{A}$$

whenever $r = q(z,\zeta)$, $s = \frac{z q'_z(z,\zeta)}{m}$, $\operatorname{Re}\left(\frac{t}{s}+1\right) \leq \frac{1}{m}\operatorname{Re}\left[\frac{z q''_{z^2}(z,\zeta)}{q'_z(z,\zeta)}+1\right]$, $z \in U$, $\zeta \in \overline{U}\setminus E(q(\cdot,\zeta))$ and $m \geq n \geq 1$. When $n=1$ we write $\Phi_1[\Omega_\zeta, q(\cdot,\zeta)]$ as $\Phi[\Omega_\zeta, q(\cdot,\zeta)]$.
In the special case when $h(\cdot,\zeta)$ is an analytic mapping of $U \times \overline{U}$ onto $\Omega_\zeta \neq \mathbb{C}$ we denote the class $\Phi_n[h(U \times \overline{U}), q(z,\zeta)]$ by $\Phi_n[h(z,\zeta), q(z,\zeta)]$.
If $\varphi : \mathbb{C}^2 \times U \times \overline{U} \to \mathbb{C}$, then the admissibility condition (A) reduces to

$$\varphi\left(q(z,\zeta), \frac{z q'_z(z,\zeta)}{m}; \xi, \zeta\right) \in \Omega_\zeta, \tag{A'}$$

where $z \in U$, $\zeta \in \overline{U}$, $\xi \in \overline{U}\setminus E(q(\cdot,\zeta))$ and $m \geq n \geq 1$.

Miller—Mocanu lemma given in [18] was rewritten in [27] for functions $p(z,\zeta)$ and $q(z,\zeta)$ as follows:

Lemma 1 ([17,27]). *Let $p(z,\zeta) \in Q(a)$ and let $q(z,\zeta) = a + a_n(\zeta)z^n + a_{n+1}(\zeta)z^{n+1} + \ldots$ with $a_k(\zeta)$ holomorphic functions in $\overline{U}$, $k \geq n$, $q(z,\zeta) \not\equiv a$ and $n \geq 1$. If $q(z,\zeta)$ is not subordinate to $p(z,\zeta)$, then there exist points $z_0 = r_0 e^{i\theta_0} \in U$ and $\xi_0 \in \partial U \setminus E(p(z,\zeta))$ and an $m \geq n \geq 1$ for which $q(U \times \overline{U}_{r_0}) \subset p(U \times \overline{U})$ and*
(i) $q(z_0,\zeta) = p(\xi_0,\zeta)$,
(ii) $z_0 q'_z(z_0,\zeta) = m\xi_0 p'_z(\xi_0,\zeta)$ and
(iii) $\operatorname{Re}\left(\frac{z_0 q''_{z^2}(z_0,\zeta)}{q'_z(z_0,\zeta)}+1\right) \geq m\operatorname{Re}\left(\frac{\xi_0 p''_{z^2}(\xi_0,\zeta)}{p'_z(\xi_0,\zeta)}+1\right)$.

This lemma will be used in the next section for proving the theorems which contain the original results. Another helpful result which will be used is the next lemma proved in [28].

Lemma 2 ([28]). *Let $h(z,\zeta)$ be convex in U for all $\zeta \in \overline{U}$ with $h(0,\zeta) = a$, $\gamma \neq 0$, $\operatorname{Re}\gamma > 0$ and $p \in H_\zeta[a,1] \cap Q$. If $p(z,\zeta) + \frac{z p'_z(z,\zeta)}{\gamma}$ is univalent in U for all $\zeta \in \overline{U}$,*

$$h(z,\zeta) \ll p(z,\zeta) + \frac{z p'_z(z,\zeta)}{\gamma}$$

and

$$q(z,\zeta) = \frac{\gamma}{z^\gamma} \int_0^z h(t,\zeta) t^{\gamma-1} dt,$$

then

$$q(z,\zeta) \ll p(z,\zeta), \quad z \in U, \zeta \in \overline{U}.$$

The function q is convex and is the best subordinant.

The connection between univalent function theory and hypergeometric functions was established in 1985 when de Branges used the generalized hypergeometric function for proving Bieberbach's conjecture [29]. Once hypergeometric functions were considered in studies regarding univalent functions, confluent hypergeometric function was used in many investigations. One of the first papers which investigated confluent hypergeometric function and gave conditions for its univalence was published in 1990 [30]. Ever since then, aspects of its univalence were further investigated [31,32], it was considered in connection with other important functions [33–37] and it was used in the definition of new operators [38]. This prolific function is used in the present paper for obtaining results related to another topic, strong differential superordinations. The function is considered as follows:

Definition 4 ([30]). *Let a and c be complex numbers with $c \neq 0, -1, -2, \ldots$ and consider*

$$\phi(a,c;z) = 1 + \frac{a}{c} \cdot \frac{z}{1!} + \frac{a(a+1)}{c(c+1)} \cdot \frac{z^2}{2!} + \ldots, \ z \in U \quad (1)$$

This function is called confluent (Kummer) hypergeometric function, is analytic in $\mathbb{C}$, and satisfies Kummer's differential equation:

$$z \cdot w''(z) + [c - z] \cdot w'(z) - a \cdot w(z) = 0.$$

If we let

$$(d)_k = \frac{\Gamma(d+k)}{\Gamma(d)} = d(d+1)(d+2) \ldots (d+k-1) \text{ and } (d)_0 = 1,$$

then (1) can be written in the form

$$\phi(a,c;z) = \sum_{k=0}^{\infty} \frac{(a)_k}{(c)_k} \cdot \frac{z^k}{k!} = \frac{\Gamma(c)}{\Gamma(a)} \cdot \sum_{k=0}^{\infty} \frac{\Gamma(a+k)}{\Gamma(c+k)} \cdot \frac{z^k}{k!} \quad (2)$$

In the study conducted for obtaining the original results presented in the next section of this paper, the operators introduced in [38] are adapted to the subclasses of $H(U \times \overline{U})$ defined in [27] as follows:

Definition 5 ([38]). *Let $\phi(a,c;z)$ be given by (1) and let $\gamma > 0$. The integral operator $B: H_\zeta[1,1] \to H_\zeta[1,1]$,*

$$B[\phi(a(\zeta),c(\zeta);z,\zeta)] = B(a(\zeta),c(\zeta);z,\zeta) = \frac{\gamma}{z^\gamma} \int_0^z \phi(a(\zeta),c(\zeta);t,\zeta) t^{\gamma-1} dt \quad (3)$$

$z \in U$, $\zeta \in \overline{U}$, is called Kummer–Bernardi integral operator.
For $\gamma = 1$ the integral operator $L: H_\zeta[1,1] \to H_\zeta[1,1]$ is defined as

$$L[\phi(a(\zeta),c(\zeta);z,\zeta)] = L(a(\zeta),c(\zeta);z,\zeta) = \frac{1}{z} \int_0^z \phi(a(\zeta),c(\zeta);t,\zeta) dt, \quad (4)$$

$z \in U, \zeta \in \overline{U}$, which is called Kummer–Libera integral operator.

The form of the confluent hypergeometric function adapted to the new classes depending on the extra parameter ζ needed in the studies related to strong differential superordination theory is given in the next section. Strong differential superordinations are proved in the theorems for which the operators given by (3) and (4) and their derivatives with respect to z are the best subordinants considering γ in relation (3) both a real number, $\gamma > 0$, and a complex number with $\text{Re } \gamma > 0$. Examples are constructed as proof of the applicability of the new results.

2. Main Results

Considering confluent hypergeometric function defined by (1) or (2), if coefficients a and c complex numbers are replaced by holomorphic functions $a(\zeta)$, $c(\zeta)$ depending on the parameter $\zeta \in \overline{U}$, the function changes its form into the following:

$$\phi(a(\zeta),c(\zeta);z,\zeta) = 1 + \frac{a(\zeta)}{c(\zeta)} \cdot \frac{z}{1!} + \frac{a(\zeta)[a(\zeta)+1]}{c(\zeta)[c(\zeta)+1]} \cdot \frac{z^2}{2!} + \ldots, z \in U, \tag{5}$$

where $(\zeta) \neq 0$, $c(\zeta) \neq 0, -1, -2, \ldots$.

In [32], Corollary 4 the convexity in the unit disc of the function $\phi(a,c;z)$ given by (1) was proved. This property extends to the new form of the function $(a(\zeta),c(\zeta);z,\zeta)$, as seen in (5).

The first original theorem presented in this paper uses the convexity of the function $\phi(a(\zeta),c(\zeta);z,\zeta)$ and the methods related to strong differential superordination theory in order to find necessary conditions for Kummer–Bernardi integral operator presented in Definition 5 to be the best subordinant of a certain strong differential superordination involving confluent hypergeometric function $\phi(a(\zeta),c(\zeta);z,\zeta)$.

Theorem 1. *Consider the confluent hypergeometric function $\phi(a(\zeta),c(\zeta);z,\zeta)$ defined by (5) and Kummer–Bernardi integral operator $B(a(\zeta),c(\zeta);z,\zeta)$ given by (3). Let $\varphi: \mathbb{C}^2 \times U \times \overline{U} \to \mathbb{C}$ be an admissible function with the properties seen in Definition 3. Suppose that $\phi(a(\zeta),c(\zeta);z,\zeta)$ is a univalent solution of the equation*

$$\phi(a(\zeta),c(\zeta);z,\zeta) = \varphi\big(B(a(\zeta),c(\zeta);z,\zeta), z \cdot B'_z(a(\zeta),c(\zeta);z,\zeta);z,\zeta\big). \tag{6}$$

If $\varphi \in \Phi_n\big[h(U \times \overline{U}), q(z,\zeta)\big]$, $p(z,\zeta) \in Q_\zeta(1)$ and $\varphi(p(z,\zeta), z \cdot p'_z(z,\zeta);z,\zeta)$ are univalent in U for all $\zeta \in \overline{U}$, then strong superordination

$$\phi(a(\zeta),c(\zeta);z,\zeta) \ll \varphi\big(p(z,\zeta), z \cdot p'_z(z,\zeta);z,\zeta\big) \tag{7}$$

implies

$$B(a(\zeta),c(\zeta);z,\zeta) \ll p(z,\zeta), \ z \in U, \ \zeta \in \overline{U}.$$

The function $q(z,\zeta) = B(a(\zeta),c(\zeta);z,\zeta)$ is the best subordinant.

Proof. Using relation (3) we obtain

$$z^\gamma \cdot B(a(\zeta),c(\zeta);z,\zeta) = \gamma \int_0^z \phi(a(\zeta),c(\zeta);t,\zeta) t^{\gamma-1} dt. \tag{8}$$

Differentiating (8) with respect to z, following a simple calculation, the next equation is obtained:

$$B(a(\zeta),c(\zeta);z,\zeta) + \frac{1}{\gamma} z \cdot B'_z(a(\zeta),c(\zeta);z,\zeta) = \phi(a(\zeta),c(\zeta);z,\zeta). \tag{9}$$

Using relation (9), strong superordination (7) becomes:

$$B(a(\zeta),c(\zeta);z,\zeta) + \frac{1}{\gamma} z \cdot B'_z(a(\zeta),c(\zeta);z,\zeta) \ll \varphi\big(p(z,\zeta), z \cdot p'_z(z,\zeta);z,\zeta\big). \tag{10}$$

Let $\varphi: \mathbb{C}^2 \times U \times \overline{U} \to \mathbb{C}$ be an admissible function, $\varphi(r,s;z,\zeta) \in \Phi_n\big[h(U \times \overline{U}), q(z,\zeta)\big]$, defined by:

$$\varphi(r,s;z,\zeta) = r + \frac{1}{\gamma} s, \ r,s \in \mathbb{C}, \ \gamma > 0. \tag{11}$$

Taking $r = B(a(\zeta),c(\zeta);z,\zeta)$, $s = z \cdot B'_z(a(\zeta),c(\zeta);z,\zeta);z,\zeta)$ relation (11) becomes:

$$\varphi(B(a(\zeta),c(\zeta);z,\zeta),z\cdot B'_z(a(\zeta),c(\zeta);z,\zeta);z,\zeta)$$
$$= B(a(\zeta),c(\zeta);z,\zeta) + \frac{1}{\gamma}z\cdot B'_z(a(\zeta),c(\zeta);z,\zeta);z,\zeta). \quad (12)$$

Using relation (12) in (10) we get:

$$\varphi\big(B(a(\zeta),c(\zeta);z,\zeta),z\cdot B'_z(a(\zeta),c(\zeta);z,\zeta);z,\zeta\big) \ll \varphi\big(p(z,\zeta),z\cdot p'_z(z,\zeta);z,\zeta\big).$$

Using Definition 1 and Remark 1, a), considering strong differential subordination (7) we get:

$$\phi(a(\zeta),c(\zeta);0,\zeta) = \varphi(p(0,\zeta),0;0,\zeta)$$

and

$$\phi(U \times \overline{U}) \subset \varphi(U \times \overline{U}). \quad (13)$$

Interpreting relation (13) we conclude that

$$\varphi\big(p(\xi,\zeta),\xi\cdot p'_z(\xi,\zeta);\xi,\zeta\big) \notin \phi(U \times \overline{U}), \xi \in \partial U, \zeta \in \overline{U}. \quad (14)$$

For $\xi = \xi_0 \in \partial U$, relation (14) becomes:

$$\varphi\big(p(\xi_0,\zeta),\xi_0\cdot p'_z(\xi_0,\zeta);\xi_0,\zeta\big) \notin \phi(U \times \overline{U}), \zeta \in \overline{U}. \quad (15)$$

Using relation (6) we get:

$$\varphi\big(B(a(\zeta),c(\zeta);z,\zeta),z\cdot B'_z(a(\zeta),c(\zeta);z,\zeta);z,\zeta\big) \in \phi(U \times \overline{U}), z \in U, \zeta \in \overline{U}. \quad (16)$$

For $z = z_0 \in U$, (16) is written as:

$$\varphi\big(B(a(\zeta),c(\zeta);z_0,\zeta),z_0\cdot B'_z(a(\zeta),c(\zeta);z_0,\zeta);z_0,\zeta\big) \in \phi(U \times \overline{U}), z_0 \in U, \zeta \in \overline{U}. \quad (17)$$

In order to finalize the proof, Lemma 1 and admissibility condition (A') will be applied. Suppose that $q(z,\zeta) = B(a(\zeta),c(\zeta);z,\zeta)$ is not subordinate to $p(z,\zeta)$ for $z \in U, \zeta \in \overline{U}$. Then, using Lemma 1, we know that there are points $z_0 = r_0 e^{i\theta_0} \in U$ and $\xi_0 \in \partial U \setminus E(p(z,\zeta))$ and an $m \geq n \geq 1$ such that

$$(z_0,\zeta) = B(a(\zeta),c(\zeta);z_0,\zeta) = p(\xi_0,\zeta) \text{ and}$$

$$z_0 \cdot q'_z(z_0,\zeta) = z_0 \cdot B'_z(a(\zeta),c(\zeta);z_0,\zeta) = m\xi_0 p'_z(\xi_0,\zeta).$$

Using those conditions with $r = q(z_0,\zeta)$ and $s = \frac{z_0 \cdot q'_z(z_0,\zeta)}{m}$ for $\xi = \xi_0$ in Definition 3 and taking into consideration the admissibility condition (A'), we obtain:

$$\varphi(p(\xi_0,\zeta),\xi_0 p'_z(\xi_0,\zeta);\xi_0,\zeta) = \varphi\left(B(a(\zeta),c(\zeta);z_0,\zeta),\frac{z_0 \cdot B'_z(a(\zeta),c(\zeta);z_0,\zeta)}{m};z_0,\zeta\right)$$
$$\in \phi(U \times \overline{U}).$$

Using $m = 1$ in the previous relation, we get

$$\varphi(p(\xi_0,\zeta),\xi_0 p'_z(\xi_0,\zeta);\xi_0,\zeta) = \varphi(B(a(\zeta),c(\zeta);z_0,\zeta),z_0\cdot B'_z(a(\zeta),c(\zeta);z_0,\zeta);z_0,\zeta)$$
$$\in \phi(U \times \overline{U})$$

and using (17) we write

$$\varphi(p(\xi_0,\zeta),\xi_0 p'_z(\xi_0,\zeta);\xi_0,\zeta) \in \phi(U \times \overline{U}), z \in U, \zeta \in \overline{U},$$

which contradicts the result obtained in relation (15). Hence, the assumption made is false and we must have:

$$B(a(\zeta),c(\zeta);z,\zeta) \ll p(z,\zeta) \text{ for } z \in U, \zeta \in \overline{U}.$$

Since $q(z,\zeta) = B(a(\zeta),c(\zeta);z,\zeta)$ satisfies the differential Equation (6), we conclude that $q(z,\zeta) = B(a(\zeta),c(\zeta);z,\zeta)$ is the best subordinant. □

Remark 2. *For $\gamma = 1$, instead of Kummer–Bernardi integral operator, Kummer–Libera integral operator defined in (4) is used in Theorem 1 and the following corollary can be written:*

Corollary 1. *Consider the confluent hypergeometric function $\phi(a(\zeta),c(\zeta);z,\zeta)$ defined by (5) and Kummer–Libera integral operator $L(a(\zeta),c(\zeta);z,\zeta)$ given by (4). Let $\varphi : \mathbb{C}^2 \times U \times \overline{U} \to \mathbb{C}$ be an admissible function with the properties seen in Definition 3. Suppose that $\phi(a(\zeta),c(\zeta);z,\zeta)$ is a univalent solution of the equation*

$$\phi(a(\zeta),c(\zeta);z,\zeta) = \varphi\big(L(a(\zeta),c(\zeta);z,\zeta), z \cdot L'_z(a(\zeta),c(\zeta);z,\zeta);z,\zeta\big).$$

If $\varphi \in \Phi_n[h(U \times \overline{U}), q(z,\zeta)]$, $p(z,\zeta) \in Q_\zeta(1)$ and $\varphi(p(z,\zeta), z \cdot p'_z(z,\zeta);z,\zeta)$ are univalent in U for all $\zeta \in \overline{U}$, then strong superordination

$$\phi(a(\zeta),c(\zeta);z,\zeta) \prec\prec \varphi(p(z,\zeta), z \cdot p'_z(z,\zeta);z,\zeta)$$

implies

$$L(a(\zeta),c(\zeta);z,\zeta) \prec\prec p(z,\zeta),\ z \in U,\ \zeta \in \overline{U}.$$

The function $q(z,\zeta) = L(a(\zeta),c(\zeta);z,\zeta)$ is the best subordinant.

Theorem 2. *Let $q(z,\zeta)$ be a convex function in the unit disc for all $\zeta \in \overline{U}$, consider the confluent hypergeometric function $\phi(a(\zeta),c(\zeta);z,\zeta)$ defined by (5) and Kummer–Bernardi integral operator $B(a(\zeta),c(\zeta);z,\zeta)$ given by (3). Let $\varphi : \mathbb{C}^2 \times U \times \overline{U} \to \mathbb{C}$ be an admissible function with the properties seen in Definition 3 and define the analytic function*

$$h(z,\zeta) = \left(1 + \frac{1}{\gamma}\right) q(z,\zeta) + \frac{1}{\gamma} z \cdot q'_z(z,\zeta), z \in U,\ \zeta \in \overline{U}.$$

If $\phi'_z(a(\zeta),c(\zeta);z,\zeta)$ and $B'_z(a(\zeta),c(\zeta);z,\zeta) \in H_\zeta[1,1] \cap Q_\zeta(1)$ are univalent functions in U for all $\zeta \in \overline{U}$, then strong differential superordination

$$h(z,\zeta) \prec\prec \phi'_z(a(\zeta),c(\zeta);z,\zeta) \tag{18}$$

implies

$$q(z,\zeta) \prec\prec B'_z(a(\zeta),c(\zeta);z,\zeta),\ z \in U,\ \zeta \in \overline{U}.$$

Proof. Using relation (9) from the proof of Theorem 1 and differentiating it with respect to z, we obtain:

$$\phi'_z(a(\zeta),c(\zeta);z,\zeta) = \left(1 + \frac{1}{\gamma}\right) B'_z(a(\zeta),c(\zeta);z,\zeta) + \frac{1}{\gamma} z \cdot B''_{z^2}(a(\zeta),c(\zeta);z,\zeta), z \in U,\ \zeta \in \overline{U}. \tag{19}$$

Using (19), strong differential superordination (18) becomes:

$$h(z,\zeta) \prec\prec \left(1 + \frac{1}{\gamma}\right) B'_z(a(\zeta),c(\zeta);z,\zeta) + \frac{1}{\gamma} z \cdot B''_{z^2}(a(\zeta),c(\zeta);z,\zeta). \tag{20}$$

For the proof of this theorem to be complete, Lemma 1 and the admissibility condition (A') will be applied.

In order to do that, we define the admissible function $\varphi : \mathbb{C}^2 \times U \times \overline{U} \to \mathbb{C}$, $\varphi(r,s;z,\zeta) \in \Phi_n[h(U \times \overline{U}), q(z,\zeta)]$, given by:

$$\varphi(r,s;z,\zeta) = \left(1 + \frac{1}{\gamma}\right) r + \frac{1}{\gamma} s,\ r,s \in \mathbb{C},\ \gamma > 0. \tag{21}$$

Taking $r = B'_z(a(\zeta), c(\zeta); z, \zeta)$, $s = z \cdot B''_{z^2}(a(\zeta), c(\zeta); z, \zeta)$ relation (21) becomes:

$$\varphi\Big(B'_z(a(\zeta), c(\zeta); z, \zeta), z \cdot B''_{z^2}(a(\zeta), c(\zeta); z, \zeta); z, \zeta\Big)$$
$$= \Big(1 + \tfrac{1}{\gamma}\Big) B'_z(a(\zeta), c(\zeta); z, \zeta) + \tfrac{1}{\gamma} z \cdot B''_{z^2}(a(\zeta), c(\zeta); z, \zeta); z, \zeta). \tag{22}$$

Using relation (22) in (20) we get:

$$h(z, \zeta) \ll \varphi\Big(B'_z(a(\zeta), c(\zeta); z, \zeta), z \cdot B''_{z^2}(a(\zeta), c(\zeta); z, \zeta); z, \zeta\Big).$$

Using Definition 1 and Remark 1, a) for this strong differential superordination, we get:

$$h(0, \zeta) = \varphi\big(B'_z(a(\zeta), c(\zeta); 0, \zeta), 0; 0, \zeta\big)$$

and

$$h(U \times \overline{U}) \subset \varphi(U \times \overline{U}). \tag{23}$$

Interpreting relation (23) we conclude that

$$\varphi\Big(B'_z(a(\zeta), c(\zeta); \xi, \zeta), \xi \cdot B''_{z^2}(a(\zeta), c(\zeta); \xi, \zeta); \xi, \zeta\Big) \notin h(U \times \overline{U}),\ \xi \in \partial U, \zeta \in \overline{U}. \tag{24}$$

For $\xi = \xi_0 \in \partial U$, relation (24) becomes:

$$\varphi\Big(B'_z(a(\zeta), c(\zeta); \xi_0, \zeta), \xi_0 \cdot B''_{z^2}(a(\zeta), c(\zeta); \xi_0, \zeta); \xi_0, \zeta\Big) \notin h(U \times \overline{U}), \zeta \in \overline{U}. \tag{25}$$

Suppose that $q(z, \zeta)$ is not subordinate to $B'_z(a(\zeta), c(\zeta); z, \zeta)$ for $z \in U, \zeta \in \overline{U}$. Then, using Lemma 1, we know that there are points $z_0 = r_0 e^{i\theta_0} \in U$ and $\xi_0 \in \partial U \setminus E(B'_z(a(\zeta), c(\zeta); z, \zeta))$ and an $m \geq n \geq 1$ such that

$$q(z_0, \zeta) = B'_z(a(\zeta), c(\zeta); z_0, \zeta) = p(\xi_0, \zeta) \text{ and}$$

$$z_0 q'_z(z_0, \zeta) = m\xi_0 B''_{z^2}(a(\zeta), c(\zeta); z_0, \zeta) = m\xi_0 p'_z(\xi_0, \zeta).$$

Using those conditions with $r = B'_z(a(\zeta), c(\zeta); z_0, \zeta)$ and $s = \xi_0 B''_{z^2}(a(\zeta), c(\zeta); z_0, \zeta)$ for $\xi = \xi_0$ in Definition 3 and taking into consideration the admissibility condition (A'), we obtain:

$$\varphi(q(z_0, \zeta), z_0 q'_z(z_0, \zeta); z_0, \zeta) = \varphi\left(B'_z(a(\zeta), c(\zeta); z_0, \zeta), \frac{\xi_0 B''_{z^2}(a(\zeta), c(\zeta); \xi_0, \zeta)}{m}; z_0, \zeta\right)$$
$$\in h(U \times \overline{U}).$$

Using $m = 1$ in the previous relation, we get

$$\varphi\Big(B'_z(a(\zeta), c(\zeta); z_0, \zeta), \xi_0 B''_{z^2}(a(\zeta), c(\zeta); z_0, \zeta); z_0, \zeta\Big) \in h(U \times \overline{U}), \zeta \in \overline{U},$$

which contradicts the result obtained in relation (25). Hence, the assumption made is false and we must have:

$$q(z, \zeta) \ll B'_z(a(\zeta), c(\zeta); z, \zeta) \text{ for } z \in U, \zeta \in \overline{U}.$$

□

Remark 3. *For $\gamma = 1$, instead of Kummer–Bernardi integral operator, Kummer–Libera integral operator defined in (4) is used in Theorem 2 and the following corollary can be written:*

Corollary 2. *Let $q(z, \zeta)$ be a convex function in the unit disc for all $\zeta \in \overline{U}$, consider the confluent hypergeometric function $\phi(a(\zeta), c(\zeta); z, \zeta)$ defined by (5) and Kummer–Libera integral operator*

$L(a(\zeta), c(\zeta); z, \zeta)$ given by (4). Let $\varphi : \mathbb{C}^2 \times U \times \overline{U} \to \mathbb{C}$ be an admissible function with the properties seen in Definition 3 and define the analytic function:

$$h(z, \zeta) = \left(1 + \frac{1}{\gamma}\right) q(z, \zeta) + \frac{1}{\gamma} z \cdot q'_z(z, \zeta), z \in U, \zeta \in \overline{U}.$$

If $\phi'_z(a(\zeta), c(\zeta); z, \zeta)$ and $L'_z(a(\zeta), c(\zeta); z, \zeta) \in H_\zeta[1,1] \cap Q_\zeta(1)$ are univalent functions in U for all $\zeta \in \overline{U}$, then strong differential superordination

$$h(z, \zeta) \prec\prec \phi'_z(a(\zeta), c(\zeta); z, \zeta)$$

implies

$$q(z, \zeta) \prec\prec L'_z(a(\zeta), c(\zeta); z, \zeta), z \in U, \zeta \in \overline{U}.$$

In Theorems 1 and 2, parameter γ is a real number, $\gamma > 0$. In the next theorem, a necessary and sufficient condition is determined such that Kummer–Bernardi integral operator is the best subordinant for a certain strong differential superordination considering γ a complex number with Re $\gamma > 0$.

Theorem 3. Let $h(z, \zeta)$ with $h(0, \zeta) = a$ be a convex function in the unit disc for all $\zeta \in \overline{U}$ and let γ be a complex number with Re $\gamma > 0$. Consider the confluent hypergeometric function $\phi(a(\zeta), c(\zeta); z, \zeta)$ defined by (5) and Kummer–Bernardi integral operator $B(a(\zeta), c(\zeta); z, \zeta)$ given by (3). Let $p(z, \zeta) \in H_\zeta[a, 1] \cap Q_\zeta(a)$.

If $p(z, \zeta) + \frac{z \cdot p'_z(z, \zeta)}{\gamma}$ is univalent in U for all $\zeta \in \overline{U}$ and the following strong differential superordination is satisfied

$$B(a(\zeta), c(\zeta); z, \zeta) + \frac{z \cdot B'_z(a(\zeta), c(\zeta); z, \zeta)}{\gamma} \prec\prec p(z, \zeta) + \frac{z \cdot p'_z(z, \zeta)}{\gamma}, \quad (26)$$

then

$$q(z, \zeta) = B(a(\zeta), c(\zeta); z, \zeta) \prec\prec p(z, \zeta), z \in U, \zeta \in \overline{U}.$$

Function $q(z, \zeta) = B(a(\zeta), c(\zeta); z, \zeta)$ is convex and is the best subordinant.

Proof. Lemma 2 will be used for the proof of this theorem. Using the definition of Kummer–Bernardi operator given by (3) and differentiating this relation with respect to z, we obtain:

$$\gamma \cdot z^{\gamma-1} \cdot B(a(\zeta), c(\zeta); z, \zeta) + z^\gamma \cdot B'_z(a(\zeta), c(\zeta); z, \zeta) = \gamma \cdot h(z, \zeta) \cdot z^{\gamma-1}, z \in U, \zeta \in \overline{U}.$$

After a simple calculation, we get:

$$B(a(\zeta), c(\zeta); z, \zeta) + \frac{z \cdot B'_z(a(\zeta), c(\zeta); z, \zeta)}{\gamma} = h(z, \zeta), z \in U, \zeta \in \overline{U}. \quad (27)$$

Using (27), the strong differential subordination (26) becomes

$$h(z, \zeta) \prec\prec p(z, \zeta) + \frac{z \cdot p'_z(z, \zeta)}{\gamma}, z \in U, \zeta \in \overline{U}.$$

Since $h(z, \zeta)$ is a convex function and $p(z, \zeta) + \frac{z \cdot p'_z(z, \zeta)}{\gamma}$ is univalent in U for all $\zeta \in \overline{U}$, by applying Lemma 2 we obtain:

$$q(z, \zeta) = B(a(\zeta), c(\zeta); z, \zeta) \prec\prec p(z, \zeta), z \in U, \zeta \in \overline{U}.$$

Since function $q(z, \zeta) = B(a(\zeta), c(\zeta); z, \zeta)$ satisfies Equation (27) and is analytic in U for all $\zeta \in \overline{U}$, we conclude that $q(z, \zeta) = B(a(\zeta), c(\zeta); z, \zeta)$ is the best subordinant. □

Example 1. Let $a = -1$, $c = \frac{i}{2\zeta}$, $\frac{i}{2\zeta} \neq 0, -1, -2, \ldots, \zeta \neq 0, \gamma \in \mathbb{C}$, Re $\gamma > 0$. We evaluate:

$$\phi\left(-1,\frac{i}{2\zeta};z,\zeta\right)=1+\frac{-1}{\frac{i}{2\zeta}}\cdot\frac{z}{1!}=1-\frac{2\zeta\cdot z}{i}=1+2i\zeta z.$$

Further, we use this expression to obtain Kummer–Bernardi integral operator's expression:

$$B\left(\phi\left(-1,\tfrac{i}{2\zeta};z,\zeta\right)\right)=\tfrac{\gamma}{z^\gamma}\int_0^z\phi\left(-1,\tfrac{i}{2\zeta};t,\zeta\right)t^{\gamma-1}dt=\tfrac{\gamma}{z^\gamma}\int_0^z(1+2i\zeta t)t^{\gamma-1}dt$$
$$=\tfrac{\gamma}{z^\gamma}\left(\tfrac{z^\gamma}{\gamma}+2i\zeta\tfrac{z^{\gamma+1}}{\gamma+1}\right)=1+2i\zeta\tfrac{\gamma}{\gamma+1}\cdot z.$$

Functions $p(z,\zeta)=1+z\zeta$ and $p(z,\zeta)+\frac{z\cdot p'_z(z,\zeta)}{\gamma}=1+z\left(\zeta+\frac{\zeta}{\gamma}\right)$ are univalent in U for all $\zeta\in\overline{U}$.

Using Theorem 3, we get:
If the following strong differential superordination is satisfied

$$1+2i\zeta\frac{\gamma}{\gamma+1}\cdot z+\frac{2i\zeta\cdot z}{\gamma+1}\prec\prec 1+z\left(\zeta+\frac{\zeta}{\gamma}\right),$$

then

$$1+2i\zeta\frac{\gamma}{\gamma+1}\cdot z\prec\prec 1+z\zeta,\ z\in U,\ \zeta\in\overline{U}.$$

Function $q(z,\zeta)=1+2i\zeta\frac{\gamma}{\gamma+1}\cdot z$ is convex and is the best subordinant.

Example 2. Let $a=-1$, $c=\frac{i}{2\zeta}$, $\frac{i}{2\zeta}\neq 0,-1,-2,\ldots$, $\zeta\neq 0$, $\gamma=1+i\in\mathbb{C}$, $\operatorname{Re}\gamma=1>0$. We evaluate:

$$\phi\left(-1,\frac{i}{2\zeta};z,\zeta\right)=1+\frac{-1}{\frac{i}{2\zeta}}\cdot\frac{z}{1!}=1-\frac{2\zeta\cdot z}{i}=1+2i\zeta z.$$

Further, we use this expression to obtain Kummer–Bernardi integral operator's expression:

$$B\left(\phi\left(-1,\tfrac{i}{2\zeta};z,\zeta\right)\right)=\tfrac{\gamma}{z^\gamma}\int_0^z\phi\left(-1,\tfrac{i}{2\zeta};t,\zeta\right)t^{\gamma-1}dt=\tfrac{1+i}{z^{1+i}}\int_0^z(1+2i\zeta t)t^{\gamma-1}dt$$
$$=\tfrac{1+i}{z^{1+i}}\left(\tfrac{z^{1+i}}{1+i}+2i\zeta\tfrac{z^{1+i+1}}{1+i+1}\right)=1+2i\zeta\tfrac{z(i+1)}{i+2}=1+\tfrac{2}{5}(-1+3i)z\zeta.$$

Functions $p(z,\zeta)=1+z\zeta$ and $p(z,\zeta)+\frac{z\cdot p'_z(z,\zeta)}{1+i}=1+\tfrac{3}{2}z\zeta(3-i)$ are univalent in U for all $\zeta\in\overline{U}$.

Using Theorem 3, we get:
If $1+\tfrac{3}{2}z\zeta(3-i)$ is univalent in U for all $\zeta\in\overline{U}$ and the following strong differential superordination is satisfied

$$1+2i\zeta t\prec\prec 1+\tfrac{3}{2}z\zeta(3-i),$$

then

$$1+\tfrac{2}{5}(-1+3i)z\zeta\prec\prec 1+z\zeta,\ z\in U,\ \zeta\in\overline{U}.$$

Function $q(z,\zeta)=1+\tfrac{2}{5}(-1+3i)z\zeta$ is convex and is the best subordinant.

3. Discussion

The study presented in this paper is inspired by the nice results published which involve confluent hypergeometric function and certain operators defined by using this interesting function. For this research, the environment of the theory of strong differential superordination is considered. Confluent hypergeometric function and Kummer–Bernardi and Kummer–Libera operators defined in [38] are used in order to obtain certain strong differential superordinations. Their best subordinants are given in the three theorems proved in the main results part. Theorems 1 and 2 use the convexity of confluent hypergeometric function $\phi(a(\zeta), c(\zeta); z, \zeta)$ given in (5) where it is adapted to certain classes of analytic functions specific for the theory of strong differential superordination. The methods related to strong differential superordination theory are applied in order to find necessary conditions for Kummer–Bernardi integral operator presented in Definition 5, relation (3), to be the best subordinant of a certain strong differential superordination involving confluent hypergeometric function $\phi(a(\zeta), c(\zeta); z, \zeta)$. As corollary, the similar result is given for Kummer–Libera operator. For those two theorems, the parameter γ is a real number, $\gamma > 0$. In Theorem 3, $\gamma \in \mathbb{C}$, with $Re\,\gamma > 0$ is considered and a necessary and sufficient condition is determined such that Kummer–Bernardi integral operator to be the best subordinant for a certain strong differential superordination. Two examples are constructed for the case when $\gamma \in \mathbb{C}$, with $Re\,\gamma > 0$.

4. Conclusions

In this paper, new strong differential superordinations are investigated using a special form of confluent hypergeometric function given in (5) and two operators previously introduced in [38]. In the three theorems proved as a result of the study, the two operators called Kummer–Bernardi and Kummer–Libera integral operators are the best subordinants of the strong differential superordinations.

The novelty of the study resides in the forms of the confluent hypergeometric function and of the two operators considered by adaptation to the new classes depending on the extra parameter ζ introduced in the theory of strong differential subordination in [27].

As future studies, the dual notion of strong differential subordination can be considered for investigations concerning confluent hypergeometric function and the two operators used in the present study. Sandwich-type results could be obtained as seen in recent papers [13,39,40].

New subclasses of univalent functions could be introduced in the context of strong differential subordination and superordination theories using the operators presented in this paper as seen in [41].

It might also be interesting to consider other hypergeometric functions and operators defined with them following the ideas presented in this paper.

Author Contributions: Conceptualization, G.I.O. and G.O.; methodology, G.I.O., G.O. and A.M.R.; software, G.I.O.; validation, G.I.O., G.O. and A.M.R.; formal analysis, G.I.O. and G.O.; investigation, G.I.O., G.O. and A.M.R.; resources, G.I.O. and G.O.; data curation, G.I.O. and G.O.; writing—original draft preparation, G.O.; writing—review and editing, G.I.O. and A.M.R.; visualization, G.I.O. and A.M.R.; supervision, G.O.; project administration, G.I.O.; funding acquisition, G.I.O. and A.M.R. All authors have read and agreed to the published version of the manuscript.

Funding: This research received no external funding.

Data Availability Statement: Not applicable.

Conflicts of Interest: The authors declare no conflict of interest.

References

1. Antonino, J.A.; Romaguera, S. Strong differential subordination to Briot-Bouquet differential equations. *J. Differ. Equ.* **1994**, *114*, 101–105. [CrossRef]
2. Miller, S.S.; Mocanu, P.T. Second order-differential inequalities in the complex plane. *J. Math. Anal. Appl.* **1978**, *65*, 298–305. [CrossRef]
3. Miller, S.S.; Mocanu, P.T. Differential subordinations and univalent functions. *Mich. Math. J.* **1981**, *28*, 157–171. [CrossRef]
4. Miller, S.S.; Mocanu, P.T. Differential Subordinations. In *Theory and Applications*; Marcel Dekker, Inc.: New York, NY, USA; Basel, Switzerland, 2000.
5. Oros, G.I.; Oros, G. Strong differential subordination. *Turk. J. Math.* **2009**, *33*, 249–257.

6. Cho, N.E.; Kwon, O.S.; Srivastava, H.M. Strong differential subordination and superordination for multivalently meromorphic functions involving the Liu–Srivastava operator. *Integral Transform. Spec. Funct.* **2010**, *21*, 589–601. [CrossRef]
7. Abubaker, A.A.; Darus, M. First order linear differential subordinations for a generalized operator. *Acta Univ. Apulensis, Math. Inform.* **2011**, *25*, 133–144.
8. Alb Lupaş, A. On special strong differential subordinations using multiplier transformation. *Appl. Math. Lett.* **2012**, *25*, 624–630. [CrossRef]
9. Alb Lupaş, A.; Oros, G.I.; Oros, G. A note on special strong differential subordinations using multiplier transformation. *J. Comput. Anal. Appl.* **2012**, *14*, 261–265.
10. Cho, N.E. Strong differential subordination properties for analytic functions involving the Komatu integral operator. *Bound. Value Probl.* **2013**, 44. [CrossRef]
11. Alb Lupaş, A. A note on strong differential subordinations using Sălăgean operator and Ruscheweyh derivative. *J. Comput. Anal. Appl.* **2014**, *9*, 144–152.
12. Andrei, L.; Choban, M. Some strong differential subordinations using a differential operator. *Carpathian J. Math.* **2015**, *31*, 143–156. [CrossRef]
13. Alb Lupaş, A. Applications of a Multiplier Transformation and Ruscheweyh Derivative for Obtaining New Strong Differential Subordinations. *Symmetry* **2021**, *13*, 1312. [CrossRef]
14. Arjomandinia, P.; Aghalary, R. Strong subordination and superordination with sandwich-type theorems using integral operators. *Stud. Univ. Babeş-Bolyai Math.* **2021**, *66*, 667–675. [CrossRef]
15. Frassu, S.; Viglialoro, G. Boundedness in a chemotaxis system with consumed chemoattractant and produced chemorepellent. *Nonlinear Anal.* **2021**, *213*, Art. 112505. [CrossRef]
16. Li, T.; Viglialoro, G. Boundedness for a nonlocal reaction chemotaxis model even in the attraction-dominated regime. *Differ. Integral Equ.* **2021**, *34*, 315–336.
17. Oros, G.I. Strong differential superordination. *Acta Univ. Apulensis* **2009**, *19*, 101–106.
18. Miller, S.S.; Mocanu, P.T. Subordinations of differential superordinations. *Complex Var.* **2003**, *48*, 815–826.
19. Oros, G.I. First order strong differential superordination. *Gen. Math.* **2007**, *15*, 77–87.
20. Aghalary, R.; Arjomandinia, P.; Ebadian, A. Application of strong differential superordination to a general equation. *Rocky Mt. J. Math.* **2017**, *47*, 383–390. [CrossRef]
21. Alb Lupaş, A. A note on strong differential superordinations using a generalized Sălăgean operator and Ruscheweyh operator. *Stud. Univ. Babeş-Bolyai Math.* **2012**, *57*, 153–165.
22. Oshah, A.; Darus, M. Strong differential subordination and superordination of new generalized derivative operator. *Korean J. Math.* **2015**, *23*, 503–519. [CrossRef]
23. Wanas, A.K.; Alb Lupaş, A. On a new strong differential subordinations and superordinations of analytic functions involving the generalized operator. *Int. J. Pure Appl. Math.* **2017**, *11*, 571–579.
24. Srivastava, H.M.; Wanas, A.K. Strong Differential Sandwich Results of λ-Pseudo-Starlike Functions with Respect to Symmetrical Points. *Math. Morav.* **2019**, *23*, 45–58. [CrossRef]
25. Wanas, A.K.; Majeed, A.H. New strong differential subordination and superordination of meromorphic multivalent quasi-convex functions. *Kragujev. J. Math.* **2020**, *44*, 27–39. [CrossRef]
26. Alb Lupaş, A.; Oros, G.I. Strong Differential Superordination Results Involving Extended Sălăgean and Ruscheweyh Operators. *Mathematics* **2021**, *9*, 2487. [CrossRef]
27. Oros, G.I. On a new strong differential subordination. *Acta Univ. Apulensis* **2012**, *32*, 243–250.
28. Oros, G.; Şendruţiu, R.; Oros, G.I. First-order strong differential superordinations. *Math. Rep.* **2013**, *15*, 115–124.
29. Branges, L. A proof of the Bieberbach conjecture. *Acta Math.* **1985**, *154*, 137–152. [CrossRef]
30. Miller, S.S.; Mocanu, P.T. Univalence of Gaussian and Confluent Hypergeometric Functions. *Proc. Am. Math. Soc.* **1990**, *110*, 333–342. [CrossRef]
31. Kanas, S.; Stankiewicz, J. Univalence of confluent hypergeometric function. *Ann. Univ. Mariae Curie-Sklodowska* **1998**, *1*, 51–56.
32. Oros, G.I. New Conditions for Univalence of Confluent Hypergeometric Function. *Symmetry* **2021**, *13*, 82. [CrossRef]
33. Ghanim, F.; Al-Shaqsi, K.; Darus, M.; Al-Janaby, H.F. Subordination Properties of Meromorphic Kummer Function Correlated with Hurwitz–Lerch Zeta-Function. *Mathematics* **2021**, *9*, 192. [CrossRef]
34. Al-Janaby, H.F.; Ghanim, F. A subclass of Noor-type harmonic p-valent functions based on hypergeometric functions. *Kragujev. J. Math.* **2021**, *45*, 499–519. [CrossRef]
35. Ghanim, F.; Al-Janaby, H.F.; Bazighifan, O. Some New Extensions on Fractional Differential and Integral Properties for Mittag-Leffler Confluent Hypergeometric Function. *Fractal Fract.* **2021**, *5*, 143. [CrossRef]
36. Ghanim, F.; Al-Janaby, H.F. An Analytical Study on Mittag-Leffler-Confluent Hypergeometric Functions with Fractional Integral Operator. *Math. Methods Appl. Sci.* **2021**, *44*, 3605–3614. [CrossRef]
37. Ghanim, F.; Bendak, S.; Al Hawarneh, A. Certain implementations in fractional calculus operators involving Mittag-Leffler-confluent hypergeometric functions. *Proc. R. Soc. A* **2022**, *478*, 20210839. [CrossRef]
38. Oros, G.I. Study on new integral operators defined using confluent hypergeometric function. *Adv. Differ. Equ.* **2021**, *2021*, 342. [CrossRef]

39. Suresh, T.K.; Reddy, D.M.; Reddy, E.K. Strong differential subordination and superordination of analytic functions in connection with a linear operator. *Malaya J. Mat.* **2019**, *5*, 263–270. [CrossRef]
40. Wanas, A.K.; Al-Ziadi, N.A.J. Strong Differential Sandwich Results for Bazilevic-Sakaguchi Type Functions Associated with Admissible Functions. *Earthline J. Math. Sci.* **2022**, *8*, 205–226. [CrossRef]
41. Wanas, A.K. Two New Classes of Analytic Functions Defined by Strong Differential Subordinations and Superordinations. *Gen. Math.* **2019**, *27*, 3–11. [CrossRef]

Article

Certain Subclasses of Bi-Starlike Function of Complex Order Defined by Erdély–Kober-Type Integral Operator

Alhanouf Alburaikan [1,†], Gangadharan Murugusundaramoorthy [2,†] and Sheza M. El-Deeb [1,3,*,†]

1. Department of Mathematics, College of Science and Arts, Al-Badaya, Qassim University, Buraidah 51911, Saudi Arabia; a.albrikan@qu.edu.sa
2. School of Advanced Sciences, Vellore Institute of Technology, Vellore 632014, India; gms@vit.ac.in or gmsmoorthy@yahoo.com
3. Department of Mathematics, Faculty of Science, Damietta University, New Damietta 34517, Egypt
* Correspondence: shezaeldeeb@yahoo.com or s.eldeeb@qu.edu.sa
† These authors contributed equally to this work.

Abstract: In the present paper, we introduce new subclasses of bi-starlike and bi-convex functions of complex order associated with Erdély–Kober-type integral operator in the open unit disc and find the estimates of initial coefficients in these classes. Moreover, we obtain Fekete-Szegő inequalities for functions in these classes. Some of the significances of our results are pointed out as corollaries.

Keywords: univalent functions; analytic functions; bi-univalent functions; coefficient bounds; bi-starlike and bi-convex functions of complex order; fractional calculus; Erdély–Kober-type integral operator

MSC: 30C45; 30C50; 30C55

1. Introduction and Preliminaries

Let $\mathfrak{A}$ signify the class of functions of the following form:

$$f(\xi) = \xi + \sum_{n=2}^{\infty} a_n \xi^n \tag{1}$$

which are analytic in the open unit disc $\mathfrak{U} = \{\xi : |\xi| < 1\}$ and normalized as $f(0) = 0$ and $f'(0) = 1$. Furthermore, let $\mathfrak{S}$ represent the class of all functions in $\mathfrak{A}$ that are univalent in $\mathfrak{U}$. Some of the imperative and well-investigated subclasses of the univalent function class $\mathfrak{S}$ include (for example) the class $\mathfrak{S}^*(\delta)$ of starlike functions of order δ in $\mathfrak{U}$ and the class $\mathfrak{K}(\delta)$ of convex functions of order δ ($0 \leq \delta < 1$) in $\mathfrak{U}$. It is known that if $f \in \mathfrak{S}$, then there exists inverse function f^{-1} because normalization is defined in some neighborhood of the origin. In some cases, f^{-1} can be defined in the entire $\mathfrak{U}$. Clearly, f^{-1} is also univalent. For this reason, class Σ is defined as follows.

It is well known that every function $f \in \mathfrak{S}$ has an inverse f^{-1} defined by the following:

$$f^{-1}(f(\xi)) = \xi \quad (\xi \in \mathfrak{U})$$
$$\text{and} \quad f(f^{-1}(w)) = w \quad (|w| < r_0(f); r_0(f) \geq 1/4)$$

where the following is the case.

$$f^{-1}(w) = g(w) = w - a_2 w^2 + (2a_2^2 - a_3) w^3 - (5a_2^3 - 5a_2 a_3 + a_4) w^4 + \cdots \tag{2}$$

A function $f(\xi) \in \mathfrak{A}$ is said to be bi-univalent in $\mathfrak{U}$ if both $f(\xi)$ and $f^{-1}(\xi)$ are univalent in $\mathfrak{U}$. Let Σ denote the class of bi-univalent functions in $\mathfrak{U}$ given by (1). Note that the following functions:

$$f_1(\xi) = \frac{\xi}{1-\xi}, \quad f_2(\xi) = \frac{1}{2}\log\frac{1+\xi}{1-\xi}, \quad f_3(\xi) = -\log(1-\xi)$$

with their corresponding inverses

$$f_1^{-1}(w) = \frac{w}{1+w}, \quad f_2^{-1}(w) = \frac{e^{2w}-1}{e^{2w}+1}, \quad f_3^{-1}(w) = \frac{e^w-1}{e^w}$$

are elements of Σ (see [1–3]). Certain subclasses of Σ are explicitly bi-starlike functions of order $\delta(0 < \delta \leq 1)$ denoted by $\mathfrak{S}^*_\Sigma(\delta)$ and bi-convex function of order δ designated by $\mathfrak{K}_\Sigma(\delta)$ familiarized by Brannan and Taha [1]. For each $f \in \mathfrak{S}^*_\Sigma(\delta)$ and $f \in \mathfrak{K}_\Sigma(\delta)$, non-sharp estimates on the first two Taylor–Maclaurin coefficients $|a_2|$ and $|a_3|$ were established [1,2], but the problem to find the general coefficient bounds on the following Taylor–Maclaurin coefficients:

$$|a_n| \quad (n \in \mathbb{N} \setminus \{1,2\}; \ \mathbb{N} := \{1,2,3,\cdots\})$$

is still an open problem (see [1–5]). Several researchers (see [6–11]) have introduced and explored some inspiring subclasses Σ and they have initiated non-sharp estimates $|a_2|$ and $|a_3|$. For two functions f_1 and $f_2 \in \mathfrak{A}$, we say that function f_1 is subordinate to f_2 if there exists a Schwarz function ω that is holomorphic in $\mathfrak{U}$ with property $w(0) = 0; |\omega(\xi)| < 1$ and satisfying $f_1(\xi) = f_2(w(\xi))$ This subordination is symbolically written as $f_1(\xi) \prec f_2(\xi)$. Lately, Ma and Minda [12]-unified subclasses of starlike and convex functions are subordinate to a general superordinate function. For this purpose, they considered an analytic function $\mathfrak{W}$ with positive real parts in the unit disk $\mathfrak{U}$, $\mathfrak{W}(0) = 1, \mathfrak{W}'(0) > 0$, and $\mathfrak{W}$ maps $\mathfrak{U}$ onto a region starlike with respect to 1 and is symmetric with respect to the real axis. In the consequence, it is assumed that $\mathfrak{W}$ is an analytic function with positive real part in the unit disk $\mathfrak{U}$, with $\mathfrak{W}(0) = 1, \mathfrak{W}'(0) > 0$, and $\mathfrak{W}(\mathfrak{U})$ is symmetric with respect to the real axis. Such functions are of the following form.

$$\mathfrak{W}(\xi) = 1 + \mathbf{m}_1 \xi + \mathbf{m}_2 \xi^2 + \mathbf{m}_3 \xi^3 + \cdots, \quad (\mathbf{m}_1 > 0). \tag{3}$$

The study of operators plays a central role in geometric function theory and its correlated fields. In the recent years, there has been an collective importance in problems concerning the evaluations of various differential and integral operators. For our study, we recall the Erdély–Kober type ([13] Ch. 5; also see [14–17]) for the integral operator definition, which shall be used throughout the paper as stated below.

Erdély–Kober Fractional-Order Derivative

Let $\kappa > 0, \varsigma, \tau \in \mathbb{C}$ be such that $\Re(\tau - \varsigma) \geq 0$, an Erdély–Kober type integral operator:

$$\mathfrak{I}^{\varsigma,\tau}_\kappa : \mathfrak{A} \to \mathfrak{A}$$

be defined for $\Re(\tau - \varsigma) > 0$ and $\Re(\varsigma) > -\kappa$ by the following.

$$\mathfrak{I}^{\varsigma,\tau}_\kappa f(\xi) = \frac{\Gamma(\tau+\kappa)}{\Gamma(\varsigma+\kappa)} \frac{1}{\Gamma(\tau-\varsigma)} \int_0^1 (1-t)^{\tau-\varsigma-1} t^{\varsigma-1} f(\xi t^\kappa) dt, \kappa > 0. \tag{4}$$

For $\kappa > 0, \Re(\tau - \varsigma) \geq 0, \Re(\vartheta) > -\kappa$ and $f \in \mathfrak{A}$ of the form (1), we have the following:

$$\mathfrak{I}_\kappa^{\varsigma,\tau} f(\xi) = \xi + \sum_{n=2}^{\infty} \frac{\Gamma(\tau+\kappa)\Gamma(\varsigma+n\kappa)}{\Gamma(\varsigma+\kappa)\Gamma(\tau+n\kappa)} a_n \xi^n \quad (\xi \in \mathfrak{U}) \tag{5}$$

$$= \xi + \sum_{n=2}^{\infty} Y_\kappa^{\varsigma,\tau}(n) a_n \xi^n \quad (\xi \in \mathfrak{U}) \tag{6}$$

where the following is the case.

$$Y_\kappa^{\varsigma,\tau}(n) = \frac{\Gamma(\tau+\kappa)\Gamma(\varsigma+n\kappa)}{\Gamma(\varsigma+\kappa)\Gamma(\tau+n\kappa)} \tag{7}$$

and $\Gamma(n+1) = n!$.

Note that the following is the case.

$$\mathfrak{I}_\kappa^{\varsigma,\varsigma} f(\xi) = f(\xi)$$

Remark 1. *By fixing the parameters $\varsigma, \tau, \vartheta$ as mentioned below, the operator $\mathfrak{I}_\kappa^{\varsigma,\tau}$ includes various operators studied in the literature as cited below:*

1. *For $\varsigma = \beta; \tau = \alpha + \beta$ and $\kappa = 1$, we obtain the operator $\mathfrak{Q}_\beta^\alpha f(\xi) (\alpha \geq 0; \beta > 1)$ studied by Jung et al. [18];*
2. *For $\varsigma = \alpha - 1; \tau = \beta - 1$ and $\kappa = 1$, we obtain the operator $\mathfrak{L}_{\alpha,\beta} f(\xi) (\alpha; \beta \in \mathbb{C} \in \mathbb{Z}_0; \mathbb{Z}_0 = \{0; -1; -2; \cdots\})$ studied by Carlson and Shafer [19];*
3. *For $\varsigma = \rho - 1; \tau = \mathfrak{l}$ and $\kappa = 1$, we obtain the operator $\mathfrak{I}_{\rho,\mathfrak{l}}(\rho > 0; \mathfrak{l} > 1)$ studied by Choi et al. [20];*
4. *For $\varsigma = \alpha; \tau = 0$ and $\kappa = 1$, we obtain the operator $\mathfrak{D}^\alpha (\alpha > 1)$ studied by Ruscheweyh [21];*
5. *For $\varsigma = 1; \tau = n$ and $\mu = 1$, we obtain the operator $\mathfrak{I}_n (n > \mathbb{N}_0)$ studied in [22,23];*
6. *For $\varsigma = \beta; \tau = \beta + 1$ and $\kappa = 1$; we obtain the integral operator $\mathfrak{I}_{\beta,1}$ which studied by Bernardi [24];*
7. *For $\varsigma = 1; \tau = 2$ and $\kappa = 1$, we obtain the integral operator $\mathfrak{I}_{1,1} = \mathfrak{I}$ studied by Libera [25] and Livingston [26].*

The motivation of our present investigation stems from (by Silverman and Silvia [27] (also see [28])) the seminal paper on bi-univalent functions by Srivastava et al. [8] and by the recent works by many authors (for example Deniz [7], Huo Tang et al. [6], El-Deeb et al. [29–31], and Murugusundaramoorthy and Janani [32]). In the present paper, we introduce two new subclasses of the function class Σ of complex order $\vartheta \in \mathbb{C}\backslash\{0\}$, involving the linear operator $\mathfrak{I}_\kappa^{\varsigma,\tau}$ given in Definition 1. We find estimates on the coefficients $|a_2|$ and $|a_3|$ for functions $f \in \mathfrak{S}_{\Sigma,\mathfrak{W}}^{\varsigma,\tau}(\vartheta,\ell)$. Several related classes are also considered, and connections to earlier known results are provided. Moreover we obtain the Fekete-Szegő inequalities for $f \in \mathfrak{S}_{\Sigma,\mathfrak{W}}^{\varsigma,\tau}(\vartheta,\ell)$ and $f \in \mathfrak{K}_{\Sigma,\mathfrak{W}}^{\varsigma,\tau}(\vartheta,\ell)$.

Definition 1. *Let $f \in \Sigma$ be assumed by (1) and $f \in \mathfrak{S}_{\Sigma,\mathfrak{W}}^{\varsigma,\tau}(\vartheta,\ell)$, if the subsequent conditions holds:*

$$1 + \frac{1}{\vartheta}\left(\frac{\xi(\mathfrak{I}_\kappa^{\varsigma,\tau} f(\xi))'}{\mathfrak{I}_\kappa^{\varsigma,\tau} f(\xi)} + \left(\frac{1+e^{i\ell}}{2}\right) \frac{\xi^2(\mathfrak{I}_\kappa^{\varsigma,\tau} f(\xi))''}{\mathfrak{I}_\kappa^{\varsigma,\tau} f(\xi)} - 1\right) \prec \mathfrak{W}(\xi) \tag{8}$$

and

$$1 + \frac{1}{\vartheta}\left(\frac{w(\mathfrak{I}_\kappa^{\varsigma,\tau} g(w))'}{\mathfrak{I}_\kappa^{\varsigma,\tau} g(w)} + \left(\frac{1+e^{i\ell}}{2}\right) \frac{w^2(\mathfrak{I}_\kappa^{\varsigma,\tau} g(w))''}{\mathfrak{I}_\kappa^{\varsigma,\tau} g(w)} - 1\right) \prec \mathfrak{W}(w), \tag{9}$$

where $\vartheta \in \mathbb{C}\backslash\{0\}$; $\ell \in (-\pi, \pi]$; $\xi, w \in \mathfrak{U}$ and g is given by (2).

Definition 2. *Let $f \in \Sigma$ be assumed by (1) and $f \in \mathfrak{K}_{\Sigma,\mathfrak{W}}^{\varsigma,\tau}(\vartheta,\ell)$, if the subsequent conditions are satisfied:*

$$1 + \frac{1}{\vartheta}\left(\frac{[\xi(\mathfrak{J}_\kappa^{\varsigma,\tau}f(\xi))' + \left(\frac{1+e^{i\ell}}{2}\right)\xi^2(\mathfrak{J}_\kappa^{\varsigma,\tau}f(\xi))'']'}{(\mathfrak{J}_\kappa^{\varsigma,\tau}f(\xi))'} - 1\right) \prec \mathfrak{W}(\xi) \tag{10}$$

and

$$1 + \frac{1}{\vartheta}\left(\frac{[w(\mathfrak{J}_\kappa^{\varsigma,\tau}g(w))' + \left(\frac{1+e^{i\ell}}{2}\right)w^2(\mathfrak{J}_\kappa^{\varsigma,\tau}g(w))'']'}{(\mathfrak{J}_\kappa^{\varsigma,\tau}g(w))'} - 1\right) \prec \mathfrak{W}(w), \tag{11}$$

where $\vartheta \in \mathbb{C}\setminus\{0\}; \ell \in (-\pi, \pi]; \xi, w \in \mathfrak{U}$ and g is given by (2).

Remark 2. *For a function $f(\xi) \in \Sigma$ specified by (1) and for $\ell = \pi$, interpret that $\mathfrak{S}_{\Sigma,\mathfrak{W}}^{\varsigma,\tau}(\vartheta, \ell) \equiv \mathfrak{S}_{\Sigma,\mathfrak{W}}^{\varsigma,\tau}(\vartheta)$ satisfies the ensuing conditions:*

$$\left[1 + \frac{1}{\vartheta}\left(\frac{\xi(\mathfrak{J}_\kappa^{\varsigma,\tau}f(\xi))'}{\mathfrak{J}_\kappa^{\varsigma,\tau}f(\xi)} - 1\right)\right] \prec \mathfrak{W}(\xi) \text{ and } \left[1 + \frac{1}{\vartheta}\left(\frac{w(\mathfrak{J}_\kappa^{\varsigma,\tau}g(w))'}{\mathfrak{J}_\kappa^{\varsigma,\tau}g(w)} - 1\right)\right] \prec \mathfrak{W}(w)$$

where $\vartheta \in \mathbb{C}\setminus\{0\}; \xi, w \in \mathfrak{U}$ and g is given by (2).

Remark 3. *A function $f(\xi) \in \Sigma$ specified by (1) and for $\ell = \pi$, we interpret that $\mathfrak{K}_{\Sigma,\mathfrak{W}}^{\varsigma,\tau}(\vartheta,\ell) \equiv \mathfrak{K}_{\Sigma,\mathfrak{W}}^{\varsigma,\tau}(\vartheta)$ satisfies the ensuing conditions correspondingly:*

$$\left[1 + \frac{1}{\vartheta}\left(\frac{\xi(\mathfrak{J}_\kappa^{\varsigma,\tau}f(\xi))''}{(\mathfrak{J}_\kappa^{\varsigma,\tau}f(\xi))'}\right)\right] \prec \mathfrak{W}(\xi) \text{ and } \left[1 + \frac{1}{\vartheta}\left(\frac{w(\mathfrak{J}_\kappa^{\varsigma,\tau}g(w))''}{(\mathfrak{J}_\kappa^{\varsigma,\tau}g(w))'}\right)\right] \prec \mathfrak{W}(w),$$

where $\vartheta \in \mathbb{C}\setminus\{0\}; \xi, w \in \mathfrak{U}$ and g is given by (2).

Remark 4. *For a function $f(\xi) \in \Sigma$ given by (1) and for $\vartheta = 1$, we note that $\mathfrak{S}_{\Sigma,\mathfrak{W}}^{\varsigma,\tau}(\vartheta, \ell) \equiv \mathfrak{S}_{\Sigma,\mathfrak{W}}^{\varsigma,\tau}(\ell)$ and satisfies the following conditions, respectively:*

$$\left(\frac{\xi(\mathfrak{J}_\kappa^{\varsigma,\tau}f(\xi))'}{\mathfrak{J}_\kappa^{\varsigma,\tau}f(\xi)} + \left(\frac{1+e^{i\ell}}{2}\right)\frac{\xi^2(\mathfrak{J}_\kappa^{\varsigma,\tau}f(\xi))''}{\mathfrak{J}_\kappa^{\varsigma,\tau}f(\xi)}\right) \prec \mathfrak{W}(\xi)$$

and the following is the case.

$$\left(\frac{w(\mathfrak{J}_\kappa^{\varsigma,\tau}g(w))'}{\mathfrak{J}_\kappa^{\varsigma,\tau}g(w)} + \left(\frac{1+e^{i\ell}}{2}\right)\frac{w^2(\mathfrak{J}_\kappa^{\varsigma,\tau}g(w))''}{\mathfrak{J}_\kappa^{\varsigma,\tau}g(w)}\right) \prec \mathfrak{W}(w).$$

Moreover, $\mathfrak{K}_{\Sigma,\mathfrak{W}}^{\varsigma,\tau}(\vartheta, \ell) \equiv \mathfrak{K}_{\Sigma,\mathfrak{W}}^{\varsigma,\tau}(\ell)$ and it satisfies the following conditions:

$$\left(\frac{[\xi(\mathfrak{J}_\kappa^{\varsigma,\tau}f(\xi))' + \left(\frac{1+e^{i\ell}}{2}\right)\xi^2(\mathfrak{J}_\kappa^{\varsigma,\tau}f(\xi))'']'}{(\mathfrak{J}_\kappa^{\varsigma,\tau}f(\xi))'}\right) \prec \mathfrak{W}(\xi)$$

and the following is the case:

$$\left(\frac{[w(\mathfrak{J}_\kappa^{\varsigma,\tau}g(w))' + \left(\frac{1+e^{i\ell}}{2}\right)w^2(\mathfrak{J}_\kappa^{\varsigma,\tau}g(w))'']'}{(\mathfrak{J}_\kappa^{\varsigma,\tau}g(w))'}\right) \prec \mathfrak{W}(w),$$

where $\ell \in (-\pi, \pi]; \xi, w \in \mathfrak{U}$ and g is given by (2).

2. Coefficient Estimates for $f \in \mathfrak{S}_{\Sigma,\mathfrak{W}}^{\varsigma,\tau}(\vartheta,\ell)$ and $f \in \mathfrak{K}_{\Sigma,\mathfrak{W}}^{\varsigma,\tau}(\vartheta,\ell)$

For notational simplicity, in the sequel we let the following be the case:

$$\kappa > 0, \mathfrak{R}(\tau - \varsigma) \geq 0, \quad \mathfrak{R}(\varsigma) > -\kappa \quad \text{and} \quad \mathfrak{I}_\kappa^{\varsigma,\tau} f(\xi)$$

and it is provided by (5):

$$Y_2 = Y_\kappa^{\varsigma,\tau}(2) = \frac{\Gamma(\tau+\kappa)\Gamma(\varsigma+2\kappa)}{\Gamma(\varsigma+\kappa)\Gamma(\tau+2\kappa)}, \tag{12}$$

$$Y_3 = Y_\kappa^{\varsigma,\tau}(3) = \frac{\Gamma(\tau+\kappa)\Gamma(\varsigma+3\kappa)}{\Gamma(\varsigma+\kappa)\Gamma(\tau+3\kappa)} \tag{13}$$

and the following.

$$\ell \in (-\pi, \pi].$$

For deriving our main results, we need the following lemma.

Lemma 1. *Ref. [33] states that if $h \in \mathfrak{P}$, then $|c_k| \leq 2$ for each k, where $\mathfrak{P}$ is the family of all functions h analytic in $\mathfrak{U}$ for which $\mathfrak{R}(h(\xi)) > 0$ and the following is the case.*

$$h(\xi) = 1 + c_1\xi + c_2\xi^2 + \cdots \quad \text{for } \xi \in \mathfrak{U}.$$

Define the functions $p(\xi)$ and $q(\xi)$ by the following:

$$p(\xi) := \frac{1+u(\xi)}{1-u(\xi)} = 1 + \wp_1\xi + \wp_2\xi^2 + \cdots$$

and the following.

$$q(w) := \frac{1+v(w)}{1-v(w)} = 1 + \mathfrak{q}_1 w + \mathfrak{q}_2 w^2 + \cdots.$$

It follows that the following is the case:

$$u(\xi) := \frac{p(\xi)-1}{p(\xi)+1} = \frac{1}{2}\left[\wp_1\xi + \left(\wp_2 - \frac{\wp_1^2}{2}\right)\xi^2 + \cdots\right]$$

and

$$v(w) := \frac{q(w)-1}{q(w)+1} = \frac{1}{2}\left[\mathfrak{q}_1 w + \left(\mathfrak{q}_2 - \frac{\mathfrak{q}_1^2}{2}\right)w^2 + \cdots\right].$$

Then, $p(\xi)$ and $q(w)$ are analytic in $\mathfrak{U}$ with $p(0) = 1 = q(0)$.

Since $u, v : \mathfrak{U} \to \mathfrak{U}$, the functions $p(\xi)$ and $q(w)$ have a positive real part in $\mathfrak{U}$, and $|\wp_i| \leq 2$ and $|\mathfrak{q}_i| \leq 2$ for each i.

Theorem 1. *Let f given by (1) be in the class $\mathfrak{S}_{\Sigma,\mathfrak{W}}^{\varsigma,\tau}(\vartheta,\ell)$, $\vartheta \in \mathbb{C}\backslash\{0\}$ and $\ell \in (-\pi,\pi]$. Then, we have the following:*

$$|a_2| \leq \frac{|\vartheta|\mathbf{m}_1\sqrt{\mathbf{m}_1}}{\sqrt{|\vartheta[(5+3e^{i\ell})Y_3 - (2+e^{i\ell})Y_2^2]\mathbf{m}_1^2 + (2+e^{i\ell})^2(\mathbf{m}_1-\mathbf{m}_2)Y_2^2|}} \tag{14}$$

and the following.

$$|a_3| \leq \frac{|\vartheta|^2\mathbf{m}_1^2}{|2+e^{i\ell}|^2 Y_2^2} + \frac{|\vartheta|\mathbf{m}_1}{|5+3e^{i\ell}|Y_3}. \tag{15}$$

Proof. It follows from (8) and (9) that we have the following:

$$1 + \frac{1}{\vartheta}\left(\frac{\xi(\mathfrak{I}_\kappa^{\varsigma,\tau} f(\xi))'}{\mathfrak{I}_\kappa^{\varsigma,\tau} f(\xi)} + \left(\frac{1+e^{i\ell}}{2}\right)\frac{\xi^2(\mathfrak{I}_\kappa^{\varsigma,\tau} f(\xi))''}{\mathfrak{I}_\kappa^{\varsigma,\tau} f(\xi)} - 1\right) = \mathfrak{W}(u(\xi)) \qquad (16)$$

and

$$1 + \frac{1}{\vartheta}\left(\frac{w(\mathfrak{I}_\kappa^{\varsigma,\tau} g(w))'}{\mathfrak{I}_\kappa^{\varsigma,\tau} g(w)} + \left(\frac{1+e^{i\ell}}{2}\right)\frac{w^2(\mathfrak{I}_\kappa^{\varsigma,\tau} g(w))''}{\mathfrak{I}_\kappa^{\varsigma,\tau} g(w)} - 1\right) = \mathfrak{W}(v(w)), \qquad (17)$$

where

$$\mathfrak{W}(u(\xi)) = \frac{1}{2}\mathbf{m}_1 \wp_1 \xi + \left(\frac{1}{2}\mathbf{m}_1(\wp_2 - \frac{\wp_1^2}{2}) + \frac{1}{4}\mathbf{m}_2 \wp_1^2\right)\xi^2 + \cdots . \qquad (18)$$

and

$$\mathfrak{W}(v(w)) = \frac{1}{2}\mathbf{m}_1 q_1 w + \left(\frac{1}{2}\mathbf{m}_1(q_2 - \frac{q_1^2}{2}) + \frac{1}{4}\mathbf{m}_2 q_1^2\right)w^2 + \cdots . \qquad (19)$$

For a given $f(z)$ of form (1), a computation shows the following:

$$\frac{zf'(z)}{f(z)} = 1 + a_2 Y_2 z + (2Y_3 a_3 - a_2^2 Y_2^2)z^2 + (3a_4 Y_4 + a_2^3 Y_2^3 - 3a_3 a_2 Y_2 Y_3)z^3 + \cdots$$

and

$$\frac{zf''(z)}{f'(z)} = 2a_2 Y_2^2 z + (6a_3 Y_3 - 4a_2^2 Y_2^2)z^2 + \cdots .$$

Using these in the left hand side of (16) and (17), a simple computation produces the following:

$$1 + \frac{1}{\vartheta}\left(\frac{\xi(\mathfrak{I}_\kappa^{\varsigma,\tau} f(\xi))'}{\mathfrak{I}_\kappa^{\varsigma,\tau} f(\xi)} + \left(\frac{1+e^{i\ell}}{2}\right)\frac{\xi^2(\mathfrak{I}_\kappa^{\varsigma,\tau} f(\xi))''}{\mathfrak{I}_\kappa^{\varsigma,\tau} f(\xi)} - 1\right) = 1 + \frac{1}{\vartheta}(2 + e^{i\ell})Y_2 a_2 \varsigma$$
$$+ \frac{1}{\vartheta}\left[(5 + 3e^{i\ell})Y_3 a_3 - (2 + e^{i\ell})Y_2^2 a_2^2\right]\varsigma^2 + \cdots$$

and

$$1 + \frac{1}{\vartheta}\left(\frac{w(\mathfrak{I}_\kappa^{\varsigma,\tau} g(w))'}{\mathfrak{I}_\kappa^{\varsigma,\tau} g(w)} + \left(\frac{1+e^{i\ell}}{2}\right)\frac{w^2(\mathfrak{I}_\kappa^{\varsigma,\tau} g(w))''}{\mathfrak{I}_\kappa^{\varsigma,\tau} g(w)} - 1\right) = 1 - \frac{1}{\vartheta}(2 + e^{i\ell})Y_2 a_2 w$$
$$+ \frac{1}{\vartheta}\left([2(5 + 3e^{i\ell})Y_3 - (2 + e^{i\ell})Y_2^2]a_2^2 - (5 + 3e^{i\ell})Y_3 a_3\right)w^2 = \cdots .$$

Thus, by equating the coefficients of ς and ς^2 in (16) and (17), we obtain the following:

$$\frac{1}{\vartheta}(2 + e^{i\ell})Y_2 a_2 = \frac{1}{2}\mathbf{m}_1 \wp_1, \qquad (20)$$

$$\frac{1}{\vartheta}\left[(5 + 3e^{i\ell})Y_3 a_3 - (2 + e^{i\ell})Y_2^2 a_2^2\right] = \frac{1}{2}\mathbf{m}_1(\wp_2 - \frac{\wp_1^2}{2}) + \frac{1}{4}\mathbf{m}_2 \wp_1^2, \qquad (21)$$

$$-\frac{1}{\vartheta}(2 + e^{i\ell})Y_2 a_2 = \frac{1}{2}\mathbf{m}_1 q_1, \qquad (22)$$

and

$$\frac{1}{\vartheta}\left([2(5 + 3e^{i\ell})Y_3 - (2 + e^{i\ell})Y_2^2]a_2^2 - (5 + 3e^{i\ell})Y_3 a_3\right) = \frac{1}{2}\mathbf{m}_1(q_2 - \frac{q_1^2}{2}) + \frac{1}{4}\mathbf{m}_2 q_1^2. \qquad (23)$$

From (20) and (22), we obtain the following:

$$\wp_1 = -q_1 \qquad (24)$$

and

$$8(2+e^{i\ell})^2 Y_2^2 a_2^2 = \vartheta^2 m_1^2(\wp_1^2 + q_1^2)$$

$$a_2^2 = \frac{\vartheta^2 m_1^2(\wp_1^2 + q_1^2)}{8(2+e^{i\ell})^2 Y_2^2}. \tag{25}$$

Now, by adding (21) and (23) and then using (25), we obtain the following.

$$a_2^2 = \frac{\vartheta^2 m_1^3(\wp_2 + q_2)}{(4\{\vartheta[(5+3e^{i\ell})Y_3 - (2+e^{i\ell})Y_2^2]m_1^2 + (2+e^{i\ell})^2(m_1 - m_2)Y_2^2\})}. \tag{26}$$

Applying Lemma (1) to the coefficients $\wp_2$ and q_2, we have the following.

$$|a_2| \leq \frac{|\vartheta| m_1 \sqrt{m_1}}{\sqrt{|\vartheta[(5+3e^{i\ell})Y_3 - (2+e^{i\ell})Y_2^2]m_1^2 + (2+e^{i\ell})^2(m_1 - m_2)Y_2^2|}}.$$

Next, in order to find the bound on $|a_3|$, by subtracting (21) from (23) and using (24), we obtain the following.

$$\frac{4}{\vartheta} \frac{(5+3e^{i\ell})}{2} Y_3(a_3 - a_2^2) = \frac{m_1}{2}(\wp_2 - q_2)$$

$$a_3 = a_2^2 + \frac{\vartheta m_1(\wp_2 - q_2)}{4(5+3e^{i\ell})Y_3}. \tag{27}$$

Substituting the value of a_2^2 given by (25), we obtain the following.

$$a_3 = \frac{\vartheta^2 m_1^2(\wp_1^2 + q_1^2)}{8(2+e^{i\ell})^2 Y_2^2} + \frac{\vartheta m_1(\wp_2 - q_2)}{4(5+3e^{i\ell})Y_3}.$$

Applying Lemma 1 once again to the coefficients $\wp_1, \wp_2, q_1$ and q_2, we obtain the following.

$$|a_3| \leq \frac{|\vartheta|^2 m_1^2}{|2+e^{i\ell}|^2 Y_2^2} + \frac{|\vartheta| m_1}{|5+3e^{i\ell}| Y_3}.$$

□

Theorem 2. *Let f given by (1) be in the following class: $\Re_{\Sigma,\mathfrak{W}}^{\varsigma,\tau}(\vartheta,\ell)$, $\vartheta \in \mathbb{C}\backslash\{0\}$ and $\ell \in (-\pi, \pi]$. Then, we have the following:*

$$|a_2| \leq \frac{|\vartheta| m_1 \sqrt{m_1}}{\sqrt{|\vartheta[3(5+3e^{i\ell})Y_3 - 4(2+e^{i\ell})Y_2^2]m_1^2 + 4(2+e^{i\ell})^2(m_1 - m_2)Y_2^2|}} \tag{28}$$

and

$$|a_3| \leq \frac{|\vartheta|^2 m_1^2}{4|2+e^{i\ell}|^2 Y_2^2} + \frac{|\vartheta| m_1}{3|5+3e^{i\ell}| Y_3}. \tag{29}$$

Proof. By Definition 2, the argument inequalities in (10) and (11) can be equivalently written as follows:

$$1 + \frac{1}{\vartheta}\left(\frac{[\xi(\mathfrak{J}_\kappa^{\varsigma,\tau} f(\xi))' + \left(\frac{1+e^{i\ell}}{2}\right)\xi^2(\mathfrak{J}_\kappa^{\varsigma,\tau} f(\xi))'']'}{(\mathfrak{J}_\kappa^{\varsigma,\tau} f(\xi))'} - 1\right) = \mathfrak{W}(u(\xi)) \tag{30}$$

and
$$1+\frac{1}{\vartheta}\left(\frac{[w(\mathfrak{J}_\kappa^{\varsigma,\tau}g(w))' + \left(\frac{1+e^{i\ell}}{2}\right)w^2(\mathfrak{J}_\kappa^{\varsigma,\tau}g(w))'']'}{(\mathfrak{J}_\kappa^{\varsigma,\tau}g(w))'} - 1\right) = \mathfrak{W}(v(w)), \quad (31)$$

and proceeding as in the proof of Theorem 1, we can arrive at the following relations:

$$1+\frac{1}{\vartheta}\left(\frac{[\xi(\mathfrak{J}_\kappa^{\varsigma,\tau}f(\xi))' + \left(\frac{1+e^{i\ell}}{2}\right)\xi^2(\mathfrak{J}_\kappa^{\varsigma,\tau}f(\xi))'']'}{(\mathfrak{J}_\kappa^{\varsigma,\tau}f(\xi))'} - 1\right) = 1+\tfrac{2}{\vartheta}(2+e^{i\ell})Y_2 a_2 \varsigma$$
$$+\frac{1}{\vartheta}[3(5+3e^{i\ell})Y_3 a_3 - 4(2+e^{i\ell})Y_2^2 a_2^2]\varsigma^2 + \cdots$$

and

$$1+\frac{1}{\vartheta}\left(\frac{[w(\mathfrak{J}_\kappa^{\varsigma,\tau}g(w))' + \left(\frac{1+e^{i\ell}}{2}\right)w^2(\mathfrak{J}_\kappa^{\varsigma,\tau}g(w))'']'}{(\mathfrak{J}_\kappa^{\varsigma,\tau}g(w))'} - 1\right) = 1-\tfrac{2}{\vartheta}(2+e^{i\ell})Y_2 a_2 w$$
$$+\frac{1}{\vartheta}[3(5+3e^{i\ell})(2a_2^2 - a_3)Y_3 - 4(2+e^{i\ell})Y_2^2 a_2^2]w^2 + \cdots.$$

From (30) and (31), equating the coefficients of ς and ς^2, we obtain the following:

$$\tfrac{2}{\vartheta}(2+e^{i\ell})Y_2 a_2 = \tfrac{1}{2}m_1 \wp_1, \quad (32)$$

$$\tfrac{1}{\vartheta}[3(5+3e^{i\ell})Y_3 a_3 - 4(2+e^{i\ell})Y_2^2 a_2^2] = \tfrac{1}{2}m_1\left(\wp_2 - \tfrac{\wp_1^2}{2}\right) + \tfrac{1}{4}m_2\wp_1^2, \quad (33)$$

and

$$-\tfrac{2}{\vartheta}(2+e^{i\ell})Y_2 a_2 = \tfrac{1}{2}m_1 q_1, \quad (34)$$

$$\tfrac{1}{\vartheta}[3(5+3e^{i\ell})(2a_2^2 - a_3)Y_3 - 4(2+e^{i\ell})Y_2^2 a_2^2] = \tfrac{1}{2}m_1\left(q_2 - \tfrac{q_1^2}{2}\right) + \tfrac{1}{4}m_2 q_1^2. \quad (35)$$

From (32) and (34), we obtain the following:

$$\wp_1 = -q_1 \quad (36)$$

and

$$32(2+e^{i\ell})^2 Y_2^2 a_2^2 = \vartheta^2 m_1^2 (\wp_1^2 + q_1^2). \quad (37)$$

If we add (33) and (35) and substitute value $\wp_1^2 + q_1^2$, we obtain the following.

$$a_2^2 = \frac{\vartheta^2 m_1^3 (\wp_2 + q_2)}{4[\vartheta[3(5+3e^{i\ell})Y_3 - 4(2+e^{i\ell})Y_2^2]m_1^2 + 4(2+e^{i\ell})^2(m_1 - m_2)Y_2^2]}. \quad (38)$$

Applying Lemma 1 to the coefficients $\wp_2$ and q_2, we have the desired inequality given in (28).

Next, if we subtract (33) from (35), we easily observe the following.

$$\frac{12}{\vartheta}\frac{(5+3e^{i\ell})}{2}(a_3 - a_2^2)Y_3 = \frac{m_1}{2}(\wp_2 - q_2)$$

$$a_3 = \frac{\vartheta m_1(\wp_2 - q_2)}{12(5+3e^{i\ell})Y_3} + a_2^2$$

Upon relieving the value of a_2^2 given in (37), the above equation leads to the following.

$$a_3 = \frac{\vartheta m_1(\wp_2 - q_2)}{12(5 + 3e^{i\ell})Y_3} + \frac{\vartheta^2 m_1^2(\wp_1^2 + q_1^2)}{32(2 + e^{i\ell})^2 Y_2^2}.$$

Applying Lemma (1) once again to the coefficients $\wp_1, \wp_2, q_1$, and q_2, we obtain the preferred coefficient provided in (29). □

Fixing $\ell = \pi$ in Theorems (1) and (2), we can state the coefficient estimates for the functions in subclasses $\mathfrak{S}_{\Sigma,\mathfrak{W}}^{\varsigma,\tau}(\vartheta)$ and $\mathfrak{K}_{\Sigma,\mathfrak{W}}^{\varsigma,\tau}(\vartheta)$, defined in Remark (2).

Corollary 1. *Let f assumed as (1) be in the class $\mathfrak{S}_{\Sigma,\mathfrak{W}}^{\varsigma,\tau}(\vartheta)$. Then, the following is the case.*

$$|a_2| \leq \frac{|\vartheta| m_1 \sqrt{m_1}}{\sqrt{|\vartheta|(2Y_3 - Y_2^2)m_1^2 + (m_1 - m_2)Y_2^2}} \quad \text{and} \quad |a_3| \leq \frac{|\vartheta|^2 m_1^2}{Y_2^2} + \frac{|\vartheta| m_1}{2Y_3}.$$

Corollary 2. *Let f assumed as (1) be in class $\mathfrak{K}_{\Sigma,\mathfrak{W}}^{\varsigma,\tau}(\vartheta)$. Then, we have the following.*

$$|a_2| \leq \frac{|\vartheta| m_1 \sqrt{m_1}}{\sqrt{2|\vartheta|(3Y_3 - 2Y_2^2)m_1^2 + 4(m_1 - m_2)Y_2^2}} \quad \text{and} \quad |a_3| \leq \frac{|\vartheta|^2 m_1^2}{4Y_2^2} + \frac{|\vartheta| m_1}{6Y_3}.$$

Fixing $\vartheta = 1$ in Theorems (1) and (2), we can state the coefficient estimates for the functions in the subclasses $\mathfrak{S}_{\Sigma,\mathfrak{W}}^{\varsigma,\tau}(\ell)$ and $\mathfrak{K}_{\Sigma,\mathfrak{W}}^{\varsigma,\tau}(\ell)$ defined in Remark (4).

Corollary 3. *Let f supposed by (1) be in class $\mathfrak{S}_{\Sigma,\mathfrak{W}}^{\varsigma,\tau}(\ell)$. Then, we have the following:*

$$|a_2| \leq \frac{m_1 \sqrt{m_1}}{\sqrt{|[(5 + 3e^{i\ell})Y_3 - (2 + e^{i\ell})Y_2^2]m_1^2 + (2 + e^{i\ell})^2(m_1 - m_2)Y_2^2|}}$$

and the following is the case.

$$|a_3| \leq \frac{m_1^2}{|2 + e^{i\ell}|^2 Y_2^2} + \frac{m_1}{|5 + 3e^{i\ell}| Y_3}.$$

Corollary 4. *Let f supposed by (1) be in class $\mathfrak{K}_{\Sigma,\mathfrak{W}}^{\varsigma,\tau}(\ell)$. Then, we have the following:*

$$|a_2| \leq \frac{m_1 \sqrt{m_1}}{\sqrt{|[3(5 + 3e^{i\ell})Y_3 - 4(2 + e^{i\ell})Y_2^2]m_1^2 + 4(2 + e^{i\ell})^2(m_1 - m_2)Y_2^2|}}$$

and

$$|a_3| \leq \frac{m_1^2}{4|2 + e^{i\ell}|^2 Y_2^2} + \frac{m_1}{3|5 + 3e^{i\ell}| Y_3}.$$

3. Fekete-Szegő Inequality

In this section, we discuss the Fekete-Szegő results [34] due to Zaprawa [35] for functions $f \in \mathfrak{S}_{\Sigma,\mathfrak{W}}^{\varsigma,\tau}(\vartheta, \ell)$ and $f \in \mathfrak{K}_{\Sigma,\mathfrak{W}}^{\varsigma,\tau}(\vartheta, \ell)$.

Theorem 3. *Let f assumed by (1) be in class $\mathfrak{S}_{\Sigma,\mathfrak{W}}^{\varsigma,\tau}(\vartheta, \ell)$ and $\varrho \in \mathbb{R}$. Then, we have the following:*

$$|a_3 - \varrho a_2^2| \leq \begin{cases} \frac{\vartheta m_1}{|5 + 3e^{i\ell}| Y_3}, & 0 \leq |\phi(\varrho)| \leq \frac{\vartheta m_1}{4|5 + 3e^{i\ell}| Y_3} \\ 4|\phi(\varrho)|, & |\phi(\varrho)| \geq \frac{\vartheta m_1}{4|5 + 3e^{i\ell}| Y_3} \end{cases}.$$

where the following is obtained.

$$\phi(\varrho) = \frac{(1-\varrho)\vartheta^2 m_1^3}{4\{\vartheta[(5+3e^{i\ell})Y_3 - (2+e^{i\ell})Y_2^2]m_1^2 + (2+e^{i\ell})^2(m_1 - m_2)Y_2^2\}}.$$

Proof. From (26) and (27), we have the following:

$$\begin{aligned}a_3 - \varrho a_2^2 &= \frac{(1-\varrho)\vartheta^2 m_1^3(\wp_2 + q_2)}{(4\{\vartheta[(5+3e^{i\ell})Y_3 - (2+e^{i\ell})Y_2^2]m_1^2 + (2+e^{i\ell})^2(m_1-m_2)Y_2^2\})} + \frac{\vartheta m_1(\wp_2 - q_2)}{4(5+3e^{i\ell})Y_3} \\ &= \left[\phi(\varrho) + \frac{\vartheta m_1}{4(5+3e^{i\ell})Y_3}\right]\wp_2 + \left[\phi(\varrho) - \frac{\vartheta m_1}{4(5+3e^{i\ell})Y_3}\right]q_2\end{aligned}$$

where the following is the case.

$$\phi(\varrho) = \frac{(1-\varrho)\vartheta^2 m_1^3}{4\{\vartheta[(5+3e^{i\ell})Y_3 - (2+e^{i\ell})Y_2^2]m_1^2 + (2+e^{i\ell})^2(m_1 - m_2)Y_2^2\}}$$

Thus, by applying Lemma 1, we obtain the following.

$$|a_3 - \varrho a_2^2| \le \begin{cases} \frac{\vartheta m_1}{|5+3e^{i\ell}|Y_3}, & 0 \le |\phi(\varrho)| \le \frac{\vartheta m_1}{4|5+3e^{i\ell}|Y_3} \\ 4|\phi(\varrho)|, & |\phi(\varrho)| \ge \frac{\vartheta m_1}{4|5+3e^{i\ell}|Y_3}. \end{cases}$$

In particular, by fixing $\varrho = 1$, we obtain the following.

$$|a_3 - a_2^2| \le \frac{\vartheta m_1}{|5+3e^{i\ell}|Y_3}.$$

□

Theorem 4. Let f given by (1) be in class $\mathfrak{K}^{\varsigma,\tau}_{\Sigma,\mathfrak{W}}(\vartheta, \ell)$ and $\aleph \in \mathbb{R}$. Then, we have the following:

$$|a_3 - \aleph a_2^2| \le \begin{cases} \frac{\vartheta m_1}{3|5+3e^{i\ell}|Y_3}, & 0 \le |\phi(\aleph)| \le \frac{\vartheta m_1}{12|5+3e^{i\ell}|Y_3} \\ 4|\phi(\aleph)|, & |\phi(\aleph)| \ge \frac{\vartheta m_1}{12|5+3e^{i\ell}|Y_3}. \end{cases}$$

where

$$\phi(\aleph) = \frac{(1-\aleph)\vartheta^2 m_1^3}{4[\vartheta[3(5+3e^{i\ell})Y_3 - 4(2+e^{i\ell})Y_2^2]m_1^2 + 4(2+e^{i\ell})^2(m_1 - m_2)Y_2^2]}.$$

Proof. From (27) and (38), we have the following.

$$\begin{aligned}a_3 - \aleph a_2^2 &= \frac{(1-\aleph)\vartheta^2 m_1^3(\wp_2 + q_2)}{4[\vartheta[3(5+3e^{i\ell})Y_3 - 4(2+e^{i\ell})Y_2^2]m_1^2 + 4(2+e^{i\ell})^2(m_1-m_2)Y_2^2]} + \frac{\vartheta m_1(\wp_2 - q_2)}{12(5+3e^{i\ell})Y_3} \\ &= \left[\phi(\aleph) + \frac{\vartheta m_1}{12(5+3e^{i\ell})Y_3}\right]\wp_2 + \left[\phi(\aleph) - \frac{\vartheta m_1}{12(5+3e^{i\ell})Y_3}\right]q_2\end{aligned}$$

where the following is the case.

$$\phi(\aleph) = \frac{(1-\aleph)\vartheta^2 m_1^3}{4[\vartheta[3(5+3e^{i\ell})Y_3 - 4(2+e^{i\ell})Y_2^2]m_1^2 + 4(2+e^{i\ell})^2(m_1 - m_2)Y_2^2]}$$

Thus, by Lemma 1, we obtain the following.

$$|a_3 - \aleph a_2^2| \le \begin{cases} \frac{\vartheta m_1}{3|5+3e^{i\ell}|Y_3}, & 0 \le |\phi(\aleph)| \le \frac{\vartheta m_1}{12|5+3e^{i\ell}|Y_3} \\ 4|\phi(\aleph)|, & |\phi(\aleph)| \ge \frac{\vartheta m_1}{12|5+3e^{i\ell}|Y_3}. \end{cases}$$

In particular, by taking $\aleph = 1$, we obtain the following.

$$|u_3 - a_2^2| \leq \frac{\vartheta m_1}{3|5 + 3e^{i\ell}|Y_3}.$$

□

4. Conclusions

By fixing $\mathfrak{W}(\zeta)$ as listed below, one can determine new results as in Theorems 1–4 for the subclasses introduced in this paper by suitably fixing m_1 and m_2:

1. For the class of strongly starlike functions, function $\mathfrak{W}$ is given by $\mathfrak{W}(\zeta) = \left(\frac{1+\zeta}{1-\zeta}\right)^\alpha = 1 + 2\alpha\zeta + 2\alpha^2\zeta^2 + \cdots$ $(0 < \alpha \leq 1)$, which gives $m_1 = 2\alpha$ and $m_2 = 2\alpha^2$, (see [36]);
2. On the other hand, if we take $\mathfrak{W}(\zeta) = \frac{1+(1-2\beta)\zeta}{1-\zeta} = 1 + 2(1-\beta)\zeta + 2(1-\beta)\zeta^2 + \cdots$ $(0 \leq \beta < 1)$, then $m_1 = m_2 = 2(1-\beta)$, (see [36]);
3. For $\mathfrak{W}(\zeta) = \frac{1+A\zeta}{1+B\zeta}$ $(-1 \leq B < A \leq 1)$, we obtain class $\mathfrak{S}^*(A, B)$ (see [37]);
4. For $\mathfrak{W}(\zeta) = 1 + \frac{2}{\pi^2}\left(\log\frac{1+\sqrt{\zeta}}{1-\sqrt{\zeta}}\right)^2$, which was considered and studied in [38];
5. For $\mathfrak{W}(\zeta) = \sqrt{1+\zeta}$, the class is denoted by $\mathfrak{S}_L^*$, which was considered and studied in [39] further in discussed [40];
6. For $\mathfrak{W}(\zeta) = \zeta + \sqrt{1+\zeta^2}$, the class is denoted by $\mathfrak{S}_l^*$ (see [41]);
7. If $\mathfrak{W}(\zeta) = 1 + \frac{4}{3}\zeta + \frac{2}{3}\zeta^2$, then such class denoted by $\mathfrak{S}_C^*$ was introduced in [42] and further studied by [43];
8. For $\mathfrak{W}(\zeta) = e^\zeta$, class $\mathfrak{S}_e^*$ was defined and studied in [44,45];
9. For $\mathfrak{W}(\zeta) = \cosh(\zeta)$, the class is denoted by $\mathfrak{S}_{\cosh}^*$ (see [46]);
10. For $\mathfrak{W}(\zeta) = 1 + \sin(\zeta)$, the class is denoted by $\mathfrak{S}_{\sin}^*$ (see [47]); for details and further investigation, (see [48]).

In the current paper, we mainly obtain the upper bounds of the initial Taylors coefficients of bi-starlike and bi-convex functions of complex order involving Erdély–Kober-type integral operators in the open unit. Furthermore, we find the Fekete-Szegő inequalities for the function in these classes. Several consequences of the results are also pointed out as examples. Moreover, we note that by assuming $\mathfrak{W}$ with some particular functions as illustrated above, one can determine new results for the subclasses introduced in this paper. Moreover, by fixing $\ell = 0$ and $\ell = \pi$ in the above Theorems, we can easily state the results for various subclasses of Σ illustrated in Remarks 2–4. By appropriately fixing the parameters in Theorems 3 and 4, we can deduce the Fekete-Szegő functional for these function classes. Moreover, motivating further research on the subject-matter of this, we have chosen to draw the attention of the concerned readers toward a significantly large number of interrelated publications(see [19 52]) and developments in the area of Geometric Function Theory of Complex Analysis. In conclusion, we choose to reiterate an important observation, which was offered in the recently published survey-cum-expository article by Srivastava ([49], p. 340), who pointed out the fact that the results for the above-mentioned or new $q-$ analogues can easily (and possibly or unimportantly) be interpreted into the equivalent results for the so-called $(p;q)-$ analogues (with $0 < |q| < p \leq 1$) by smearing some recognizable parametric and argument variations with the additional parameter p being redundant.

Author Contributions: Conceptualization, A.A., G.M. and S.M.E.-D.; methodology, A.A., G.M. and S.M.E.-D.; validation, A.A., G.M. and S.M.E.-D.; formal analysis, A.A., G.M. and S.M.E.-D.; investigation, A.A., G.M. and S.M.E.-D.; resources, A.A., G.M. and S.M.E.-D.; writing—original draft preparation, A.A., G.M. and S.M.E.-D.; writing—review and editing, A.A., G.M. and S.M.E.-D.; supervision, A.A., G.M. and S.M.E.-D.; project administration, A.A., G.M. and S.M.E.-D. All authors have read and agreed to the published version of the manuscript.

Funding: This research received no external funding.

Institutional Review Board Statement: Not applicable.

Informed Consent Statement: Not applicable.

Data Availability Statement: Not applicable.

Acknowledgments: The researchers would like to thank the Deanship of Scientific Research, Qassim University, for funding the publication of this project. The authors are grateful to the referees of this article who provided valuable comments and advice that allowed us to revise and improve the content of the paper.

Conflicts of Interest: The authors declare no conflict of interest.

References

1. Brannan, D.A.; Taha, T.S. On some classes of bi-univalent functions. *Studia Univ. Babeş-Bolyai Math.* **1986**, *31*, 70–77.
2. Taha, T.S. Topics in Univalent Function Theory. Ph.D. Thesis, University of London, London, UK, 1981.
3. Brannan, D.A.; Clunie, J. *Aspects of Contemporary Complex Analysis*; Academic Press: New York, NY, USA; London, UK, 1980.
4. Lewin, M. On a coefficient problem for bi-univalent functions. *Proc. Am. Math. Soc.* **1967**, *18*, 63–68. [CrossRef]
5. Netanyahu, E. The minimal distance of the image boundary from the origin and the second coefficient of a univalent function in $|z| < 1$. *Arch. Rational. Mech. Anal.* **1969**, *32*, 100–112.
6. Tang, H.; Deng, G.T.; Li, S.H. Coefficient estimates for new subclasses of Ma-Minda bi-univalent functions. *J. Inequal. Appl.* **2013**, *2013*, 317. [CrossRef]
7. Deniz, E. Certain subclasses of bi-univalent functions satisfying subordinate conditions. *J. Class. Anal.* **2013**, *2*, 49–60. [CrossRef]
8. Srivastava, H.M.; Mishra, A.K.; Gochhayat, P. Certain subclasses of analytic and bi-univalent functions. *Appl. Math. Lett.* **2010**, *23* 1188–1192. [CrossRef]
9. Çaglar, M.; Orhan, H.; Yagmur, N. Coefficient bounds for new subclasses of bi-univalent functions. *Filomat* **2013**, *27*, 1165–1171. [CrossRef]
10. Xu, Q.-H.; Gui, Y.-C.; Srivastava, H.M. Coefficient estimates for a certain subclass of analytic and bi-univalent functions. *Appl. Math. Lett.* **2012**, *25*, 990–994. [CrossRef]
11. Xu, Q.-H.; Xiao, H.-G.; Srivastava, H.M. A certain general subclass of analytic and bi-univalent functions and associated coefficient estimate problems. *Appl. Math. Comput.* **2012**, *218*, 11461–11465. [CrossRef]
12. Ma, W.C.; Minda, D. A unified treatment of some special classes of functions. In Proceedings of the Conference on Complex Analysis, Tianjin, China, 19–23 June 1992; pp. 157–169.
13. Kiryakova, V. *Generalized Fractional Calculus and Applications*; Pitman Research Notes in Mathematics Series, 301; John Willey & Sons, Inc.: New York, NY, USA, 1994.
14. Erdelyi, A.; Magnus,W.; Oberhettinger, F.; Tricomi, F.G. *Higher Transcendental Functions*; McGraw-Hill: New York, NY, USA; Toronto, ON, Canada; London, UK, 1953; Volume I.
15. Akdemir, A.O.; Karaoblan, A.; Ragusa, M.A.; Set, E. Fractional integral inequalities via Atangana-Baleanu operators for convex and concave functions. *J. Funct.* **2021**, *2021*, 1055434. [CrossRef]
16. Luchko, Y. The four-parameters Wright function of the second kind and its applications in FC. *Mathematics* **2020**, *8*, 970. [CrossRef]
17. Tang, J.H.; Yin, C.T. Analysis of the generalized fractional diferential system. *Aims Math.* **2022**, *7*, 8654–8684. [CrossRef]
18. Jung, I.B.; Kim Y.C.; Srivastava, H.M. The Hardy space of analytic functions associated with certain one-parameter families of integral operators. *J. Math. Anal. Appl.* **1993**, *176*, 138–147. [CrossRef]
19. Carlson, B.C.; Shafer, D.B. Starlike and prestarlike Hypergeometric functions. *J. Math. Anal.* **1984**, *15*, 737–745. [CrossRef]
20. Choi, J.H.; Saigo, M.; Srivastava, H.M. Some inclusion properties of a certain family of integral operators. *J. Math. Anal. Appl.* **2002**, *276*, 432–445. [CrossRef]
21. Ruscheweyh, S. New criteria for univalent functions. *Proc. Am. Math. Soc.* **1975**, *49*, 109–115. [CrossRef]
22. Noor, K.I. On new classes of integral operators. *J. Nat. Geom.* **1999**, *16*, 71–80.
23. Noor, K.I.; Noor, M.A. On integral operators. *J. Math. Anal. Appl.* **1999**, *238*, 341–352. [CrossRef]
24. Bernardi, S.D. Convex and starlike univalent functions. *Trans. Am. Math. Soc.* **1969**, *135*, 429–446. [CrossRef]
25. Libera, R.J. Some classes of regular univalent functions. *Proc. Am. Math. Soc.* **1965**, *16*, 755–758. [CrossRef]
26. Livingston, A.E. On the radius of univalence of certain analytic functions. *Proc. Am. Math. Soc.* **1966**, *17*, 352–357. [CrossRef]
27. Silverman, H.; Silvia, E.M. Characterizations for subclasses of univalent functions. *Math. Jpn.* **1999**, *50*, 103–109.
28. Silverman, H. A class of bounded starlike functions. *Int. J. Math. Math. Sci.* **1994**, *17*, 249–252. [CrossRef]
29. El-Deeb, S.M. Maclaurin Coefficient estimates for new subclasses of bi-univalent functions connected with a q-analogue of Bessel function. *Abstr. Appl. Anal.* **2020**, *2020*, 1–7. [CrossRef]
30. El-Deeb, S.M.; Bulboacă, T.; El-Matary, B.M. Maclaurin coefficient estimates of bi-univalent functions connected with the q-derivative. *Mathematics* **2020**, *8*, 418. [CrossRef]
31. El-Deeb, S.M.; El-Matary, B.M. Subclasses of bi-univalent functions associated with q-confluent hypergeometric distribution based upon the Horadam polynomials. *Adv. Theory Nonlinear Anal. Appl.* **2021**, *5*, 82–93. [CrossRef]

32. Murugusundaramoorthy, G.; Janani, T. Bi-starlike function of complex order associated with double Zeta functions. *Afr. Mat.* **2015**, *26*, 1025–1036. [CrossRef]
33. Pommerenke, C. *Univalent Functions*; Vandenhoeck & Ruprecht, Göttingen: Göttingen, Germany, 1975.
34. Fekete, M.; Szegő, G. Eine Bemerkungüber ungerade schlichte Funktionen. *J. Lond. Math. Soc.* **1933**, *8*, 85–89. [CrossRef]
35. Zaprawa, P. On the Fekete Szegö problem for classes of bi-univalent functions. *Bull. Belg. Math. Soc. Simon Stevin* **2014**, *21*, 169–178. [CrossRef]
36. Robertson, M.S. Certain classes of starlike functions. *Mich. Math. J.* **1985**, *32*, 135–140. [CrossRef]
37. Janowski, W. Extremal problems for a family of functions with positive real part and for some related families. *Ann. Pol. Math.* **1970**, *23*, 159–177. [CrossRef]
38. Ronning, F. Uniformly convex functions and a corresponding class of starlike functions. *Proc. Am. Math. Soc.* **1993**, *118*, 189–196. [CrossRef]
39. Sokół, J. Radius problem in the class $\mathcal{SL}^*$. *Appl. Math. Comput.* **2009**, *214*, 569–573. [CrossRef]
40. Mohsin, M.; Malik, S.N. Upper bound of third hankel determinant for class of analytic functions related with lemniscate of bernoulli. *J. Inequal. Appl.* **2013**, *2013*, 412. [CrossRef]
41. Raina, R.K.; Sokół, J. On coefficient estimates for a class of starlike functions. *Hacet. J. Math. Statist.* **2015**, *44*, 1427–1433. [CrossRef]
42. Sharma, K.; Jain, N.K.; Ravichandran, V. Starlike functions associated with a cardioid. *Afr. Mat.* **2016**, *27*, 923–939. [CrossRef]
43. Shi, L.; Izaz, A.; Arif, M.; Cho, N.E.; Hussain, S.; Hassan, K.A. Study of third hankel determinant problem for certain subfamilies of analytic functions involving cardioid domain. *Mathematics* **2019**, *7*, 418. [CrossRef]
44. Mendiratta, R.; Nagpal, S.; Ravichandran, V. On a subclass of strongly starlike functions associated with exponential function. *Bull. Malays. Math. Sci. Soc.* **2015**, *38*, 365–386. [CrossRef]
45. Shi, L.; Srivastava, H.M.; Arif, M.; Hussain, S.; Khan, H. An investigation of the third Hankel determinant problem for certain subfamilies of univalent functions involving the exponential function. *Symmetry* **2019**, *11*, 598. [CrossRef]
46. Alotaibi, A.; Arif, M.; Alghamdi, M.A.; Hussain, S. Starlikeness associated with cosine hyperbolic function. *Mathematics* **2020**, *8*, 16. [CrossRef]
47. Cho, N.E.; Kumar, V.; Kumar, S.S.; Ravichandran, V. Radius problems for starlike functions associated with the sine function. *Bull. Iran. Math. Soc.* **2019**, *45*, 213–232. [CrossRef]
48. Arif, M.; Raza, M.; Huo, T.; Hussain, S.; Khan, H. Hankel determinant of order three for familiar subsets of analytic functions related with sine function. *Open Math.* **2019**, *17*, 1615–1630. [CrossRef]
49. Srivastava, H.M. Operators of basic (or q-) calculus and fractional q-calculus and their applications in Geometric Function theory of Complex Analysis. *Iran. J. Sci. Technol. Trans. Sci.* **2020**, *44*, 327–344. [CrossRef]
50. Srivastava, H.M.; Karlsson, P.W. *Multiple Gaussian Hypergeometric Series*; Wiley: New York, NY, USA, 1985.
51. Srivastava, H.M.; Raducanu, D.; Zaprawa, P.A. Certain subclass of analytic functions defined by means of differential subordination. *Filomat* **2016**, *30*, 3743–3757. [CrossRef]
52. Srivastava, H.M. Certain q-polynomial expansions for functions of several variables. I and II. *IMA J. Appl. Math.* **1983**, *30*, 205–209. [CrossRef]

Article

An Avant-Garde Construction for Subclasses of Analytic Bi-Univalent Functions

Feras Yousef [1,*], Ala Amourah [2], Basem Aref Frasin [3] and Teodor Bulboacă [4]

1. Department of Mathematics, The University of Jordan, Amman 11942, Jordan
2. Department of Mathematics, Irbid National University, Irbid 21110, Jordan; ala.amourah@siswa.ukm.edu.my
3. Department of Mathematics, Al al-Bayt University, Mafraq 25113, Jordan; bafrasin@aabu.edu.jo
4. Faculty of Mathematics and Computer Science, Babeş-Bolyai University, 400084 Cluj-Napoca, Romania; bulboaca@math.ubbcluj.ro
* Correspondence: fyousef@ju.edu.jo

Abstract: The zero-truncated Poisson distribution is an important and appropriate model for many real-world applications. Here, we exploit the zero-truncated Poisson distribution probabilities to construct a new subclass of analytic bi-univalent functions involving Gegenbauer polynomials. For functions in the constructed class, we explore estimates of Taylor–Maclaurin coefficients $|a_2|$ and $|a_3|$, and next, we solve the Fekete–Szegő functional problem. A number of new interesting results are presented to follow upon specializing the parameters involved in our main results.

Keywords: analytic bi-univalent functions; zero-truncated Poisson distribution; Gegenbauer polynomials; Fekete–Szegő functional problem

MSC: 30C45; 33C45; 60E05

1. Introduction

In discrete probability distributions, the Poisson distribution has found an extensive and varied application in formulating probability models for a wide variety of real-life phenomena dealing with counts of rare events, such as reliability theory, queueing systems, epidemiology, medicine, industry, and many others. In some practical situations, only positive counts would be available and the zero count is ignored or is impossible to be observed at all. For instance: the length of stay in a hospital is recorded as a minimum of at least one day, the number of journal articles published in different disciplines, the number of occupants in passenger cars, etc. An appropriate Poisson distribution that applies to such a case is called a zero-truncated Poisson distribution.

The probability density function of a discrete random variable X that follows a zero-truncated Poisson distribution can be written as

$$P_m(X=s) = \frac{m^s}{(e^m-1)s!}, \quad s=1,2,3,\ldots,$$

where the parameter mean $m > 0$.

Now, we introduce a novel power series whose coefficients are probabilities of the zero-truncated Poisson distribution

$$\mathbb{P}(m,z) := z + \sum_{n=2}^{\infty} \frac{m^{n-1}}{(e^m-1)(n-1)!} z^n, \quad z \in \mathbb{U},$$

where $m > 0$ and $\mathbb{U} := \{z \in \mathbb{C} : |z| < 1\}$ is the *open unit disk*. By ratio test, it is clear that the radius of convergence of the above series is infinity.

Orthogonal polynomials have been extensively studied in recent years from various perspectives due to their importance in mathematical statistics, probability theory, mathematical physics, approximation theory, and engineering. From a mathematical point of view, orthogonal polynomials often arise from solutions of ordinary differential equations under certain conditions imposed by certain model. Orthogonal polynomials that appear most commonly in applications are the classical orthogonal polynomials (Hermite polynomials, Laguerre polynomials, and Jacobi polynomials). The general subclass of Jacobi polynomials is the set of Gegenbauer polynomials, this class includes Legendre polynomials and Chebyshev polynomials as subclasses. To study the basic definitions and the most important properties of the classical orthogonal polynomials, we refer the reader to [1–4]. For a recent connection between the classical orthogonal polynomials and geometric function theory, we mention [5–10].

Gegenbauer polynomials $C_n^\alpha(x)$ for $n = 2, 3, \ldots$, and $\alpha > -\frac{1}{2}$ are defined by the following three-term recurrence formula

$$C_0^\alpha(x) = 1;$$
$$C_1^\alpha(x) = 2\alpha x; \qquad (1)$$
$$C_n^\alpha(x) = \frac{1}{n}\left[2x(n+\alpha-1)C_{n-1}^\alpha(x) - (n+2\alpha-2)C_{n-2}^\alpha(x)\right].$$

It is worth mentioning that by setting $\alpha = \frac{1}{2}$ and $\alpha = 1$ in Equation (1), we immediately obtain Legendre polynomials $P_n(x) = C_n^{\frac{1}{2}}(x)$ and Chebyshev polynomials of the second kind $U_n(x) = C_n^1(x)$, respectively.

The generating function of Gegenbauer polynomials is given as

$$H_\alpha(x, z) = \frac{1}{(1 - 2xz + z^2)^\alpha},$$

where $x \in [-1, 1]$ and $z \in \mathbb{U}$. For fixed x, the function H_α is analytic in $\mathbb{U}$, so it can be expanded in a Taylor–Maclaurin series, as follows:

$$H_\alpha(x, z) = \sum_{n=0}^\infty C_n^\alpha(x) z^n, \quad z \in \mathbb{U}. \qquad (2)$$

2. Preliminaries and Definitions

Let $\mathcal{A}$ denote the class of all normalized analytic functions f written as

$$f(z) = z + \sum_{n=2}^\infty a_n z^n, \quad z \in \mathbb{U}. \qquad (3)$$

Differential subordination of analytic functions provides excellent tools for study in geometric function theory. The earliest problem in differential subordination was introduced by Miller and Mocanu [11], see also [12]. The book of Miller and Mocanu [13] sums up most of the advancement in the field and the references to the date of its publication.

Definition 1. *Let f and g be two analytic functions in $\mathbb{U}$. The function f is said to be subordinate to g, written as $f(z) \prec g(z)$, if there is an analytic function ω in $\mathbb{U}$ with the properties*

$$\omega(0) = 0 \quad \text{and} \quad |\omega(z)| < 1, \, z \in \mathbb{U},$$

such that

$$f(z) = g(\omega(z)), \, z \in \mathbb{U}.$$

Definition 2. *A single-valued one-to-one function f defined in a simply connected domain is said to be a univalent function.*

Let $\mathcal{S}$ denote the class of all functions $f \in \mathcal{A}$, given by (3), that are univalent in $\mathbb{U}$. Hence, every function $f \in \mathcal{S}$ has an inverse given by

$$f^{-1}(w) = w - a_2 w^2 + \left(2a_2^2 - a_3\right) w^3 - \left(5a_2^3 - 5a_2 a_3 + a_4\right) w^4 + \dots. \tag{4}$$

Definition 3. *A univalent function f is said to be bi-univalent in $\mathbb{U}$ if its inverse function $f^{-1}(w)$ has an analytic univalent extension in $\mathbb{U}$.*

Let Σ denote the class of all functions $f \in \mathcal{A}$ that are bi-univalent in $\mathbb{U}$ given by (3). For interesting subclasses of functions in the class Σ, see [14–24].

The coefficient functional

$$\Delta_\eta(f) = a_3 - \eta a_2^2 = \frac{1}{6}\left(f'''(0) - \frac{3\eta}{2}\left(f''(0)\right)^2\right) \tag{5}$$

of the analytic function f given by (3) is very important in the theory of analytic and univalent functions. Thus, it is quite natural to ask about inequalities for $\Delta_\eta(f)$ corresponding to subclasses of bi-univalent functions in the open unit disk $\mathbb{U}$. The problem of maximizing the absolute value of the functional $\Delta_\eta(f)$ is called the Fekete–Szegö problem [25]. There are now several results of this type in the literature, each of them dealing with $|a_3 - \eta a_2^2|$ for various classes of functions defined in terms of subordination (see, e.g., [26–31]).

Now, let us define the linear operator

$$\chi : \mathcal{A} \to \mathcal{A}$$

by

$$\chi_m f(z) := \mathbb{P}(m, z) * f(z) = z + \sum_{n=2}^{\infty} \frac{m^{n-1}}{(e^m - 1)(n-1)!} a_n z^n, \quad z \in \mathbb{U},$$

where the symbol "$*$" denotes the Hadamard product of the two series.

To obtain our results we need the following lemma:

Lemma 1 ([32], p. 172). *Assume that $\omega(z) = \sum_{n=1}^{\infty} \omega_n z^n$, $z \in \mathbb{U}$, is an analytic function in $\mathbb{U}$ such that $|\omega(z)| < 1$ for all $z \in \mathbb{U}$. Then, $|\omega_1| \leq 1$, $|\omega_n| \leq 1 - |\omega_1|^2$, $n = 2, 3, \dots$.*

Motivated essentially by the earlier work of Amourah et al. [33], we construct, in the next section, a new subclass of bi-univalent functions governed by the zero-truncated Poisson distribution series and Gegenbauer polynomials. Then, we investigate the optimal bounds for the Taylor–Maclaurin coefficients $|a_2|$ and $|a_3|$ and solve the Fekete–Szegö functional problem for functions in our new subclass.

3. The Class $\zeta_\Sigma(x, \alpha, \delta, \mu)$

Consider the function $f \in \Sigma$ given by (3), the function $g = f^{-1}$ given by (4), and H_α is the generating function of Gegenbauer polynomials given by (2). Now, we are ready to define our new subclass of bi-univalent functions $\zeta_\Sigma(x, \alpha, \delta, \mu)$ as follows.

Definition 4. *A function f is said to be in the class $\zeta_\Sigma(x, \alpha, \delta, \mu)$, if the following subordinations are fulfilled:*

$$(1-\mu)\frac{\chi_m f(z)}{z} + \mu(\chi_m f(z))' + \delta z(\chi_m f(z))'' \prec H_\alpha(x, z),$$

and

$$(1-\mu)\frac{\chi_m g(w)}{w} + \mu(\chi_m g(w))' + \delta w(\chi_m g(w))'' \prec H_\alpha(x, w),$$

where $\alpha > 0$, $\mu, \delta \geq 0$, and $x \in \left(\frac{1}{2}, 1\right]$.

Upon allocating the parameters μ and δ, one can obtain several new subclasses of Σ, as illustrated in the following two examples.

Example 1. *A function f is said to be in the class $\zeta_\Sigma(x, \alpha, \mu) := \zeta_\Sigma(x, \alpha, 0, \mu)$, if the following subordinations are fulfilled:*

$$(1-\mu)\frac{\chi_m f(z)}{z} + \mu(\chi_m f(z))' \prec H_\alpha(x, z),$$

and

$$(1-\mu)\frac{\chi_m g(w)}{w} + \mu(\chi_m g(w))' \prec H_\alpha(x, w),$$

where $\alpha > 0$, $\mu \geq 0$, and $x \in \left(\frac{1}{2}, 1\right]$.

Example 2. *A function f is said to be in the class $\zeta_\Sigma(x, \alpha) := \zeta_\Sigma(x, \alpha, 0, 1)$, if the following subordinations are fulfilled:*

$$(\chi_m f(z))' \prec H_\alpha(x, z),$$

and

$$(\chi_m g(w))' \prec H_\alpha(x, w),$$

where $\alpha > 0$ and $x \in \left(\frac{1}{2}, 1\right]$.

4. Main Results

Theorem 1. *If the function f belongs to the class $\zeta_\Sigma(x, \alpha, \delta, \mu)$, then*

$$|a_2| \leq \frac{2\alpha x(e^m - 1)\sqrt{2x}}{m\sqrt{\left|\left[2\alpha(1 + 2\mu + 6\delta)(e^m - 1) - 2(1+\alpha)(1+\mu+2\delta)^2\right]x^2 + (1+\mu+2\delta)^2\right|}}, \quad (6)$$

and

$$|a_3| \leq \frac{4\alpha^2 x^2 (e^m - 1)^2}{m^2(1+\mu+2\delta)^2} + \frac{4\alpha x(e^m - 1)}{m^2(1+2\mu+6\delta)}.$$

Proof. If $f \in \zeta_\Sigma(x, \alpha, \delta, \mu)$, from the Definition 4 there exist two analytic functions in $\mathbb{U}$ that are w and v, such that $w(0) = v(0) = 0$ and $|\omega(z)| < 1$, $|v(w)| < 1$ for all $z, w \in \mathbb{U}$, and

$$(1-\mu)\frac{\chi_m f(z)}{z} + \mu(\chi_m f(z))' + \delta z(\chi_m f(z))'' = H_\alpha(x, \omega(z)), \quad z \in \mathbb{U}, \quad (7)$$

and

$$(1-\mu)\frac{\chi_m g(w)}{w} + \mu(\chi_m g(w))' + \delta w(\chi_m g(w))'' = H_\alpha(x, v(w)), \quad w \in \mathbb{U}. \quad (8)$$

From the equalities (7) and (8), we obtain

$$(1-\mu)\frac{\chi_m f(z)}{z} + \mu(\chi_m f(z))' + \delta z(\chi_m f(z))''$$
$$= 1 + C_1^\alpha(x)c_1 z + \left[C_1^\alpha(x)c_2 + C_2^\alpha(x)c_1^2\right]z^2 + \ldots, \quad z \in \mathbb{U}, \quad (9)$$

and

$$(1-\mu)\frac{\chi_m g(w)}{w} + \mu(\chi_m g(w))' + \delta w(\chi_m g(w))''$$
$$= 1 + C_1^\alpha(x)d_1 w + \left[C_1^\alpha(x)d_2 + C_2^\alpha(x)d_1^2\right]w^2 + \ldots, \quad w \in \mathbb{U}, \quad (10)$$

where

$$w(z) = \sum_{j=1}^{\infty} c_j z^j, \ z \in \mathbb{U}, \quad \text{and} \quad v(w) = \sum_{j=1}^{\infty} d_j w^j, \ w \in \mathbb{U}. \quad (11)$$

According to Lemma 1, if the above function w and v has the form (11), then

$$|c_j| \leq 1 \quad \text{and} \quad |d_j| \leq 1 \quad \text{for all} \quad j \in \mathbb{N}. \quad (12)$$

Thus, upon comparing and equating the corresponding coefficients in (9) and (10), we have

$$\frac{(1+\mu+2\delta)m}{e^m - 1} a_2 = C_1^{\alpha}(x) c_1, \quad (13)$$

$$\frac{(1+2\mu+6\delta)m^2}{2(e^m - 1)} a_3 = C_1^{\alpha}(x) c_2 + C_2^{\alpha}(x) c_1^2, \quad (14)$$

$$-\frac{(1+\mu+2\delta)m}{e^m - 1} a_2 = C_1^{\alpha}(x) d_1, \quad (15)$$

and

$$\frac{(1+2\mu+6\delta)m^2}{2(e^m - 1)} \left[2a_2^2 - a_3\right] = C_1^{\alpha}(x) d_2 + C_2^{\alpha}(x) d_1^2. \quad (16)$$

It follows from (13) and (15) that

$$c_1 = -d_1, \quad (17)$$

and

$$\frac{2(1+\mu+2\delta)^2 m^2}{(e^m - 1)^2} a_2^2 = [C_1^{\alpha}(x)]^2 \left(c_1^2 + d_1^2\right). \quad (18)$$

If we add (14) and (16), we get

$$\frac{(1+2\mu+6\delta)m^2}{(e^m - 1)} a_2^2 = C_1^{\alpha}(x)(c_2 + d_2) + C_2^{\alpha}(x)\left(c_1^2 + d_1^2\right). \quad (19)$$

Substituting the value of $(c_1^2 + d_1^2)$ from (18) in the right hand side of (19), we deduce that

$$\left[(1+2\mu+6\delta) - \frac{2(1+\mu+2\delta)^2}{(e^m - 1)} \frac{C_2^{\alpha}(x)}{[C_1^{\alpha}(x)]^2}\right] \frac{m^2}{(e^m - 1)} a_2^2 = C_1^{\alpha}(x)(c_2 + d_2). \quad (20)$$

Now, using (1), (12) and (20), we find that (6) holds.
Moreover, if we subtract (16) from (14), we obtain

$$\frac{(1+2\mu+6\delta)m^2}{(e^m - 1)} \left(a_3 - a_2^2\right) = C_1^{\alpha}(x)(c_2 - d_2) + C_2^{\alpha}(x)\left(c_1^2 - d_1^2\right). \quad (21)$$

Then, in view of (17) and (18), Equation (21) becomes

$$a_3 = \frac{(e^m - 1)^2 [C_1^{\alpha}(x)]^2}{2m^2(1+\mu+2\delta)^2}\left(c_1^2 + d_1^2\right) + \frac{(e^m - 1)C_1^{\alpha}(x)}{m^2(1+2\mu+6\delta)}(c_2 - d_2).$$

Thus, applying (1), we conclude that

$$|a_3| \leq \frac{4\alpha^2 x^2 (e^m - 1)^2}{m^2(1+\mu+2\delta)^2} + \frac{4\alpha x(e^m - 1)}{m^2(1+2\mu+6\delta)},$$

and the proof of the theorem is complete. □

The following result addresses the Fekete–Szegő functional problem for functions in the class $\zeta_\Sigma(x, \alpha, \delta, \mu)$.

Theorem 2. *If the function f belongs to the class $\zeta_\Sigma(x, \alpha, \delta, \mu)$, then*

$$\left|a_3 - \eta a_2^2\right| \leq \begin{cases} \dfrac{4\alpha x(e^m-1)}{m^2(1+2\mu+6\delta)}, & \text{if } |\eta - 1| \leq M, \\[2ex] \dfrac{8\alpha^2 x^3(e^m-1)^2|1-\eta|}{\left|m^2\left\{[2\alpha(1+2\mu+6\delta)(e^m-1)-2(1+\alpha)(1+\mu+2\delta)^2]x^2+(1+\mu+2\delta)^2\right\}\right|}, & \text{if } |\eta - 1| \geq M, \end{cases}$$

where

$$M := \left|1 - \frac{(1+\mu+2\delta)^2\left[2(1+\alpha)x^2 - 1\right]}{2\alpha x^2(e^m-1)(1+2\mu+6\delta)}\right|.$$

Proof. If $f \in \zeta_\Sigma(x, \alpha, \delta, \mu)$, from (20) and (21) we get

$$a_3 - \eta a_2^2 = (1-\eta)\frac{(e^m-1)^2\left[C_1^\alpha(x)\right]^3(c_2+d_2)}{m^2\left[(e^m-1)(1+2\mu+6\delta)\left[C_1^\alpha(x)\right]^2 - 2(1+\mu+2\delta)^2 C_2^\alpha(x)\right]}$$

$$+ \frac{(e^m-1)C_1^\alpha(x)}{m^2(1+2\mu+6\delta)}(c_2-d_2)$$

$$= C_1^\alpha(x)\left[h(\eta) + \frac{(e^m-1)}{m^2(1+2\mu+6\delta)}\right]c_2 + \left[h(\eta) - \frac{(e^m-1)}{m^2(1+2\mu+6\delta)}\right]d_2,$$

where

$$h(\eta) = \frac{(e^m-1)^2\left[C_1^\alpha(x)\right]^2(1-\eta)}{m^2\left[(e^m-1)(1+2\mu+6\delta)\left[C_1^\alpha(x)\right]^2 - 2(1+\mu+2\delta)^2 C_2^\alpha(x)\right]}.$$

Then, in view of (1), we conclude that

$$\left|a_3 - \eta a_2^2\right| \leq \begin{cases} \dfrac{4\alpha x(e^m-1)}{m^2(1+2\mu+6\delta)}, & \text{if } 0 \leq |h(\eta)| \leq \dfrac{(e^m-1)}{m^2(1+2\mu+6\delta)}, \\[2ex] 4\alpha x|h(\eta)|, & \text{if } |h(\eta)| \geq \dfrac{(e^m-1)}{m^2(1+2\mu+6\delta)}, \end{cases}$$

which completes the proof of Theorem 2. □

5. Corollaries and Consequences

Corresponding essentially to the Example 1 (setting $\delta = 0$) and Example 2 (setting $\delta = 0$ and $\mu = 1$), from Theorems 1 and 2 we get the following consequences, respectively.

Corollary 1. *If the function f belongs to the class $\zeta_\Sigma(x, \alpha, \mu)$, then*

$$|a_2| \leq \frac{2\alpha x(e^m-1)\sqrt{2x}}{m\sqrt{\left|\left[2\alpha(1+2\mu)(e^m-1) - 2(1+\alpha)(1+\mu)^2\right]x^2 + (1+\mu)^2\right|}},$$

$$|a_3| \leq \frac{4\alpha^2 x^2(e^m-1)^2}{m^2(1+\mu)^2} + \frac{4\alpha x(e^m-1)}{m^2(1+2\mu)},$$

and
$$\left|a_3 - \eta a_2^2\right| \leq \begin{cases} \frac{4\alpha x(e^m-1)}{m^2(1+2\mu)}, & \text{if } |\eta - 1| \leq N, \\ \frac{8\alpha^2 x^3(e^m-1)^2|1-\eta|}{\left|m^2\left\{[2\alpha(1+2\mu)(e^m-1)-2(1+\alpha)(1+\mu)^2]x^2+(1+\mu)^2\right\}\right|}, & \text{if } |\eta - 1| \geq N, \end{cases}$$

where
$$N := \left|1 - \frac{(1+\mu)^2\left[2(1+\alpha)x^2-1\right]}{2\alpha x^2(e^m-1)(1+2\mu)}\right|.$$

Corollary 2. *If the function f belongs to the class* $\zeta_\Sigma(x,\alpha)$, *then*

$$|a_2| \leq \frac{2\alpha x(e^m-1)\sqrt{2x}}{m\sqrt{|[6\alpha(e^m-1)-8(1+\alpha)]x^2+4|}},$$

$$|a_3| \leq \frac{\alpha^2 x^2(e^m-1)^2}{m^2} + \frac{4\alpha x(e^m-1)}{3m^2},$$

and
$$\left|a_3 - \eta a_2^2\right| \leq \begin{cases} \frac{4\alpha x(e^m-1)}{3m^2}, & \text{if } |\eta - 1| \leq L, \\ \frac{8\alpha^2 x^3(e^m-1)^2|1-\eta|}{\left|m^2\left\{[6\alpha(e^m-1)-8(1+\alpha)]x^2+4\right\}\right|}, & \text{if } |\eta - 1| \geq L, \end{cases}$$

where
$$L := \left|1 - \frac{2\left[2(1+\alpha)x^2-1\right]}{3\alpha x^2(e^m-1)}\right|.$$

6. Concluding Remarks

In the present work we have constructed a new subclass $\zeta_\Sigma(x,\alpha,\delta,\mu)$ of normalized analytic and bi-univalent functions governed with the zero-truncated Poisson distribution series and Gegenbauer polynomials. For functions belonging to this class, we have made estimates of Taylor–Maclaurin coefficients, $|a_2|$ and $|a_3|$, and solved the Fekete–Szegő functional problem. Furthermore, by suitably specializing the parameters δ and μ, one can deduce the results for the subclasses $\zeta_\Sigma(x,\alpha,\mu)$ and $\zeta_\Sigma(x,\alpha)$ which are defined, respectively, in Examples 1 and 2.

The results offered in this paper would lead to other different new results for the classes $\zeta_\Sigma(x,1/2,\delta,\mu)$ for Legendre polynomials and $\zeta_\Sigma(x,1,\delta,\mu)$ for Chebyshev polynomials.

It remains an open problem to derive estimates on the bounds of $|a_n|$ for $n \geq 4, n \in \mathbb{N}$, for the subclasses that have been introduced here.

Author Contributions: Conceptualization, F.Y. and A.A.; methodology, A.A.; validation, F.Y., A.A., B.A.F. and T.B.; formal analysis, A.A.; investigation, F.Y., B.A.F. and T.B.; writing—original draft preparation, F.Y. and A.A.; writing—review and editing, F.Y., T.B.; supervision, B.A.F. All authors have read and agreed to the published version of the manuscript.

Funding: This research received no external funding.

Institutional Review Board Statement: Not applicable.

Informed Consent Statement: Not applicable.

Data Availability Statement: No data were used to support this study.

Conflicts of Interest: The authors declare no conflict of interest.

References

1. Agarwal, P.; Agarwal, R.P.; Ruzhansky, M. *Special Functions and Analysis of Differential Equations*; CRC Press: Boca Raton, FL, USA, 2020.
2. Doman, B. *The Classical Orthogonal Polynomials*; World Scientific: Singapore, 2015.
3. Chihara, T.S. *An Introduction to Orthogonal Polynomials*; Courier Corporation: Mineola, NY, USA, 2011.
4. Ismail, M.; Ismail, M.E.; van Assche, W. *Classical and Quantum Orthogonal Polynomials in One Variable*; Cambridge University Press: Cambridge, UK, 2005.
5. Wanas, A.K. New Families of Bi-univalent Functions Governed by Gegenbauer Polynomials. *Ear. J. Math. Sci.* **2021**, *7*, 403–427. [CrossRef]
6. Frasin, B.A.; Yousef, F.; Al-Hawary, T.; Aldawish, I. Application of Generalized Bessel Functions to Classes of Analytic Functions. *Afr. Mat.* **2021**, *32*, 431–439. [CrossRef]
7. Frasin, B.A.; Al-Hawary, T.; Yousef, F.; Aldawish, I. On Subclasses of Analytic Functions Associated with Struve Functions. *Nonlinear Func. Anal. Appl.* **2022**, *27*, 99–110. [CrossRef]
8. Altınkaya, Ş.; Yalçın, S. Estimates on Coefficients of a General Subclass of Bi-univalent Functions Associated with Symmetric q-Derivative Operator by Means of the Chebyshev Polynomials. *Asia Pac. J. Math.* **2017**, *8*, 90–99.
9. Bulut, S.; Magesh, N.; Balaji, V.K. Initial Bounds for Analytic and Bi-Univalent Functions by Means of Chebyshev Polynomials. *J. Class. Anal.* **2017**, *11*, 83–89. [CrossRef]
10. Amourah, A.; Frasin, B.A.; Abdeljawad, T. Fekete-Szegő Inequality for Analytic and Bi-Univalent Functions Subordinate to Gegenbauer Polynomials. *J. Funct. Spaces* **2021**, *2021*, 5574673.
11. Miller, S.S.; Mocanu, P.T. Second Order Differential Inequalities in the Complex Plane. *J. Math. Anal. Appl.* **1978**, *65*, 289–305. [CrossRef]
12. Miller, S.S.; Mocanu, P.T. Differential Subordinations and Univalent Functions. *Mich. Math. J.* **1981**, *28*, 157–172 [CrossRef]
13. Miller, S.S.; Mocanu, P.T. *Differential Subordinations. Theory and Applications*; Marcel Dekker, Inc.: New York, NY, USA, 2000.
14. Ahmad, I.; Ali Shah, S.G.; Hussain, S.; Darus, M.; Ahmad, B. Fekete-Szegő Functional for Bi-univalent Functions Related with Gegenbauer Polynomials. *J. Math.* **2022**, *2022*, 2705203. [CrossRef]
15. Murugusundaramoorthy, G.; Bulboacă, T. Subclasses of Yamakawa-Type Bi-Starlike Functions Associated with Gegenbauer Polynomials. *Axioms* **2022**, *11*, 92. [CrossRef]
16. Sakar, F.M.; Doğan, E. Problem on Coefficients of Bi-Univalent Function Class Using Chebyshev Polynomials. In *Mathematical, Computational Intelligence and Engineering Approaches for Tourism, Agriculture and Healthcare*; Lecture Notes in Networks and Systems; Srivastava, P., Thakur, S.S., Oros, G.I., AlJarrah, A.A., Laohakosol, V., Eds.; Springer: Singapore, 2022; Volume 214. [CrossRef]
17. Wanas, A.K.; Cotîrlă, L.-I. Applications of (M,N)-Lucas Polynomials on a Certain Family of Bi-Univalent Functions. *Mathematics* **2022**, *10*, 595. [CrossRef]
18. Frasin, B.A.; Swamy, S.R.; Nirmala, J. Some Special Families of Holomorphic and Al-Oboudi Type Bi-Univalent Functions Rrelated to k-Fibonacci Numbers Involving Modified Sigmoid Activation Function. *Afr. Mat.* **2021**, *32*, 631–643. [CrossRef]
19. Srivastava, H.M.; Wanas, A.K.; Srivastava, R. Applications of the q-Srivastava-Attiya Operator Involving a Certain Family of Bi-univalent Functions Associated with the Horadam Polynomials. *Symmetry* **2021**, *13*, 1230. [CrossRef]
20. Kanas, S.; Sivasankari, P.V.; Karthiyayini, R.; Sivasubramanian, S. Second Hankel Determinant for a Certain Subclass of Bi-Close to Convex Functions Defined by Kaplan. *Symmetry* **2021**, *13*, 567. [CrossRef]
21. Atshan, W.G.; Rahman, I.A.R.; Lupaş, A.A. Some Results of New Subclasses for Bi-Univalent Functions Using Quasi-Subordination. *Symmetry* **2021**, *13*, 1653. [CrossRef]
22. Yousef, F.; Alroud, S.; Illafe, M. New Subclasses of Analytic and Bi-univalent Functions Endowed with Coefficient Estimate Problems. *Anal. Math. Phys.* **2021**, *11*, 58. [CrossRef]
23. Bulut, S. Coefficient Estimates for a Class of Analytic and Bi-univalent Functions. *Novi. Sad. J. Math.* **2013**, *43*, 59–65.
24. Murugusundaramoorthy, G.; Magesh, N.; Prameela, V. Coefficient Bounds for Certain Subclasses of Bi-univalent Function. *Abstr. Appl. Anal.* **2013**, *2013*, 573017. [CrossRef]
25. Fekete, M.; Szegő, G. Eine Bemerkung über ungerade schlichte funktionen. *J. Lond. Math. Soc.* **1933**, *1*, 85–89. [CrossRef]
26. Illafe, M.; Amourah, A.; Haji Mohd, M. Coefficient Estimates and Fekete-Szegő Functional Inequalities for a Certain Subclass of Analytic and Bi-Univalent Functions. *Axioms* **2022**, *11*, 147. [CrossRef]
27. Wanas, A.K.; Yalçın, S. Coefficient Estimates and Fekete-Szegő Inequality for Family of Bi-Univalent Functions Defined by the Second Kind Chebyshev Polynomial. *Int. J. Open Problems Compt. Math* **2020**, *13*, 25–33.
28. Karthikeyan, K.R.; Murugusundaramoorthy, G. Unified Solution of Initial Coefficients and Fekete-Szegő Problem for Subclasses of Analytic Functions Related to a Conic Region. *Afr. Mat.* **2022**, *33*, 44. [CrossRef]
29. Swamy, S.R.; Altınkaya, Ş. Fekete-Szegő Functional for Regular Functions Based on Quasi-Subordination. *Int. J. Nonlinear Anal. Appl.* **2022**, *14*, 1–11.
30. Swamy, S.R.; Sailaja, Y. On the Fekete-Szegő Coefficient Functional for Quasi-Subordination Class. *Palas. J. Math.* **2021**, *10*, 666–672.
31. Bulut, S. Fekete-Szegő Problem for Starlike Functions Connected with k-Fibonacci Numbers. *Math. Slov.* **2021**, *71*, 823–830. [CrossRef]
32. Nehari, Z. *Conformal Mapping*; McGraw-Hill: New York, NY, USA, 1952.
33. Amourah, A.; Frasin, B.A.; Ahmad, M.; Yousef, F. Exploiting the Pascal Distribution Series and Gegenbauer Polynomials to Construct and Study a New Subclass of Analytic Bi-Univalent Functions. *Symmetry* **2022**, *14*, 147. [CrossRef]

Article

Sharp Bounds for the Second Hankel Determinant of Logarithmic Coefficients for Strongly Starlike and Strongly Convex Functions

Sevtap Sümer Eker [1,*], Bilal Şeker [1], Bilal Çekiç [1] and Mugur Acu [2]

[1] Department of Mathematics, Faculty of Science, Dicle University, 21280 Diyarbakır, Turkey; bilal.seker@dicle.edu.tr (B.Ş.); bilalc@dicle.edu.tr (B.Ç.)
[2] Department of Mathematics and Informatics, Faculty of Science, Lucian Blaga University of Sibiu, Street Dr. I. Ratiu 5–7, 550012 Sibiu, Romania; mugur.acu@ulbsibiu.ro
* Correspondence: sevtaps@dicle.edu.tr

Abstract: The logarithmic coefficients are very essential in the problems of univalent functions theory. The importance of the logarithmic coefficients is due to the fact that the bounds on logarithmic coefficients of f can transfer to the Taylor coefficients of univalent functions themselves or to their powers, via the Lebedev–Milin inequalities; therefore, it is interesting to investigate the Hankel determinant whose entries are logarithmic coefficients. The main purpose of this paper is to obtain the sharp bounds for the second Hankel determinant of logarithmic coefficients of strongly starlike functions and strongly convex functions.

Keywords: logarithmic coefficient; Hankel determinant; strongly starlike; strongly convex

MSC: 30C45; 30C50

1. Introduction

Let $\mathcal{A}$ stand for the standard class of analytic functions of the form

$$f(z) = z + \sum_{k=2}^{\infty} a_k z^k, \qquad z \in \mathbb{U} = \{z \in \mathbb{C} : |z| < 1\}, \tag{1}$$

and let $\mathcal{S}$ be the class of functions in $\mathcal{A}$, which are univalent in $\mathbb{U}$.

A function f of the form (1) is said to be *starlike of order α* in $\mathbb{U}$ if

$$\Re\left\{\frac{zf'(z)}{f(z)}\right\} > \alpha \qquad (z \in \mathbb{U}).$$

The set of all such functions is denoted by $\mathcal{S}^*(\alpha)$.

Next, by $\mathcal{K}(\alpha)$, we denote the class of *convex functions of order α* in $\mathbb{U}$ that satisfy the following inequality:

$$\Re\left\{1 + \frac{zf''(z)}{f'(z)}\right\} > \alpha \qquad (z \in \mathbb{U}).$$

A function f of the form (1) is said to be *strongly starlike of order α*, $(0 < \alpha \leq 1)$, in $\mathbb{U}$ if

$$\left|\arg \frac{zf'(z)}{f(z)}\right| < \frac{\pi\alpha}{2} \qquad (z \in \mathbb{U}). \tag{2}$$

The set of all such functions is denoted by $\mathcal{S}_s^*(\alpha)$. Moreover, a function f of the form (1) is said to be *strongly convex of order* α, $(0 < \alpha \leq 1)$, in $\mathbb{U}$ if

$$\left| \arg\left(1 + \frac{zf''(z)}{f'(z)}\right) \right| < \frac{\pi\alpha}{2} \qquad (z \in \mathbb{U}). \tag{3}$$

The set of all such functions is denoted by $\mathcal{K}_c(\alpha)$.

The class $\mathcal{S}_s^*(\alpha)$ was independently introduced by Brannan and Kirwan [1] and Stankiewicz [2] (see also [3]). Clearly, $\mathcal{S}_s^*(1) = \mathcal{S}^*$ is the class of starlike functions and $\mathcal{K}_c^*(1) = \mathcal{K}$ is the class of convex functions in $\mathbb{U}$. We should observe that as α increases the sets $\mathcal{S}^*(\alpha)$ and $\mathcal{K}(\alpha)$ become smaller; however as α increases the sets $\mathcal{S}_s^*(\alpha)$ and $\mathcal{K}_c(\alpha)$ become larger. Furthermore, although the sharp coefficient bounds of the functions in the classes $\mathcal{S}^*(\alpha)$ and $\mathcal{K}(\alpha)$ are known, sharp coefficient bounds for the functions in the sets $\mathcal{S}_s^*(\alpha)$ and $\mathcal{K}_c(\alpha)$ are much harder to obtain, and only partial results are known [1,4].

Let $\mathcal{P}$ denote the class of analytic functions $p(z)$ in $\mathbb{U}$ satisfying $p(0) = 1$ and $\Re(p(z)) > 0$. Thus, if $p \in \mathcal{P}$, then have the following form:

$$p(z) = 1 + \sum_{k=1}^{\infty} c_k z^k, \qquad z \in \mathbb{U}. \tag{4}$$

Functions in $\mathcal{P}$ are called *Carathedory functions*.

Associated with each $f \in \mathcal{S}$, is a well-defined logarithmic function

$$\mathcal{F}_f := \log \frac{f(z)}{z} = 2 \sum_{k=1}^{\infty} \gamma_k z^k, \qquad z \in \mathbb{U}. \tag{5}$$

The numbers γ_k are called the *logarithmic coefficients of* f. The logarithmic coefficients are very essential in the problems of univalent functions coefficients. The importance of the logarithmic coefficients is due to the fact that the bounds on logarithmic coefficients of f can transfer to the Taylor coefficients of univalent functions themselves or to their powers, via the Lebedev–Milin inequalities.

Relatively little exact information is known about the logarithmic coefficients of f when $f \in \mathcal{S}$. The logarithmic coefficients of the Koebe function $\mathcal{K}(z) = z(1-z)^{-2}$ are $\gamma_k = 1/k$. Because of the extremal properties of the Koebe function, one could expect that $\gamma_k \leq 1/k$, for each $f \in \mathcal{S}$; however, this conjecture is false even in the case $k = 2$. For the whole class $\mathcal{S}$, the sharp estimates of single logarithmic coefficients are known only for

$$|\gamma_1| \leq 1 \quad \text{and} \quad |\gamma_2| \leq \frac{1}{2} + \frac{1}{e^2} = 0.6353\ldots$$

and are unknown for $k \geq 3$. Recently, logarithmic coefficients have been studied by various authors and upper bounds of logarithmic coefficients of functions in some important subclasses of $\mathcal{S}$ have been obtained (e.g., [5–10]). For a summary of some of the significant results concerning the logarithmic coefficients for univalent functions, we refer to [11].

For $q, n \in \mathbb{N}$, the Hankel determinant $H_{q,n}(f)$ of $f \in \mathcal{A}$ of form (1) is defined as

$$H_{q,n}(f) = \begin{vmatrix} a_n & a_{n+1} & \cdots & a_{n+q-1} \\ a_{n+1} & a_{n+2} & \cdots & a_{n+q} \\ \vdots & \vdots & & \vdots \\ a_{n+q-1} & a_{n+q} & \cdots & a_{n+2(q-1)} \end{vmatrix}.$$

The Hankel determinant $H_{2,1}(f) = a_3 - a_2^2$ is the well-known Fekete–Szegö functional. The second Hankel determinant $H_{2,2}(f)$ is given by $H_{2,2}(f) = a_2 a_4 - a_3^2$.

The problem of computing the upper bound of $H_{q,n}$ over various subfamilies of $\mathcal{A}$ is interesting and widely studied in the literature on the geometric function theory of complex analysis. The upper bounds of $H_{2,2}$, $H_{3,1}$ and higher-order Hankel determinants for subclasses of analytic functions were obtained by various authors [12–24].

Very recently, Kowalczyk and Lecko [25] introduced the Hankel determinant $H_{q,n}(F_f/2)$, which are logarithmic coefficients of f, i.e.,

$$H_{q,n}(F_f/2) = \begin{vmatrix} \gamma_n & \gamma_{n+1} & \cdots & \gamma_{n+q-1} \\ \gamma_{n+1} & \gamma_{n+2} & \cdots & \gamma_{n+q} \\ \vdots & \vdots & & \vdots \\ \gamma_{n+q-1} & \gamma_{n+q} & \cdots & \gamma_{n+2(q-1)} \end{vmatrix}.$$

For a function $f \in \mathcal{S}$ given in (1), by differentiating (5) one can obtain the following:

$$\gamma_1 = \frac{1}{2}a_2, \quad \gamma_2 = \frac{1}{2}\left(a_3 - \frac{1}{2}a_2^2\right), \quad \gamma_3 = \frac{1}{2}\left(a_4 - a_2 a_3 + \frac{1}{3}a_2^3\right). \tag{6}$$

Therefore, the second Hankel determinant of $F_f/2$ can be obtained by

$$H_{2,1}(F_f/2) = \gamma_1 \gamma_3 - \gamma_2^2 = \frac{1}{4}\left(a_2 a_4 - a_3^2 + \frac{1}{12}a_2^4\right). \tag{7}$$

Furthermore, if $f \in \mathcal{S}$, then for

$$f_\theta(z) = e^{-i\theta} f(e^{i\theta} z) \quad (\theta \in \mathbb{R}),$$

we find that (see [26])

$$H_{2,1}\left(\frac{F_{f_\theta}}{2}\right) = e^{4i\theta} H_{2,1}\left(\frac{F_f}{2}\right).$$

Kowalczyk and Lecko [26] obtained sharp bounds for $H_{2,1}(F_f/2)$ for the classes of starlike and convex functions of order α. The problem of computing the sharp bounds of $H_{2,1}(F_f/2)$ for starlike and convex functions with respect to symmetric points in the open unit disk has been considered by Allu and Arora [27].

In this paper, we calculate the sharp bounds for $H_{2,1}(F_f/2) = \gamma_1 \gamma_3 - \gamma_2^2$ for the classes $\mathcal{S}_s^*(\alpha)$ and $\mathcal{K}_c(\alpha)$.

To establish our main results, we will require the following Lemmas:

Lemma 1 ([28] (see also [26])). *If $p \in \mathcal{P}$ is of the form (4) with $c_1 \geq 0$, then*

$$\begin{aligned} c_1 &= 2d_1, \\ c_2 &= 2d_1^2 + 2(1 - d_1^2)d_2, \\ c_3 &= 2d_1^3 + 4(1 - d_1^2)d_1 d_2 - 2(1 - d_1^2)d_1 d_2^2 + 2(1 - d_1^2)(1 - |d_2|^2)d_3 \end{aligned} \tag{8}$$

for some $d_1 \in [0, 1]$ and $d_2, d_3 \in \overline{\mathbb{U}} = \{z \in \mathbb{C} : |z| \leq 1\}$.

For $d_1 \in \mathbb{U}$ and $d_2 \in \partial \mathbb{U} = \{z \in \mathbb{C} : |z| = 1\}$, there is a unique function $p \in \mathcal{P}$ with c_1 and c_2 as in (8), namely

$$p(z) = \frac{1 + (\overline{d_1} d_2 + d_1)z + d_2 z^2}{1 + (\overline{d_1} d_2 - d_1)z - d_2 z^2}, \quad z \in \mathbb{U}.$$

Lemma 2 ([29]). *Given real numbers A, B, C, let*

$$Y(A, B, C) = \max\left\{|A + Bz + Cz^2| + 1 - |z|^2 : z \in \overline{\mathbb{U}}\right\}.$$

I. If $AC \geq 0$, then

$$Y(A,B,C) = \begin{cases} |A| + |B| + |C|, & |B| \geq 2(1-|C|), \\ 1 + |A| + \frac{B^2}{4(1-|C|)}, & |B| < 2(1-|C|). \end{cases}$$

II. If $AC < 0$, then

$$Y(A,B,C) = \begin{cases} 1 - |A| + \frac{B^2}{4(1-|C|)}, & -4AC(C^{-2}-1) \leq B^2 \wedge |B| < 2(1-|C|), \\ 1 + |A| + \frac{B^2}{4(1+|C|)}, & B^2 < \min\{4(1+|C|)^2, -4AC(C^{-2}-1)\}, \\ R(A,B,C), & \text{otherwise.} \end{cases}$$

where

$$R(A,B,C) = \begin{cases} |A| + |B| - |C|, & |C|(|B|+4|A|) \leq |AB|, \\ -|A| + |B| + |C|, & |AB| \leq |C|(|B|-4|A|), \\ (|A|+|C|)\sqrt{1 - \frac{B^2}{4AC}}, & \text{otherwise.} \end{cases}$$

2. Second Hankel Determinant of Logarithmic Coefficients for the Class $\mathcal{S}_s^*(\alpha)$

Theorem 1. Let $\alpha \in (0,1]$. If $f \in \mathcal{S}_s^*(\alpha)$, then

$$\left|\gamma_1 \gamma_3 - \gamma_2^2\right| \leq \frac{\alpha^2}{4}. \tag{9}$$

This inequality is sharp. Equality holds for the function

$$f(z) = z \exp \int_0^z \frac{(1-u^2)^{-2\alpha} - 1}{u} du, \quad z \in \mathbb{U}. \tag{10}$$

Proof. Let $\alpha \in (0,1]$ and $f \in \mathcal{S}_s^*(\alpha)$ be of the form (1). Then by (2) we have

$$\frac{zf'(z)}{f(z)} = (p(z))^\alpha, \quad z \in \mathbb{U}, \tag{11}$$

for some function $p \in \mathcal{P}$ of the form (4). Since the class $\mathcal{P}$ and the functional $|H_{2,1}(F_f/2)|$ are rotationally invariant, we may assume that $c_1 \in [0,2]$ (i.e., in view of (8) that $d_1 \in [0,1]$). Equating the coefficients, we obtain

$$\begin{aligned} a_2 &= \alpha c_1 \\ a_3 &= \frac{\alpha}{2}\left(c_2 - \frac{1-3\alpha}{2}c_1^2\right) \\ a_4 &= \frac{\alpha}{3}\left(c_3 + \frac{5\alpha-2}{2}c_1 c_2 + \frac{17\alpha^2 - 15\alpha + 4}{12}c_1^3\right). \end{aligned} \tag{12}$$

Hence by using (6)–(8) we obtain

$$\gamma_1\gamma_3 - \gamma_2^2 = \frac{1}{4}\left(a_2 a_4 - a_3^2 + \frac{1}{12}a_2^4\right)$$

$$= \frac{\alpha^2}{576}\left[(7+\alpha)(1-\alpha)c_1^4 - 12(1-\alpha)c_1^2 c_2 + 48 c_1 c_3 - 36 c_2^2\right]$$

$$= \frac{\alpha^2}{36}\Big[(4-\alpha^2)d_1^4 + 6\alpha(1-d_1^2)d_1^2 d_2 - (1-d_1^2)\left[12 d_1^2 + 9(1-d_1^2)\right]d_2^2 \qquad (13)$$

$$+ 12(1-d_1^2)(1-|d_2|^2) d_1 d_3\Big].$$

Now, we may have the following cases on d_1:
Case 1. Suppose that $d_1 = 1$. Then by (13) we obtain

$$\left|\gamma_1\gamma_3 - \gamma_2^2\right| = \frac{\alpha^2}{36}(4-\alpha^2)$$

Case 2. Suppose that $d_1 = 0$. Then by (13) we obtain

$$\left|\gamma_1\gamma_3 - \gamma_2^2\right| = \frac{\alpha^2}{4}|d_2|^2 \leq \frac{\alpha^2}{4}.$$

Case 3. Suppose that $d_1 \in (0,1)$. By the fact that $|d_3| \leq 1$, applying the triangle inequality to (13) we can write

$$\left|\gamma_1\gamma_3 - \gamma_2^2\right| = \left|\frac{\alpha^2(1-d_1^2)}{3}\left[\frac{4-\alpha^2}{12(1-d_1^2)}d_1^4 + \frac{\alpha}{2}d_1^2 d_2 - \frac{12 d_1^2 + 9(1-d_1^2)}{12}d_2^2 + (1-|d_2|^2)d_1 d_3\right]\right|$$

$$\leq \frac{\alpha^2 d_1(1-d_1^2)}{3}\left[\left|\frac{4-\alpha^2}{12(1-d_1^2)}d_1^3 + \frac{\alpha}{2}d_1 d_2 - \frac{12 d_1^2 + 9(1-d_1^2)}{12 d_1}d_2^2\right| + 1 - |d_2|^2\right] \qquad (14)$$

$$= \frac{\alpha^2 d_1(1-d_1^2)}{3}\left[\left|A + B d_2 + C d_2^2\right| + 1 - |d_2|^2\right]$$

where

$$A = \frac{4-\alpha^2}{12(1-d_1^2)}d_1^3 \qquad B = \frac{\alpha}{2}d_1 \qquad C = -\frac{d_1^2+3}{4 d_1}.$$

Since $AC < 0$, we apply Lemma 2 only for the case II.
We consider the following sub-cases.
3 (a) Since

$$-4AC\left(\frac{1}{C^2}-1\right) - B^2 = \frac{(4-\alpha^2)d_1^2(d_1^2+3)}{12(1-d_1^2)}\left(\frac{16 d_1^2}{(d_1^2+3)^2}-1\right) - \frac{\alpha^2 d_1^2}{4} \leq 0$$

equivalent to $(1-\alpha^2)d_1^2 \leq 9$, which evidently holds for $d_1 \in (0,1)$. Further, the inequality $|B| < 2(1-|C|)$ is equivalent to $3 + (1+\alpha)d_1^2 - 4 d_1 < 0$ which is false for $d_1 \in (0,1)$.
3 (b) Since

$$4(1+|C|)^2 = \frac{(d_1^2 + 4 d_1 + 3)^2}{4 d_1^2} > 0$$

and

$$-4AC\left(\frac{1}{C^2}-1\right) = \frac{(4-\alpha^2)d_1^2(d_1^2-9)}{12(d_1^2+3)} < 0,$$

we see that the inequality

$$\frac{\alpha^2 d_1^2}{4} < \min\left\{4(1+|C|)^2, -4AC\left(\frac{1}{C^2}-1\right)\right\}$$

is false for $d_1 \in (0,1)$.

3 (c) The inequality

$$|C|\Big(|B|+4|A|\Big) - |AB| = \frac{(d_1^2+3)}{4d_1}\left(\frac{\alpha d_1}{2} + \frac{(4-\alpha^2)d_1^3}{3(1-d_1^2)}\right) - \frac{\alpha(4-\alpha^2)d_1^4}{24(1-d_1^2)} \leq 0,$$

is equivalent to

$$d^4(8+\alpha^3 - 2\alpha^2 - 7\alpha) + d^2(24 - 6\alpha^2 - 6\alpha) + 9\alpha \leq 0.$$

It is easy to verify that

$$d^4(8+\alpha^3 - 2\alpha^2 - 7\alpha) + d^2(24 - 6\alpha^2 - 6\alpha) + 9\alpha$$
$$> d^4(32 + \alpha^3 - 8\alpha^2 - 13\alpha) + 9\alpha > 0.$$

for $d_1 \in (0,1)$. Thus, the inequality $|C|\Big(|B|+4|A|\Big) \leq |AB|$ does not hold for $\alpha \in (0,1]$ and $d_1 \in (0,1)$.

3 (d) We can write

$$|AB| - |C|\Big(|B|-4|A|\Big) = \frac{\alpha(4-\alpha^2)d_1^4}{24(1-d_1^2)} - \frac{(d_1^2+3)}{4d_1}\left(\frac{\alpha d_1}{2} - \frac{(4-\alpha^2)d_1^3}{3(1-d_1^2)}\right)$$
$$= \frac{1}{24(1-t)}(K_1 t^2 + L_1 t + M_1)$$

where $t = d_1^2 \in (0,1)$ and

$$K_1 = -\alpha^3 - 2\alpha^2 + 7\alpha + 8$$
$$L_1 = 6(4 + \alpha - \alpha^2)$$
$$M_1 = -9\alpha.$$

It is easy to see that $K_1 > 0$, $L_1 > 0$ and $M_1 < 0$, for $\alpha \in (0,1]$.

For the equation $K_1 t^2 + L_1 t + M_1$, we have $\Delta = 144(4+4\alpha - \alpha^3) > 0$. Since $K_1 > 0$, $\frac{M_1}{K_1} < 0$ and $K_1 + L_1 + M_1 = 32 - \alpha^3 - 8\alpha^2 + 4\alpha > 0$, for $\alpha \in (0,1]$, the equation $K_1 t^2 + L_1 t + M_1$ has positive unique root such that

$$0 < t_1 = \frac{-L_1 + \sqrt{\Delta}}{2K_1} < 1,$$

Therefore, for $d_1^* = \sqrt{t_1}$, it follows that $|AB| = |C|\Big(|B|-4|A|\Big)$.

Moreover, $|AB| \leq |C|\Big(|B|-4|A|\Big)$, when $d_1 \in (0, d_1^*]$, and $|AB| \geq |C|\Big(|B|-4|A|\Big)$, when $d_1 \in [d_1^*, 1)$.

Then for $d_1 \in (0, d_1^*]$, we can write from (14) and Lemma 2, we obtain

$$\left|\gamma_1\gamma_3 - \gamma_2^2\right| \leq \frac{\alpha^2 d_1(1-d_1^2)}{3}\Big(-|A|+|B|+|C|\Big) = \Phi(d_1)$$

where

$$\Phi(d_1) = \frac{\alpha^2}{36}\left(-(4-\alpha^2)d_1^4 + 3(1+2\alpha)d_1^2(1-d_1^2) + 9(1-d_1^2)\right).$$

Since
$$\Phi'(d_1) = \frac{-\alpha^2 d_1}{9}\left[(7+6\alpha-\alpha^2)d_1^2 + 3(1-\alpha)\right] < 0,$$

for $d_1 \in [0, d_1^*]$, Φ is a decreasing function on $[0, d_1^*]$. This implies that

$$\left|\gamma_1\gamma_3 - \gamma_2^2\right| \le \Phi(0) = \frac{\alpha^2}{4}.$$

3 (e) Next consider the case $d_1 \in [d_1^*, 1]$. Using the last case of Lemma 2,

$$\left|\gamma_1\gamma_3 - \gamma_2^2\right| \le \frac{\alpha^2 d_1(1-d_1^2)}{3}\left((|A|+|C|)\sqrt{1-\frac{B^2}{4AC}}\right) = \Psi(d_1)$$

where
$$\Psi(d_1) = \frac{\alpha^2}{18}[9 + (1-\alpha^2)d_1^4 - 6d_1^2]\sqrt{\frac{(1-\alpha^2)d_1^2 + 3}{(4-\alpha^2)(d_1^2+3)}}.$$

To find the maximum of the function $\Psi(d_1)$ on the interval $d_1 \in [d_1^*, 1]$, let us investigate the derivative of $\Psi(d_1)$:

$$\Psi'(d_1) = \frac{-d_1^2\alpha^2}{18(4-\alpha^2)(d_1^2+3)^2}\sqrt{\frac{(4-\alpha^2)(d_1^2+3)}{(1-\alpha^2)d_1^2+3}}$$
$$\times \left[4(3-(1-\alpha^2)d_1^2)(d_1^2+3)((1-\alpha^2)d_1^2+3) + 3\alpha^2(9+(1-\alpha^2)d_1^4 - 6d_1^2))\right] < 0,$$

since
$$4(3-(1-\alpha^2)d_1^2 \ge 8 + 4\alpha^2 > 0$$

and
$$9 + (1-\alpha^2)d_1^4 - 6d_1^2 \ge 9 - d_1^2(6-(1-\alpha^2)d_1^2) = 3 + (1-\alpha^2)d_1^2 > 0$$

for $\alpha \in (0,1]$ and $d_1 \in [d_1^*, 1]$. Thus Ψ is a decreasing function on $[d_1^*, 1]$.
Furthermore, $\Phi(d_1^*) = \Psi(d_1^*)$. This implies that

$$\left|\gamma_1\gamma_3 - \gamma_2^2\right| \le \Psi(d_1) \le \Psi(d_1^*) = \Phi(d_1^*) \le \Phi(0) = \frac{\alpha^2}{4}.$$

Summarizing parts from Cases 1–3, it follows the desired inequality.

In order to show that the inequality is sharp, let us set $c_1 = 0$ and $d_2 = 1$ into (8). Then, we obtain $c_2 = 2$ and $c_3 = 0$. Hence by (12) we have $a_2 = a_4 = 0$ and $a_3 = \alpha$. This shows that equality is attained for the function given in (10).

This completes the proof of the theorem. □

For $\alpha = 1$ we obtain the bounds for the class $\mathcal{S}^*$ of starlike functions given in [25].

Corollary 1. *Let $f(z) \in \mathcal{S}^*$. Then*

$$\left|\gamma_1\gamma_3 - \gamma_2^2\right| \le \frac{1}{4}.$$

The inequality is sharp.

3. Second Hankel Determinant of Logarithmic Coefficients for the Class $\mathcal{K}_c(\alpha)$

Theorem 2. *Let $\alpha \in (0,1]$. If $f \in \mathcal{K}_c(\alpha)$, then*

$$|\gamma_1\gamma_3 - \gamma_2^2| \leq \begin{cases} \frac{\alpha^2}{36}, & 0 < \alpha \leq \frac{1}{3} \\ \frac{\alpha^2(13\alpha^2+18\alpha+17)}{144(\alpha^2+6\alpha+4)}, & \frac{1}{3} < \alpha \leq 1. \end{cases} \quad (15)$$

The inequalities in (15) are sharp.

Proof. Let $\alpha \in (0,1]$ and $f \in \mathcal{K}_c(\alpha)$ be of the form (1). Then, by (3), we have

$$1 + \frac{zf''(z)}{f'(z)} = (p(z))^\alpha, \quad z \in \mathbb{U}, \quad (16)$$

for some function $p \in \mathcal{P}$ of the form (4). As in the proof of Theorem 1, we may assume that $c_1 \in [0,2]$ (i.e., in view of (8) that $d_1 \in [0,1]$). Equating the coefficients, we obtain

$$a_2 = \frac{\alpha}{2}c_1$$

$$a_3 = \frac{\alpha}{6}\left(c_2 - \frac{1-3\alpha}{2}c_1^2\right) \quad (17)$$

$$a_4 = \frac{\alpha}{144}\left((17\alpha^2 - 15\alpha + 4)c_1^3 + 6(5\alpha - 2)c_1c_2 + 12c_3\right).$$

Hence, by using (6)–(8) we obtain

$$\begin{aligned}\gamma_1\gamma_3 - \gamma_2^2 &= \frac{1}{4}\left(a_2a_4 - a_3^2 + \frac{1}{12}a_2^4\right) \\ &= \frac{\alpha^2}{2304}\left[(\alpha^2 - 6\alpha + 4)c_1^4 + 4(3\alpha - 2)c_1^2c_2 + 24c_1c_3 - 16c_2^2\right] \\ &= \frac{\alpha^2}{144}\Big[(2+\alpha^2)d_1^4 + 6\alpha(1-d_1^2)d_1^2d_2 - (1-d_1^2)[6d_1^2 + 4(1-d_1^2)]d_2^2 \\ &\quad + 6(1-d_1^2)(1-|d_2|^2)d_1d_3\Big]. \end{aligned} \quad (18)$$

Now, we may have the following cases on d_1:

Case 1. Suppose that $d_1 = 1$. Then, by (18) we obtain

$$|\gamma_1\gamma_3 - \gamma_2^2| = \frac{\alpha^2}{144}(2+\alpha^2)$$

Case 2. Suppose that $d_1 = 0$. Then, by (18) we obtain

$$|\gamma_1\gamma_3 - \gamma_2^2| = \frac{\alpha^2}{36}|d_2|^2 \leq \frac{\alpha^2}{36}.$$

Case 3. Suppose that $d_1 \in (0,1)$. By the fact that $|d_3| \leq 1$, applying the triangle inequality to (18) we can write

$$\begin{aligned}
\left|\gamma_1\gamma_3 - \gamma_2^2\right| &= \left|\frac{\alpha^2}{144}\left[(2+\alpha^2)d_1^4 + 6\alpha(1-d_1^2)d_1^2 d_2\right.\right.\\
&\quad \left.\left. - (1-d_1^2)[6d_1^2 + 4(1-d_1^2)]d_2^2 + 6(1-d_1^2)(1-|d_2|^2)d_1 d_3\right]\right| \\
&< \frac{\alpha^2 d_1(1-d_1^2)}{24}\left[\left|\frac{(2+\alpha^2)}{6(1-d_1^2)}d_1^3 + \alpha d_1 d_2 - \frac{4+2d_1^2}{6d_1}d_2^2\right| + 1 - |d_2|^2\right] \\
&= \frac{\alpha^2 d_1(1-d_1^2)}{24}\left[\left|A + B d_2 + C d_2^2\right| + 1 - |d_2|^2\right]
\end{aligned} \quad (19)$$

where

$$A = \frac{2+\alpha^2}{6(1-d_1^2)}d_1^3 \qquad B = \alpha d_1 \qquad C = -\frac{2+d_1^2}{3d_1}.$$

Since $AC < 0$, we apply Lemma 2 only for the case II.
We consider the following sub-cases.
3 (a) Note that

$$\begin{aligned}
-4AC\left(\frac{1}{C^2}-1\right) - B^2 &= \frac{-d_1^2[d_1^2(7\alpha^2 - 4) + 26\alpha^2 + 16]}{9(d_1^2+2)} \\
&= \frac{-d_1^2[\alpha^2(7d_1^2+26) + 4(4-d_1^2)]}{9(d_1^2+2)} \leq 0.
\end{aligned}$$

for $d_1 \in (0,1)$ and $\alpha \in (0,1]$. On the other hand, we have

$$|B| - 2(1-|C|) = \frac{d_1^2(3\alpha+2) - 6d_1 + 4}{3d_1}.$$

Since $\Delta = 4(1-12\alpha) \leq 0$ for $\frac{1}{12} \leq \alpha < 1$, we have

$$d_1^2(3\alpha+2) - 6d_1 + 4 \geq 0.$$

Further, since $\Delta = 4(1-12\alpha) > 0$ for $0 < \alpha < \frac{1}{12}$, the equation

$$d_1^2(3\alpha+2) - 6d_1 + 4 = 0$$

has the roots

$$s_{1,2} = \frac{3 \pm \sqrt{1-12\alpha}}{3\alpha+2}$$

which are greater than 1. So

$$d_1^2(3\alpha+2) - 6d_1 + 4 > 0$$

for $d_1 \in (0,1)$ and $\alpha \in (0,1]$.
Consequently $|B| < 2(1-|C|)$ does not hold for $d_1 \in (0,1)$ and $\alpha \in (0,1]$.
3 (b) Since

$$4(1+|C|)^2 = \frac{4(d_1^2 + 3d_1 + 2)^2}{9d_1^2} > 0$$

and

$$-4AC\left(\frac{1}{C^2}-1\right) = -\frac{2d_1^2(4-d_1^2)(\alpha^2+2)}{9(d_1^2+2)} < 0,$$

we see that the inequality

$$\alpha^2 d_1^2 < \min\left\{4(1+|C|)^2, -4AC\left(\frac{1}{C^2}-1\right)\right\}$$

is false for $d_1 \in (0,1)$.

3 (c) We can write

$$|C|\Big(|B|+4|A|\Big) - |AB| = \frac{1}{18(1-d_1^2)}(K_2 d_1^4 + L_2 d_1^2 + M_2)$$

where

$$K_2 = -3\alpha^3 + 4\alpha^2 - 12\alpha + 8$$
$$L_2 = 8\alpha^2 - 6\alpha + 16$$
$$M_2 = 12\alpha.$$

It is easy to see that $L_2 > 0$ and $M_2 > 0$, for $\alpha \in (0,1]$.

There are two cases according to the sign of K_2:

(i) If $K_2 \geq 0$, then we have

$$|C|\Big(|B|+4|A|\Big) - |AB| = \frac{1}{18(1-d_1^2)}(K_2 d_1^4 + L_2 d_1^2 + M_2) > 0.$$

(ii) If $K_2 < 0$, then using the fact that $\alpha \in (0,1]$ and $d_1 \in (0,1)$, we can write

$$|C|\Big(|B|+4|A|\Big) - |AB| = \frac{1}{18(1-d_1^2)}(K_2 d_1^4 + L_2 d_1^2 + M_2)$$
$$> \frac{1}{18(1-d_1^2)}(K_2 + L_2 d_1^2 + M_2)$$
$$= \frac{1}{18(1-d_1^2)}\left(L_2 d_1^2 - 3\alpha^3 + 4\alpha^2 + 8\right)$$
$$\geq \frac{1}{18(1-d_1^2)}\left(L_2 d_1^2 + 5 + 4\alpha^2\right) > 0.$$

Therefore, the inequality $|C|\Big(|B|+4|A|\Big) \leq |AB|$ does not hold for $\alpha \in (0,1]$ and $d_1 \in (0,1)$.

3 (d) We can write

$$|AB| - |C|\Big(|B|-4|A|\Big) = \frac{\alpha(\alpha^2+2)}{6(1-d_1^2)}d_1^4 - \frac{d_1^2+2}{3d_1}\left(\alpha d_1 - 4\frac{\alpha^2+2}{6(1-d_1^2)}d_1^3\right)$$
$$= \frac{1}{18(1-t)}\left(K_3 t^2 + L_3 t + M_3\right)$$

where $t = d_1^2 \in (0,1)$ and

$$K_3 = 3\alpha^3 + 4\alpha^2 + 12\alpha + 8$$
$$L_3 = 8\alpha^2 + 6\alpha + 16$$
$$M_3 = -12\alpha.$$

It is easy to see that $K_3 > 0$, $L_3 > 0$ and $M_3 < 0$, for $\alpha \in (0,1]$.

For the equation $K_3 t^2 + L_3 t + M_3 = 0$, we have $\Delta > 0$. Since $\frac{M_3}{K_3} < 0$ and $K_3 + L_3 + M_3 > 0$, for $\alpha \in (0,1]$, the equation $K_3 t^2 + L_3 t + M_3 = 0$ has a unique positive root $t_1 < 1$.

Thus, the inequality $|AB| - |C|(|B| - 4|A|) \leq 0$ holds for $(0, d_1^{**}]$, where $d_1^{**} = \sqrt{t_1}$. So we can write from (19) and Lemma 2,

$$\left|\gamma_1\gamma_3 - \gamma_2^2\right| \leq \frac{\alpha^2 d_1(1-d_1^2)}{24}\left(-|A| + |B| + |C|\right)$$

$$= \frac{\alpha^2}{144}\Phi_1(d_1)$$

where

$$\Phi_1(d_1) = \left(Dd_1^4 + Ed_1^2 + 4\right),$$

and

$$D = -(\alpha^2 + 6\alpha + 4)$$
$$E = 6\alpha - 2.$$

If $\Phi_1'(d_1) = 2d_1(2Dd_1^2 + E) = 0$, then $d_1^2 = -\frac{E}{2D}$. So if $E = 6\alpha - 2 > 0$, i.e., $\frac{1}{3} < \alpha \leq 1$, then we have a critical point:

$$\xi = \sqrt{-\frac{E}{2D}} = \sqrt{\frac{3\alpha - 1}{\alpha^2 + 6\alpha + 4}}. \tag{20}$$

Since

$$K_3\xi^4 + L_3\xi^2 + M_3 = K_3\left(\frac{3\alpha-1}{\alpha^2+6\alpha+4}\right)^2 + L_3\left(\frac{3\alpha-1}{\alpha^2+6\alpha+4}\right) + M_3$$

$$= \frac{39\alpha^5 + 28\alpha^4 - 243\alpha^3 - 296\alpha^2 - 156\alpha - 56}{(\alpha^2 + 6\alpha + 4)^2}$$

$$\leq \frac{-243\alpha^3 - 296\alpha^2 - 89\alpha - 56}{(\alpha^2 + 6\alpha + 4)^2}$$

$$< 0,$$

we have $0 < \xi < d_1^{**}$; therefore, we obtain

$$\left|\gamma_1\gamma_3 - \gamma_2^2\right| \leq \frac{\alpha^2}{144}\Phi_1(\xi)$$

$$= \frac{\alpha^2(13\alpha^2 + 18\alpha + 17)}{144(\alpha^2 + 6\alpha + 4)},$$

for $\frac{1}{3} < \alpha \leq 1$.

Furthermore, if $0 < \alpha \leq \frac{1}{3}$, then the function $\Phi_1(d_1)$ is decreasing on $(0, d_1^{**}]$. Thus we have

$$\left|\gamma_1\gamma_3 - \gamma_2^2\right| \leq \frac{\alpha^2}{144}\Phi_1(d_1)$$

$$\leq \frac{\alpha^2}{36}.$$

3 (e) Next consider the case $d_1 \in [d_1^{**}, 1]$. Using the last case of the Lemma 2,

$$\left|\gamma_1\gamma_3 - \gamma_2^2\right| \le \frac{\alpha^2 d_1(1-d_1^2)}{24}\left((|A|+|C|)\sqrt{1-\frac{B^2}{4AC}}\right)$$
$$= \frac{\alpha^2}{144}\Psi_1(d_1)$$

where
$$\Psi_1(d_1) = (\alpha^2 d_1^4 - 2d_1^2 + 4)\sqrt{1 + \frac{9\alpha^2(1-d_1^2)}{2(\alpha^2+2)(d_1^2+2)}}.$$

To find the maximum of the function $\Psi_1(d_1)$ on the interval $d_1 \in [d_1^{**}, 1]$, let us investigate the derivative of $\Psi_1(d_1)$:

$$\Psi_1'(d_1) = \frac{-d_1}{(\alpha^2+2)(d_1^2+2)^2}\sqrt{\frac{(\alpha^2+2)(d_1^2+2)}{(4-7\alpha^2)d_1^2+13\alpha^2+8}} \times$$
$$\left\{4(d_1^2+2)\left(1-\alpha^2 d_1^2\right)\left[\left(4-7\alpha^2\right)d_1^2 + 13\alpha^2 + 8\right] + \left(\alpha^2 d_1^4 - 2d_1^2 + 4\right)27\alpha^2\right\}.$$

Since for $d_1 \in [d_1^{**}, 1]$
$$\left(4 - 7\alpha^2\right)d_1^2 + 13\alpha^2 + 8 = \alpha^2(13-7d_1^2) + 4(d_1^2+2) > 0$$

and
$$\left(\alpha^2 d_1^4 - 2d_1^2 + 4\right) = 4 - d_1^2(2-\alpha^2 d_1^2) \ge 4 - (2-\alpha^2 d_1^2) = 2 + \alpha^2 d_1^2 > 0,$$

for $\alpha \in (0,1]$ and $d_1 \in [d_1^{**}, 1]$. Thus $\Psi_1(d_1)$ is a decreasing function on the interval $[d_1^{**}, 1]$. This implies that

$$\left|\gamma_1\gamma_3 - \gamma_2^2\right| \le \frac{\alpha^2}{144}\Psi_1(d_1) \le \frac{\alpha^2}{144}\Psi_1(d_1^{**}) = \frac{\alpha^2}{144}\Phi_1(d_1^{**}).$$

Summarizing parts from Cases 1–3, it follows the desired inequalities.
To show the sharpness for the case $0 < \alpha \le \frac{1}{3}$, consider the function

$$p_1(z) = \frac{1-z^2}{1+z^2}, \quad (z \in \mathbb{U}).$$

It is obvious that the function p_1 is in $\mathcal{P}$ with $c_1 = c_3 = 0$ and $c_2 = -2$. The corresponding function f_1 can be obtained from (16). Hence, by (17) we have $a_2 = a_4 = 0$ and $a_3 = -\frac{\alpha}{3}$. From (18) we obtain

$$\left|\gamma_1\gamma_3 - \gamma_2^2\right| = \frac{\alpha^2}{36},$$

for $0 < \alpha \le \frac{1}{3}$.
For the case $\frac{1}{3} < \alpha \le 1$, consider the function

$$p_2(z) = \frac{1-z^2}{1-2\xi z + z^2}, \quad (z \in \mathbb{U})$$

where ξ is given in (20). From Lemma 1, it is obvious that the function p_2 is in $\mathcal{P}$. The corresponding function f_2 can be obtained from (16), having the following coefficients:

$$a_2 = \alpha\xi,$$
$$a_3 = \frac{1}{3}\alpha\left((1+3\alpha)\xi^2 - 1\right),$$
$$a_4 = \frac{1}{18}\alpha\xi\left((17\alpha^2 + 15\alpha + 4)\xi^2 - 15\alpha - 3\right).$$

Hence from (18) we obtain

$$\left|\gamma_1\gamma_3 - \gamma_2^2\right| = \frac{\alpha^2(13\alpha^2 + 18\alpha + 17)}{144(\alpha^2 + 6\alpha + 4)}.$$

This completes the proof. □

For $\alpha = 1$ we obtain the bounds for the class $\mathcal{K}$ of convex functions given in [25].

Corollary 2. *Let* $f(z) \in \mathcal{K}$. *Then*

$$\left|\gamma_1\gamma_3 - \gamma_2^2\right| \leq \frac{1}{33}.$$

The inequality is sharp.

4. Discussion

In this work, we have obtained the sharp bounds for the second Hankel determinant of logarithmic coefficients of strongly starlike functions and strongly convex functions. Because of the importance of the logarithmic coefficients of univalent functions, our results provide a basis for research on the Hankel determinant of the logarithmic coefficients of the class of strongly starlike and strongly convex functions and other classes associated with these classes. Furthermore, our results could also inspire further studies taking other subclasses of $\mathcal{S}$ into consideration and/or obtaining the bounds for higher-order Hankel determinants.

Author Contributions: Conceptualization, S.S.E., B.Ş., B.Ç. and M.A.; methodology, S.S.E., B.Ş., B.Ç. and M.A.; writing—original draft preparation, S.S.E., B.Ş., B.Ç. and M.A.; investigation, S.S.E., B.Ş., B.Ç. and M.A. All authors have read and agreed to the published version of the manuscript.

Funding: This research received no external funding.

Data Availability Statement: Not applicable.

Conflicts of Interest: The authors declare no conflict of interest.

References

1. Brannan, D.A.; Kirwan, W.E. On some classes of bounded univalent functions. *J. Lond. Math. Soc.* **1969**, *2*, 431–443. [CrossRef]
2. Stankiewicz, J. On a family of starlike functions. *Ann. Univ. Mariae Curie-Sklodowska Sect. A* **1968**, *22–24*, 175–181.
3. Goodman, A.W. *Univalent Functions*; Mariner Comp.: Tampa, FL, USA, 1983; Volume 1.
4. Brannan, D.; Clunie, J.; Kirwan, W. Coefficient Estimates for a Class of Star-Like Functions. *Can. J. Math.* **1970**, *22*, 476–485. [CrossRef]
5. Ali, M.F.; Vasudevarao, A. On logarithmic coefficients of some close-to-convex functions. *Proc. Am. Math. Soc.* **2018**, *146*, 1131–1142 [CrossRef]
6. Ali, M.F.; Vasudevarao, A.; Thomas, D.K. On the third logarithmic coefficients of close-to-convex functions. *Curr. Res. Math. Comput. Sci. II* **2018**, 271–278.
7. Cho, N.E.; Kowalczyk, B.; Kwon, O.S.; Lecko, A.; Sim, Y.J. On the third logarithmic coefficient in some subclasses of close-to-convex functions. *Rev. Real. Acad. Cienc. Exactas Fis. Nat. Ser. A Mat.* **2020**, *114*, 1–14. [CrossRef]
8. Kumar, U.P.; Vasudevarao, A. Logarithmic coefficients for certain subclasses of close-to-convex functions. *Monats. Math.* **2018**, *187*, 543–563. [CrossRef]
9. Thomas, D.K. On logarithmic coefficients of close to convex functions. *Proc. Am. Math. Soc.* **2016**, *144*, 1681–1687. [CrossRef]
10. Zaprawa, P. Initial logarithmic coefficients for functions starlike with respect to symmetric points. *Bol. Soc. Mat. Mex.* **2021**, *27*, 1–13. [CrossRef]

11. Vasudevarao, A.; Thomas, D.K. The logarithmic coefficients of univalent functions—An overview. *Curr. Res. Math. Comput. Sci. II* **2018**, 257–269.
12. Cho, N.E.; Kowalczyk, B.; Kwon, O.S.; Lecko, A.; Sim, Y.J. Some Coefficient Inequalities Related to the Hankel Determinant for Strongly Starlike Functions of Order Alpha. *J. Math. Ineq.* **2017**, *11*, 429–439. [CrossRef]
13. Janteng, A.; Halim, S.A.; Darus, M. Hankel determinant for starlike and convex functions. *Int. J. Math. Anal.* **2007**, *1*, 619–625.
14. Kowalczyk, B.; Lecko, A.; Sim, Y.J. The sharp bound for the Hankel determinant of the third kind for convex functions. *Bull. Aust. Math. Soc.* **2018**, *97*, 435–445. [CrossRef]
15. Krishna, D.V.; Ramreddy, T. Hankel determinant for starlike and convex functions of order alpha. *Tbilisi Math. J.* **2012**, *5*, 65–76. [CrossRef]
16. Lee, S.K.; Ravichandran, V.; Supramaniam, S. Bounds for the second Hankel determinant of certain univalent functions. *J. Inequal. Appl.* **2013**, *2013*, 281. [CrossRef]
17. Sokol, J.; Thomas, D.K. The second Hankel determinant for alpha-convex functions. *Lith. Math. J.* **2018**, *58*, 212–218. [CrossRef]
18. Srivastava, H.M.; Ahmad, Q.Z.; Darus, M.; Khan, N.; Khan, B.; Zaman, N.; Shah, H.H. Upper bound of the third Hankel determinant for a subclass of close-to-convex functions associated with the lemniscate of Bernoulli. *Mathematics* **2019**, *7*, 848. [CrossRef]
19. Sim, Y.J.; Lecko, A.; Thomas, D.K. The second Hankel determinant for strongly convex and Ozaki close-to-convex functions. *Ann. Mat.* **2021**, *200*, 2515–2533. [CrossRef]
20. Shi, L.; Srivastava, H.M.; Arif, M.; Hussain, S.; Khan, H. An investigation of the third Hankel determinant problem for certain subfamilies of univalent functions involving the exponential function. *Symmetry* **2019**, *11*, 598. [CrossRef]
21. Breaz, V.D.; Cătaş, A.; Cotîrlă, L. On the Upper Bound of the Third Hankel Determinant for Certain Class of Analytic Functions Related with Exponential Function. *An. Şt. Univ. Ovidius Constanţa* **2022**, *30*, 75–89 [CrossRef]
22. Khan, B.; Aldawish, I.; Araci, S.; Khan, M.G. Third Hankel Determinant for the Logarithmic Coefficients of Starlike Functions Associated with Sine Function. *Fractal Fract.* **2022**, *6*, 261. [CrossRef]
23. Shi, L.; Khan, M.G.; Ahmad, B.; Mashwani, W.K.; Agarwal, P.; Momani, S. Certain Coefficient Estimate Problems for Three-Leaf-Type Starlike Functions. *Fractal Fract.* **2021**, *5*, 137. [CrossRef]
24. Rahman, I.A.R.; Atshan, W.G.; Oros, G.I. New concept on fourth Hankel determinant of a certain subclass of analytic functions. *Afr. Mat.* **2022**, *33*, 7. [CrossRef]
25. Kowalczyk, B.; Lecko, A. Second Hankel determinant of logarithmic coefficients of convex and starlike functions. *Bull. Aust. Math. Soc.* **2022**, *105*, 458–467. [CrossRef]
26. Kowalczyk, B.; Lecko, A. Second hankel determinant of logarithmic coefficients of convex and starlike functions of order alpha. *Bull. Malays. Math. Sci. Soc.* **2022**, *45*, 727–740. [CrossRef]
27. Allu, V.; Arora, V. Second Hankel determinant of logarithmic coefficients of certain analytic functions. *arXiv* **2021**, arXiv:2110.05161.
28. Cho, N.; Kowalczyk, B.; Lecko, A. Sharp Bounds of Some Coefficient Functionals Over The Class of Functions Convex in The Direction of the Imaginary Axis. *Bull. Aust. Math. Soc.* **2019**, *100*, 86–96. [CrossRef]
29. Choi, J.H.; Kim, Y.C.; Sugawa, T. A general approach to the Fekete–Szegö problem. *J. Math. Soc. Jpn.* **2007**, *59*, 707–727. [CrossRef]

Article

New Results about Radius of Convexity and Uniform Convexity of Bessel Functions

Luminița-Ioana Cotîrlă [1,*], **Pál Aurel Kupán** [2] **and Róbert Szász** [2]

[1] Department of Mathematics, Technical University of Cluj-Napoca, 400114 Cluj-Napoca, Romania
[2] Department of Mathematics and Informatics, Sapientia Hungarian University of Transylvania, 540485 Târgu Mureș, Romania; kupanp@ms.sapientia.ro (P.A.K.); rszasz@ms.sapientia.ro (R.S.)
* Correspondence: luminita.cotirla@math.utcluj.ro

Abstract: We determine in this paper new results about the radius of uniform convexity of two kinds of normalization of the Bessel function J_ν in the case $\nu \in (-2, -1)$, and provide an alternative proof regarding the radius of convexity of order alpha. We then compare results regarding the convexity and uniform convexity of the considered functions and determine interesting connections between them.

Keywords: Bessel function; convex function; uniformly convex functions; radius of convexity

MSC: 33C10

1. Introduction

Let $U(r) = \{z \in \mathbb{C} : |z| < r\}$ be the disk, centered at zero, of radius r, where $r > 0$. We denote by $U(r) = U(0, r)$.
We say that a function f of the form

$$f(z) = z + a_2 z^2 + \ldots \quad (1)$$

is convex on $U(r)$ if and only if $f(U(r))$ is a convex domain in the set $\mathbb{C}$ and the function f is univalent.
We know that the function f is convex on $U(r)$ if and only if

$$\operatorname{Re}\left(1 + \frac{zf''(z)}{f'(z)}\right) > 0, \ z \in U(r).$$

We say that f is a convex function of order α on $U(r)$ if

$$\operatorname{Re}\left(1 + \frac{zf''(z)}{f'(z)}\right) > \alpha, \ z \in U(r).$$

The radius of convexity of order α for f is defined by the equality

$$r_f^c(\alpha) = \sup\left\{r \in (0, \infty) : \operatorname{Re}\left(1 + \frac{zf''(z)}{f'(z)}\right) > \alpha, \ z \in U(r)\right\}. \quad (2)$$

We say that f is uniformly convex in the disk $U(r)$ if the function f has the form in (1), it is a convex function, and it has the property that the arc $f(\gamma)$ is convex for every circular arc γ contained in the disk $U(r)$ with center ζ, also in $U(r)$. The function f is uniformly convex in the disk $U(r)$ if and only if

$$\operatorname{Re}\left(1 + \frac{zf''(z)}{f'(z)}\right) > \left|\frac{zf''(z)}{f'(z)}\right|, \ z \in U(r).$$

We know that the radius of uniform convexity is defined by

$$r_f^{uc}(\alpha) = \sup\left\{r \in (0,\infty) : \text{Re}\left(1 + \frac{zf''(z)}{f'(z)}\right) > \left|\frac{zf''(z)}{f'(z)}\right|, \ z \in U(r)\right\}. \qquad (3)$$

The Bessel function of the first kind is defined by

$$J_\nu(z) = \sum_{n=0}^{\infty} \frac{(-1)^n}{n!\Gamma(n+\nu+1)} (z/2)^{2n+\nu}.$$

Consider the following normalized forms:

$$g_\nu(z) = 2^\nu \Gamma(1+\nu) z^{1-\nu} J_\nu(z) = z - \frac{1}{4(\nu+1)} z^3 + \ldots, \qquad (4)$$

and

$$h_\nu(z) = 2^\nu \Gamma(1+\nu) z^{1-\nu/2} J_\nu(z^{\frac{1}{2}}) = z - \frac{1}{4(\nu+1)} z^2 + \ldots, \qquad (5)$$

where ν is a real number and $-2 < \nu < -1$, and g_ν and h_ν are entire functions.

This article can be considered a continuation of previous papers [1,2] which dealt with geometric properties of Bessel functions.

For more details about the geometric properties of Bessel functions, interested readers are referred to the following papers: [1,3–13].

The aim of this work is to determine the radius of convexity of order α, $r_f^c(\alpha)$ for $f = g_\nu$ and $f = h_\nu$ and the radius of uniform convexity $r_f^{uc}(\alpha)$ for the case $\nu \in (-2,-1)$ and to derive an interesting connection between the convexity and uniform convexity.

In the next section, we provide several results which are necessary later in this work.

2. Preliminaries

Lemma 1 ([14], p. 483, Hurwitz). *If $\nu \in (-2,-1)$, then $J_\nu(z)$ has exactly two purely imaginary conjugate complex zeros, and all the other zeros are real.*

The zeros $z^{-\nu} J_\nu(z)$ are taken to be $\pm j_{\nu,n}$, where $n \in \mathbb{N}^* = \{1,2,3,\ldots\}$. We may suppose, without restricting the generality, that $j_{\nu,1} = ia$, $a > 0$, and $0 < a < j_{\nu,2} < j_{\nu,3} < \cdots < j_{\nu,n} < \cdots$.

Lemma 2 ([14], p. 502). *The following equality holds*

$$\sum_{n=1}^{\infty} \frac{1}{j_{\nu,n}^2} = \frac{1}{4(\nu+1)}. \qquad (6)$$

Lemma 3 ([8]). *In the notations of Lemma 2, we have*

$$\frac{zg'_\nu(z)}{g_\nu(z)} = 1 - 2\sum_{n=1}^{\infty} \frac{z^2}{j_{\nu,n}^2 - z^2}, \qquad (7)$$

and

$$\frac{zh'_\nu(z)}{h_\nu(z)} = 1 - \sum_{n=1}^{\infty} \frac{z}{j_{\nu,n}^2 - z}. \qquad (8)$$

The series are uniformly convergent on every compact subset of $\mathbb{C} \setminus \{\pm j_{\nu,n} : n \in \mathbb{N}^*\}$.

Lemma 4 ([9]). *If $v \in \mathbb{C}$, $\delta \in \mathbb{R}$, and $\delta > \rho \geq |v|$, then*

$$\left|\frac{v}{\delta - v}\right| \leq \frac{\rho}{\delta - \rho} \quad \text{and} \quad \left|\frac{v}{(\delta - v)^2}\right| \leq \frac{\rho}{(\delta - \rho)^2}.$$

Proof. The following implications hold

$$|\delta - v| \geq \delta - \rho \Rightarrow \frac{1}{|\delta - v|} \leq \frac{1}{\delta - \rho} \Rightarrow \left|\frac{1}{(\delta - v)^2}\right| \leq \frac{1}{(\delta - \rho)^2}.$$

If the last two inequalities are multiplied by the inequality $|v| \leq \rho$, we obtain the desired results. □

Lemma 5. *If $v \in \mathbb{C}$, $\delta, \gamma \in \mathbb{R}$, $\gamma \geq \delta > \rho \geq |v|$, then*

$$\left|\frac{v^2}{(\delta + v)(\gamma - v)}\right| \leq \frac{\rho^2}{(\delta - \rho)(\gamma + \rho)}. \tag{9}$$

Proof. We can prove the second inequality of the following equivalence:

$$\left|\frac{1}{(\delta + v)(\gamma - v)}\right| \leq \frac{1}{(\delta - \rho)(\gamma + \rho)} \Leftrightarrow (\delta - \rho)(\gamma + \rho) \leq |(\delta + v)(\gamma - v)|, \tag{10}$$

where $\gamma \geq \delta > \rho \geq |v|$.

We prove the inequality (10) in two steps.

Let $v = x + iy$; then, it is obvious that

$$|(\delta + v)(\gamma - v)| = \sqrt{[(\delta + x)^2 + y^2][(+y^2 + \gamma - x)^2]} \geq |(\gamma - x)(\delta + x)|, \tag{11}$$

where $\gamma \geq \delta > \rho \geq \sqrt{x^2 + y^2}$.

On the other hand, a simple calculation results in

$$(\delta + x)(\gamma - x) \geq (\delta - \rho)(\gamma + \rho), \; x \in [-\rho, \rho]. \tag{12}$$

It is easily seen that (11) and (12) imply the second inequality of (10). Finally, multiplying the inequality $\rho^2 \geq |v|^2$ by the first inequality of (10), we obtain (9) and the proof is complete. □

Lemma 6. *If $v \in \mathbb{C}$, $\delta, \gamma \in \mathbb{R}$, and $\gamma \geq \delta > \rho \geq |v|$, then*

$$\left|\frac{2v^2[2\gamma\delta + (\gamma - \delta)v]}{(\gamma - v)^2(\delta + v)^2}\right| \leq \frac{2r^2|2\gamma\delta - (\gamma - \delta)\rho|}{(\gamma + \rho)^2(\delta - \rho)^2}. \tag{13}$$

Proof. The inequality obviously holds provided that $\gamma = \delta$ (see (10)), thus, we have to prove it in the case that $\gamma > \delta$.

We can then prove the following inequality:

$$\left|\frac{2\gamma\delta + (\gamma - \delta)v}{(\delta + v)(\gamma - v)}\right| \leq \frac{2\gamma\delta - (\gamma - \delta)\rho}{(\delta - \rho)(\gamma + \rho)}, \; \gamma \geq \delta > \rho \geq |v|. \tag{14}$$

We define $z = x + iy$ and define the mapping

$$\phi : [-\rho, \rho] \to \mathbb{R}, \; \phi(y) = \frac{(\omega + x)^2 + y^2}{[(\delta + x)^2 + y^2][(\gamma - x)^2 + y^2]}, \; \omega = \frac{2\gamma\delta}{\gamma - \delta}.$$

Then, we have

$$\phi'(y) = 2y\frac{[(\delta+x)^2+y^2][(\gamma-x)^2+y^2]-[(\delta+x)^2+(\gamma-x)^2+2y^2][(\omega+x)^2+y^2]}{[(\delta+x)^2+y^2]^2[(\gamma-x)^2+y^2]^2}.$$

As $\phi'(y) < 0$, $y \in (0, \rho)$ and $\phi'(y) > 0$, $y \in (-\rho, 0)$, it follows that

$$\phi(y) \leq \phi(0) = \frac{(\omega+x)^2}{[(\delta+x)^2][(\gamma-x)^2]}, \ y \in [-\rho, \rho]. \tag{15}$$

We can determine the maximum of the function

$$\varphi : [-\rho, \rho] \to \mathbb{R}, \ \varphi(x) = \frac{\omega+x}{(\delta+x)(\gamma-x)}.$$

We have

$$\varphi'(x) = \frac{x^2 + 2\omega x - \gamma\delta}{(\delta+x)^2(\gamma-x)^2}.$$

The derivative $\varphi'(x) = 0$ has one positive root, $x_1 = \sqrt{\omega^2 + \gamma\delta} - \omega$, and one negative root, $x_2 = -\sqrt{\omega^2 + \gamma\delta} - \omega$. As $x_2 < -r$ and $x_1 \in (-\rho, \rho)$, it follows the inequality

$$\frac{\omega+x}{(\delta+x)(\gamma-x)} = \varphi(x) \leq \max\{\varphi(-\rho), \varphi(\rho)\} = \varphi(-\rho) = \frac{\omega-\rho}{(\delta-\rho)(\gamma+\rho)} \tag{16}$$

for every $x \in [-\rho, \rho]$. From (15) and (16), we have (14). Finally, multiplying the inequalities (14), $|v^2| \leq \rho^2$ and the first inequality of (10), we infer (13). □

Lemma 7. *If the functions g_ν and h_ν are defined by (4) and (5), respectively, then*

$$\frac{zg_\nu''(z)}{g_\nu'(z)} = z\frac{zJ_{\nu+2}(z) - 3J_{\nu+1}(z)}{J_\nu(z) - zJ_{\nu+1}(z)}. \tag{17}$$

$$\frac{zh_\nu''(z)}{h_\nu'(z)} = \frac{zJ_{\nu+2}(z^{\frac{1}{2}}) - 4z^{\frac{1}{2}}J_{\nu+1}(z^{\frac{1}{2}})}{4J_\nu(z^{\frac{1}{2}}) - 2z^{\frac{1}{2}}J_{\nu+1}(z^{\frac{1}{2}})}. \tag{18}$$

Proof. We differentiate the equality (4), and at the second time we differentiate it logarithmically. After multiplying by z, we obtain the following equality:

$$\frac{zg_\nu''(z)}{g_\nu'(z)} = \frac{z^2J_\nu''(z) + 2z(1-\nu)J_\nu'(z) + \nu(\nu-1)J_\nu(z)}{zJ_\nu'(z) + (1-\nu)J_\nu(z)}.$$

The function J_ν is a solution of the Bessel differential equation; thus, we can replace the function $z^2 J_\nu''$ using the equality $z^2 J_\nu''(z) = (\nu^2 - z^2)J_\nu(z) - zJ_\nu'(z)$, and it follows that

$$\frac{zg_\nu''(z)}{g_\nu'(z)} = \frac{z(1-2\nu)J_\nu'(z) + (2\nu^2 - \nu - z^2)J_\nu(z)}{zJ_\nu'(z) + (1-\nu)J_\nu(z)}.$$

In the second step, we use the following well-known equality: $zJ_\nu'(z) = \nu J_\nu(z) - zJ_{\nu+1}(z)$, and infer

$$\frac{zg_\nu''(z)}{g_\nu'(z)} = \frac{z(2\nu-1)J_{\nu+1}(z) - z^2J_\nu(z)}{J_\nu(z) - zJ_{\nu+1}(z)}.$$

Finally, we replace $zJ_\nu(z)$ in the numerator by $zJ_\nu(z) = 2(\nu+1)J_{\nu+1}(z) - zJ_{\nu+2}(z)$, and obtain (17).

We differentiate equality (5) twice, similarly to the case of the function g_ν, and obtain

$$\frac{zh_\nu''(z)}{h_\nu'(z)} = \frac{\nu(\nu-2)J_\nu(z^{\frac{1}{2}}) + (3-2\nu)z^{\frac{1}{2}}J_\nu'(z^{\frac{1}{2}}) + zJ_\nu''(z^{\frac{1}{2}})}{2(2-\nu)J_\nu(z^{\frac{1}{2}}) + 2z^{\frac{1}{2}}J_\nu'(z^{\frac{1}{2}})}.$$

We use the equality $zJ_\nu''(z^{\frac{1}{2}}) = (\nu^2 - z)J_\nu(z^{\frac{1}{2}}) - z^{\frac{1}{2}}J_\nu'(z^{\frac{1}{2}})$, and obtain

$$\frac{zh_\nu''(z)}{h_\nu'(z)} = \frac{(2\nu^2 - 2\nu - z)J_\nu(z^{\frac{1}{2}}) + (2-2\nu)z^{\frac{1}{2}}J_\nu'(z^{\frac{1}{2}})}{2(2-\nu)J_\nu(z^{\frac{1}{2}}) + 2z^{\frac{1}{2}}J_\nu'(z^{\frac{1}{2}})}.$$

Now, using the equality $z^{\frac{1}{2}}J_\nu'(z^{\frac{1}{2}}) = \nu J_\nu(z^{\frac{1}{2}}) - z^{\frac{1}{2}}J_{\nu+1}(z^{\frac{1}{2}})$, we infer

$$\frac{zh_\nu''(z)}{h_\nu'(z)} = \frac{(2\nu-2)z^{\frac{1}{2}}J_{\nu+1}(z^{\frac{1}{2}}) - zJ_\nu(z^{\frac{1}{2}})}{4J_\nu(z^{\frac{1}{2}}) - 2z^{\frac{1}{2}}J_{\nu+1}(z^{\frac{1}{2}})},$$

and combining this with the equality $z^{\frac{1}{2}}J_\nu(z^{\frac{1}{2}}) = 2(\nu+1)J_{\nu+1}(z^{\frac{1}{2}}) - z^{\frac{1}{2}}J_{\nu+2}(z^{\frac{1}{2}})$, (18) follows. □

3. Main Results

Theorem 1. *If $\alpha \in [0,1)$ and $\nu \in (-2,-1)$, then the radius of convexity of order α for the mapping g_ν is $r_\nu^c(\alpha) = r_1$, where r_1 is the unique root of the equation*

$$1 + r\frac{I_{\nu+2}(r) + 3I_{\nu+1}(r)}{I_{\nu+1}(r) + rI_\nu(r)} = \alpha \tag{19}$$

in the interval $(0, a)$.

Proof. According to the proof of Theorem 1 [2], the equalities

$$\frac{zg_\nu'(z)}{g_\nu(z)} = 1 - 2\sum_{n=1}^{\infty} \frac{z^2}{j_{\nu,n}^2 - z^2}, \quad \sum_{n=1}^{\infty} \frac{1}{j_{\nu,n}^2} = \frac{1}{4(\nu+1)}.$$

imply

$$\frac{zg_\nu'(z)}{g_\nu(z)} = 1 - \frac{a^2}{2(1+\nu)} \frac{z^2}{a^2 + z^2} - 2\sum_{n=2}^{\infty} \frac{a^2 + j_{\nu,n}^2}{j_{\nu,n}^2} \frac{z^4}{(a^2+z^2)(j_{\nu,n}^2 - z^2)}.$$

The logarithmic differentation of this equality leads to

$$1 + \frac{zg_\nu''(z)}{g_\nu'(z)} =$$

$$1 - \frac{a^2}{2(1+\nu)}\frac{z^2}{a^2+z^2} - 2\sum_{n=2}^{\infty}\frac{a^2+j_{\nu,n}^2}{j_{\nu,n}^2}\frac{z^4}{(a^2+z^2)(j_{\nu,n}^2-z^2)} - \frac{\frac{a^2}{1+\nu}\frac{a^2z^2}{(a^2+z^2)^2} + 2\sum_{n=2}^{\infty}\frac{a^2+j_{\nu,n}^2}{j_{\nu,n}^2}\frac{2z^4[2a^2j_{\nu,n}^2+z^2(j_{\nu,n}^2-a^2)]}{(a^2+z^2)^2(j_{\nu,n}^2-z^2)^2}}{1 - \frac{a^2}{2(1+\nu)}\frac{z^2}{a^2+z^2} - 2\sum_{n=2}^{\infty}\frac{a^2+j_{\nu,n}^2}{j_{\nu,n}^2}\frac{z^4}{(a^2+z^2)(j_{\nu,n}^2-z^2)}}. \tag{20}$$

It is proven in Theorem 1 [2] that the radius of starlikeness, $r_{g_\nu}^*$, for the function g_ν is the smallest root of the equation

$$1 + \frac{a^2}{2(1+\nu)}\frac{r^2}{a^2 - r^2}$$

$$-2\sum_{n=2}^{\infty}\frac{a^2 + j_{\nu,n}^2}{j_{\nu,n}^2}\frac{r^4}{(a^2-r^2)(j_{\nu,n}^2+r^2)} = ir\frac{g_\nu'(ir)}{g_\nu(ir)} = 0,$$

in the interval $(0, a)$. Thus, we have

$$0 < r_{g_\nu}^* < a < j_{\nu,2} < j_{\nu,3} < \cdots < j_{\nu,n} < \cdots. \tag{21}$$

Taking into account that $\nu + 1 < 0$, the equality (20) implies the following inequality:

$$\operatorname{Re}\left(1 + \frac{zg_\nu''(z)}{g_\nu'(z)}\right) \geq$$

$$\frac{1 + \frac{a^2}{2(1+\nu)}\left|\frac{z^2}{a^2+z^2}\right| - 2\sum_{n=2}^{\infty}\frac{a^2+j_{\nu,n}^2}{j_{\nu,n}^2}\left|\frac{z^4}{(a^2+z^2)(j_{\nu,n}^2-z^2)}\right| -}{1 + \frac{a^2}{2(1+\nu)}\left|\frac{z^2}{a^2+z^2}\right| - 2\sum_{n=2}^{\infty}\frac{a^2+j_{\nu,n}^2}{j_{\nu,n}^2}\left|\frac{z^4}{(a^2+z^2)(j_{\nu,n}^2-z^2)}\right|} \tag{22}$$

$$\frac{-\frac{a^2}{1+\nu}\left|\frac{a^2z^2}{(a^2+z^2)^2}\right| + 2\sum_{n=2}^{\infty}\frac{a^2+j_{\nu,n}^2}{j_{\nu,n}^2}\left|\frac{2z^4[2a^2j_{\nu,n}^2+z^2(j_{\nu,n}^2-a^2)]}{(a^2+z^2)^2(j_{\nu,n}^2-z^2)^2}\right|}{1 + \frac{a^2}{2(1+\nu)}\left|\frac{z^2}{a^2+z^2}\right| - 2\sum_{n=2}^{\infty}\frac{a^2+j_{\nu,n}^2}{j_{\nu,n}^2}\left|\frac{z^4}{(a^2+z^2)(j_{\nu,n}^2-z^2)}\right|}$$

for every $z \in U(r_\nu^*)$.

Using $\delta = a^2, \rho = r^2$ and $v = z^2$ in Lemma 4, we obtain

$$\frac{a^2}{2(1+\nu)}\left|\frac{z^2}{a^2+z^2}\right| \geq \frac{a^2}{2(1+\nu)}\frac{r^2}{a^2-r^2} \text{ and } \frac{a^2}{2(1+\nu)}\left|\frac{z^2}{(a^2+z^2)^2}\right| \geq \tag{23}$$

$$\frac{a^2}{(a^2-r^2)^2}\frac{r^2}{2(1+\nu)}.$$

In a similar manner, Lemma 5 and Lemma 6 imply that

$$\left|\frac{z^4}{(a^2+z^2)(j_{\nu,n}^2-z^2)}\right| \leq \frac{r^4}{(a^2-r^2)(j_{\nu,n}^2+r^2)} \tag{24}$$

$$\left|\frac{2z^4[2a^2j_{\nu,n}^2+z^2(j_{\nu,n}^2-a^2)]}{(a^2+z^2)^2(j_{\nu,n}^2-z^2)^2}\right| \leq \frac{2r^4[2a^2j_{\nu,n}^2-r^2(j_{\nu,n}^2-a^2)]}{(a^2-r^2)^2(j_{\nu,n}^2+r^2)^2}.$$

Now, inequalities (22)–(24) imply the following inequality:

$$\operatorname{Re}\left(1 + \frac{zg_\nu''(z)}{g_\nu'(z)}\right) \geq$$

$$\frac{1 + \frac{a^2}{2(1+\nu)}\frac{r^2}{a^2-r^2} - 2\sum_{n=2}^{\infty}\frac{a^2+j_{\nu,n}^2}{j_{\nu,n}^2}\frac{r^4}{(a^2-r^2)(j_{\nu,n}^2+r^2)} -}{1 + \frac{a^2}{2(1+\nu)}\frac{z^2}{a^2-r^2} - 2\sum_{n=2}^{\infty}\frac{a^2+j_{\nu,n}^2}{j_{\nu,n}^2}\frac{r^4}{(a^2-r^2)(j_{\nu,n}^2+r^2)}} \tag{25}$$

$$\frac{-\frac{a^2}{1+\nu}\frac{a^2r^2}{(a^2-r^2)^2} + 2\sum_{n=2}^{\infty}\frac{a^2+j_{\nu,n}^2}{j_{\nu,n}^2}\frac{2r^4[2a^2j_{\nu,n}^2-r^2(j_{\nu,n}^2-a^2)]}{(a^2-r^2)^2(j_{\nu,n}^2+r^2)^2}}{\cdots} = 1 + \frac{irg_\nu''(ir)}{g_\nu'(ir)} = \Phi(r),$$

provided that $a > r_{g_\nu}^* > |z|$, where $r_{g_\nu}^*$ verifies the inequalities (21).

The following equalities hold: $\Phi(0) = 1$ and $\lim_{r \nearrow r_{g_\nu}^*} \Phi(r) = -\infty$. Consequently, equation $1 + \frac{irg_\nu''(ir)}{g_\nu'(ir)} = \alpha$ has a real root in the interval $(0, r_{g_\nu}^*)$. The smallest positive real root of the equation $1 + \frac{irg_\nu''(ir)}{g_\nu'(ir)} = \alpha$ is denoted by $r_{g_\nu}^c(\alpha)$, and this root is the radius of convexity of order α of the function g_ν. The first equality of Lemma 7 and the equality $J_\nu(iz) = i^\nu I_\nu(z)$ imply that the equation $1 + \frac{irg_\nu''(ir)}{g_\nu'(ir)} = \alpha$ is equivalent to (19).
□

We determine the radius of uniform convexity of the mapping g_ν in the next theorem.

Theorem 2. If $\nu \in (-2, -1)$, then the radius of uniform convexity for the mapping g_ν is $r_\nu^*(\alpha) = r_2$, where r_2 is the smallest positive root of the equation

$$\frac{1}{2} + r\frac{I_{\nu+2}(r) + 3I_{\nu+1}(r)}{I_{\nu+1}(r) + rI_\nu(r)} = 0 \tag{26}$$

in the interval $(0, r_\nu^*)$.

Proof. Equality (20) implies the following inequality:

$$\left|\frac{zg_\nu''(z)}{g_\nu'(z)}\right| \leq \frac{-\frac{a^2}{2(1+\nu)}\left|\frac{z^2}{a^2+z^2}\right| + 2\sum_{n=2}^{\infty}\frac{a^2+j_{\nu,n}^2}{j_{\nu,n}^2}\left|\frac{z^4}{(a^2+z^2)(j_{\nu,n}^2-z^2)}\right| + \frac{-\frac{a^2}{1+\nu}\left|\frac{a^2z^2}{(a^2+z^2)^2}\right| + 2\sum_{n=2}^{\infty}\frac{a^2+j_{\nu,n}^2}{j_{\nu,n}^2}\left|\frac{2z^4[2a^2j_{\nu,n}^2+z^2(j_{\nu,n}^2-a^2)]}{(a^2+z^2)^2(j_{\nu,n}^2-z^2)^2}\right|}{1+\frac{a^2}{2(1+\nu)}\left|\frac{z^2}{a^2+z^2}\right| - 2\sum_{n=2}^{\infty}\frac{a^2+j_{\nu,n}^2}{j_{\nu,n}^2}\left|\frac{z^4}{(a^2+z^2)(j_{\nu,n}^2-z^2)}\right|}}. \tag{27}$$

We can again use inequalities (22) and (23), and in combination with (27), we have

$$\left|\frac{zg_\nu''(z)}{g_\nu'(z)}\right| \leq \frac{-\frac{a^2}{2(1+\nu)}\frac{r^2}{a^2-r^2} + 2\sum_{n=2}^{\infty}\frac{a^2+j_{\nu,n}^2}{j_{\nu,n}^2}\frac{r^4}{(a^2-r^2)(j_{\nu,n}^2+r^2)} + \frac{-\frac{a^2}{1+\nu}\frac{a^2r^2}{(a^2-r^2)^2} + 2\sum_{n=2}^{\infty}\frac{a^2+j_{\nu,n}^2}{j_{\nu,n}^2}\frac{2r^4[2a^2j_{\nu,n}^2-r^2(j_{\nu,n}^2-a^2)]}{(a^2-r^2)^2(j_{\nu,n}^2+r^2)^2}}{1+\frac{a^2}{2(1+\nu)}\frac{r^2}{a^2-r^2} - 2\sum_{n=2}^{\infty}\frac{a^2+j_{\nu,n}^2}{j_{\nu,n}^2}\frac{r^4}{(a^2-r^2)(j_{\nu,n}^2+r^2)}}} = -\frac{irg_\nu''(ir)}{g_\nu'(ir)}.$$

Inequalities (25) and (27) imply

$$\operatorname{Re}\left(1 + \frac{zg_\nu''(z)}{g_\nu'(z)}\right) - \left|\frac{zg_\nu''(z)}{g_\nu'(z)}\right| \geq 1 + 2\frac{irg_\nu''(ir)}{g_\nu'(ir)}, \quad z \in U(r_\nu^*). \tag{28}$$

The smallest positive root of the equation $1 + 2\frac{irg_\nu''(ir)}{g_\nu'(ir)} = 0$ in the interval $(0, r_\nu^*)$ is denoted by r_ν^{uc}. According to (28), the value r_ν^{uc} is the biggest with the property that

$$\operatorname{Re}\left(1 + \frac{zg_\nu''(z)}{g_\nu'(z)}\right) - \left|\frac{zg_\nu''(z)}{g_\nu'(z)}\right| > 0, \quad z \in U(r_\nu^{uc}).$$

Lemma 7 and the equality $J_\nu(iz) = i^\nu I_\nu(z)$ imply that the equation $1 + 2\frac{irg_\nu''(ir)}{g_\nu'(ir)} = 0$ is equivalent to (26), completing the proof. □

Theorems 1 and 2 imply the following result.

Corollary 1. The mapping g_ν is uniformly convex in the disk $U(r)$ if and only if it is convex of order $\frac{1}{2}$.

Theorem 3. If $\alpha \in [0, 1)$ and $\nu \in (-2, -1)$, then the radius of convexity of order α for the mapping h_ν is $r_{h_\nu}^c(\alpha) = r_3$, where r_3 is the smallest real root of the equation

$$1 + \frac{rI_{\nu+2}(r^{\frac{1}{2}}) + 4r^{\frac{1}{2}}I_{\nu+1}(r^{\frac{1}{2}})}{4I_\nu(r^{\frac{1}{2}}) + 2r^{\frac{1}{2}}I_{\nu+1}(r^{\frac{1}{2}})} = \alpha \tag{29}$$

in the interval $(0, r_{h_\nu}^*)$.

Proof. According to the proof of Theorem 2 [2], the equalities

$$\frac{zh'_\nu(z)}{h_\nu(z)} = 1 - \sum_{n=1}^{\infty} \frac{z}{j_{\nu,n}^2 - z}, \quad \sum_{n=1}^{\infty} \frac{1}{j_{\nu,n}^2} = \frac{1}{4(\nu+1)}$$

imply

$$\frac{zh'_\nu(z)}{h_\nu(z)} = 1 - \frac{a^2}{4(\nu+1)} \cdot \frac{z}{a^2+z} - \sum_{n=2}^{\infty} \frac{a^2 + j_{\nu,n}^2}{j_{\nu,n}^2} \cdot \frac{z^2}{(a^2+z)(j_{\nu,n}^2 - z)},$$

where $z \in U(0,r)$.

The logarithmic differentiation of the equality leads to

$$1 + \frac{zh''_\nu(z)}{h'_\nu(z)} = 1 - \frac{a^2}{4(\nu+1)} \cdot \frac{z}{a^2+z} - \sum_{n=2}^{\infty} \frac{a^2 + j_{\nu,n}^2}{j_{\nu,n}^2} \cdot \frac{z^2}{(a^2+z)(j_{\nu,n}^2 - z)} -$$

$$\frac{\frac{a^2}{4(1+\nu)} \cdot \frac{a^2 z}{(a^2+z)^2} + \sum_{n=2}^{\infty} \frac{a^2 + j_{\nu,n}^2}{j_{\nu,n}^2} \cdot \frac{z^2[2a^2 j_{\nu,n}^2 + z(j_{\nu,n}^2 - a^2)]}{(j_{\nu,n}^2 - z)^2 (a^2+z)^2}}{1 - \frac{a^2}{4a^2 + z} \cdot \frac{z}{(\nu+1)} - \sum_{n=2}^{\infty} \frac{a^2 + j_{\nu,n}^2}{j_{\nu,n}^2} \cdot \frac{z^2}{(j_{\nu,n}^2 - z)(a^2+z)}}. \quad (30)$$

It is proven in [2] that the radius of starlikeness, $r^*_{h_\nu}$, for function h_ν is the smallest root of the equation

$$\frac{-rh'_\nu(-r)}{h_\nu(-r)} = 0, \; r \in \left(0, a^2\right), \; z \in U(0,r).$$

However,

$$\frac{-rh'_\nu(-r)}{h_\nu(-r)} = 1 + \frac{a^2}{4(\nu+1)} \cdot \frac{r}{a^2 - r} -$$

$$- \sum_{n=2}^{\infty} \frac{a^2 + j_{\nu,n}^2}{j_{\nu,n}^2} \cdot \frac{r^2}{(a^2-r)(j_{\nu,n}^2 + r)} = 0, \; r \in \left(0, a^2\right).$$

Taking into the account that $\nu + 1 < 0$, we obtain from relation (30)

$$\operatorname{Re}\left(1 + \frac{zh''_\nu(z)}{h'_\nu(z)}\right) \geq \frac{a^2}{4(\nu+1)} \cdot \left|\frac{z}{a^2+z}\right| - \sum_{n=2}^{\infty} \frac{a^2 + j_{\nu,n}^2}{j_{\nu,n}^2} \cdot \left|\frac{z^2}{(a^2+z)(j_{\nu,n}^2 - z)}\right| -$$

$$\frac{\frac{-a^2}{4(\nu+1)} \cdot \left|\frac{a^2 z}{(a^2+z)^2}\right| + \sum_{n=2}^{\infty} \frac{a^2 + j_{\nu,n}^2}{j_{\nu,n}^2} \cdot \left|\frac{z^2[2a^2 j_{\nu,n}^2 + z(j_{\nu,n}^2 - a^2)]}{(a^2+z)^2 (j_{\nu,n}^2 - z)^2}\right|}{1 + \frac{a^2}{4(\nu+1)} \cdot \left|\frac{z}{a^2+z}\right| - \sum_{n}^{\infty} \frac{a^2 + j_{\nu,n}^2}{j_{\nu,n}^2} \cdot \left|\frac{z^2}{(a^2+z)(j_{\nu,n}^2 - z)}\right|} \quad (31)$$

and $z \in U(0,r), r \in \left(0, r^*_{h_\nu}\right)$. We obtain from Lemmas 4 and 5 the following inequality:

$$\operatorname{Re}\left(1 + \frac{zh''_\nu(z)}{h'_\nu(z)}\right) \geq 1 + \frac{a^2}{4(\nu+1)} \cdot \frac{r}{a^2 - r} - \sum_{n=2}^{\infty} \frac{a^2 + j_{\nu,n}^2}{j_{\nu,n}^2} \cdot \frac{r^2}{(a^2-r)(a^2+r)} -$$

$$\frac{-\frac{a^2}{4(\nu+1)} \cdot \frac{a^2 r}{(a^2-r)^2} + \sum_{n=2}^{\infty} \frac{a^2 + j_{\nu,n}^2}{j_{\nu,n}^2} \cdot \frac{r^2[2a^2 j_{\nu,n}^2 - r(j_{\nu,n}^2 - a^2)]}{(a^2-r)^2 (j_{\nu,n}^2 + r)^2}}{1 + \frac{a^2}{4(\nu+1)} \cdot \frac{r}{a^2 - r} - \sum_{n=2}^{\infty} \frac{a^2 + j_{\nu,n}^2}{j_{\nu,n}^2} \cdot \frac{r^2}{(a^2-r)(j_{\nu,n}^2 - r)}} = \quad (32)$$

$$= 1 - \frac{rh''_\nu(-r)}{h'_\nu(-r)} = \psi(r), \; a > r^*_{h_\nu} > |z|,$$

similarly to the proof of Theorem 1. The mapping

$$\psi : \left(0, r_{h_\nu}^*\right) \to \mathbb{R}, \ \psi(r) = 1 + \frac{-rh_\nu''(-r)}{h_\nu'(-r)},$$

is strictly decreasing, and $a > r_{h_\nu}^* > |z|$.

We then have $\lim_{r \nearrow r_{h_\nu}^*} \psi(r) = -\infty$, $\psi(0) = 1$, and the equation

$$1 + \frac{-rh_\nu''(-r)}{h_\nu'(-r)} = \alpha$$

has at least one real root in the interval $\left(0, r_{h_\nu}^*\right)$.

The smallest positive real root of the equation $1 - \frac{rh_\nu''(-r)}{h_\nu'(-r)} = \alpha$ is denoted by $r_{h_\nu}^c(\alpha)$, and this root is the radius of convexity of order α of the function h_ν. The second equality of Lemma 7 and the equality $J_\nu(iz) = i^\nu I_\nu(z)$ imply that the equation $1 - \frac{rh_\nu''(-r)}{h_\nu'(-r)} = \alpha$ is equivalent to (29). □

Theorem 4. *If $\alpha \in [0, 1)$ and $\nu \in (-2, -1)$, then the radius of uniform convexity of h_ν is $r_{h_\nu}^*(\alpha) = r_4$, where r_4 is the smallest positive root of the equation*

$$\frac{r I_{\nu+2}(r^{\frac{1}{2}}) + 4r^{\frac{1}{2}} I_{\nu+1}(r^{\frac{1}{2}})}{4 I_\nu(r^{\frac{1}{2}}) + 2r^{\frac{1}{2}} I_{\nu+1}(r^{\frac{1}{2}})} = \frac{1}{2} \tag{33}$$

in the interval $(0, r_{h_\nu}^*)$.

Proof. Equality (30) implies the following inequality:

$$\left| \frac{zh_\nu''(z)}{h_\nu'(z)} \right| \leq -\frac{a^2}{4(\nu+1)} \cdot \left| \frac{z}{a^2+z} \right| + \sum_{n=2}^{\infty} \frac{a^2 + j_{\nu,n}^2}{j_{\nu,n}^2} \cdot \left| \frac{z^2}{(a^2+z)(j_{\nu,n}^2 - z)} \right| +$$

$$+ \frac{\frac{-a^2}{4(\nu+1)} \cdot \left| \frac{a^2 z}{(a^2+z)^2} \right| + \sum_{n=2}^{\infty} \frac{a^2 + j_{\nu,n}^2}{j_{\nu,n}^2} \cdot \left| \frac{z^2 [2a^2 j_{\nu,n}^2 + z(j_{\nu,n}^2 - a^2)]}{(a^2+z)^2 (j_{\nu,n}^2 - z)^2} \right|}{1 + \frac{a^2}{4(\nu+1)} \cdot \left| \frac{z}{a^2+z} \right| - \sum_{n=2}^{\infty} \frac{a^2 + j_{\nu,n}^2}{j_{\nu,n}^2} \cdot \left| \frac{z^2}{(a^2+z)(j_{\nu,n}^2 - z)} \right|}. \tag{34}$$

We obtain the following from the relation (31), Lemma 4, and the relation (34):

$$\left| \frac{zh_\nu''(z)}{h_\nu'(z)} \right| \leq -\frac{a^2}{4(\nu+1)} \cdot \frac{r}{a^2 - r} + \sum_{n=2}^{\infty} \frac{a^2 + j_{\nu,n}^2}{j_{\nu,n}^2} \cdot \frac{r^2}{(a^2 - r)(j_{\nu,n}^2 + r)} +$$

$$+ \frac{\frac{a^2}{4(\nu+1)} \cdot \frac{a^2 r}{(a^2-r)^2} + \sum_{n=2}^{\infty} \frac{a^2 + j_{\nu,n}^2}{j_{\nu,n}^2} \cdot \frac{r^2[2a^2 j_{\nu,n}^2 - r(j_{\nu,n}^2 - a^2)]}{(a^2-r)^2 (j_{\nu,n}^2 + r)^2}}{1 - \frac{a^2}{4(a^2-r)} \cdot \frac{r}{\nu+1} - \sum_{n=2}^{\infty} \frac{a^2 + j_{\nu,n}^2}{j_{\nu,n}^2} \cdot \frac{r^2}{(a^2-r)(j_{\nu,n}^2 + r)}} = \frac{rh_\nu''(-r)}{h_\nu'(-r)}, |z| \leq r < a^2.$$

Inequalities (32) and (34) imply

$$\mathrm{Re}\left(1 + \frac{zh_\nu''(z)}{h_\nu'(z)}\right) - \left|\frac{zh_\nu''(z)}{h_\nu'(z)}\right| \geq 1 - \frac{2rh_\nu''(-r)}{h_\nu'(-r)}, \ z \in U(r_{h_\nu}^*). \tag{35}$$

The smallest positive root of the equation $1 - \frac{2rh_\nu''(-r)}{h_\nu'(-r)} = 0$ in the interval $(0, r_{h_\nu}^*)$ is denoted by $r_{h_\nu}^{uc}$.

According to (35), the value $r_{h_\nu}^{uc}$ is the biggest with the property that

$$\text{Re}\left(1 + \frac{zh_\nu''(z)}{h_\nu'(z)}\right) - \left|\frac{zh_\nu''(z)}{h_\nu'(z)}\right| > 0, \ z \in U(r_{h_\nu}^{uc}).$$

The equation $1 - \frac{2rh_\nu''(-r)}{h_\nu'(-r)} = 0$ is equivalent to (33), completing the proof. Lemma 7 and the equality $J_\nu(iz) = i^\nu I_\nu(z)$ imply that the equation $1 - \frac{2rh_\nu''(-r)}{h_\nu'(-r)} = 0$ is equivalent to (33). □

From Theorems 3 and 4, we obtain the following corollary.

Corollary 2. *The function h_ν is uniformly convex in the disk $U(r)$ if and only if it is convex of order $\frac{1}{2}$.*

Author Contributions: Conceptualization, L.-I.C., R.S. and P.A.K.; methodology, R.S.; software, L.-I.C., R.S. and P.A.K.; validation, R.S.; formal analysis, L.-I.C., R.S. and P.A.K.; investigation, L.-I.C., R.S. and P.A.K.; resources, L.-I.C., R.S. and P.A.K.; data curation, L.-I.C., R.S. and P.A.K.; writing—original draft preparation, L.-I.C., R.S. and P.A.K.; writing—review and editing, L.-I.C., R.S. and P.A.K.; visualization, L.-I.C., R.S. and P.A.K.; supervision, R.S.; project administration, L.-I.C., R.S. and P.A.K.; funding acquisition, L.-I.C., R.S. and P.A.K. All authors have read and agreed to the published version of the manuscript.

Funding: This research received no external funding.

Institutional Review Board Statement: Not applicable.

Informed Consent Statement: Not applicable.

Data Availability Statement: Not applicable.

Acknowledgments: The authors would like to express their sincere thanks to the referees for their valuable suggestions.

Conflicts of Interest: The authors declare no conflict of interest.

References

1. Deniz, E.; Szász, R. The radius of uniform convexity of Bessel functions. *J. Math. Anal. Appl.* **2017**, *453*, 572–588. [CrossRef]
2. Szász, R. About the radius of starlikeness of Bessel functions of the first kind. *Monatsh. Math.* **2015**, *176*, 323–330. [CrossRef]
3. Baricz, Á.; Szakál, A.; Szász, R.; Yagmur, N. Radii of starlikeness and convexity of a product and cross-product of Bessel functions. *Results Math.* **2018**, *73*, 62. [CrossRef]
4. Baricz, Á. Geometric properties of generalized Bessel functions. *Publ. Math. Debrecen* **2008**, *73*, 155–178.
5. Baricz, Á; *Generalized Bessel Functions of the First Kind*; Lecture Notes in Mathematics, 1994; Springer: Berlin/Heidelberg, Germany, 2010; Volume XIV, p. 206, ISBN: 978-3-642-12229-3.
6. Baricz, Á; Ponnusamy, S. Starlikeness and convexity of generalized Bessel functions. *Integral Transform. Spec. Funct.* **2010**, *21*, 641–653. [CrossRef]
7. Baricz, R. The radius of convexity of normalized Bessel functions. *Anal. Math.* **2015**, *41*, 141–151. [CrossRef]
8. Baricz Á.; Kupán, A.P.; Szász, R. The radius of starlikeness of normalized Bessel functions of the first kind. *Proc. AMS* **2014**, *142*, 2019–2025. [CrossRef]
9. Bulut, S.; Engel, O. The radius of starlikeness, Convexity and uniform convexity of the Legendre polynomials of odd degree. *Results Math.* **2019**, *74*, 48. [CrossRef]
10. Liang, Ch.Y.; Engel, O. Certain properties of the generalized Mittag-Leffler function.. *Electronic J. Math. Anal. Appl.* **2018**, *6*, 288–294.
11. Murat, Ç.; Deniz, E.; Szász, R. Radii of a-convexity of some normalized Bessel functions of the first kind. *Results Math.* **2017**, *72*, 2023–2035.
12. Engel, O.; Kupán, A.P.; Páll-Szabó, Á.O. About the radius of convexity of some analytic functions. *Creat. Math. Inform.* **2015**, *24*, 155–161. [CrossRef]
13. Engel, O.; Páll-Szabó, Á.O. The radius of convexity of particular functions and applications to the study of a second order differential inequality. *Izv. Nats. Akad. Nauk Armenii Mat.* **2017**, *52*, 127–132. Reprinted in *J. Contemp. Math. Anal.* **2017**, *52*, 118–127. [CrossRef]
14. Watson, G.N. *A Treatise of the Theory of Bessel Functions*; Cambridge University Press: Cambridge, UK, 1944.

Article

Cauchy Integral and Boundary Value for Vector-Valued Tempered Distributions

Richard D. Carmichael

Department of Mathematics, Wake Forest University, Winston-Salem, NC 27109, USA; carmicha@wfu.edu

Abstract: Using the historically general growth condition on scalar-valued analytic functions, which have tempered distributions as boundary values, we show that vector-valued analytic functions in tubes $T^C = \mathbb{R}^n + iC$ obtain vector-valued tempered distributions as boundary values. In a certain vector-valued case, we study the structure of this boundary value, which is shown to be the Fourier transform of the distributional derivative of a vector-valued continuous function of polynomial growth. A set of vector-valued functions used to show the structure of the boundary value is shown to have a one–one and onto relationship with a set of vector-valued distributions, which generalize the Schwartz space $\mathcal{D}'_{L^2}(\mathbb{R}^n)$; the tempered distribution Fourier transform defines the relationship between these two sets. By combining the previously stated results, we obtain a Cauchy integral representation of the vector-valued analytic functions in terms of the boundary value.

Keywords: analytic functions; vector-valued tempered distributions; boundary value; Cauchy integral

MSC: 32A26; 32A40; 46F12; 46F20

1. Introduction

Tillmann [1] introduced the analysis of analytic functions, which obtain tempered distributional boundary values in $\mathcal{S}'(\mathbb{R}^n)$. In [1], Tillmann worked with scalar-valued analytic functions in tubes $T^{C_\mu} = \mathbb{R}^n + iC_\mu$, where the $C_\mu = \{y \in \mathbb{R}^n : (-1)^{\mu_j} y_j > 0, j = 1, \ldots, n\}$ with $\mu = (\mu_1, \mu_2, \ldots, \mu_n)$ being any of the 2^n n-tuples, whose components are either 0 or 1 and characterize the growth conditions on the analytic functions, which obtain the $\mathcal{S}'(\mathbb{R}^n)$ boundary values. This analysis by Tillmann was motivated by the work by Köthe in [2,3].

Using a more restrictive growth on the analytic functions, we showed in [4] that vector-valued analytic functions in tubes $T^C = \mathbb{R}^n + iC$, where C is an open convex cone, having this more restrictive growth obtain vector-valued tempered distributions in $\mathcal{S}'(\mathbb{R}^n, \mathcal{X})$, with $\mathcal{X}$ being a specified topological vector space. In this paper, our first objective is to generalize this result of [4] to the general growth form of Tillmann for the vector-valued analytic functions. We obtain this boundary value generalization in Section 4 of this paper.

Moreover, in Section 4, we study the structure of this boundary value in $\mathcal{S}'(\mathbb{R}^n, \mathcal{X})$. To do this, we first restrict the topological vector space $\mathcal{X}$ by imposing certain conditions on it to ensure that the boundary value is the Fourier transform of a distributional derivative of a continuous vector-valued function **g**, which has polynomial growth in the norm of the space $\mathcal{X}$. By further restricting $\mathcal{X}$ to be a Hilbert space, we show that function **g** is in a set that has a one–one and onto relationship with a set of vector-valued distributions, which generalize the $\mathcal{D}'_{L^2}(\mathbb{R}^n)$ distributions of Schwartz. The relationship between these two sets is obtained using the tempered distribution Fourier transform; the proof of this relationship is proved in Section 3 of this paper. Using the relationships of these noted two sets, we are able to obtain an additional structure of the tempered distribution boundary value of the analytic functions in Section 4.

A few papers have been written concerning the construction of a Cauchy integral for tempered distributions. All of these papers concern scalar-valued analytic functions

Citation: Carmichael, R.D. Cauchy Integral and Boundary Value for Vector-Valued Tempered Distributions. *Axioms* **2022**, *11*, 392. https://doi.org/10.3390/axioms11080392

Academic Editor: Georgia Irina Oros

Received: 12 July 2022
Accepted: 7 August 2022
Published: 10 August 2022

Publisher's Note: MDPI stays neutral with regard to jurisdictional claims in published maps and institutional affiliations.

Copyright: © 2022 by the authors. Licensee MDPI, Basel, Switzerland. This article is an open access article distributed under the terms and conditions of the Creative Commons Attribution (CC BY) license (https://creativecommons.org/licenses/by/4.0/).

and scalar-valued tempered distributions. The first paper known to this author was by J. Sebastião e Silva [5] (Section 5) and concerned scalar-valued analytic functions and tempered distributions in one dimension. An associated analysis by Sebastião e Silva is contained in [6]. Carmichael [7] defined a Cauchy integral for tempered distributions in the $\mathbb{C}^n$ setting corresponding to analytic functions in each of the 2^n quadrant tubes $T^{C_\mu} \subset \mathbb{C}^n$ and showed that the analytic functions with growth, such as that of Tillmann in $(\mathbb{C} - \mathbb{R})^n$ could be recovered as the defined Cauchy integral of the tempered distribution boundary value; the results of [7] can be extended to the vector-valued analytic functions in T^{C_μ} and the tempered distribution setting considered in this paper by the same techniques as those of [7]. The Cauchy integrals introduced by Sebastião e Silva in [5] and by Carmichael in [7] are in fact equivalence classes of analytic functions defined by an integral involving the Cauchy kernel.

Vladimirov [8–10] defined a Cauchy integral for tempered distributions associated with analytic functions in general tubes $T^C = \mathbb{R}^n + iC \subset \mathbb{C}^n$ corresponding to open convex cones C with the functions satisfying a growth condition similar to that of Tillmann. Vladimirov has shown that the analytic functions that he has considered can be recovered by a Cauchy integral involving the tempered distribution boundary values of the analytic functions. An associated analysis by Vladimirov is contained in [11,12]. The works mentioned in this paragraph and the previous paragraph all concern scalar valued analytic functions and scalar-valued tempered distributions.

In Section 5 of this paper, we build on our analysis of Sections 3 and 4 to obtain a Cauchy integral representation of the vector-valued analytic functions, which are shown to have tempered vector-valued distributions as the boundary values in Section 4. The proof of our result here and the form of the Cauchy integral representation are substantially different from any of the previous results concerning Cauchy integral representation of the analytic functions having tempered distribution boundary values.

2. Definitions and Notation

Throughout, $\mathcal{X}$ will denote a topological vector space with the stated appropriate properties corresponding to the results that we wish to prove. For $\mathcal{X}$ being a normed space, we denote the norm by $\mathcal{N}$. Θ will denote the zero element of $\mathcal{X}$; and if $\mathcal{X}$ is a Hilbert space, we denote the space by $\mathcal{H}$. For integration of the vector-valued functions and vector-valued analytic functions, we refer to Dunford and Schwartz [13]. For foundational information concerning vector-valued distributions, we refer to Schwartz [14,15].

The n-dimensional notation to be used in this paper will be the same as in [16,17]. Note $\overline{0} = (0,0,\ldots,0)$ is the origin in $\mathbb{R}^n$. The information concerning cones $C \subset \mathbb{R}^n$ needed is explicitly stated in [16] (Section 2) and [17] (Chapter 1). We do not repeat the definitions and notations concerning cones as stated in [16] (Section 2), and we ask the reader to refer to this reference.

The $L^p(\mathbb{R}^n, \mathcal{X})$ functions, $1 \leq p \leq \infty$, with values in a Banach space $\mathcal{X}$ and their norm $|\mathbf{h}|_p$ [13] (p. 119) are noted in [13] (Chapter III). The Fourier transform on $L^1(\mathbb{R}^n)$ or $L^1(\mathbb{R}^n, \mathcal{X})$ is given in [17] (p. 3). All Fourier (inverse Fourier) transforms on scalar or vector-valued functions will be denoted $\hat{\phi}(x) = \mathcal{F}[\phi(t); x]$ ($\mathcal{F}^{-1}[\phi(t); x]$). As stated in [18,19], the Plancherel theory is not true for vector-valued functions, except when $\mathcal{X} = \mathcal{H}$, a Hilbert space. The Plancherel theory is complete in the $L^2(\mathbb{R}^n, \mathcal{H})$ setting in that the inverse Fourier transform is the inverse mapping of the Fourier transform with $\mathcal{F}^{-1}\mathcal{F} = I = \mathcal{F}\mathcal{F}^{-1}$ with I being the identity mapping.

We denote $\mathcal{S}(\mathbb{R}^n)$ as the tempered functions with associated distributions being $\mathcal{S}'(\mathbb{R}^n)$ or associated vector-valued distributions being $\mathcal{S}'(\mathbb{R}^n, \mathcal{X})$. The Fourier (inverse Fourier) transform on $\mathcal{S}'(\mathbb{R}^n)$ and $\mathcal{S}'(\mathbb{R}^n, \mathcal{X})$ is the usual definition and is given in [14] (p. 73).

3. Fourier and Inverse Fourier Transform on a Function Subset of $\mathcal{S}'(\mathbb{R}^n, \mathcal{H})$

Let $\mathcal{X}$ be a Banach space. We defined the space $\mathcal{S}'_p(\mathbb{R}^n, \mathcal{X}), 1 \leq p < \infty$, in [16]. We repeat the definition here because of the importance of these functions for our results in this paper.

Definition 1. *For a Banach space $\mathcal{X}$, $\mathcal{S}'_p(\mathbb{R}^n, \mathcal{X}), 1 \leq p < \infty$, is the set of all measurable functions $g(t), t \in \mathbb{R}^n$, with values in $\mathcal{X}$ such that there exists a real number $m \geq 0$ for which $(1 + |t|^p)^{-m} g(t) \in L^p(\mathbb{R}^n, \mathcal{X})$.*

Note that m can be taken as a nonnegative integer in Definition 1. As noted in [16], $\mathcal{S}'_p(\mathbb{R}^n, \mathcal{X}) \subset \mathcal{S}'(\mathbb{R}^n, \mathcal{X})$, $1 \leq p < \infty$. The spaces $\mathcal{S}'_p(\mathbb{R}^n, \mathcal{X})$ will be important in this paper. Throughout this paper, the differential operator D_t, $t \in \mathbb{R}^n$ will take the form

$$D_t = \frac{-1}{2\pi i} \left(\frac{\partial}{\partial t_1}, \frac{\partial}{\partial t_2}, \ldots, \frac{\partial}{\partial t_n} \right).$$

Thus, for α being any n-tuple of nonnegative integers,

$$D_t^\alpha = \left(\frac{-1}{2\pi i} \right)^{|\alpha|} \left(\frac{\partial^{\alpha_1}}{\partial t_1^{\alpha_1}}, \frac{\partial^{\alpha_2}}{\partial t_2^{\alpha_2}}, \ldots, \frac{\partial^{\alpha_n}}{\partial t_n^{\alpha_n}} \right).$$

The goal of this section is to show a one–one and onto relationship between the set of functions $\mathcal{S}'_2(\mathbb{R}^n, \mathcal{H})$ and another subset of $\mathcal{S}'(\mathbb{R}^n, \mathcal{H})$, where $\mathcal{H}$ is a Hilbert space. This relationship is obtained by both the Fourier and inverse Fourier transforms in $\mathcal{S}'(\mathbb{R}^n, \mathcal{H})$. We define the space that has this stated relationship to $\mathcal{S}'_2(\mathbb{R}^n, \mathcal{H})$, as follows.

Definition 2. *Let m be any nonnegative integer. The set of Hilbert space $\mathcal{H}$-valued generalized functions in $\mathcal{S}'(\mathbb{R}^n, \mathcal{H})$ of the form*

$$V_t = \sum_{|\alpha| \leq m} D_t^\alpha g_\alpha(t)$$

where $g_\alpha \in L^2(\mathbb{R}^n, \mathcal{H})$, $|\alpha| \leq m$, will be denoted as $L2(\mathbb{R}^n, \mathcal{H})$.

We emphasize that $L2(\mathbb{R}^n, \mathcal{H}) \subset \mathcal{S}'(\mathbb{R}^n, \mathcal{H})$. When $\mathcal{H} = \mathbb{C}^1$, note that $L2(\mathbb{R}^n, \mathbb{C}^1) = \mathcal{D}'_{L^2}(\mathbb{R}^n)$, the Schwartz space of distributions contained in $\mathcal{S}'(\mathbb{R}^n)$ of the form of finite sums of distributional derivatives of $L^2(\mathbb{R}^n)$ functions. For $\phi \in \mathcal{D}_{L^2}(\mathbb{R}^n)$, the Schwartz space that is the set of test functions for $\mathcal{D}'_{L^2}(\mathbb{R}^n)$, the application $\langle V, \phi \rangle$, $V \in \mathcal{D}'_{L^2}(\mathbb{R}^n)$, yields a complex number. In exactly the same way, for $V \in L2(\mathbb{R}^n, \mathcal{H})$ and $\phi \in \mathcal{D}_{L^2}(\mathbb{R}^n)$, the application $\langle V, \phi \rangle$ yields an element of $\mathcal{H}$; and the algebraic and differentiation calculations on the form $\langle V, \phi \rangle$ hold for $V \in L2(\mathbb{R}^n, \mathcal{H})$, as usual, just as these calculations hold on the form $\langle V, \phi \rangle$ for $V \in \mathcal{S}'(\mathbb{R}^n, \mathcal{H})$ and $\phi \in \mathcal{S}(\mathbb{R}^n)$. This is an important note in relation to our construction of the Cauchy Integral (later in this paper).

We now obtain the relationship between $\mathcal{S}'_2(\mathbb{R}^n, \mathcal{H})$ and $L2(\mathbb{R}^n, \mathcal{H})$ for any Hilbert space $\mathcal{H}$.

Lemma 1. *The $\mathcal{S}'(\mathbb{R}^n, \mathcal{H})$ Fourier transform maps $\mathcal{S}'_2(\mathbb{R}^n, \mathcal{H})$ one-one and onto $L2(\mathbb{R}^n, \mathcal{H})$. The $\mathcal{S}'(\mathbb{R}^n, \mathcal{H})$ inverse Fourier transform maps $L2(\mathbb{R}^n, \mathcal{H})$ one-one and onto $\mathcal{S}'_2(\mathbb{R}^n, \mathcal{H})$.*

Proof. Let the function $\mathbf{g} \in \mathcal{S}'_2(\mathbb{R}^n, \mathcal{H})$. From Definition 1, there is a real number $m \geq 0$ for which $(1 + |t|^2)^{-m} \mathbf{g}(t) \in L^2(\mathbb{R}^n, \mathcal{H})$, and m can be taken as a nonnegative integer. Since $\mathbf{g} \in \mathcal{S}'_2(\mathbb{R}^n, \mathcal{H}) \subset \mathcal{S}'(\mathbb{R}^n, \mathcal{H})$, the Fourier transform of $\mathbf{g}$ in $\mathcal{S}'(\mathbb{R}^n, \mathcal{H})$ is an element of $\mathcal{S}'(\mathbb{R}^n, \mathcal{H})$; we put $V_x = \mathcal{F}[\mathbf{g}]_x$. Let $\phi \in \mathcal{S}(\mathbb{R}^n)$, and let Δ denote the Laplace operator in the variable $x \in \mathbb{R}^n$. Using integration by parts, we have

$$\langle V_x, \phi(x) \rangle = \langle \mathbf{g}(t), \mathcal{F}[\phi(x); t] \rangle$$
$$= \langle \frac{\mathbf{g}(t)}{(1+|t|^2)^m}, \int_{\mathbb{R}^n} \phi(x)(1+|t|^2)^m e^{2\pi i \langle x,t \rangle} dx \rangle \qquad (1)$$
$$= \langle \frac{\mathbf{g}(t)}{(1+|t|^2)^m}, \mathcal{F}[(1-(4\pi^2)^{-1}\Delta)^m \phi(x); t] \rangle$$
$$= \langle \mathcal{F}[\frac{\mathbf{g}(t)}{(1+|t|^2)^m}; x], (1-(4\pi^2)^{-1}\Delta)^m \phi(x) \rangle.$$

Since $(1+|t|^2)^{-m}\mathbf{g}(t) \in L^2(\mathbb{R}^n, \mathcal{H})$, then $\mathbf{h}(x) = \mathcal{F}[(1+|t|^2)^{-m}\mathbf{g}(t); x] \in L^2(\mathbb{R}^n, \mathcal{H})$. From (1), we have

$$\langle V_x, \phi(x) \rangle = \langle (1-(4\pi^2)^{-1}\Delta)^m \mathbf{h}(x), \phi(x) \rangle,$$

and $V_x = \mathcal{F}[\mathbf{g}]_x = (1-(4\pi^2)^{-1}\Delta)^m \mathbf{h}(x) \in L2(\mathbb{R}^n, \mathcal{H})$. Thus, the $\mathcal{S}'(\mathbb{R}^n, \mathcal{H})$ Fourier transform maps $\mathcal{S}'_2(\mathbb{R}^n, \mathcal{H})$ to $L2(\mathbb{R}^n, \mathcal{H})$.

We now desire to prove that any element of $L2(\mathbb{R}^n, \mathcal{H})$ is the $\mathcal{S}'(\mathbb{R}^n, \mathcal{H})$ Fourier transform of an element in $\mathcal{S}'_2(\mathbb{R}^n, \mathcal{H})$. Let $V \in L2(\mathbb{R}^n, \mathcal{H})$ and $\phi \in \mathcal{S}(\mathbb{R}^n)$. By Definition 2, there is a nonnegative integer m, such that

$$V_t = \sum_{|\alpha| \leq m} D_t^\alpha \mathbf{g}_\alpha(t)$$

with $\mathbf{g}_\alpha(t) \in L^2(\mathbb{R}^n, \mathcal{H})$, $|\alpha| \leq m$. Since $L2(\mathbb{R}^n, \mathcal{H}) \subset \mathcal{S}'(\mathbb{R}^n, \mathcal{H})$, $\mathcal{F}^{-1}[V]_x$ exists in $\mathcal{S}'(\mathbb{R}^n, \mathcal{H})$, and we have for the nonnegative integer m

$$\langle \mathcal{F}^{-1}[V]_x, \phi(x) \rangle = \sum_{|\alpha| \leq m} \langle D_t^\alpha \mathbf{g}_\alpha(t), \mathcal{F}^{-1}[\phi(x); t] \rangle$$
$$= \sum_{|\alpha| \leq m} (-1)^{|\alpha|} \langle \mathbf{g}_\alpha(t), D_t^\alpha \int_{\mathbb{R}^n} \phi(x) e^{-2\pi i \langle x,t \rangle} dx \rangle$$
$$= \sum_{|\alpha| \leq m} (-1)^{|\alpha|} \langle \mathbf{g}_\alpha(t), (-1/2\pi i)^{|\alpha|} \int_{\mathbb{R}^n} \phi(x)(-2\pi i)^{|\alpha|} x^\alpha e^{-2\pi i \langle x,t \rangle} dx \rangle$$
$$= \sum_{|\alpha| \leq m} \langle (-1)^{|\alpha|} \mathbf{g}_\alpha(t), \int_{\mathbb{R}^n} x^\alpha \phi(x) e^{-2\pi i \langle x,t \rangle} dx \rangle$$
$$= \sum_{|\alpha| \leq m} \langle (-1)^{|\alpha|} \mathbf{g}_\alpha(t), \mathcal{F}^{-1}[x^\alpha \phi(x); t] \rangle$$
$$= \sum_{|\alpha| \leq m} \langle \mathcal{F}^{-1}[(-1)^{|\alpha|} \mathbf{g}_\alpha(t); x], x^\alpha \phi(x) \rangle.$$

For each α, $|\alpha| \leq m$, put $\mathbf{h}_\alpha(x) = \mathcal{F}^{-1}[(-1)^{|\alpha|} \mathbf{g}_\alpha(t); x]$. We have $\mathbf{h}_\alpha(x) \in L^2(\mathbb{R}^n, \mathcal{H})$, $|\alpha| \leq m$, since each $\mathbf{g}_\alpha(t) \in L^2(\mathbb{R}^n, \mathcal{H})$; moreover, $\sum_{|\alpha| \leq m} \mathbf{h}_\alpha(x) \in L^2(\mathbb{R}^n, \mathcal{H})$. Thus, we have

$$\langle \mathcal{F}^{-1}[V]_x, \phi(x) \rangle = \sum_{|\alpha| \leq m} \langle \mathbf{h}_\alpha(x), x^\alpha \phi(x) \rangle$$
$$= \langle \sum_{|\alpha| \leq m} x^\alpha \mathbf{h}_\alpha(x), \phi(x) \rangle, \qquad (2)$$

and $\mathcal{F}^{-1}[V]_x = \sum_{|\alpha| \leq m} x^\alpha \mathbf{h}_\alpha(x)$ in $\mathcal{S}'(\mathbb{R}^n, \mathcal{H})$. For the $L^2(\mathbb{R}^n, \mathcal{H})$ norm $|\cdot|_2$ and the order m of the summation defining V, we consider

$$|(1+|x|^2)^{-m-2} \sum_{|\alpha| \leq m} x^\alpha \mathbf{h}_\alpha(x)|_2. \qquad (3)$$

For $|\alpha| \leq m$, note that $|x^\alpha| \leq |x|^{|\alpha|} \leq (1+|x|)^{|\alpha|} \leq (1+|x|)^m$. Since $(1+|x|)^m \leq 2^m$ if $|x| \leq 1$ and $(1+|x|)^m \leq (1+|x|^2)^m$ if $|x| \geq 1$, then

$$|x^\alpha (1+|x|^2)^{-m-2}| \leq (1+|x|)^m (1+|x|^2)^{-m-2}$$
$$\leq \max_{x \in \mathbb{R}^n}\{2^m, (1+|x|^2)^m\}(1+|x|^2)^{-m-2}$$
$$\leq \max\{2^m, 1\} = 2^m$$

for $|\alpha| \leq m$ since $m \geq 0$ is a nonnegative integer. Thus, for the $L^2(\mathbb{R}^n, \mathcal{H})$ norm in (3), we have

$$\left|(1+|x|^2)^{-m-2} \sum_{|\alpha|\leq m} x^\alpha \mathbf{h}_\alpha(x)\right|_2 \leq 2^m \left|\sum_{|\alpha|\leq m} \mathbf{h}_\alpha(x)\right|_2 < \infty \quad (4)$$

since $\sum_{|\alpha|\leq m} \mathbf{h}_\alpha(x) \in L^2(\mathbb{R}^n, \mathcal{H})$. Recalling (2), we have by (4) that $\mathcal{F}^{-1}[V]_x = \sum_{|\alpha|\leq m} x^\alpha \mathbf{h}_\alpha(x) \in \mathcal{S}'_2(\mathbb{R}^n, \mathcal{H})$ for any $V \in L2(\mathbb{R}^n, \mathcal{H})$; and $V_t = \mathcal{F}[\sum_{|\alpha|\leq m} x^\alpha \mathbf{h}_\alpha(x)]_t$ in $\mathcal{S}'(\mathbb{R}^n, \mathcal{H})$. Thus, the $\mathcal{S}'(\mathbb{R}^n, \mathcal{H})$ Fourier transform maps $\mathcal{S}'_2(\mathbb{R}^n, \mathcal{H})$ onto $L2(\mathbb{R}^n, \mathcal{H})$; the fact that this mapping is one–one follows directly from the fact that the Fourier transform is a one–one mapping on $\mathcal{S}'(\mathbb{R}^n, \mathcal{H})$. The same statements and proofs as in this proof of Lemma 1 for the Fourier transform hold in exactly the same way for the inverse Fourier transform on $\mathcal{S}'(\mathbb{R}^n, \mathcal{H})$; and we have that the $\mathcal{S}'(\mathbb{R}^n, \mathcal{H})$ inverse Fourier transform maps $L2(\mathbb{R}^n, \mathcal{H})$ one–one and onto $\mathcal{S}'_2(\mathbb{R}^n, \mathcal{H})$. The proof of Lemma 1 is complete. □

Let C be a regular cone in $\mathbb{R}^n$; that is, C is an open convex cone in $\mathbb{R}^n$, which does not contain any entire straight line. $C^* = \{t \in \mathbb{R}^n : \langle t, y \rangle \geq 0 \text{ for all } y \in C\}$ is the dual cone of C. We consider now the Cauchy kernel

$$K(z-t) = \int_{C^*} e^{2\pi i \langle z-t, u \rangle} du, \quad z \in T^C = \mathbb{R}^n + iC, \ t \in \mathbb{R}^n.$$

The ultradistributional test function spaces $\mathcal{D}(*, L^p) \subset \mathcal{D}_{L^p}(\mathbb{R}^n), 1 < p \leq \infty$, where $*$ is Beurling (M_p) or Roumieu $\{M_p\}$, defined in [17] (Section 2.3, p. 21). For C being a regular cone, we proved in [17] (Section 4.1, Theorem 4.1.1) that $K(z - \cdot) \in \mathcal{D}(*, L^p) \subset \mathcal{D}_{L^p}(\mathbb{R}^n)$ for $z \in T^C, 1 < p \leq \infty$, under specified conditions on the sequence M_p of positive numbers, which we assume here. (See [17] (pp. 13–14, Theorem 4.1.1) for assumptions on the sequence M_p.) The Schwartz space $\mathcal{D}'_{L^2}(\mathbb{R}^n)$ consists of finite sums of distributional derivatives of $L^2(\mathbb{R}^n)$ functions; thus, the space $L2(\mathbb{R}^n, \mathcal{H}|)$ is the extension of $\mathcal{D}'_{L^2}(\mathbb{R}^n)$ to vector-valued distributions with values in $\mathcal{H}$. Thus, for $p = 2$, we emphasize that the form $\langle V_t, K(z-t) \rangle, z \in T^C$, is well defined for $V \in L2(\mathbb{R}^n, \mathcal{H})$, and yields an element of $\mathcal{H}$; the algebraic and differentiation calculations on the form $\langle V, \phi \rangle$ hold for $V \in L2(\mathbb{R}^n, \mathcal{H})$ and $\phi \in \mathcal{D}_{L^2}(\mathbb{R}^n)$, as usual, just as these calculations hold for the form $\langle V, \phi \rangle$ for $V \in \mathcal{S}'(\mathbb{R}^n, \mathcal{H})$ and $\phi \in \mathcal{S}(\mathbb{R}^n)$. We use this information in Section 5 of this paper.

4. Boundary Values in $\mathcal{S}'(\mathbb{R}^n, \mathcal{X})$

Let C be an open convex cone in $\mathbb{R}^n$. In [4] (Theorem 8), we proved that an analytic function $\mathbf{f}(z), z \in T^C$, with values in a specified topological vector space $\mathcal{X}$ and satisfying a certain norm growth obtained a vector-value-tempered distributional boundary value, as $y \to \overline{0}, y \in C' \subset\subset C$, for any compact subcone C' of C. The norm growth used in [4] (Theorem 8) was not as general as the growth of Tillmann [1] in which the original tempered distributional boundary value results in the scalar-valued case were obtained. In this section, we extend the result [4] (Theorem 8) by assuming a norm growth on the analytic function equivalent to that of Tillmann [1]; our result here also contains new information concerning the boundary value. As a corollary of our result, we obtain a precise representation of the boundary value when the conditions on the topological vector space $\mathcal{X}$ are restricted.

Following Vladimirov [11] (p. 230), we shall use the term "spectral function" but will extend the definition of this term to the vector-valued case. For an analytic function

$f(z)$, $z \in T^C = \mathbb{R}^n + iC \subset \mathbb{C}^n$, with values in a topological vector space $\mathcal{X}$, the spectral function of $f(z)$ is that vector-valued distribution $V \in \mathcal{D}'(\mathbb{R}^n, \mathcal{X})$, such that $e^{-2\pi \langle y,t \rangle} V_t \in \mathcal{S}'(\mathbb{R}^n, \mathcal{X})$, $y \in C$; and $f(x+iy) = \mathcal{F}[e^{-2\pi \langle y,t \rangle} V_t]_x$ in $\mathcal{S}'(\mathbb{R}^n, \mathcal{X})$ for $z = x + iy \in T^C$.

We begin by assuming that the topological vector space $\mathcal{X}$ is locally convex, separable, and quasi-complete where quasi-complete is in the sense of Schwartz [15] (p. 198). We further assume that $\mathcal{X}$ is a normed space with norm $\mathcal{N}$. These stated assumptions on $\mathcal{X}$ were the assumptions under which we obtained [4] (Theorem 8) and are the assumptions on the topological vector space $\mathcal{X}$ under which we obtain Theorem 1 below.

Throughout the paper, by $y \to \bar{0}$, $y \in C$, we mean that $y \to \bar{0}$, $y \in C' \subset\subset C$ for every compact subcone $C' \subset\subset C$.

The following theorem generalizes and extends [4] (Theorem 8) for $\mathcal{X}$, satisfying the properties noted above.

Theorem 1. *Let C be an open convex cone. Let $f(z)$ be analytic in T^C and have values in $\mathcal{X}$. Let*

$$\mathcal{N}(f(x+iy)) \leq M(1+|z|)^q |y|^{-r}, \quad z = x + iy \in T^C, \tag{5}$$

where $M > 0$ is a real constant, q is a nonnegative integer, $r > 1$ is an integer, and M, q, and r are independent of $z = x + iy \in T^C$. There exists an element $U \in \mathcal{S}'(\mathbb{R}^n, \mathcal{X})$, such that

$$\lim_{y \to \bar{0}, y \in C} f(x+iy) = U \tag{6}$$

in the weak and strong topologies of $\mathcal{S}'(\mathbb{R}^n, \mathcal{X})$. Further, $U = \mathcal{F}[V]$ with $V \in \mathcal{S}'(\mathbb{R}^n, \mathcal{X})$ being the spectral function of $f(z)$, $z \in T^C$,, such that $\mathrm{supp}(V) \subseteq C^*$.

Proof. We apply the proofs of [4] (Theorems 3 and 8). Note that in the second sentence of the proof of [4] (Theorem 8) that the value of $\eta \geq 1$ is arbitrary but fixed; in the present proof, we simply take $\eta = 1$, where it is appropriate to use $\eta = 1$. Let $\lambda > 0$; put $\rho = \sigma + i\lambda$, $\sigma \in \mathbb{R}^1$; and define $f'(\rho; x, y) = f(x + \rho y)$, $y \in pr(C)$, where $pr(C)$ denotes the projection of C, which is the intersection of C with the unit sphere in $\mathbb{R}^n$. (Thus, $|y| = 1$ if $y \in pr(C)$.) $f'(\rho; x, y)$ is an analytic function of ρ in the half plane $\lambda = \mathrm{Im}(\rho) > 0$ and has values in $\mathcal{X}$. We have $f'(\rho; x, y) = f(x + \rho y) = f((x + \sigma y) + i\lambda y)$, $\lambda > 0$, for $z = x + iy$ with $y \in pr(C)$; and note that $\lambda y \in C$ for $\lambda > 0$ and $y \in pr(C)$. Now for $y = \mathrm{Im}(z) \in pr(C)$ and $0 < \lambda \leq \eta = 1$ we have

$$\begin{aligned}
\mathcal{N}(f'(\rho; x, y)) &\leq M(1 + |(x + \sigma y) + i\lambda y|)^q |\lambda y|^{-r} \\
&= M(1 + (\lambda^2 + |x + \sigma y|^2)^{1/2})^q \lambda^{-r} \\
&\leq M(1 + (1 + (|x| + |\sigma|)^2)^{1/2})^q \lambda^{-r} \\
&\leq M(1 + ((1 + |x| + |\sigma|)^2)^{1/2})^q \lambda^{-r} \\
&= M(2 + |x| + |\sigma|)^q \lambda^{-r}
\end{aligned} \tag{7}$$

which is of the form, with norm $\mathcal{N}$ replacing the absolute value, of [4] (15), which is used in exactly the same way in the proof of [4] (Theorem 8) as in the proof of [4] (Theorem 3). Thus, for $y = \mathrm{Im}(z) \in pr(C)$ and $0 < \lambda \leq \eta = 1$ the bound on $\mathcal{N}(f'(\rho; x, y))$ is in the proper form to proceed with the proof of this present Theorem 1 exactly as in the form of the proofs of [4] (Theorems 3 and 8). We obtain the structured function of the form $\Lambda^{(-r-1)} f'(\rho; x, y)$, $y \in pr(C)$, which satisfies the growth (similar to [4] (37))

$$\mathcal{N}(\Lambda^{(-r-1)} f'(\rho; x, y)) \leq M^{(r+1)} (2 + |x| + |\sigma|)^q (2 + |\sigma|)^{r+1}$$

for $0 < \lambda \leq \eta = 1$ where $M^{(r+1)}$ is a positive constant, and obtains the representation (similar to [4] (38))

$$f(x + \rho y) = f'(\rho; x, y) = \frac{\partial^{r+1} (\Lambda^{(-r-1)} f'(\rho; x, y))}{\partial \sigma^{r+1}}, \quad \sigma = \mathrm{Re}(\rho).$$

Now, we proceed in our proof of Theorem 1 in exactly the same way as in [4] (Theorem 8) (p. 328) to obtain the desired boundedness properties leading to the existence of an element $V \in \mathcal{D}'(\mathbb{R}^n, \mathcal{X})$, such that $e^{-2\pi\langle y,t\rangle} V_t \in \mathcal{S}'(\mathbb{R}^n, \mathcal{X})$, $y \in C$, and $\mathbf{f}(z) = \mathcal{F}[e^{-2\pi\langle y,t\rangle} V_t]_x$, $z = x + iy \in T^C$, in $\mathcal{S}'(\mathbb{R}^n, \mathcal{X})$ from the results of Schwartz [14] (Prop. 22, p. 76). (These results of Schwartz [14] (Prop. 22, p. 76) were obtained in their original scalar-valued case in [20]; the related results were then obtained by Lions [21]). Thus, $V \in \mathcal{D}'(\mathbb{R}^n, \mathcal{X})$ is the spectral function of $\mathbf{f}(z)$, $z \in T^C$. The remainder of the proof of [4] (Theorem 8, pp. 329–330) and the succeeding discussion after the conclusion of the proof of [4] (Theorem 8) can be applied to the present proof of Theorem 1 in the same way to yield that, in fact, $V \in \mathcal{S}'(\mathbb{R}^n, \mathcal{X})$ and that

$$\lim_{y \to 0, y \in C} \mathbf{f}(x + iy) = \lim_{y \to 0, y \in C} \mathcal{F}[e^{-2\pi\langle y,t\rangle} V_t] = \mathcal{F}[V] = U \tag{8}$$

in the weak topology of $\mathcal{S}'(\mathbb{R}^n, \mathcal{X})$. However, $\mathcal{S}(\mathbb{R}^n)$ is a Montel space; thus, the convergence in (8) is in the strong topology of $\mathcal{S}'(\mathbb{R}^n, \mathcal{X})$ as well. We emphasize that $V \in \mathcal{S}'(\mathbb{R}^n, \mathcal{X})$ and that $U = \mathcal{F}[V] \in \mathcal{S}'(\mathbb{R}^n, \mathcal{X})$ is the desired boundary value in (6) as obtained in (8).

We now prove that $\mathrm{supp}(V) \subseteq C^*$. Let $t_o \in C_* = \mathbb{R}^n \setminus C^*$; C_* is an open set in $\mathbb{R}^n$ since C^* is a closed set. From the definition of C^*, for $t_o \in C_*$, there is a point $y_o \in C$, such that $\langle y_o, t_o \rangle < 0$. Using the fact that C_* is open and the continuity of $\langle t, y_o \rangle$ at $t_o \in C_*$ as a function of t, there is a fixed $\tau > 0$ and a fixed neighborhood $N(t_o; \gamma) = \{t \in \mathbb{R}^n : |t - t_o| < \gamma, \ \gamma > 0\} \subset C_*$, such that $\langle t, y_o \rangle < -\tau < 0$ for all $t \in N(t_o; \gamma)$. Let $\phi \in \mathcal{D}(\mathbb{R}^n)$, such that $\mathrm{supp}(\phi) \subset N(t_o, \gamma)$. Recall that $V \in \mathcal{S}'(\mathbb{R}^n, \mathcal{X})$, such that $e^{-2\pi\langle y,t\rangle} V_t \in \mathcal{S}'(\mathbb{R}^n, \mathcal{X})$, $y \in C$, and $\mathbf{f}(x + iy) = \mathcal{F}[e^{-2\pi\langle y,t\rangle} V_t]_x$, $z = x + iy \in T^C$, in $\mathcal{S}'(\mathbb{R}^n, \mathcal{X})$. Thus $e^{-2\pi\langle y,t\rangle} V_t = \mathcal{F}^{-1}[\mathbf{f}(x + iy)]_t$, $x + iy \in T^C$, in $\mathcal{S}'(\mathbb{R}^n, \mathcal{X})$; or $V_t = e^{2\pi\langle y,t\rangle} \mathcal{F}^{-1}[(x + iy)]_t$, $x + iy \in T^C$, in $\mathcal{S}'(\mathbb{R}^n, \mathcal{X})$. Let $y = \beta y_o$, $y_o \in C$, $\beta > 0$, now. We have $y = \beta y_o \in C$ and

$$\begin{aligned}
\langle V, \phi \rangle &= \langle e^{2\pi\langle \beta y_o, t\rangle} \mathcal{F}^{-1}[\mathbf{f}(x + i\beta y_o)]_t, \phi(t) \rangle \\
&= \langle \mathcal{F}^{-1}[\mathbf{f}(x + i\beta y_o)]_t, e^{2\pi\langle \beta y_o, t\rangle} \phi(t) \rangle \\
&= \langle \mathbf{f}(x + i\beta y_o), \mathcal{F}^{-1}[e^{2\pi\langle \beta y_o, t\rangle} \phi(t); x] \rangle \\
&= \int_{\mathbb{R}^n} \mathbf{f}(x + i\beta y_o) \int_{\mathrm{supp}(\phi)} e^{2\pi\langle \beta y_o, t\rangle} \phi(t) e^{-2\pi i \langle x, t\rangle} dt\, dx
\end{aligned} \tag{9}$$

for the function $\phi \in \mathcal{D}(\mathbb{R}^n)$ chosen above. Using integration by parts and letting Δ denote the Laplacian in the $t \in \mathbb{R}^n$ variable, we have for any positive integer m

$$\mathcal{N}\left(\int_{\mathbb{R}^n} \mathbf{f}(x + i\beta y_o) \int_{\mathrm{supp}(\phi)} e^{2\pi\langle \beta y_o, t\rangle} \phi(t) e^{-2\pi i \langle x, t\rangle} dt\, dx\right) \tag{10}$$

$$= \mathcal{N}\left(\int_{\mathbb{R}^n} \frac{\mathbf{f}(x + i\beta y_o)}{(1 + |x|^2)^m} \int_{\mathrm{supp}(\phi)} e^{2\pi\langle \beta y_o, t\rangle} \phi(t)(1 + |x|^2)^m e^{-2\pi i \langle x, t\rangle} dt\, dx\right)$$

$$= \mathcal{N}\left(\int_{\mathbb{R}^n} \frac{\mathbf{f}(x + i\beta y_o)}{(1 + |x|^2)^m} \int_{\mathrm{supp}(\phi)} \left(1 - \frac{\Delta}{4\pi^2}\right)^m (e^{2\pi\langle \beta y_o, t\rangle} \phi(t)) e^{-2\pi i \langle x, t\rangle} dt\, dx\right).$$

(For the present, the positive integer m is arbitrary; later, we explicitly choose m to obtain the desired convergence of all integrals through Equation (15) below). For the interior integral over $\mathrm{supp}(\phi)$ in (10), we note that by applying $(1 - (\Delta/4\pi^2))^m$ to the product $e^{2\pi\langle \beta y_o, t\rangle} \phi(t)$ and then bounding the terms in the resulting sum, including the terms involving 2π or it powers, we obtain a finite sum of terms involving powers of $\beta(y_o)_j$, $j = 1, \ldots, n$, multiplied by $e^{2\pi\langle \beta y_o, t\rangle}$, where $(y_o)_j$ is the jth component of y_o, $j = 1, \ldots, n$, and multiplied by bounds on $\phi(t)$ or one of its partial derivatives with $e^{2\pi\langle \beta y_o, t\rangle}$ in each term of the sum. Of course, the boundedness of $\phi(t)$ and any of its partial derivatives are valid because of the compact support of $\phi(t)$. Moreover, note that $|\beta(y_o)_j| \leq \beta|y_o|$, $j = 1, \ldots, n$. Thus, since the interior integral in (10) is over $\operatorname{supp}(\phi) \subset N(t_0; \gamma)$, we obtain the following bound on this interior integral:

$$\left| \int_{\operatorname{supp}(\phi)} (1 - \frac{\Delta}{4\pi^2})^m (e^{2\pi \langle \beta y_0, t \rangle} \phi(t)) e^{-2\pi i \langle x,t \rangle} dt \right|$$
$$\leq \int_{\operatorname{supp}(\phi)} |(1 - \frac{\Delta}{4\pi^2})^m (e^{2\pi \langle \beta y_0, t \rangle} \phi(t))| dt \quad (11)$$
$$\leq T_{\operatorname{supp}(\phi)} (1 + \beta|y_0|)^{4(m+1)} \sup_{t \in \operatorname{supp}(\phi)} e^{2\pi \langle \beta y_0, t \rangle}$$

where $T_{\operatorname{supp}(\phi)}$ is a positive constant depending only on $\operatorname{supp}(\phi)$. Using (11) in (10), we have

$$\mathcal{N}\left(\int_{\mathbb{R}^n} \frac{\mathbf{f}(x + i\beta y_0)}{(1 + |x|^2)^m} \int_{\operatorname{supp}(\phi)} (1 - \frac{\Delta}{4\pi^2})^m (e^{2\pi \langle \beta y_0, t \rangle} \phi(t)) e^{-2\pi i \langle x,t \rangle} dt dx \right)$$
$$\leq T_{\operatorname{supp}(\phi)} (1 + \beta|y_0|)^{4(m+1)} \sup_{t \in \operatorname{supp}(\phi)} e^{2\pi \langle \beta y_0, t \rangle} \int_{\mathbb{R}^n} \frac{\mathcal{N}(\mathbf{f}(x + i\beta y_0))}{(1 + |x|^2)^m} dx \quad (12)$$

where $y_0 \in C$, $\beta > 0$ is arbitrary, and $\operatorname{supp}(\phi) \subset N(t_0; \gamma) \subset C_*$, $t_0 \in C_*$, $\gamma > 0$ and fixed. As noted before, since $\langle y_0, t_0 \rangle < 0$ and C_* is open, by the continuity of $\langle t, y_0 \rangle$ at $t_0 \in C_*$ as a function of $t \in \mathbb{R}^n$, the fixed $\tau > 0$ is chosen and the fixed $N(t_0; \gamma) \subset C_*$ is chosen, such that $\langle t, y_0 \rangle < -\tau < 0$ for all $t \in N(t_0; \gamma) \subset C_*$. Since $\operatorname{supp}(\phi) \subset N(t_0; \gamma)$, we have

$$\sup_{t \in \operatorname{supp}(\phi)} e^{2\pi \langle \beta y_0, t \rangle} \leq e^{-2\pi \tau \beta},$$

which yields from (12)

$$\mathcal{N}\left(\int_{\mathbb{R}^n} \frac{\mathbf{f}(x + i\beta y_0)}{(1 + |x|^2)^m} \int_{\operatorname{supp}(\phi)} (1 - \frac{\Delta}{4\pi^2})^m (e^{2\pi \langle \beta y_0, t \rangle} \phi(t)) e^{-2\pi i \langle x,t \rangle} dt dx \right)$$
$$\leq T_{\operatorname{supp}(\phi)} e^{-2\pi \tau \beta} (1 + \beta|y_0|)^{4(m+1)} \int_{\mathbb{R}^n} \frac{\mathcal{N}(\mathbf{f}(x + i\beta y_0))}{(1 + |x|^2)^m} dx \quad (13)$$

where $y_0 \in C$, $\tau > 0$, and $\gamma > 0$ are fixed and are independent of the arbitrary $\beta > 0$. We now bound the integral on the right of the inequality in (13) using the assumed growth (5) on $\mathbf{f}(z)$, $z \in T^C$; (13) holds for all $\beta > 0$. To obtain the $\operatorname{supp}(V)$ containment result, we are going to let $\beta \to \infty$ in (13); thus, we may assume that $\beta > 1$ in the remainder of this proof. By simple calculations and for $\beta > 1$, we have

$$1 + |x + i\beta y_0| = \beta(\frac{1}{\beta} + ((\frac{|x|}{\beta})^2 + |y_0|^2)^{1/2}) \leq \beta(1 + (|x|^2 + |y_0|^2)^{1/2})$$

and

$$(1 + |x + i\beta y_0|)^q \leq \beta^q (1 + (|x|^2 + |y_0|^2)^{1/2})^q \leq \beta^q (1 + |y_0| + |x|)^q.$$

Hence, from (5),

$$\mathcal{N}(\mathbf{f}(x + i\beta y_0)) \leq M \beta^q (1 + |y_0| + |x|)^q |\beta y_0|^{-r}$$

and

$$\int_{\mathbb{R}^n} \frac{\mathcal{N}(\mathbf{f}(x + i\beta y_0))}{(1 + |x|^2)^m} dx \leq M \beta^{q-r} |y_0|^{-r} \int_{\mathbb{R}^n} \frac{(1 + |y_0| + |x|)^q}{(1 + |x|^2)^m} dx. \quad (14)$$

Combining (10), (12), (13), and (14) yields

$$\mathcal{N}\left(\int_{\mathbb{R}^n} \mathbf{f}(x+i\beta y_o) \int_{supp(\phi)} e^{2\pi\langle\beta y_o,t\rangle}\phi(t)e^{-2\pi i\langle x,t\rangle}dtdx\right) \qquad (15)$$

$$\leq MT_{supp(\phi)}(1+\beta|y_o|)^{4(m+1)}\beta^{q-r}|y_o|^{-r}e^{-2\pi\tau\beta}\int_{\mathbb{R}^n}\frac{(1+|y_o|+|x|)^q}{(1+|x|^2)^m}dx.$$

The positive integer m in (15) was introduced in (10), and at that point in the proof, m was arbitrary. We now choose m, such that $m > 2(q+n+1)$. With this choice of m, the integral in (15) converges where $y_o \in C$ is a fixed point in C; further, with this choice of m, all calculations from (10) leading to (15) are valid and the integrals converge. Because of the exponential term $e^{-2\pi\tau\beta}$, where $\tau > 0$ is fixed and now $\beta > 1$ is arbitrary, the right side of (15) has limit 0 as $\beta \to \infty$. Thus, from (9) $\langle V,\phi\rangle = \Theta$ for $\phi \in \mathcal{D}(\mathbb{R}^n)$, such that $supp(\phi) \subset N(t_o,\gamma) \subset C_*$ for t_o being an arbitrary but fixed point in the open set $C_* = \mathbb{R}^n \setminus C^*$. That is, for each fixed point, $t_o \in C_* = \mathbb{R}^n \setminus C^*$, with C_* being an open set, there is a neighborhood $N(t_o;\gamma) \subset C_*$ of t_o, such that for all $\phi \in \mathcal{D}(\mathbb{R}^n)$ with $supp(\phi) \subset N(t_o;\gamma)$, we have $\langle V,\phi\rangle = \Theta$. Thus, V vanishes on a neighborhood of each point of C_*; this proves that V vanishes on the open set $C_* = \mathbb{R}^n \setminus C^*$. Thus, $supp(V) \subseteq C^*$, which is a closed set in $\mathbb{R}^n$. The proof of Theorem 1 is complete. □

Yoshinaga [22] (Proposition 3) provides a representation of the tempered vector-valued distributions in the case of the topological vector space $\mathcal{X}$ being a complete space of type (DF). Yoshinaga's result is as follows for $\mathcal{X}$, being a complete space of type (DF): $V \in \mathcal{S}'(\mathbb{R}^n,\mathcal{X})$, if and only if there exists a continuous function $\mathbf{g}$ on $\mathbb{R}^n$ with values in $\mathcal{X}$, an integer $k \geq 0$, and a n-tuple α of nonnegative integers, such that $V = D^\alpha \mathbf{g}$ and $\{\mathbf{g}(t)/(1+|t|^2)^{kn}; t \in \mathbb{R}^n\}$ is a bounded subset of $\mathcal{X}$. (In fact, in Yoshinaga's symbolism, $\alpha = (k,k,...,k)$.)

The functions $\mathcal{S}'_2(\mathbb{R}^n,\mathcal{X})$ of Definition 1 are an integral part of the following corollary to Theorem 1; recall that these functions are defined by the necessity for $\mathcal{X}$ being a Banach space. We know that a Banach space satisfies all of the conditions on $\mathcal{X}$ stated prior to Theorem 1 and also is a complete norm space of type (DF); since a Hilbert space is a Banach space, a Hilbert space also satisfies all of these stated conditions on $\mathcal{X}$. Thus, the above-stated result of Yoshinaga and Theorem 1 of this paper both hold for $\mathcal{X}$ being a Banach or Hilbert space.

We obtain a corollary of Theorem 1 now in which more precise information is obtained concerning the spectral function V and the boundary value U of Theorem 1.

Corollary 1. *Let C be an open convex cone and $\mathcal{X}$ be a Banach space. Let $f(z)$ be analytic in $T^C = \mathbb{R}^n + iC$, have values in $\mathcal{X}$, and satisfy (5). There is a continuous function $\mathbf{g} \in \mathcal{S}'_2(\mathbb{R}^n,\mathcal{X})$ with $supp(\mathbf{g}) \subseteq C^*$ a.e. and an n-tuple α of nonnegative integers, such that the spectral function $V \in \mathcal{S}'(\mathbb{R}^n,\mathcal{X})$ of Theorem 1 has the form $V_t = D_t^\alpha \mathbf{g}(t)$, and there is $U = \mathcal{F}[V] \in \mathcal{S}'(\mathbb{R}^n,\mathcal{X})$ such that*

$$\lim_{y\to\overline{0},y\in C} f(x+iy) = U$$

in the weak and strong topologies of $\mathcal{S}'(\mathbb{R}^n,\mathcal{X})$. Further, for $\mathcal{X} = \mathcal{H}$ being a Hilbert space, we have $\mathcal{F}[\mathbf{g}] \in L^2(\mathbb{R}^n,\mathcal{H})$; and the boundary value $U \in \mathcal{S}'(\mathbb{R}^n,\mathcal{H})$ has the form

$$U_x = x^\alpha \mathcal{F}[\mathbf{g}]_x = x^\alpha(1-\frac{\Delta}{4\pi^2})^m h(x) \qquad (16)$$

in $\mathcal{S}'(\mathbb{R}^n,\mathcal{H})$ where $h \in L^2(\mathbb{R}^n,\mathcal{X})$, α is an n-tuple of nonnegative integers, and $m \geq 0$ is a real number that can be taken to be a nonnegative integer.

Proof. We apply the results of Theorem 1 and consider the spectral function $V \in \mathcal{S}'(\mathbb{R}^n,\mathcal{X})$ obtained in Theorem 1 where $\mathcal{X}$ is a Banach space in this corollary. As per the result of Yoshinaga [22] (Proposition 3) stated above, there is a continuous function $\mathbf{g}$ on $\mathbb{R}^n$

with values in $\mathcal{X}$, an n-tuple α of nonnegative integers, and an integer $k \geq 0$, such that $V_t = D_t^\alpha \mathbf{g}(t)$ and $\{\frac{\mathbf{g}(t)}{(1+|t|^2)^{kn}}; t \in \mathbb{R}^n\}$ is a bounded subset of $\mathcal{X}$. (In Yoshinaga's symbolism, α is the n-tuple with all components being k.) Thus, there is a real constant $R > 0$, such that

$$\mathcal{N}\left(\frac{\mathbf{g}(t)}{(1+|t|^2)^{kn}}\right) = \frac{\mathcal{N}(\mathbf{g}(t))}{(1+|t|^2)^{kn}} \leq R,\ t \in \mathbb{R}^n.$$

For the integer $k \geq 0$, we have

$$\int_{\mathbb{R}^n} (\mathcal{N}\left(\frac{\mathbf{g}(t)}{(1+|t|^2)^{(k+2)n}}\right))^2 dt$$

$$= \int_{\mathbb{R}^n} \left(\frac{1}{(1+|t|^2)^{2n}}\right)^2 (\mathcal{N}\left(\frac{\mathbf{g}(t)}{(1+|t|^2)^{kn}}\right))^2 dt$$

$$\leq R^2 \int_{\mathbb{R}^n} \frac{1}{(1+|t|^2)^{4n}} dt < \infty$$

which proves that $\mathbf{g} \in \mathcal{S}'_2(\mathbb{R}^n, \mathcal{X})$. Further, $\mathrm{supp}(\mathbf{g}) \subseteq C^*$ a.e. since $\mathrm{supp}(V) \subseteq C^*$. From Theorem 1, the boundary value $U \in \mathcal{S}'(\mathbb{R}^n, \mathcal{X})$ in (6) is $U = \mathcal{F}[V]$, the Fourier transform of the spectral function $V \in \mathcal{S}'(\mathbb{R}^n, \mathcal{X})$ in $\mathcal{S}'(\mathbb{R}^n, \mathcal{X})$. Moreover, from Theorem 1, the boundary value U is obtained in both the weak and strong topologies of $\mathcal{S}'(\mathbb{R}^n, \mathcal{X})$.

Now, let $\mathcal{X} = \mathcal{H}$, a Hilbert space, in this Corollary 1. Since $\mathbf{g} \in \mathcal{S}'_2(\mathbb{R}^n, \mathcal{H})$, then $\mathcal{F}[\mathbf{g}] \in L2(\mathbb{R}^n, \mathcal{H})$ in $\mathcal{S}'(\mathbb{R}^n, \mathcal{H})$ by Lemma 1. We know from the above that the boundary value $U \in \mathcal{S}'(\mathbb{R}^n, \mathcal{H})$ is $U = \mathcal{F}[V]$, and $V \in \mathcal{S}'(\mathbb{R}^n, \mathcal{H})$ has the form $V_t = D_t^\alpha \mathbf{g}(t)$ in $\mathcal{S}'(\mathbb{R}^n, \mathcal{H})$. Let $\phi \in \mathcal{S}(\mathbb{R}^n)$. We have

$$\langle U, \phi \rangle = \langle \mathcal{F}[V], \phi \rangle = \langle V, \hat{\phi} \rangle = \langle D_t^\alpha \mathbf{g}(t), \hat{\phi}(t) \rangle$$

$$= (-1)^{|\alpha|} \int_{\mathbb{R}^n} \mathbf{g}(t) D_t^\alpha \int_{\mathbb{R}^n} \phi(x) e^{2\pi i \langle x, t \rangle} dx dt$$

$$= (-1)^{|\alpha|} \int_{\mathbb{R}^n} \mathbf{g}(t) \int_{\mathbb{R}^n} \phi(x) (-1/2\pi i)^{|\alpha|} (2\pi i)^{|\alpha|} x^\alpha e^{2\pi i \langle x, t \rangle} dx dt$$

$$= \langle \mathbf{g}(t), \mathcal{F}[x^\alpha \phi(x); t] \rangle = \langle \mathcal{F}[\mathbf{g}]_x, x^\alpha \phi(x) \rangle = \langle x^\alpha \mathcal{F}[\mathbf{g}]_x, \phi(x) \rangle.$$

Thus, $U_x = x^\alpha \mathcal{F}[\mathbf{g}]_x$ in $\mathcal{S}'(\mathbb{R}^n, \mathcal{H})$ with $\mathbf{g} \in \mathcal{S}'_2(\mathbb{R}^n, \mathcal{H})$. Since $\mathbf{g} \in \mathcal{S}'_2(\mathbb{R}^n, \mathcal{H})$, by definition there is a real number $m \geq 0$, such that $\mathbf{g}(t)/(1+|t|^2)^m \in L^2(\mathbb{R}^n, \mathcal{H})$, and m can be taken to be a nonnegative integer. We have—by the proof of Lemma 1—that $\mathcal{F}[\mathbf{g}]_x = (1-(4\pi^2)^{-1}\Delta)^m \mathbf{h}(x) \in L2(\mathbb{R}^n, \mathcal{H})$ in $\mathcal{S}'(\mathbb{R}^n, \mathcal{H})$, where $\mathbf{h} \in L^2(\mathbb{R}^n, \mathcal{H})$ and Δ is the Laplace operator in the $x \in \mathbb{R}^n$ variable. Combining equalities, we have

$$U_x = x^\alpha \mathcal{F}[\mathbf{g}]_x = x^\alpha (1 - \frac{\Delta}{4\pi^2})^m \mathbf{h}(x)$$

in $\mathcal{S}'(\mathbb{R}^n, \mathcal{H})$ with $\mathbf{h} \in L^2(\mathbb{R}^n, \mathcal{H})$, which is (16). The proof is complete. □

5. Cauchy Integral

A Cauchy integral of tempered distributions $\mathcal{S}'(\mathbb{R}^n)$ has been defined in one and many dimensions. Of course, the main problem in making such a definition is that the Cauchy kernel is not a tempered function in $\mathcal{S}(\mathbb{R}^n)$; an arbitrary element of $\mathcal{S}'(\mathbb{R}^n)$ applied to the Cauchy kernel is not well defined.

Let C be a regular cone in $\mathbb{R}^n$; that is, C is an open convex cone that does not contain an entirely straight line. With C^* being the dual cone of C, the Cauchy kernel function is

$$K(z-t) = \int_{C^*} e^{2\pi i \langle z-t, u \rangle} du,\ z \in T^C,\ t \in \mathbb{R}^n,$$

as defined in Section 3. For the tube T^C being the upper or lower half-planes in $\mathbb{C}^1$ or the tube defined by one of the 2^n quadrant cones $C_\mu = \{y \in \mathbb{R}^n : (-1)^{\mu_j} y_j > 0,\ j = 1, \ldots, n\}$

where μ is any of the 2^n n-tuples whose components are either 0 or 1, the Cauchy kernel takes the usual form. In order to generate an element of $\mathcal{S}(\mathbb{R}^n)$ from the Cauchy kernel in the half plane setting in $\mathbb{C}^1$ and the tube defined by a quadrant cone, one divides the Cauchy kernel by a certain specifically chosen polynomial.

Sebastião e Silva [5] introduced a Cauchy integral for tempered distributions in the half-plane setting. Carmichael [7] defined a Cauchy integral for tempered distributions in the $\mathbb{C}^n$ setting corresponding to analytic functions in the quadrant cone setting T^{C_μ} in $\mathbb{C}^n$ and showed that the analytic functions in $(\mathbb{C} - \mathbb{R})^n$, which have distributional boundary values in $\mathcal{S}'(\mathbb{R}^n)$, can be recovered as the Cauchy integral of the boundary value; the results of [7] can be extended to the vector-valued tempered distributions considered in this paper by the same techniques as those in [7]. The Cauchy integrals introduced by both Sebastião e Silva and Carmichael are in fact equivalence classes of analytic functions defined by an integral involving the Cauchy kernel. Vladimirov [8–10] has defined a Cauchy integral for tempered distributions associated with analytic functions in general tubes $T^C = \mathbb{R}^n + iC \subset \mathbb{C}^n$ corresponding to regular cones C similar to the analytic functions we considered in this paper. Vladimirov showed that the analytic functions that he considered can be recovered by a Cauchy integral involving the tempered distributional boundary values of the analytic functions. The papers mentioned in this paragraph all concern scalar-valued analytic functions and distributions.

In this section, we build on our analyses of Sections 3 and 4 to obtain a Cauchy integral representation of the vector-valued analytic functions, which we considered in Theorem 1 and in Corollary 1. The proof of our results here—and the forms of our results—are different from any of the previous results concerning the Cauchy integral of the tempered distribution representation of the analytic functions. By our technique here, we do not need to divide the Cauchy kernel or the boundary value in (16) by a specified form of the polynomial and do not need to apply other special features of proof previously used by the authors in order to obtain that our Cauchy integral is well defined and that the analytic function considered is represented by a Cauchy integral involving the boundary value.

The Cauchy integral representation of the analytic functions that we considered in this paper follows. Note that cone C in the following result is assumed to be a regular cone. In Theorem 1 and Corollary 1, we assumed that cone C was an open convex cone. However, an open convex cone could contain an entirely straight line; in this case, the dual cone has measure 0 and $K(z - t) = 0$, $z \in T^C$, $t \in \mathbb{R}^n$. To avoid this triviality, we assume that cone C in the following Cauchy integral representation is a regular cone.

Theorem 2. *Let C be a regular cone in $\mathbb{R}^n$ and $\mathcal{H}$ be a Hilbert space. Let $f(z)$ be analytic in $T^C = \mathbb{R}^n + iC$, have values in $\mathcal{H}$, and satisfy (5). There is a continuous function $g \in \mathcal{S}'_2(\mathbb{R}^n, \mathcal{H})$ with $\operatorname{supp}(g) \subseteq C^*$ a.e. and an n-tuple α of nonnegative integers, such that*

$$f(z) = z^\alpha \langle \mathcal{F}[g]_\nu, K(z-\nu)\rangle, \ z \in T^C, \tag{17}$$

in $\mathcal{S}'(\mathbb{R}^n, \mathcal{H})$. Further,

$$\langle \mathcal{F}[g]_\nu, K(z-\nu)\rangle = \Theta, \ z \in T^{-C}, \tag{18}$$

in $\mathcal{S}'(\mathbb{R}^n, \mathcal{H})$.

Proof. From Theorem 1, there is an element $V \in \mathcal{S}'(\mathbb{R}^n, \mathcal{H})$, the spectral function of $\mathbf{f}(z)$, $z \in T^C$, such that $e^{-2\pi\langle y,t\rangle}V_t \in \mathcal{S}'(\mathbb{R}^n, \mathcal{H})$, $y \in C$; $\operatorname{supp}(V) \subseteq C^*$; and $\mathbf{f}(z) = \mathcal{F}[e^{-2\pi\langle y,t\rangle}V_t]_x$, $y \in C$, in $\mathcal{S}'(\mathbb{R}^n, \mathcal{H})$. Further, by Corollary 1, there is a continuous function $\mathbf{g} \in \mathcal{S}'_2(\mathbb{R}^n, \mathcal{H})$ with $\operatorname{supp}(\mathbf{g}) \subseteq C^*$ a.e. and an n-tuple α of nonnegative integers, such that $V_t = D_t^\alpha \mathbf{g}(t)$, $t \in \mathbb{R}^n$. Now, let $\phi \in \mathcal{S}(\mathbb{R}^n)$ and $z = x + iy \in T^C$. Recall that we have defined the differential operator D to be $D_t = (-1/2\pi i)(\frac{\partial}{\partial t_1}, \ldots, \frac{\partial}{\partial t_n})$. We have

$$\begin{aligned}
\langle \mathbf{f}(x+iy), \phi(x) \rangle &= \langle \mathcal{F}[e^{-2\pi\langle y,t \rangle} V_t]_x, \phi(x) \rangle \\
&= \langle e^{-2\pi\langle y,t \rangle} V_t, \hat{\phi}(t) \rangle = \langle V_t, \int_{\mathbb{R}} \phi(x) e^{2\pi i \langle z,t \rangle} dx \rangle \\
&= \langle D_t^\alpha \mathbf{g}(t), \int_{\mathbb{R}^n} \phi(x) e^{2\pi i \langle z,t \rangle} dx \rangle \\
&= (-1)^{|\alpha|} \int_{C^*} \mathbf{g}(t) \int_{\mathbb{R}^n} \phi(x)(-1/2\pi i)^{|\alpha|} (2\pi i)^{|\alpha|} z^\alpha e^{2\pi i \langle z,t \rangle} dxdt \\
&= \int_{C^*} \mathbf{g}(t) \int_{\mathbb{R}^n} \phi(x) z^\alpha e^{-2\pi\langle y,t \rangle} e^{2\pi i \langle x,t \rangle} dxdt \\
&= \int_{C^*} e^{-2\pi\langle y,t \rangle} \mathbf{g}(t) \mathcal{F}[z^\alpha \phi(x); t] dt \\
&= \langle z^\alpha \mathcal{F}[I_{C^*}(t) e^{-2\pi\langle y,t \rangle} \mathbf{g}(t)]_x, \phi(x) \rangle
\end{aligned} \quad (19)$$

where $I_{C^*}(t)$ is the characteristic function of C^*. We have proven in [17] (Lemma 4.2.1, p. 62) that $I_{C^*}(t) e^{-2\pi\langle y,t \rangle} \in L^p$, $y \in C$, for all p, $1 \leq p \leq \infty$. Since $\mathbf{g} \in \mathcal{S}'_2(\mathbb{R}^n, \mathcal{H})$, then $\mathcal{F}[\mathbf{g}]_x \in L2(\mathbb{R}^n, \mathcal{H})$ in $\mathcal{S}'(\mathbb{R}^n, \mathcal{H})$ by Lemma 1. Recall also from Section 3 that the Cauchy kernel $K(z - \cdot) \in \mathcal{D}(*, L^p) \subset \mathcal{D}_{L^p}(\mathbb{R}^n)$, $1 < p \leq \infty$, for $z \in T^C$ with C being a regular cone and that an element of $L2(\mathbb{R}^n, \mathcal{H})$ applied to $K(z - \cdot)$, $z \in T^C$, is a well-defined function of $z \in T^C$. Continuing (19) and using convolution, we now have

$$\begin{aligned}
\langle \mathbf{f}(x+iy), \phi(x) \rangle &= \langle z^\alpha (\mathcal{F}[\mathbf{g}] * \mathcal{F}[I_{C^*}(t) e^{-2\pi\langle y,t \rangle}])_x, \phi(x) \rangle \\
&= \langle z^\alpha \langle \mathcal{F}[\mathbf{g}]_v, \mathcal{F}[I_{C^*}(t) e^{-2\pi\langle y,t \rangle}]_{(x-v)} \rangle, \phi(x) \rangle \\
&= \langle z^\alpha \langle \mathcal{F}[\mathbf{g}]_v, \int_{C^*} e^{2\pi i \langle z-v, t \rangle} dt \rangle, \phi(x) \rangle \\
&= \langle z^\alpha \langle \mathcal{F}[\mathbf{g}]_v, K(z-v) \rangle, \phi(x) \rangle
\end{aligned} \quad (20)$$

where $I_{C^*}(t)$ is the characteristic function of C^*. Since $\mathbf{g} \in \mathcal{S}'_2(\mathbb{R}^n, \mathcal{H})$, then $\mathcal{F}[\mathbf{g}] \in L2(\mathbb{R}^n, \mathcal{H})$ by Lemma 1; and as previously noted, $\mathcal{F}[\mathbf{g}]$ applied to the Cauchy kernel is a well-defined function of $z \in T^C$ and is an analytic function of $z \in T^C$ with values in $\mathcal{H}$. Thus, from (20) we have obtained

$$\mathbf{f}(z) = z^\alpha \langle \mathcal{F}[\mathbf{g}]_v, K(z-v) \rangle, \; z \in T^C,$$

in $\mathcal{S}'(\mathbb{R}^n, \mathcal{H})$, and (17) is obtained.

To prove (18), first note that for a regular cone, C, $-C$ is also a regular cone; and $(-C)^* = -C^*$. Thus, for $z \in T^{-C}$ and $\phi \in \mathcal{S}(\mathbb{R}^n)$,

$$\begin{aligned}
\langle \langle \mathcal{F}[\mathbf{g}]_v, K(z-v) \rangle, \phi(x) \rangle &= \langle \langle \mathcal{F}[\mathbf{g}]_v, \int_{-C^*} e^{-2\pi\langle y,t \rangle} e^{2\pi i \langle x-v, t \rangle} dt \rangle, \phi(x) \rangle \\
&= \langle \langle \mathcal{F}[\mathbf{g}]_v, \mathcal{F}[I_{-C^*}(t) e^{-2\pi\langle y,t \rangle}]_{(x-v)} \rangle, \phi(x) \rangle \\
&= \langle \langle (\mathcal{F}[\mathbf{g}] * \mathcal{F}[I_{-C^*}(t) e^{-2\pi\langle y,t \rangle}])_x \rangle, \phi(x) \rangle \\
&= \langle \mathcal{F}[I_{-C^*}(t) e^{-2\pi\langle y,t \rangle} \mathbf{g}(t)]_x, \phi(x) \rangle.
\end{aligned} \quad (21)$$

Now $I_{-C^*}(t) = 0$ if $t \notin -C^*$ and, hence, if $t \in C^*$. This fact coupled with the fact that $\operatorname{supp}(\mathbf{g}) \subseteq C^*$ a.e. yields $I_{-C^*}(t) e^{-2\pi\langle y,t \rangle} \mathbf{g}(t) = \Theta$ a.e. for $t \in \mathbb{R}^n$ and $y \in -C$. Hence $\mathcal{F}[I_{-C^*}(t) e^{-2\pi\langle y,t \rangle} \mathbf{g}(t)]_x = \Theta$, $x \in \mathbb{R}^n$, $y \in -C$, in (21). Thus, from (21), we have $\langle \mathcal{F}[\mathbf{g}]_v, K(z-v) \rangle = \Theta$, $z \in T^{-C}$, in $\mathcal{S}'(\mathbb{R}^n, \mathcal{H})$; and (18) is obtained. □

6. Conclusions

Tillmann [1] obtained the original analysis concerning the scalar-valued tempered distributions $\mathcal{S}'(\mathbb{R}^n)$ as boundary values of analytic functions. We proved a boundary value result concerning vector-valued tempered distributions $\mathcal{S}'(\mathbb{R}^n, \mathcal{X})$ as boundary values of vector-valued analytic functions in [4] (Theorem 8) but used a norm growth condition on the analytic functions, which was a special case for the growth of Tillmann. We desired to obtain a result, such as [4] (Theorem 8), but under the general norm growth on the analytic function, which was equivalent to the growth of Tillmann. We achieved this first goal of this paper in Theorem 1 for vector-valued analytic functions $f(z)$ on tubes $T^C = \mathbb{R}^n + iC$ with C being an open convex cone. The values of the analytic functions and the tempered distributions were in a very general type of topological vector space. We achieved additional information in Theorem 1 concerning the spectral function of the analytic function.

We asked if additional information concerning the spectral function and the boundary value could be obtained if the topological vector space $\mathcal{X}$ was restricted somewhat. We obtained the desired information in Corollary 1 by restricting $\mathcal{X}$ to be a Banach space and then a Hilbert space; we showed the structure of the spectral function and the boundary value in these cases for $\mathcal{X}$. Integral to this analysis was the Lemma 1 result, which proved the relation under the Fourier transform between two important subsets of $\mathcal{S}'(\mathbb{R}^n, \mathcal{H})$ for our results in Corollary 1. It is important to note that the reason to restrict to Hilbert space $\mathcal{H}$ (which we do in our results) is that the Plancherel theory for the Fourier transform of the functions holds if and only if the functions have value in the Hilbert space.

The second principal goal of this paper was to obtain a Cauchy integral representation of the analytic functions considered in Theorem 1 and Corollary 1. Sebastião e Silva, Carmichael, and Vladimirov have obtained and studied the Cauchy integral of tempered distributions $\mathcal{S}'(\mathbb{R}^n)$ in the scalar-valued case and in one and several dimensions; see the papers of these authors in the references. Their analyses basically concerned dividing the Cauchy kernel or the boundary value by a suitable polynomial whose order was large enough to make the quotient when evaluated by the tempered distribution to be well defined, or used other special features of proof that we do not use here.

In Section 5 of this paper, we constructed our Cauchy integral used in the representation of the assumed analytic function in a different manner by using the general known structure of the spectral function and our proven structure of the tempered distributional boundary value in $\mathcal{S}'(\mathbb{R}^n, \mathcal{H})$ for $\mathcal{H}$ being a Hilbert space. The analytic function obtaining the boundary value in $\mathcal{S}'(\mathbb{R}^n, \mathcal{H})$ was shown to be equated to the product of a polynomial and the constructed Cauchy integral.

This paper concerns theoretical mathematics, yet the topics considered find applications in mathematical physics and in mathematics that are applied to physical problems. We survey historically some areas of application in the scalar-valued case. We recall the work of Streater and Wightman [23] in studying quantum field theory. In a field theory, the "vacuum expectation values" are tempered distributions, which are boundary values in the tempered distribution topology of analytic functions with the analytic functions being Fourier–Laplace transforms. In addition, a field theory can be recovered from its "vacuum expectation values"; see [23] (Chapter 3). A similar field theory analysis using boundary values of analytic functions is contained in the work by Simon [24]. We also reference Raina [25] concerning "form factor bounds" in particle physics in which tempered distributional boundary values, which are of a special form, imply that the analytic functions that obtain these boundary values are Hardy H^p functions; this fact is then used in the analysis of the "form factor bounds". See also the associated papers listed in the references of [25].

As noted in Vladimirov [8], scalar-valued analytic functions of the type that we considered in this paper can arise in applying the Fourier–Laplace transform to convolution equations, which describe linear homogeneous processes with causality that find application in the quantum field theory, theory of electrical circuits, scattering of electromagnetic waves, and linear thermodynamic systems; refer to the list of references in [8]. We also note paper [26] by Vladimirov, concerning the linear conjugacy of scalar-valued analytic functions of several complex variables, which are again of the type that we considered in this paper with respect to growth. The linear conjugacy analysis involves scalar-valued tempered distributional boundary values of analytic functions represented as Fourier–

Laplace integrals. Vladimirov [26] (p. 207) states that many problems arising in mathematical physics reduce to the problem of linear conjugacy involving tempered distributions; Vladimirov [26] provides examples of such problems.

The survey of applications above (concerning the type of analysis used in this paper) involve scalar-valued functions and distributions. Yet, a close consideration of the linear conjugacy problem of [26], together with the vector-valued analysis of this paper, leads one to believe that the linear conjugacy problem can be extended to the vector-valued case. Further, in an analysis of the stated applications above, one must sometimes obtain a distributional solution of a partial differential equation; such calculations can be extended to the vector-valued case. We suggest that the considerable related analyses to the results of this paper and the results of related references in this paper can be achieved in the vector-valued case and will work toward this end in the future.

Funding: This research received no external funding.

Institutional Review Board Statement: Not applicable.

Informed Consent Statement: Not applicable.

Data Availability Statement: Not applicable.

Conflicts of Interest: The author declares no conflict of interest.

References

1. Tillmann, H.-G. Darstellung der Schwartzschen Distributionen durch analytische Funktionen. *Math. Z.* **1961**, *77*, 106–124. [CrossRef]
2. Köthe, G. Die Randverteilungen analytischer Funktionen. *Math. Z.* **1952**, *57*, 13–33. [CrossRef]
3. Köthe, G. Dualität in der Funktionentheorie. *J. Reine Angew. Math.* **1953**, *191*, 30–49. [CrossRef]
4. Carmichael, R.D.; Walker, W.W. Representation of distributions with compact support. *Manuscr. Math.* **1974**, *11*, 305–338. [CrossRef]
5. Sebastião e Silva, J. Les séries de multipôles des physiciens et la théorie des ultradistributions. *Math. Annalen* **1967**, *174*, 109–142. [CrossRef]
6. Sebastião e Silva, J. Les fonctions analytiques comme ultra-distributions dan le calcul opérationnel. *Math. Annalen* **1958**, *136*, 58–96. [CrossRef]
7. Carmichael, R.D. n-dimensional Cauchy integral of tempered distributions. *J. Elisha Mitchell Sci. Soc.* **1977**, *93*, 115–135.
8. Vladimirov, V.S. Generalization of the Cauchy-Bochner integral representation. *Math. USSR Izv.* **1969**, *3*, 87–104. [CrossRef]
9. Vladimirov, V.S. On Cauchy-Bochner representations. *Math. USSR Izv.* **1972**, *6*, 529–535. [CrossRef]
10. Vladimirov, V.S. The Laplace transform of tempered distributions. *Glob. Anal. Appl. Int. Sem. Course Trieste.* **1974**, *III*, 243–270.
11. Vladimirov, V.S. *Methods of the Theory of Functions of Many Complex Variables*; The M.I.T. Press: Cambridge, MA, USA, 1966.
12. Vladimirov, V.S. *Generalized Functions in Mathematical Physics*; Mir Publishers: Moscow, Russia, 1979.
13. Dunford, N.; Schwartz, J. *Linear Operators Part I*; Interscience Publishers Inc.: New York, NY, USA, 1966.
14. Schwartz, L. Théorie des Distributions a Valeurs Vectorielles I. *Ann. Inst. Fourier* **1957**, *7*, 1–149. [CrossRef]
15. Schwartz, L. Théorie des Distributions a Valeurs Vectorielles II. *Ann. Inst. Fourier* **1958**, *8*, 1–209. [CrossRef]
16. Carmichael, R.D. Generalized vector-valued Hardy functions. *Axioms* **2022**, *11*, 39. [CrossRef]
17. Carmichael, R.D.; Kamiński, A.; Pilipović, S. *Boundary Values and Convolution in Ultradistribution Spaces*; World Scientific Publishing: Singapore, 2007.
18. Arendt, W.; Batty, C.; Hieber, M.; Neubrander, F. *Vector-Valued Laplace Transforms and Cauchy Problems*, 2nd ed.; Birkhauser/Springer: Basel, Switzerland, 2011.
19. Kwapień, S. Isomorphic characterizations of inner product spaces by orthogonal series with vector valued coefficients. *Studia Math.* **1972**, *44*, 583–595. [CrossRef]
20. Schwartz, L. Transformation de Laplace des distributions. *Comm. Sém. Math. Univ. Lund (Tome Suppl.)* **1952**, 196–206.
21. Lions, J.L. Supports dans la Tranformation de Laplace. *J. Analyse Math.* **1952–1953**, *11*, 369–380. [CrossRef]
22. Yoshinaga, K. Values of vector-valued distributions and smoothness of semi-group distributions. *Bull. Kyushu Inst. Tech.* **1965**, *12*, 1–27.
23. Streater, R.F.; Wightman, A.S. *PCT, Spin and Statistics, and All That*; W. A. Benjamin, Inc.: New York, NY, USA, 1964.
24. Simon, B. *The $P(\Phi)_2$ Euclidean (Quantum) Field Theory*; Princeton University Press: Princeton, NJ, USA, 1974.
25. Raina, A.K. On the role of Hardy spaces in form factor bounds. *Lett. Math. Phys.* **1978**, *2*, 513–519. [CrossRef]
26. Vladimirov, V.S. Problems of linear conjugacy of holomorphic functions of several complex variables. *Amer. Math. Soc. Transl.* **1968**, *71*, 203–232.

Article

On Special Fuzzy Differential Subordinations Obtained for Riemann–Liouville Fractional Integral of Ruscheweyh and Sălăgean Operators

Alina Alb Lupaş

Department of Mathematics and Computer Science, University of Oradea, 1 Universitatii Street, 410087 Oradea, Romania; alblupas@gmail.com

Abstract: New results concerning fuzzy differential subordination theory are obtained in this paper using the operator denoted by $D_z^{-\lambda} L_\alpha^n$, previously introduced by applying the Riemann–Liouville fractional integral to the convex combination of well-known Ruscheweyh and Sălăgean differential operators. A new fuzzy subclass $DL_n^{\mathcal{F}}(\delta, \alpha, \lambda)$ is defined and studied involving the operator $D_z^{-\lambda} L_\alpha^n$. Fuzzy differential subordinations are obtained considering functions from class $DL_n^{\mathcal{F}}(\delta, \alpha, \lambda)$ and the fuzzy best dominants are also given. Using particular functions interesting corollaries are obtained and an example shows how the obtained results can be applied.

Keywords: differential operator; fuzzy differential subordination; fuzzy best dominant; fractional integral

MSC: 30C45; 30A10; 33C05

1. Introduction

The concept of fuzzy set, introduced by Lotfi A. Zadeh in 1965 [1], has opened the way for a new theory called fuzzy set theory. It has developed intensely, nowadays having applications in many branches of science and technology.

The fuzzy set concept was applied for developing new directions of study in many mathematical theories. In geometric function theory, it was used for introducing the new concepts of fuzzy subordination [2] and fuzzy differential subordinations [3] as generalizations of the classical notion of differential subordination due to Miller and Mocanu [4,5]. The main aspects regarding the theory of differential subordination can be found in [6]. Steps in the evolution of the theory of fuzzy differential subordination can be followed in [7].

The general context of the study presented in this paper contains notions familiar to geometric function theory merged with fuzzy set theory. We first present the main classes of analytic functions involved and the definitions regarding fuzzy differential subordination theory.

$U = \{z \in \mathbb{C} : |z| < 1\}$ represents the unit disc of the complex plane and $\mathcal{H}(U)$ the space of holomorphic functions in U.

Consider $\mathcal{A} = \{f \in \mathcal{H}(U) : f(z) = z + a_2 z^2 + \ldots, z \in U\}$, and $\mathcal{H}[a, m] = \{f \in \mathcal{H}(U) : f(z) = a + a_m z^m + a_{m+1} z^{m+1} + \ldots, z \in U\}$, for $a \in \mathbb{C}$ and $m \in \mathbb{N}$.

We remember the usual definitions needed for fuzzy differential subordination:

Definition 1 ([8]). *A fuzzy subset of X is a pair (M, F_A), with $M = \{x \in X : 0 < F_M(x) \le 1\}$ the support of the fuzzy set and $F_M : X \to [0, 1]$ the membership function of the fuzzy set. It is denoted $M = \text{supp}(M, F_M)$.*

Remark 1. *When $M \subset X$, we have $F_M(x) = \begin{cases} 1, & \text{if } x \in M, \\ 0, & \text{if } x \notin M. \end{cases}$*

Evidently $F_\emptyset(x) = 0$, $x \in X$, and $F_X(x) = 1$, $x \in X$.

Definition 2 ([2]). *Let $D \subset \mathbb{C}$ and let $z_0 \in D$ be a fixed point. We take the functions $f, g \in \mathcal{H}(D)$. The function f is said to be fuzzy subordinate to g and we write $f \prec_F g$, if there exists a function $F : \mathbb{C} \to [0, 1]$ such that $f(z_0) = g(z_0)$ and $F_{f(D)}f(z) \leq F_{g(D)}g(z)$, $z \in D$.*

Remark 2. *(1) If g is univalent, then $f \prec_F g$ if and only if $f(z_0) = g(z_0)$ and $f(D) \subset g(D)$.*
(2) Such a function $F : \mathbb{C} \to [0,1]$ can be consider $F(z) = \frac{|z|}{1+|z|}$, $F(z) = \frac{1}{1+|z|}$.
(3) If $D = U$ the conditions become $f(0) = g(0)$ and $f(U) \subset g(U)$, which is equivalent to the classical definition of subordination.

Definition 3 ([3]). *Consider h an univalent function in U and $\psi : \mathbb{C}^3 \times U \to \mathbb{C}$, such that $h(0) = \psi(a, 0; 0) = a$. When the fuzzy differential subordination*

$$F_{\psi(\mathbb{C}^3 \times U)}\psi(p(z), zp'(z), z^2 p''(z); z) \leq F_{h(U)} h(z), \quad z \in U, \tag{1}$$

is satisfied for an analytic function p in U, such that $p(0) = a$, then p is called a fuzzy solution of the fuzzy differential subordination. A fuzzy dominant of the fuzzy solutions of the fuzzy differential subordination is an univalent function q for which $F_{p(U)} p(z) \leq F_{q(U)} q(z)$, $z \in U$, for all p satisfying (1). The fuzzy best dominant of (1) is a fuzzy dominant $\tilde{q}$, such that $F_{\tilde{q}(U)} \tilde{q}(z) \leq F_{q(U)} q(z)$, $z \in U$, for all fuzzy dominants q of (1).

Lemma 1 ([6]). *Consider $h \in \mathcal{A}$. If $\operatorname{Re}\left(\frac{zh''(z)}{h'(z)} + 1\right) > -\frac{1}{2}$, $z \in U$, then $\frac{1}{z}\int_0^z h(t)dt$ is a convex function, $z \in U$.*

Lemma 2 ([9]). *Consider a convex function h with $h(0) = a$, and $\gamma \in \mathbb{C}^*$ such that $\operatorname{Re}\gamma \geq 0$. When $p \in \mathcal{H}[a, m]$, $\psi : \mathbb{C}^2 \times U \to \mathbb{C}$, $\psi(p(z), zp'(z); z) = \frac{1}{\gamma} zp'(z) + p(z)$ is an analytic function in U and*

$$F_{\psi(\mathbb{C}^2 \times U)}\left(\frac{1}{\gamma} zp'(z) + p(z)\right) \leq F_{h(U)} h(z), \quad z \in U,$$

then

$$F_{p(U)} p(z) \leq F_{g(U)} g(z) \leq F_{h(U)} h(z), \quad z \in U,$$

with the convex function $g(z) = \frac{\gamma}{mz^{\frac{\gamma}{m}}} \int_0^z h(t) t^{\frac{\gamma}{m}-1} dt$, $z \in U$ as the fuzzy best dominant.

Lemma 3 ([9]). *Consider a convex function g in U and define $h(z) = m\alpha zg'(z) + g(z)$, $z \in U$, with $m \in \mathbb{N}$ and $\alpha > 0$.*
If $p(z) = g(0) + p_m z^m + p_{m+1} z^{m+1} + \ldots$, $z \in U$, is a holomorphic function in U and

$$F_{p(U)}(p(z) + \alpha z p'(z)) \leq F_{h(U)} h(z), \quad z \in U,$$

then we obtain the sharp result

$$F_{p(U)} p(z) \leq F_{g(U)} g(z), z \in U.$$

The original results exposed in this paper are obtained using the well-known Ruscheweyh and Sălăgean differential operators combined with Riemann–Liouville fractional integral. The resulting operator was introduced in [10], where it was used for obtaining results involving classical differential subordination theory. The necessary definitions are reminded:

Definition 4 (Ruscheweyh [11]). *The Ruscheweyh operator R^n is introduced by $R^n : \mathcal{A} \to \mathcal{A}$,*

$$R^0 f(z) = f(z),$$
$$R^1 f(z) = z f'(z),$$
$$\ldots$$
$$(n+1) R^{n+1} f(z) = n R^n f(z) + z(R^n f(z))',$$

for $f \in \mathcal{A}, n \in \mathbb{N}, z \in U$.

Remark 3. *For a function $f(z) = z + \sum_{j=2}^{\infty} a_j z^j \in \mathcal{A}$, the Ruscheweyh operator can be written using the following form $R^n f(z) = z + \sum_{j=2}^{\infty} \frac{\Gamma(n+j)}{\Gamma(n+1)\Gamma(j)} a_j z^j$, $z \in U$, where Γ denotes the gamma function.*

Definition 5 (Sălăgean [12]). *The Sălăgean operator S^n is introduced by $S^n : \mathcal{A} \to \mathcal{A}$,*

$$S^0 f(z) = f(z),$$
$$S^1 f(z) = z f'(z),$$
$$\ldots$$
$$S^{n+1} f(z) = z(S^n f(z))',$$

for $f \in \mathcal{A}, n \in \mathbb{N}, z \in U$.

Remark 4. *For a function $f(z) = z + \sum_{j=2}^{\infty} a_j z^j \in \mathcal{A}$, the Sălăgean operator can be written using the following form $S^n f(z) = z + \sum_{j=2}^{\infty} j^n a_j z^j$, $z \in U$.*

Definition 6 ([13]). *Define the linear operator $L_\alpha^n : \mathcal{A} \to \mathcal{A}$, given by*

$$L_\alpha^n f(z) = \alpha S^n f(z) + (1-\alpha) R^n f(z), \quad z \in U,$$

where $\alpha \geq 0, n \in \mathbb{N}$.

Remark 5. *For a function $f(z) = z + \sum_{j=2}^{\infty} a_j z^j \in \mathcal{A}$, the defined operator can be written using the following form $L_\alpha^n f(z) = z + \sum_{j=2}^{\infty} \left[\alpha j^n + (1-\alpha) \frac{\Gamma(n+j)}{\Gamma(n+1)\Gamma(j)} \right] a_j z^j$, $z \in U$.*

We also remind the definition of Riemann–Liouville fractional integral:

Definition 7 ([14]). *The Riemann–Liouville fractional integral of order λ applied to an analytic function f is defined by*

$$D_z^{-\lambda} f(z) = \frac{1}{\Gamma(\lambda)} \int_0^z \frac{f(t)}{(z-t)^{1-\lambda}} dt,$$

with $\lambda > 0$.

In [10] we defined the Riemann–Liouville fractional integral applied to the operator L_α^n as follows:

Definition 8 ([10]). *The Riemann–Liouville fractional integral applied to the differential operator $L_\alpha^n f$ is introduced by*

$$D_z^{-\lambda} L_\alpha^n f(z) = \frac{1}{\Gamma(\lambda)} \int_0^z \frac{L_\alpha^n f(t)}{(z-t)^{1-\lambda}} dt =$$

$$\frac{1}{\Gamma(\lambda)} \int_0^z \frac{t}{(z-t)^{1-\lambda}} dt + \sum_{j=2}^{\infty} \left(\alpha j^n + (1-\alpha) \frac{\Gamma(n+j)}{\Gamma(n+1)\Gamma(j)} \right) a_j \int_0^z \frac{t^j}{(z-t)^{1-\lambda}} dt,$$

where $\alpha \geq 0$, $\lambda > 0$ and $n \in \mathbb{N}$.

Remark 6. *For a function $f(z) = z + \sum_{j=2}^{\infty} a_j z^j \in \mathcal{A}$, the Riemann–Liouville fractional integral of $L_\alpha^n f$ has the following form*

$$D_z^{-\lambda} L_\alpha^n f(z) = \frac{1}{\Gamma(2+\lambda)} z^{1+\lambda} + \sum_{j=2}^{\infty} \left[\frac{\alpha j^m \Gamma(j+1)}{\Gamma(j+\lambda+1)} + \frac{(1-\alpha)j\Gamma(m+j)}{\Gamma(m+1)\Gamma(j+\lambda+1)} \right] a_j z^{j+\lambda},$$

and $D_z^{-\lambda} L_\alpha^n f(z) \in \mathcal{H}[0, \lambda+1]$.

The results exposed in this paper follow a line of research concerned with fuzzy differential subordinations which is popular nowadays, namely introducing new operators and using them for defining and studying new fuzzy classes of functions.

Fuzzy differential subordinations involving Ruscheweyh and Sălăgean differential operators were obtained in many studies, such as [15]. New operators introduced using fractional integral and applied in fuzzy differential subordination theory were studied in [16] where Riemann–Liouville fractional integral is applied for Gaussian hypergeometric function and in [17] where Riemann–Liouville fractional integral is combined with confluent hypergeometric function.

Motivated by the nice results obtained in fuzzy differential subordination theory using Ruscheweyh and Sălăgean differential operators and fractional integral applied to different known operators, the study presented in this paper uses the previously defined operator $D_z^{-\lambda} L_\alpha^n$ given in Definition 8 applied for obtaining new fuzzy differential subordinations. In the next section, a new fuzzy class will be defined and studied in order to obtain fuzzy differential subordinations inspired by recently published studies concerned with the same topic seen in [18–20].

The main results contained in Section 2 of the paper, begin with the definition of a new fuzzy class $DL_n^{\mathcal{F}}(\delta, \alpha, \lambda)$ for which the operator $D_z^{-\lambda} L_\alpha^n$ given in Definition 8 is used. The property of this class to be convex is proved and certain fuzzy differential subordinations involving functions from the class and the operator $D_z^{-\lambda} L_\alpha^n$ are obtained. The fuzzy best dominants are given for the considered fuzzy differential subordinations in theorems which generate interesting corollaries when specific functions with remarkable geometric properties are used as fuzzy best dominants. An example is also shown in order to prove the applicability of the new results.

2. Main Results

The usage of the operator $D_z^{-\lambda} L_\alpha^n$ seen in Definition 8 defines a new fuzzy subclass of analytic functions as follows:

Definition 9. *The class $DL_n^{\mathcal{F}}(\delta, \alpha, \lambda)$ is composed of all functions $f \in \mathcal{A}$ with the property*

$$F_{\left(D_z^{-\lambda} L_\alpha^n f\right)'(U)} \left(D_z^{-\lambda} L_\alpha^n f(z) \right)' > \delta, \quad z \in U,$$

where $n \in \mathbb{N}$, $\delta \in [0,1)$, $\alpha \geq 0$, $\lambda > 0$.

We begin studying this subclass of functions:

Theorem 1. *$DL_n^{\mathcal{F}}(\delta, \alpha, \lambda)$ is a convex set.*

Proof. Taking the functions

$$f_k(z) = z + \sum_{j=2}^{\infty} a_{jk} z^j, \quad k = 1, 2, \quad z \in U,$$

belonging to the class $DL_n^{\mathcal{F}}(\delta,\alpha,\lambda)$, we have to prove that the function

$$h(z) = \gamma_1 f_1(z) + \gamma_2 f_2(z)$$

belongs to the class $DL_n^{\mathcal{F}}(\delta,\alpha,\lambda)$ with $\gamma_1, \gamma_2 \geq 0$, $\gamma_1 + \gamma_2 = 1$.

We have $h'(z) = (\gamma_1 f_1 + \gamma_2 f_2)'(z) = \gamma_1 f_1'(z) + \gamma_2 f_2'(z)$, $z \in U$, and $\left(D_z^{-\lambda} L_\alpha^n h(z)\right)' = \left(D_z^{-\lambda} L_\alpha^n (\gamma_1 f_1 + \gamma_2 f_2)(z)\right)' = \gamma_1 \left(D_z^{-\lambda} L_\alpha^n f_1(z)\right)' + \gamma_2 \left(D_z^{-\lambda} L_\alpha^n f_2(z)\right)'$. and we can write

$$F_{\left(D_z^{-\lambda} L_\alpha^n h\right)'(U)} \left(D_z^{-\lambda} L_\alpha^n h(z)\right)' = F_{\left(D_z^{-\lambda} L_\alpha^n (\gamma_1 f_1 + \gamma_2 f_2)\right)'(U)} \left(D_z^{-\lambda} L_\alpha^n (\gamma_1 f_1 + \gamma_2 f_2)(z)\right)' =$$

$$F_{\left(D_z^{-\lambda} L_\alpha^n (\gamma_1 f_1 + \gamma_2 f_2)\right)'(U)} \left(\gamma_1 \left(D_z^{-\lambda} L_\alpha^n f_1(z)\right)' + \gamma_2 \left(D_z^{-\lambda} L_\alpha^n f_2(z)\right)'\right) =$$

$$\frac{F_{\left(\gamma_1 D_z^{-\lambda} L_\alpha^n f_1\right)'(U)} \left(\gamma_1 \left(D_z^{-\lambda} L_\alpha^n f_1(z)\right)'\right) + F_{\left(\gamma_2 D_z^{-\lambda} L_\alpha^n f_2\right)'(U)} \left(\gamma_2 \left(D_z^{-\lambda} L_\alpha^n f_2(z)\right)'\right)}{2} =$$

$$\frac{F_{\left(D_z^{-\lambda} L_\alpha^n f_1\right)'(U)} \left(D_z^{-\lambda} L_\alpha^n f_1(z)\right)' + F_{\left(D_z^{-\lambda} L_\alpha^n f_2\right)'(U)} \left(D_z^{-\lambda} L_\alpha^n f_2(z)\right)'}{2}.$$

Having $f_1, f_2 \in DL_n^{\mathcal{F}}(\delta,\alpha,\lambda)$ we get $\delta < F_{\left(D_z^{-\lambda} L_\alpha^n f_1\right)'(U)} \left(D_z^{-\lambda} L_\alpha^n f_1(z)\right)' \leq 1$ and $\delta < F_{\left(D_z^{-\lambda} L_\alpha^n f_2\right)'(U)} \left(D_z^{-\lambda} L_\alpha^n f_2(z)\right)' \leq 1$, $z \in U$.

In these conditions $\delta < \dfrac{F_{\left(D_z^{-\lambda} L_\alpha^n f_1\right)'(U)} \left(D_z^{-\lambda} L_\alpha^n f_1(z)\right)' + F_{\left(D_z^{-\lambda} L_\alpha^n f_2\right)'(U)} \left(D_z^{-\lambda} L_\alpha^n f_2(z)\right)'}{2} \leq 1$ and we get $\delta < F_{\left(D_z^{-\lambda} L_\alpha^n h\right)'(U)} \left(D_z^{-\lambda} L_\alpha^n h(z)\right)' \leq 1$, equivalently with $h \in DL_n^{\mathcal{F}}(\delta,\alpha,\lambda)$ and $DL_n^{\mathcal{F}}(\delta,\alpha,\lambda)$ is a convex set. □

We give fuzzy differential subordinations obtained for the operator $D_z^{-\lambda} L_\alpha^n$.

Theorem 2. *Considering a convex function g in U and defining $h(z) = g(z) + \frac{1}{c+2} z g'(z)$, with $c > 0$, $z \in U$, when $f \in DL_n^{\mathcal{F}}(\delta,\alpha,\lambda)$ and $G(z) = \frac{c+2}{z^{c+1}} \int_0^z t^c f(t) dt$, $z \in U$, then*

$$F_{\left(D_z^{-\lambda} L_\alpha^n f\right)'(U)} \left(D_z^{-\lambda} L_\alpha^n f(z)\right)' \leq F_{h(U)} h(z), \quad z \in U, \tag{2}$$

implies the sharp result

$$F_{\left(D_z^{-\lambda} L_\alpha^n G\right)'(U)} \left(D_z^{-\lambda} L_\alpha^n G(z)\right)' \leq F_{g(U)} g(z), \quad z \in U.$$

Proof. Differentiating relation

$$z^{c+1} G(z) = (c+2) \int_0^z t^c f(t) dt,$$

considering z as variable, we get $(c+1) G(z) + z G'(z) = (c+2) f(z)$ and

$$(c+1) D_z^{-\lambda} L_\alpha^n G(z) + z \left(D_z^{-\lambda} L_\alpha^n G(z)\right)' = (c+2) D_z^{-\lambda} L_\alpha^n f(z), \quad z \in U,$$

and differentiating it again with respect to z, we obtain

$$\left(D_z^{-\lambda} L_\alpha^n G(z)\right)' + \frac{1}{c+2} z \left(D_z^{-\lambda} L_\alpha^n G(z)\right)'' = \left(D_z^{-\lambda} L_\alpha^n f(z)\right)', \quad z \in U.$$

and the inequality (2) representing the fuzzy differential subordination can be written

$$F_{D_z^{-\lambda} L_\alpha^n G(U)} \left(\frac{1}{c+2} z \left(D_z^{-\lambda} L_\alpha^n G(z)\right)'' + \left(D_z^{-\lambda} L_\alpha^n G(z)\right)'\right) \leq F_{g(U)} \left(\frac{1}{c+2} z g'(z) + g(z)\right).$$

Denoted
$$p(z) = \left(D_z^{-\lambda} L_\alpha^n G(z)\right)', \quad z \in U,$$

where $p \in \mathcal{H}[1,n]$, we obtain

$$F_{p(U)}\left(\frac{1}{c+2}zp'(z) + p(z)\right) \leq F_{g(U)}\left(\frac{1}{c+2}zg'(z) + g(z)\right), \quad z \in U.$$

Applying Lemma 3, we get

$$F_{(D_z^{-\lambda}L_\alpha^n G)'(U)}\left(D_z^{-\lambda}L_\alpha^n G(z)\right)' \leq F_{g(U)}g(z), \quad z \in U,$$

and g is the best dominant. □

We give an inclusion result for the class $DL_n^{\mathcal{F}}(\delta, \alpha, \lambda)$:

Theorem 3. *Taking $h(z) = \frac{1+(2\delta-1)z}{1+z}$ and $G(z) = \frac{c+2}{z^{c+1}}\int_0^z t^c f(t)dt$, $z \in U$, with $\delta \in [0,1)$, $c > 0$, $n \in \mathbb{N}$, $\alpha \geq 0$, $\lambda > 0$, then*

$$G\left[DL_n^{\mathcal{F}}(\delta, \alpha, \lambda)\right] \subset DL_n^{\mathcal{F}}(\delta^*, \alpha, \lambda), \tag{3}$$

where $\delta^* = 2\delta - 1 + 2(2+c)(1-\delta)\int_0^1 \frac{t^{c+1}}{t+1}dt$.

Proof. Making the same steps such as in the proof of Theorem 2, taking account the hypothesis of Theorem 3 and that $h(z) = \frac{1+(2\delta-1)z}{1+z}$ is a convex function, we obtain

$$F_{p(U)}\left(\frac{1}{c+2}zp'(z) + p(z)\right) \leq f_{h(U)}h(z),$$

with $p(z) = \left(D_z^{-\lambda} L_\alpha^n G(z)\right)', z \in U$.

Applying Lemma 2, we get

$$F_{(D_z^{-\lambda}L_\alpha^n G)'(U)}\left(D_z^{-\lambda}L_\alpha^n G(z)\right)' \leq F_{g(U)}g(z) \leq F_{h(U)}h(z),$$

where

$$g(z) = \frac{2+c}{nz^{\frac{2+c}{n}}}\int_0^z t^{\frac{2+c}{n}-1}\frac{1+(2\delta-1)t}{1+t}dt = (2\delta-1) + \frac{2(c+2)(1-\delta)}{nz^{\frac{c+2}{n}}}\int_0^z \frac{t^{\frac{2+c}{n}-1}}{t+1}dt.$$

Since the function g is convex and $g(U)$ is symmetric with respect to the real axis, we can write

$$F_{D_z^{-\lambda}L_\alpha^n G(U)}\left(D_z^{-\lambda}L_\alpha^n G(z)\right)' \geq \min_{|z|=1} F_{g(U)}g(z) = F_{g(U)}g(1) \tag{4}$$

and $\delta^* = g(1) = 2\delta - 1 + \frac{2(2+c)(1-\delta)}{n}\int_0^1 \frac{t^{\frac{2+c}{n}-1}}{t+1}dt$, that give the inclusion (3). □

Theorem 4. *Taking a convex function g with the property $g(0) = 0$, define $h(z) = g(z) + zg'(z)$, $z \in U$. When $f \in \mathcal{A}$, $n \in \mathbb{N}$, $\alpha \geq 0$, $\lambda > 0$, and the fuzzy differential subordination holds*

$$F_{(D_z^{-\lambda}L_\alpha^n f)'(U)}\left(D_z^{-\lambda}L_\alpha^n f(z)\right)' \leq F_{h(U)}h(z), \quad z \in U, \tag{5}$$

then we get the sharp result

$$F_{D_z^{-\lambda}L_\alpha^n f(U)}\frac{D_z^{-\lambda}L_\alpha^n f(z)}{z} \leq F_{g(U)}g(z), \quad z \in U.$$

Proof. Considering $p(z) = \frac{D_z^{-\lambda} L_\alpha^n f(z)}{z} \in \mathcal{H}[0, \lambda]$, we can write $zp(z) = D_z^{-\lambda} L_\alpha^n f(z), z \in U$, and differentiating it we get $zp'(z) + p(z) = \left(D_z^{-\lambda} L_\alpha^n f(z)\right)', z \in U$.

The inequality (5) can be written as following

$$F_{p(U)}(zp'(z) + p(z)) \leq F_{h(U)} h(z) = F_{g(U)}(zg'(z) + g(z)), \quad z \in U,$$

and applying Lemma 3, we get the sharp result

$$F_{\left(D_z^{-\lambda} L_\alpha^n f\right)'(U)} \frac{D_z^{-\lambda} L_\alpha^n f(z)}{z} \leq F_{g(U)} g(z), \quad z \in U.$$

□

Example 1. *Consider*

$$g(z) = \frac{-2z}{1+z}$$

a convex function in U and we obtain that $g(0) = 0$, $g'(z) = \frac{-2}{(1+z)^2}$. *Define*

$$h(z) = g(z) + zg'(z) = \frac{-2z}{1+z} - \frac{2z}{(1+z)^2} = \frac{-2z^2 - 4z}{(1+z)^2}.$$

Take $\alpha = 2$, $n = 1$, $f(z) = z + z^2$, $z \in U$, *and after a short computation we obtain*

$$L_2^1 f(z) = z + 2z^2$$

and

$$D_z^{-\lambda} L_2^1 f(z) = \frac{1}{\Gamma(\lambda)} \int_0^z \frac{L_2^1 f(t)}{(z-t)^{1-\lambda}} dt = \frac{1}{\Gamma(\lambda)} \int_0^z \frac{t + 2t^2}{(z-t)^{1-\lambda}} dt$$

$$= \frac{1}{\Gamma(\lambda+2)} z^{1+\lambda} + \frac{4}{\Gamma(\lambda+3)} z^{2+\lambda}$$

and differentiating it

$$\left(D_z^{-\lambda} L_2^1 f(z)\right)' = \frac{1}{\Gamma(\lambda+1)} z^\lambda + \frac{4}{\Gamma(\lambda+2)} z^{\lambda+1}.$$

Applying Theorem 4 we get the following fuzzy differential subordination

$$\frac{1}{\Gamma(1+\lambda)} z^\lambda + \frac{4}{\Gamma(2+\lambda)} z^{1+\lambda} \prec_\mathcal{F} \frac{-2z^2 - 4z}{(1+z)^2}, \quad z \in U,$$

induce the following fuzzy differential subordination

$$\frac{1}{\Gamma(2+\lambda)} z^\lambda + \frac{4}{\Gamma(3+\lambda)} z^{1+\lambda} \prec_\mathcal{F} \frac{-2z}{1+z}, \quad z \in U.$$

Theorem 5. *Taking a holomorphic function h, such that* $h(0) = 0$ *and* $\operatorname{Re}\left(1 + \frac{zh''(z)}{h'(z)}\right) > -\frac{1}{2}$, $z \in U$, *when* $f \in \mathcal{A}$, $n \in \mathbb{N}$, $\alpha \geq 0$, $\lambda > 0$, *and the fuzzy differential subordination holds*

$$F_{\left(D_z^{-\lambda} L_\alpha^n f\right)'(U)} \left(D_z^{-\lambda} L_\alpha^n f(z)\right)' \leq F_{h(U)} h(z), \quad z \in U, \tag{6}$$

then

$$F_{D_z^{-\lambda} L_\alpha^n f(U)} \frac{D_z^{-\lambda} L_\alpha^n f(z)}{z} \leq F_{q(U)} q(z), \quad z \in U,$$

where the fuzzy best dominant $q(z) = \frac{1}{z} \int_0^z h(t) dt$ *is convex.*

Proof. Considering $\operatorname{Re}\left(1+\frac{zh''(z)}{h'(z)}\right) > -\frac{1}{2}$, $z \in \mathcal{U}$, and using Lemma 1, we deduce that $q(z) = \frac{1}{z}\int_0^z h(t)dt$ is a convex function and it is a solution of the differential equation defining the fuzzy differential subordination (6) $zq'(z) + q(z) = h(z)$, therefore it is the fuzzy best dominant.

Differentiating $zp(z) = D_z^{-\lambda}L_\alpha^n f(z)$, we get $\left(D_z^{-\lambda}L_\alpha^n f(z)\right)' = zp'(z) + p(z)$, $z \in \mathcal{U}$, and (6) can be written

$$F_{p(\mathcal{U})}(zp'(z) + p(z)) \leq F_{h(\mathcal{U})}h(z), \quad z \in \mathcal{U}.$$

Applying Lemma 3, we get

$$F_{D_z^{-\lambda}L_\alpha^n f(\mathcal{U})}\frac{D_z^{-\lambda}L_\alpha^n f(z)}{z} \leq F_{q(\mathcal{U})}q(z), \quad z \in \mathcal{U}.$$

□

Corollary 1. *Taking the convex function in $\mathcal{U}$, $h(z) = \frac{1+(2\delta-1)z}{1+z}$, with $\delta \in [0,1)$, when $f \in \mathcal{A}$ and the fuzzy differential subordination holds*

$$F_{(D_z^{-\lambda}L_\alpha^n f)'(\mathcal{U})}\left(D_z^{-\lambda}L_\alpha^n f(z)\right)' \leq F_{h(\mathcal{U})}h(z), z \in \mathcal{U}, \tag{7}$$

then

$$F_{D_z^{-\lambda}L_\alpha^n f(\mathcal{U})}\frac{D_z^{-\lambda}L_\alpha^n f(z)}{z} \leq F_{q(\mathcal{U})}q(z), z \in \mathcal{U},$$

where the fuzzy best dominant $q(z) = 2\delta - 1 + 2(1-\delta)\frac{\ln(z+1)}{z}$, $z \in \mathcal{U}$, is convex.

Proof. Taking $h(z) = \frac{1+(2\delta-1)z}{1+z}$, we obtain $h(0) = 1$, $h'(z) = \frac{-2(1-\delta)}{(1+z)^2}$ and $h''(z) = \frac{4(1-\delta)}{(1+z)^3}$, therefore $\operatorname{Re}\left(\frac{zh''(z)}{h'(z)} + 1\right) = \operatorname{Re}\left(\frac{1-z}{1+z}\right) = \operatorname{Re}\left(\frac{1-\rho\cos\theta - i\rho\sin\theta}{1+\rho\cos\theta + i\rho\sin\theta}\right) = \frac{1-\rho^2}{1+2\rho\cos\theta+\rho^2} > 0 > -\frac{1}{2}$.

Following the same steps like in the proof of Theorem 5 with $p(z) = \frac{D_z^{-\lambda}L_\alpha^n f(z)}{z}$, the fuzzy differential subordination (7) can be written

$$F_{D_z^{-\lambda}L_\alpha^n f(\mathcal{U})}(zp'(z) + p(z)) \leq F_{h(\mathcal{U})}h(z), \quad z \in \mathcal{U}.$$

Applying Lemma 2 for $m = 1$ and $\gamma = 1$, we obtain

$$F_{D_z^{-\lambda}L_\alpha^n f(\mathcal{U})}\frac{D_z^{-\lambda}L_\alpha^n f(z)}{z} \leq F_{q(\mathcal{U})}q(z),$$

where

$$q(z) = \frac{1}{z}\int_0^z h(t)dt = \frac{1}{z}\int_0^z \frac{1+(2\delta-1)t}{t+1}dt =$$

$$2\delta - 1 + \frac{2(1-\delta)}{z}\int_0^z \frac{1}{t+1}dt = 2\delta - 1 + 2(1-\delta)\frac{\ln(z+1)}{z}, \quad z \in \mathcal{U}.$$

□

Example 2. *Consider*

$$h(z) = \frac{-2z}{1+z}$$

and we obtain that $h(0) = 0$, $h'(z) = \frac{-2}{(1+z)^2}$ and $h''(z) = \frac{4}{(1+z)^3}$. Taking account that

$$\operatorname{Re}\left(1 + \frac{zh''(z)}{h'(z)}\right) = \operatorname{Re}\left(\frac{1-z}{1+z}\right) = \operatorname{Re}\left(\frac{1-\rho\cos\theta - i\rho\sin\theta}{1+\rho\cos\theta + i\rho\sin\theta}\right)$$

$$= \frac{1-\rho^2}{1+2\rho\cos\theta+\rho^2} > 0 > -\frac{1}{2},$$

h is a convex function in U.

Taking $\alpha = 2$, $n = 1$, $f(z) = z + z^2$, $z \in U$, as in Example 1, we have

$$L_2^1 f(z) = z + 2z^2$$

and

$$D_z^{-\lambda} L_2^1 f(z) = \frac{1}{\Gamma(\lambda+2)} z^{1+\lambda} + \frac{4}{\Gamma(\lambda+3)} z^{2+\lambda}$$

and differentiating it

$$\left(D_z^{-\lambda} L_2^1 f(z)\right)' = \frac{1}{\Gamma(\lambda+1)} z^{\lambda} + \frac{4}{\Gamma(\lambda+2)} z^{\lambda+1}.$$

Additionally, we get

$$q(z) = \frac{1}{z} \int_0^z \frac{-2t}{1+t} dt = \frac{2\ln(1+z)}{z} - 2.$$

Applying Theorem 5 we get the following fuzzy differential subordination

$$\frac{1}{\Gamma(1+\lambda)} z^{\lambda} + \frac{4}{\Gamma(2+\lambda)} z^{1+\lambda} \prec_F \frac{2z}{1+z}, \quad z \in U,$$

induce the following fuzzy differential subordination

$$\frac{1}{\Gamma(2+\lambda)} z^{1+\lambda} + \frac{4}{\Gamma(3+\lambda)} z^{2+\lambda} \prec_F \frac{2\ln(1+z)}{z} - 2, \quad z \in U.$$

Theorem 6. *Taking a convex function g with the property $g(0) = 0$ and defining $h(z) = zg'(z) + g(z)$, $z \in U$, when $f \in \mathcal{A}$, $n \in \mathbb{N}$, $\alpha \geq 0$, $\lambda > 0$, and the fuzzy differential subordination*

$$F_{D_z^{-\lambda} L_\alpha^n f(U)} \left(\frac{z D_z^{-\lambda} L_\alpha^{n+1} f(z)}{D_z^{-\lambda} L_\alpha^n f(z)} \right)' \leq F_{h(U)} h(z), \quad z \in U, \tag{8}$$

holds, then we obtain the sharp result

$$F_{D_z^{-\lambda} L_\alpha^n f(U)} \frac{z D_z^{-\lambda} L_\alpha^{n+1} f(z)}{D_z^{-\lambda} L_\alpha^n f(z)} \leq F_{g(U)} g(z), \quad z \in U.$$

Proof. Considering $p(z) = \frac{D_z^{-\lambda} L_\alpha^{n+1} f(z)}{D_z^{-\lambda} L_\alpha^n f(z)}$ and differentiating it we get $zp'(z) + p(z) = \left(\frac{z L_\alpha^{n+1} f(z)}{L_\alpha^n f(z)}\right)'$. With this notation, inequality (8) can be written as

$$F_{p(U)}(zp'(z) + p(z)) \leq F_{h(U)} h(z) = F_{g(U)}(zg'(z) + g(z)), \quad z \in U.$$

Applying Lemma 3, we get

$$F_{D_z^{-\lambda} L_\alpha^n f(U)} \frac{D_z^{-\lambda} L_\alpha^{n+1} f(z)}{D_z^{-\lambda} L_\alpha^n f(z)} \leq F_{g(U)} g(z), \quad z \in U.$$

□

Example 3. *Consider*

$$g(z) = \frac{-2z}{1+z}$$

and
$$h(z) = g(z) + zg'(z) = \frac{-2z^2 - 4z}{(1+z)^2}$$

as given in Example 1.

Taking $\alpha = 2, n = 1, f(z) = z + z^2, z \in U$, as in Example 1, we get
$$L_2^1 f(z) = z + 2z^2$$

and
$$L_2^2 f(z) = z + 2z^2$$

and applying Riemann–Liouville fractional integral of order λ we have
$$D_z^{-\lambda} L_2^1 f(z) = \frac{1}{\Gamma(\lambda+2)} z^{1+\lambda} + \frac{4}{\Gamma(\lambda+3)} z^{2+\lambda} = D_z^{-\lambda} L_2^2 f(z).$$

Applying Theorem 6 we get the following fuzzy differential subordination
$$1 \prec_F \frac{-2z^2 - 4z}{(1+z)^2}, \quad z \in U,$$

induce the following fuzzy differential subordination
$$z \prec_F \frac{-2z}{1+z}, \quad z \in U.$$

Theorem 7. *Taking a convex function g with the property $g(0) = 0$ and defining $h(z) = \lambda z g'(z) + g(z), z \in U, \alpha \geq 0, \lambda, \delta > 0$, when $f \in \mathcal{A}$ and the fuzzy differential subordination*
$$F_{D_z^{-\lambda} L_\alpha^n f(U)} \left(\left(\frac{D_z^{-\lambda} L_\alpha^n f(z)}{z} \right)^{\delta-1} \left(D_z^{-\lambda} L_\alpha^n f(z) \right)' \right) \leq F_{h(U)} h(z), \quad z \in U, \quad (9)$$

holds, then we obtain the sharp result
$$F_{D_z^{-\lambda} L_\alpha^n f(U)} \left(\frac{D_z^{-\lambda} L_\alpha^n f(z)}{z} \right)^{\delta} \leq F_{g(U)} g(z), \quad z \in U.$$

Proof. Considering $p(z) = \left(\frac{D_z^{-\lambda} L_\alpha^n f(z)}{z} \right)^{\delta} \in \mathcal{H}[0, \lambda \delta]$, and differentiating it we obtain
$$zp'(z) = \delta \left(\frac{D_z^{-\lambda} L_\alpha^n f(z)}{z} \right)^{\delta-1} \left(D_z^{-\lambda} L_\alpha^n f(z) \right)' - \delta \left(\frac{D_z^{-\lambda} L_\alpha^n f(z)}{z} \right)^{\delta}$$

$$= \delta \left(\frac{D_z^{-\lambda} L_\alpha^n f(z)}{z} \right)^{\delta-1} \left(D_z^{-\lambda} L_\alpha^n f(z) \right)' - \delta p(z),$$

and $\frac{1}{\delta} zp'(z) + p(z) = \left(\frac{D_z^{-\lambda} L_\alpha^n f(z)}{z} \right)^{\delta-1} \left(D_z^{-\lambda} L_\alpha^n f(z) \right)', z \in U$.

Inequality (9) can be written
$$F_{p(U)} \left(\frac{1}{\delta} zp'(z) + p(z) \right) \leq F_{h(U)} h(z) = F_{g(U)} \left(\lambda z g'(z) + g(z) \right), \quad z \in U.$$

Applying Lemma 3 for $\alpha = \frac{1}{\delta}$ and $m = \lambda \delta$, we get
$$F_{D_z^{-\lambda} L_\alpha^n f(U)} \left(\frac{D_z^{-\lambda} L_\alpha^n f(z)}{z} \right)^{\delta} \leq F_{g(U)} g(z), \quad z \in U.$$

Example 4. Consider
$$g(z) = \frac{-2z}{1+z}$$
and
$$h(z) = g(z) + zg'(z) = \frac{-2z^2 - 4z}{(1+z)^2}$$
as given in Example 1.
    Taking $\alpha = 2$, $n = 1$, $f(z) = z + z^2$, $z \in U$, as in Example 1, we obtain
$$L_2^1 f(z) = z + 2z^2$$
and
$$D_z^{-\lambda} L_2^1 f(z) = \frac{1}{\Gamma(\lambda+2)} z^{1+\lambda} + \frac{4}{\Gamma(\lambda+3)} z^{2+\lambda}$$
and differentiating it
$$\left(D_z^{-\lambda} L_2^1 f(z)\right)' = \frac{1}{\Gamma(\lambda+1)} z^\lambda + \frac{4}{\Gamma(\lambda+2)} z^{\lambda+1}.$$

Applying Theorem 7 we get the following fuzzy differential subordination
$$\left(\frac{1}{\Gamma(\lambda+2)} z^\lambda + \frac{4}{\Gamma(\lambda+3)} z^{1+\lambda}\right)^{\delta-1} \left(\frac{1}{\Gamma(1+\lambda)} z^\lambda + \frac{4}{\Gamma(2+\lambda)} z^{1+\lambda}\right) \prec_\mathcal{F} \frac{-2z^2 - 4z}{(1+z)^2}, \ z \in U,$$
induce the following fuzzy differential subordination
$$\left(\frac{1}{\Gamma(\lambda+2)} z^\lambda + \frac{4}{\Gamma(\lambda+3)} z^{1+\lambda}\right)^\delta \prec_\mathcal{F} \frac{-2z}{1+z}, \ z \in U.$$

Theorem 8. *Considering a holomorphic function h, such that $h(0) = 0$ and $\text{Re}\left(1 + \frac{zh''(z)}{h'(z)}\right) > -\frac{1}{2}$, $z \in U$, when $f \in \mathcal{A}$, $\alpha \geq 0$, $\lambda, \delta > 0$, and the fuzzy differential subordination*
$$F_{D_z^{-\lambda} L_\alpha^n f(U)} \left(\left(\frac{D_z^{-\lambda} L_\alpha^n f(z)}{z}\right)^{\delta-1} \left(D_z^{-\lambda} L_\alpha^n f(z)\right)'\right) \leq F_{h(U)} h(z), \ z \in U, \quad (10)$$
holds, then
$$F_{D_z^{-\lambda} L_\alpha^n f(U)} \left(\frac{D_z^{-\lambda} L_\alpha^n f(z)}{z}\right)^\delta \leq F_{q(U)} q(z), \ z \in U,$$
where the fuzzy best dominant $q(z) = \frac{1}{z} \int_0^z h(t) dt$ is convex.

Proof. Considering $p(z) = \left(\frac{D_z^{-\lambda} L_\alpha^n f(z)}{z}\right)^\delta \in \mathcal{H}[0, \lambda\delta]$, after differentiating it and making an easy computation, we get
$$\frac{1}{\delta} zp'(z) + p(z) = \left(\frac{D_z^{-\lambda} L_\alpha^n(z)}{z}\right)^{\delta-1} \left(D_z^{-\lambda} L_\alpha^n f(z)\right)', \ z \in U,$$
and inequality (10) can be written
$$F_{p(U)} \left(\frac{1}{\delta} zp'(z) + p(z)\right) \leq F_{h(U)} h(z), \ z \in U.$$

Applying Lemma 2, we obtain

$$F_{D_z^{-\lambda}L_\alpha^n f(U)}\left(\frac{D_z^{-\lambda}L_\alpha^n f(z)}{z}\right)^\delta \leq F_{q(U)}q(z), \quad z \in U.$$

Taking into account that $\operatorname{Re}\left(1+\frac{zh''(z)}{h'(z)}\right) > -\frac{1}{2}$, $z \in U$, applying Lemma 1 we obtain that $q(z) = \frac{1}{z}\int_0^z h(t)dt$ is a convex function and it is a solution of the differential equation of the fuzzy differential subordination (10) $zq'(z) + q(z) = h(z)$, thus it is the fuzzy best dominant. □

Example 5. Considering

$$h(z) = \frac{-2z}{1+z},$$

as in Example 2, a convex function which satisfy conditions from Theorem 8, and taking $\alpha = 2$, $n = 1$, $f(z) = z + z^2$, $z \in U$, we obtain

$$L_2^1 f(z) = z + 2z^2$$

and

$$D_z^{-\lambda}L_2^1 f(z) = \frac{1}{\Gamma(\lambda+2)}z^{1+\lambda} + \frac{4}{\Gamma(\lambda+3)}z^{2+\lambda}$$

and differentiating it

$$\left(D_z^{-\lambda}L_2^1 f(z)\right)' = \frac{1}{\Gamma(\lambda+1)}z^\lambda + \frac{4}{\Gamma(\lambda+2)}z^{\lambda+1}.$$

Additionally, we get

$$q(z) = \frac{1}{z}\int_0^z \frac{-2t}{1+t}dt = \frac{2\ln(1+z)}{z} - 2.$$

Applying Theorem 8 we get the following fuzzy differential subordination

$$\left(\frac{1}{\Gamma(\lambda+2)}z^\lambda + \frac{4}{\Gamma(\lambda+3)}z^{1+\lambda}\right)^{\delta-1}\left(\frac{1}{\Gamma(1+\lambda)}z^\lambda + \frac{4}{\Gamma(2+\lambda)}z^{1+\lambda}\right) \prec_\mathcal{F} \frac{2z}{1+z}, \quad z \in U,$$

induce the following fuzzy differential subordination

$$\left(\frac{1}{\Gamma(\lambda+2)}z^\lambda + \frac{4}{\Gamma(\lambda+3)}z^{1+\lambda}\right)^\delta \prec_\mathcal{F} \frac{2\ln(1+z)}{z} - 2, \quad z \in U.$$

Theorem 9. Considering a convex function g with the property $g(0) = \frac{1}{\lambda+1}$ and defining $h(z) = zg'(z) + g(z)$, $z \in U$, $\lambda > 0$, $\alpha \geq 0$, $n \in \mathbb{N}$, when $f \in \mathcal{A}$ and the fuzzy differential subordination

$$F_{D_z^{-\lambda}L_\alpha^n f(U)}\left(1 - \frac{D_z^{-\lambda}L_\alpha^n f(z)\left(D_z^{-\lambda}L_\alpha^n f(z)\right)''}{\left[\left(D_z^{-\lambda}L_\alpha^n f(z)\right)'\right]^2}\right) \leq F_{h(U)}h(z), \quad z \in U,$$

holds, then we obtain the sharp result

$$F_{D_z^{-\lambda}L_\alpha^n f(U)}\left(\frac{D_z^{-\lambda}L_\alpha^n f(z)}{z\left(D_z^{-\lambda}L_\alpha^n f(z)\right)'}\right) \leq F_{g(U)}g(z), \quad z \in U.$$

Proof. Differentiating $p(z) = \dfrac{D_z^{-\lambda}L_\alpha^n f(z)}{z\left(D_z^{-\lambda}L_\alpha^n f(z)\right)'}$ we obtain $zp'(z) + p(z) = 1 - \dfrac{D_z^{-\lambda}L_\alpha^n f(z)\left(D_z^{-\lambda}L_\alpha^n f(z)\right)''}{\left[\left(D_z^{-\lambda}L_\alpha^n f(z)\right)'\right]^2}$, $z \in U$.

Using this notation, the fuzzy differential subordination can be written

$$F_{p(U)}(zp'(z) + p(z)) \leq F_{h(U)}h(z) - \Gamma_{g(U)}(zg'(z) + g(z)), \quad z \in U,$$

and applying Lemma 3, we obtain the sharp result

$$F_{D_z^{-\lambda}L_\alpha^n f(U)}\left(\dfrac{D_z^{-\lambda}L_\alpha^n f(z)}{z\left(D_z^{-\lambda}L_\alpha^n f(z)\right)'}\right) \leq F_{g(U)}g(z), \quad z \in U.$$

□

3. Conclusions

Applying the theory of fuzzy differential subordination, we studied a subclass of analytic function $DL_n^{\mathcal{F}}(\delta, \alpha, \lambda)$ newly introduced regarding the operator $D_z^{-\lambda}L_\alpha^n$. Several interesting properties are obtained for the defining subclass $DL_n^{\mathcal{F}}(\delta, \alpha, \lambda)$. New fuzzy differential subordinations are obtained for $D_z^{-\lambda}L_\alpha^n$. To show how the results would be applied it is give an example. The operator $D_z^{-\lambda}L_\alpha^n$ introduced in Definition 8 and the subclass $DL_n^{\mathcal{F}}(\delta, \alpha, \lambda)$ introduced in Definition 9 can be objects in other future studies. Other subclasses of analytic functions can be introduced regarding this operator and some properties for these subclasses can be investigated regarding coefficient estimates, closure theorems, distortion theorems, neighborhoods, and the radii of starlikeness, convexity, or close-to-convexity.

The dual theory of fuzzy differential superordination introduced in [21] could be used for obtaining similar results involving the operator $D_z^{-\lambda}L_\alpha^n$ and the class $L_n^{\mathcal{F}}(\delta, \alpha, \lambda)$ which could be combined with the results presented here for sandwich-type theorems, as seen in [17].

Funding: This research received no external funding.

Institutional Review Board Statement: Not applicable.

Informed Consent Statement: Not applicable.

Data Availability Statement: Not applicable.

Conflicts of Interest: The author declares no conflict of interest.

References

1. Zadeh, L.A. Fuzzy Sets. *Inf. Control* **1965**, *8*, 338–353. [CrossRef]
2. Oros, G.I.; Oros, G. The notion of subordination in fuzzy sets theory. *Gen. Math.* **2011**, *19*, 97–103.
3. Oros, G.I.; Oros, G. Fuzzy differential subordination. *Acta Univ. Apulensis* **2012**, *3*, 55–64.
4. Miller, S.S.; Mocanu, P.T. Second order differential inequalities in the complex plane. *J. Math. Anal. Appl.* **1978**, *65*, 289–305. [CrossRef]
5. Miller, S.S.; Mocanu, P.T. Differential subordinations and univalent functions. *Mich. Math. J.* **1981**, *28*, 157–172. [CrossRef]
6. Miller, S.S.; Mocanu, P.T. *Differential Subordinations: Theory and Applications*; Marcel Dekker, Inc.: New York, NY, USA; Basel, Switzerland, 2000.
7. Oros, G.I. Univalence criteria for analytic functions obtained using fuzzy differential subordinations. *Turk. J. Math.* **2022**, *46*, 1478–1491. [CrossRef]
8. Gal, S.G.; Ban, A.I. *Elements of Fuzzy Mathematics*; Universității din Oradea: Oradea, Romania, 1996. (In Romanian)
9. Oros, G.I.; Oros, G. Dominants and best dominants in fuzzy differential subordinations. *Stud. Univ. Babes-Bolyai Math.* **2012**, *57*, 239–248.
10. Alb Lupaș, A.; Oros, G.I. On Special Differential Subordinations Using Fractional Integral of Sălăgean and Ruscheweyh Operators. *Symmetry* **2021**, *13*, 1553. [CrossRef]
11. Ruscheweyh, S. New criteria for univalent functions. *Proc. Am. Math. Soc.* **1975**, *49*, 109–115. [CrossRef]

12. Sălăgean, G.S. *Subclasses of Univalent Functions*; Lecture Notes in Math; Springer: Berlin, Germany, 1983; Volume 1013; pp. 362–372.
13. Alb Lupaş, A. On special differential subordinations using Sălăgean and Ruscheweyh operators. *Math. Inequal. Appl.* **2009**, *12*, 781–790. [CrossRef]
14. Cho, N.E.; Aouf, A.M.K. Some applications of fractional calculus operators to a certain subclass of analytic functions with negative coefficients. *Turk. J. Math.* **1996**, *20*, 553–562.
15. Alb Lupaş, A.; Oros, G.I. New Applications of Sălăgean and Ruscheweyh Operators for Obtaining Fuzzy Differential Subordinations. *Mathematics* **2021**, *9*, 2000. [CrossRef]
16. Oros, G.I.; Dzitac, S. Applications of Subordination Chains and Fractional Integral in Fuzzy Differential Subordinations. *Mathematics* **2022**, *10*, 1690. [CrossRef]
17. Alb Lupaş, A. Fuzzy Differential Sandwich Theorems Involving the Fractional Integral of Confluent Hypergeometric Function. *Symmetry* **2021**, *13*, 1992. [CrossRef]
18. El-Deeb, S.M.; Oros, G.I. Fuzzy differential subordinations connected with the linear operator. *Math. Bohem.* **2021**, *146*, 397–406. [CrossRef]
19. Srivastava H.M. ; El-Deeb, S.M. Fuzzy Differential Subordinations Based upon the Mittag-Leffler Type Borel Distribution. *Symmetry* **2021**, *13*, 1023. [CrossRef]
20. Noor, K.I; Noor, M.A. Fuzzy Differential Subordination Involving Generalized Noor-Salagean Operator. *Inf. Sci. Lett.* **2022**, *11*, 1–7.
21. Atshan, W.G.; Hussain, K.O. Fuzzy Differential Superordination. *Theory Appl. Math. Comput. Sci.* **2017**, *7*, 27–38.

Article

Applications of Beta Negative Binomial Distribution and Laguerre Polynomials on Ozaki Bi-Close-to-Convex Functions

Isra Al-Shbeil [1], Abbas Kareem Wanas [2], Afis Saliu [3,4] and Adriana Cătaş [5,*]

[1] Department of Mathematics, Faculty of Science, The University of Jordan, Amman 11942, Jordan
[2] Department of Mathematics, College of Science, University of Al-Qadisiyah, Al Diwaniyah 58002, Iraq
[3] Department of Mathematics, University of the Gambia, Birkama Campus, MDI Road, Kanifing Serrekunda P.O. Box 3530, The Gambia
[4] Department of Mathematics, Gombe State University, P.M.B 127, Gombe 760253, Nigeria
[5] Department of Mathematics and Computer Science, University of Oradea, 1 University Street, 410087 Oradea, Romania
* Correspondence: acatas@gmail.com

Abstract: In the present paper, due to beta negative binomial distribution series and Laguerre polynomials, we investigate a new family $\mathcal{F}_\Sigma(\delta, \eta, \lambda, \theta; h)$ of normalized holomorphic and bi-univalent functions associated with Ozaki close-to-convex functions. We provide estimates on the initial Taylor–Maclaurin coefficients and discuss Fekete–Szegő type inequality for functions in this family.

Keywords: bi-univalent function; Laguerre polynomial; coefficient bound; Fekete–Szegő problem; beta negative binomial distribution; subordination

1. Introduction

Consider the set $\mathcal{A}$ of functions f which are holomorphic in the unit disk $\mathbb{D} = \{|z| < 1\}$ in the complex plane $\mathbb{C}$, of the form:

$$f(z) = z + \sum_{n=2}^{\infty} a_n z^n, \quad z \in \mathbb{D}. \qquad (1)$$

Let $\mathcal{S}$ be the subset of $\mathcal{A}$ which contains univalent functions in $\mathbb{D}$ having the form (1). As we can see in [1], due to the Koebe one-quarter theorem, every function $f \in \mathcal{S}$ has an inverse f^{-1} such that $f^{-1}(f(z)) = z$, $(z \in \mathbb{D})$ and $f(f^{-1}(w)) = w$, $(|w| < r_0(f), r_0(f) \geq \frac{1}{4})$. With f on the form (1), we have

$$f^{-1}(w) = w - a_2 w^2 + \left(2a_2^2 - a_3\right) w^3 - \left(5a_2^3 - 5a_2 a_3 + a_4\right) w^4 + \cdots, \quad |w| < r_0(f). \qquad (2)$$

We called a function $f \in \mathcal{A}$ as bi-univalent in $\mathbb{D}$, if both f and f^{-1} are univalent in $\mathbb{D}$. The set of bi-univalent functions in $\mathbb{D}$ is denoted by Σ.

In recent years, Srivastava et al. [2] reconsidered the study of holomorphic and bi-univalent functions. In this sense, we pursued a kind of surveys represented by those of Ali et al. [3], Bulut et al. [4], Srivastava et al. [5] and others (see, for example, [6–18]).

The polynomial solution $\phi(\tau)$ of the differential equation (see [19])

$$\tau \phi'' + (1 + \gamma - \tau)\phi' + n\phi = 0,$$

consists on the generalized Laguerre polynomial $L_n^\gamma(\tau)$, where $\gamma > -1$ and n is non-negative integers.

We defined by

$$H_\gamma(\tau, z) = \sum_{n=0}^{\infty} L_n^\gamma(\tau) z^n = \frac{e^{-\frac{\tau z}{1-z}}}{(1-z)^{\gamma+1}}, \qquad (3)$$

the generating function of generalized Laguerre polynomial $L_n^\gamma(\tau)$, where $\tau \in \mathbb{R}$ and $z \in \mathbb{D}$. Similarly, the generalized Laguerre polynomials is given by the following recurrence relations:

$$L_{n+1}^\gamma(\tau) = \frac{2n+1+\gamma-\tau}{n+1} L_n^\gamma(\tau) - \frac{n+\gamma}{n+1} L_{n-1}^\gamma(\tau) \quad (n \geq 1),$$

with the initial conditions

$$L_0^\gamma(\tau) = 1, \quad L_1^\gamma(\tau) = 1 + \gamma - \tau \quad \text{and} \quad L_2^\gamma(\tau) = \frac{\tau^2}{2} - (\gamma+2)\tau + \frac{(\gamma+1)(\gamma+2)}{2}. \quad (4)$$

Obviously, if $\gamma = 0$ the generalized Laguerre polynomial implies the simple Laguerre polynomial, i.e., $L_n^0(\tau) = L_n(\tau)$.

Consider two functions f and g holomorphic in $\mathbb{D}$. We say that the function f is subordinate to g, if there exists a function w, holomorphic in $\mathbb{D}$ with $w(0) = 0$, and $|w(z)| < 1$, $(z \in \mathbb{D})$ such that $f(z) = g(w(z))$. We denote this relation by $f \prec g$ or $f(z) \prec g(z)$ $(z \in \mathbb{D})$. In addition, if the function g is univalent in $\mathbb{D}$, then we get the following equivalence (see [20]), $f(z) \prec g(z) \iff f(0) = g(0)$ and $f(\mathbb{D}) \subset g(\mathbb{D})$.

From a theoretical standpoint, the Poisson, Pascal, logarithmic, binomial and Borel distributions have all been examined in some depth in geometric function theory (see for example [21–26]).

For a discrete random variable x, we say that it has a beta negative binomial distribution if it takes the values $0, 1, 2, 3, \cdots$ with the probabilities

$$\frac{B(\eta+\theta,\lambda)}{B(\eta,\lambda)}, \quad \theta\frac{B(\eta+\theta,\lambda+1)}{B(\eta,\lambda)}, \quad \frac{1}{2}\theta(\theta+1)\frac{B(\eta+\theta,\lambda+2)}{B(\eta,\lambda)}, \cdots,$$

respectively, where η, θ and λ are the parameters.

$$\text{Prob}(x = \tau) = \binom{\theta+\tau-1}{\tau}\frac{B(\eta+\theta,\lambda+\tau)}{B(\eta,\lambda)}$$

$$= \frac{\Gamma(\theta+\tau)}{\tau!\Gamma(\theta)} \frac{\Gamma(\eta+\theta)\Gamma(\lambda+\tau)\Gamma(\eta+\lambda)}{\Gamma(\eta+\theta+\lambda+\tau)\Gamma(\eta)\Gamma(\lambda)}$$

$$= \frac{(\eta)_\theta(\theta)_\tau(\lambda)_\tau}{(\eta+\lambda)_\theta(\theta+\eta+\lambda)_\tau \tau!},$$

where $(\alpha)_n$ is the Pochhammer symbol defined by

$$(\alpha)_n = \frac{\Gamma(\alpha+n)}{\Gamma(\alpha)} = \begin{cases} 1 & (n = 0), \\ \alpha(\alpha+1)\ldots(\alpha+n-1) & (n \in \mathbb{N}). \end{cases}$$

Wanas and Al-Ziadi [27] developed the following power series whose coefficients are beta negative binomial distribution probabilities:

$$\mathfrak{X}_{\eta,\lambda}^\theta(z) = z + \sum_{n=2}^\infty \frac{(\eta)_\theta(\theta)_{n-1}(\lambda)_{n-1}}{(\eta+\lambda)_\theta(\theta+\eta+\lambda)_{n-1}(n-1)!} z^n \quad (z \in \mathbb{D}; \eta, \lambda, \theta > 0).$$

By the well-known ratio test, we deduce that the radius of convergence of the above power series is infinity.

We recall the linear operator $\mathfrak{B}_{\eta,\lambda}^\theta : \mathcal{A} \longrightarrow \mathcal{A}$, as can be found in (see [27])

$$\mathfrak{B}_{\eta,\lambda}^\theta f(z) = \mathfrak{X}_{\eta,\lambda}^\theta(z) * f(z) = z + \sum_{n=2}^\infty \frac{(\eta)_\theta(\theta)_{n-1}(\lambda)_{n-1}}{(\eta+\lambda)_\theta(\theta+\eta+\lambda)_{n-1}(n-1)!} a_n z^n \quad z \in \mathbb{D},$$

where $(*)$ represents the Hadamard product (or convolution) of two series.

2. Main Results

We open the main section by introducing the family $\mathcal{F}_\Sigma(\delta, \eta, \lambda, \theta; h)$ as follows:

Definition 1. *Suppose that $\frac{1}{2} \leq \delta \leq 1$, $\eta, \lambda, \theta > 0$ and h is analytic in $\mathbb{D}$, $h(0) = 1$. We say that the function $f \in \Sigma$ is in the family $\mathcal{F}_\Sigma(\delta, \eta, \lambda, \theta; h)$ if the following subordinations hold:*

$$\frac{2\delta - 1}{2\delta + 1} + \frac{2}{2\delta + 1}\left(1 + \frac{z\left(\mathfrak{B}^\theta_{\eta,\lambda}f(z)\right)''}{\left(\mathfrak{B}^\theta_{\eta,\lambda}f(z)\right)'}\right) \prec h(z)$$

and

$$\frac{2\delta - 1}{2\delta + 1} + \frac{2}{2\delta + 1}\left(1 + \frac{w\left(\mathfrak{B}^\theta_{\eta,\lambda}f^{-1}(w)\right)''}{\left(\mathfrak{B}^\theta_{\eta,\lambda}f^{-1}(w)\right)'}\right) \prec h(w),$$

where f^{-1} is given by (2).

For $\delta = \frac{1}{2}$ in Definition 1, the family $\mathcal{F}_\Sigma(\delta, \eta, \lambda, \theta; h)$ reduces to the family $\mathcal{S}_\Sigma(\eta, \lambda, \theta; h)$ of bi-starlike functions such that the following subordinations hold:

$$1 + \frac{z\left(\mathfrak{B}^\theta_{\eta,\lambda}f(z)\right)''}{\left(\mathfrak{B}^\theta_{\eta,\lambda}f(z)\right)'} \prec h(z)$$

and

$$1 + \frac{w\left(\mathfrak{B}^\theta_{\eta,\lambda}f^{-1}(w)\right)''}{\left(\mathfrak{B}^\theta_{\eta,\lambda}f^{-1}(w)\right)'} \prec h(w).$$

Theorem 1. *Suppose that $\frac{1}{2} \leq \delta \leq 1$ and $\eta, \lambda, \theta > 0$. If $f \in \Sigma$ of the form (1) is in the family $\mathcal{F}_\Sigma(\delta, \eta, \lambda, \theta; h)$, with $h(z) = 1 + e_1 z + e_2 z^2 + \cdots$, then*

$$|a_2| \leq \frac{(2\delta + 1)\Gamma(\eta + \theta + \lambda + 1)\Gamma(\eta)\Gamma(\lambda)|e_1|}{4\theta \Gamma(\eta + \theta)\Gamma(\lambda + 1)\Gamma(\eta + \lambda)} = \frac{|e_1|}{Y} \qquad (5)$$

and

$$|a_3| \leq \min\left\{\max\left\{\left|\frac{e_1}{\Phi}\right|, \left|\frac{e_2}{\Phi} + \frac{\Psi e_1^2}{Y^2 \Phi}\right|\right\}, \max\left\{\left|\frac{e_1}{\Phi}\right|, \left|\frac{e_2}{\Phi} - \frac{(2\Phi - \Psi)e_1^2}{Y^2 \Phi}\right|\right\}\right\}, \qquad (6)$$

where

$$Y = \frac{4\theta \Gamma(\eta+\theta)\Gamma(\lambda+1)\Gamma(\eta+\lambda)}{(2\delta+1)\Gamma(\eta+\theta+\lambda+1)\Gamma(\eta)\Gamma(\lambda)},$$

$$\Phi = \frac{6\theta(\theta+1)\Gamma(\eta+\theta)\Gamma(\lambda+2)\Gamma(\eta+\lambda)}{(2\delta+1)\Gamma(\eta+\theta+\lambda+2)\Gamma(\eta)\Gamma(\lambda)}, \qquad (7)$$

$$\Psi = \frac{8\theta^2 \Gamma^2(\eta+\theta)\Gamma^2(\lambda+1)\Gamma^2(\eta+\lambda)}{(2\delta+1)\Gamma^2(\eta+\theta+\lambda+1)\Gamma^2(\eta)\Gamma^2(\lambda)}.$$

Proof. Assume that $f \in \mathcal{F}_\Sigma(\delta, \eta, \lambda, \theta; h)$. Then, there exist two holomorphic functions $\phi, \psi : \mathbb{D} \longrightarrow \mathbb{D}$ given by

$$\phi(z) = r_1 z + r_2 z^2 + r_3 z^3 + \cdots \quad (z \in \mathbb{D}) \qquad (8)$$

and

$$\psi(w) = s_1 w + s_2 w^2 + s_3 w^3 + \cdots \quad (w \in \mathbb{D}), \qquad (9)$$

with $\phi(0) = \psi(0) = 0$, $|\phi(z)| < 1$, $|\psi(w)| < 1$, $z, w \in \mathbb{D}$ such that

$$1 + \frac{2}{2\delta + 1} \frac{z\left(\mathcal{B}^{\theta}_{\eta,\lambda} f(z)\right)''}{\left(\mathcal{B}^{\theta}_{\eta,\lambda} f(z)\right)'} = 1 + e_1 \phi(z) + e_2 \phi^2(z) + \cdots \tag{10}$$

and

$$1 + \frac{2}{2\delta + 1} \frac{w\left(\mathcal{B}^{\theta}_{\eta,\lambda} f^{-1}(w)\right)''}{\left(\mathcal{B}^{\theta}_{\eta,\lambda} f^{-1}(w)\right)'} = 1 + e_1 \psi(w) + e_2 \psi^2(w) + \cdots. \tag{11}$$

Using (8)–(11), one obtains

$$1 + \frac{2}{2\delta + 1} \frac{z\left(\mathcal{B}^{\theta}_{\eta,\lambda} f(z)\right)''}{\left(\mathcal{B}^{\theta}_{\eta,\lambda} f(z)\right)'} = 1 + e_1 r_1 z + \left[e_1 r_2 + e_2 r_1^2\right] z^2 + \cdots \tag{12}$$

and

$$1 + \frac{2}{2\delta + 1} \frac{w\left(\mathcal{B}^{\theta}_{\eta,\lambda} f^{-1}(w)\right)''}{\left(\mathcal{B}^{\theta}_{\eta,\lambda} f^{-1}(w)\right)'} = 1 + e_1 s_1 w + \left[e_1 s_2 + e_2 s_1^2\right] w^2 + \cdots. \tag{13}$$

Since $|\phi(z)| < 1$ and $|\psi(w)| < 1$, $z, w \in \mathbb{D}$, we deduce

$$|r_j| \leq 1 \quad \text{and} \quad |s_j| \leq 1 \ (j \in \mathbb{N}). \tag{14}$$

In view of (12) and (13), after simplifying, we obtain

$$\frac{4\theta \Gamma(\eta + \theta)\Gamma(\lambda + 1)\Gamma(\eta + \lambda)}{(2\delta + 1)\Gamma(\eta + \theta + \lambda + 1)\Gamma(\eta)\Gamma(\lambda)} a_2 = e_1 r_1, \tag{15}$$

$$\frac{6\theta(\theta + 1)\Gamma(\eta + \theta)\Gamma(\lambda + 2)\Gamma(\eta + \lambda)}{(2\delta + 1)\Gamma(\eta + \theta + \lambda + 2)\Gamma(\eta)\Gamma(\lambda)} a_3 - \frac{8\theta^2 \Gamma^2(\eta + \theta)\Gamma^2(\lambda + 1)\Gamma^2(\eta + \lambda)}{(2\delta + 1)\Gamma^2(\eta + \theta + \lambda + 1)\Gamma^2(\eta)\Gamma^2(\lambda)} a_2^2 \tag{16}$$
$$= e_1 r_2 + e_2 r_1^2,$$

$$-\frac{4\theta \Gamma(\eta + \theta)\Gamma(\lambda + 1)\Gamma(\eta + \lambda)}{(2\delta + 1)\Gamma(\eta + \theta + \lambda + 1)\Gamma(\eta)\Gamma(\lambda)} a_2 = e_1 s_1 \tag{17}$$

and

$$\frac{6\theta(\theta + 1)\Gamma(\eta + \theta)\Gamma(\lambda + 2)\Gamma(\eta + \lambda)}{(2\delta + 1)\Gamma(\eta + \theta + \lambda + 2)\Gamma(\eta)\Gamma(\lambda)} \left(2a_2^2 - a_3\right) - \frac{8\theta^2 \Gamma^2(\eta + \theta)\Gamma^2(\lambda + 1)\Gamma^2(\eta + \lambda)}{(2\delta + 1)\Gamma^2(\eta + \theta + \lambda + 1)\Gamma^2(\eta)\Gamma^2(\lambda)} a_2^2 \tag{18}$$
$$= e_1 s_2 + e_2 s_1^2.$$

From (15) and (17), we derive inequality (5). Applying (7), then (15) and (16) become

$$\Upsilon a_2 = e_1 r_1, \quad \Phi a_3 - \Psi a_2^2 = e_1 r_2 + e_2 r_1^2 \tag{19}$$

which yields

$$\frac{\Phi}{e_1} a_3 = r_2 + \left(\frac{e_2}{e_1} + \frac{\Psi e_1}{\Upsilon^2}\right) r_1^2, \tag{20}$$

and on using the known sharp result ([28], p. 10):

$$|r_2 - \mu r_1^2| \leq \max\{1, |\mu|\} \tag{21}$$

for all $\mu \in \mathbb{C}$, we obtain

$$\left|\frac{\Phi}{e_1}\right||a_3| \leq \max\left\{1, \left|\frac{e_2}{e_1} + \frac{\Psi e_1}{Y^2}\right|\right\}. \tag{22}$$

Similarly, (17) and (18) become

$$-Y a_2 = e_1 s_1, \quad \Phi(2a_2^2 - a_3) - \Psi a_2^2 = e_1 s_2 + e_2 s_1^2. \tag{23}$$

These equalities provide

$$-\frac{\Phi}{e_1} a_3 = s_2 + \left(\frac{e_2}{e_1} - \frac{(2\Phi - \Psi)e_1}{Y^2}\right) s_1^2. \tag{24}$$

Applying (21), we deduce

$$\left|\frac{\Phi}{e_1}\right||a_3| \leq \max\left\{1, \left|\frac{e_2}{e_1} - \frac{(2\Phi - \Psi)e_1}{Y^2}\right|\right\}. \tag{25}$$

Inequality (6) follows from (22) and (25). □

Furthermore, we use the generating function (3) of the generalized Laguerre polynomials $L_n^\gamma(\tau)$ as $h(z)$. As a consequence, from (4), we obtain $e_1 = 1 + \gamma - \tau$ and $e_2 = \frac{\tau^2}{2} - (\gamma + 2)\tau + \frac{(\gamma+1)(\gamma+2)}{2}$, and then, Theorem 1 is reduced to the following corollary.

Corollary 1. *If $f \in \Sigma$ of the form (1) is in the class $\mathcal{F}_\Sigma(\delta, \eta, \lambda, \theta; H_\gamma(\tau, z))$, then*

$$|a_2| \leq \frac{(2\delta + 1)\Gamma(\eta + \theta + \lambda + 1)\Gamma(\eta)\Gamma(\lambda)|1 + \gamma - \tau|}{4\theta\Gamma(\eta + \theta)\Gamma(\lambda + 1)\Gamma(\eta + \lambda)} = \frac{|1 + \gamma - \tau|}{Y}$$

and

$$|a_3| \leq \min\left\{\max\left\{\left|\frac{1 + \gamma - \tau}{\Phi}\right|, \left|\frac{\frac{\tau^2}{2} - (\gamma + 2)\tau + \frac{(\gamma+1)(\gamma+2)}{2}}{\Phi} + \frac{\Psi(1 + \gamma - \tau)^2}{Y^2 \Phi}\right|\right\},\right.$$
$$\left.\max\left\{\left|\frac{1 + \gamma - \tau}{\Phi}\right|, \left|\frac{\frac{\tau^2}{2} - (\gamma + 2)\tau + \frac{(\gamma+1)(\gamma+2)}{2}}{\Phi} - \frac{(2\Phi - \Psi)(1 + \gamma - \tau)^2}{Y^2 \Phi}\right|\right\}\right\},$$

for all $\delta, \eta, \lambda, \theta$ such that $\frac{1}{2} \leq \delta \leq 1$ and $\eta, \lambda, \theta > 0$, where Y, Φ, Ψ are defined by (7) and $H_\gamma(\tau, z)$ is given by (3).

In the following theorem, we develop "the Fekete–Szegő Problem" for the family $\mathcal{F}_\Sigma(\delta, \eta, \lambda, \theta; h)$.

Theorem 2. *If $f \in \Sigma$ of the form (1) is in the class $\mathcal{F}_\Sigma(\delta, \eta, \lambda, \theta; h)$, then*

$$\left|a_3 - \eta a_2^2\right| \leq \frac{|e_1|}{\Phi} \min\left\{\max\left\{1, \left|\frac{e_2}{e_1} + \frac{(\Psi + \eta\Phi)e_1}{Y^2}\right|\right\}, \max\left\{1, \left|\frac{e_2}{e_1} - \frac{(2\Phi - \Psi - \eta\Phi)e_1}{Y^2}\right|\right\}\right\}, \tag{26}$$

for all $\delta, \eta, \lambda, \theta$ such that $\frac{1}{2} \leq \delta \leq 1$ and $\eta, \lambda, \theta > 0$, where Y, Φ, Ψ are defined by (7).

Proof. According to the notations from the proof of Theorem 1 and from (19) and (20), we obtain

$$a_3 - \eta a_2^2 = \frac{e_1}{\Phi}\left(r_2 + \left(\frac{e_2}{e_1} + \frac{(\Psi + \eta\Phi)e_1}{Y^2}\right)r_1^2\right). \tag{27}$$

Applying the well-known sharp result $|r_2 - \mu r_1^2| \leq \max\{1, |\mu|\}$, one obtains

$$\left|a_3 - \eta a_2^2\right| \leq \frac{|e_1|}{\Phi}\max\left\{1, \left|\frac{e_2}{e_1} + \frac{(\Psi + \eta\Phi)e_1}{Y^2}\right|\right\}. \tag{28}$$

Similarly, from (23) and (24), we derive

$$a_3 - \eta a_2^2 = -\frac{e_1}{\Phi}\left(s_2 + \left(\frac{e_2}{e_1} - \frac{(2\Phi - \Psi - \eta\Phi)e_1}{Y^2}\right)s_1^2\right) \qquad (29)$$

and in view of $|s_2 - \mu s_1^2| \leq \max\{1, |\mu|\}$, we get

$$|a_3 - \eta a_2^2| \leq \frac{|e_1|}{\Phi}\max\left\{1, \left|\frac{e_2}{e_1} - \frac{(2\Phi - \Psi - \eta\Phi)e_1}{Y^2}\right|\right\}. \qquad (30)$$

Inequality (26) follows from (28) and (30). □

Corollary 2. *If $f \in \Sigma$ of the form (1) is in the class $\mathcal{F}_\Sigma(\delta, \eta, \lambda, \theta; H_\gamma(\tau, z))$, then*

$$\begin{aligned}&\left|a_3 - \eta a_2^2\right|\\ &\leq \frac{|1 + \gamma - \tau|}{\Phi}\min\left\{\max\left\{1, \left|\frac{\frac{\tau^2}{2} - (\gamma + 2)\tau + \frac{(\gamma+1)(\gamma+2)}{2}}{1 + \gamma - \tau} + \frac{(\Psi + \eta\Phi)(1 + \gamma - \tau)}{Y^2}\right|\right\},\right.\\ &\left.\max\left\{1, \left|\frac{\frac{\tau^2}{2} - (\gamma + 2)\tau + \frac{(\gamma+1)(\gamma+2)}{2}}{1 + \gamma - \tau} - \frac{(2\Phi - \Psi - \eta\Phi)(1 + \gamma - \tau)}{Y^2}\right|\right\}\right\},\end{aligned}$$

for all $\delta, \eta, \lambda, \theta$ such that $\frac{1}{2} \leq \delta \leq 1$ and $\eta, \lambda, \theta > 0$, where Y, Φ, Ψ are given by (7) and $H_\gamma(\tau, z)$ is given by (3).

3. Conclusions

In the present survey, we considered a certain class of bi-univalent functions, denoted by $\mathcal{F}_\Sigma(\delta, \eta, \lambda, \theta; h)$, representable in the form of a Hadamard product of two power series. The coefficients of the first one, developed by Wanas and Al-Ziadi in [27], are beta negative binomial distribution probabilities. Furthermore, the Fekete–Szegő Problem was developed, by making use of the newly introduced family. Consequently, inequalities of Fekete–Szegő type were obtained in the special case of generalized Laguerre polynomials.

Author Contributions: Conceptualization, I.A.-S., A.K.W. and A.C.; Formal analysis, I.A.-S., A.K.W., A.C. and A.S.; Investigation, I.A.-S., A.K.W., A.C. and A.S.; Methodology, I.A.-S., A.K.W. and A.C.; Validation, I.A.-S., A.K.W. and A.C.; Writing—original draft, I.A.-S., A.K.W.; Writing—review and editing, I.A.-S., A.K.W. and A.C. All authors have read and agreed to the published version of the manuscript.

Funding: This research received no external funding.

Institutional Review Board Statement: Not applicable.

Informed Consent Statement: Not applicable.

Data Availability Statement: Not applicable

Conflicts of Interest: The authors declare no conflict of interest.

References

1. Duren, P.L. *Univalent Functions*; Grundlehren der Mathematischen Wissenschaften, Band 259; Springer: New York, NY, USA; Berlin/Heidelberg, Germany; Tokyo, Japan, 1983.
2. Srivastava, H.M.; Mishra, A.K.; Gochhayat, P. Certain subclasses of analytic and bi-univalent functions. *Appl. Math. Lett.* **2010**, *23*, 1188–1192. [CrossRef]
3. Ali, R.M.; Lee, S.K.; Ravichandran, V.; Supramaniam, S. Coefficient estimates for bi-univalent Ma-Minda starlike and convex functions. *Appl. Math. Lett.* **2012**, *25*, 344–351. [CrossRef]
4. Bulut, S.; Magesh, N.; Abirami, C. A comprehensive class of analytic bi-univalent functions by means of Chebyshev polynomials. *J. Fract. Calc. Appl.* **2017**, *8*, 32–39.

5. Srivastava, H.M.; Wanas, A.K.; Srivastava, R. Applications of the q-Srivastava-Attiya operator involving a certain family of bi-univalent functions associated with the Horadam polynomials. *Symmetry* **2021**, *13*, 1230. [CrossRef]
6. Akgül, A. (P,Q)-Lucas polynomial coefficient inequalities of the bi-univalent function class. *Turkish J. Math.* **2019**, *43*, 2170–2176. [CrossRef]
7. Al-Amoush, A.G. Coefficient estimates for a new subclasses of λ-pseudo biunivalent functions with respect to symmetrical points associated with the Horadam Polynomials. *Turk. J. Math.* **2019**, *43*, 2865–2875. [CrossRef]
8. Altınkaya, Ş. Inclusion properties of Lucas polynomials for bi-univalent functions introduced through the q-analogue of the Noor integral operator. *Turkish J. Math.* **2019**, *43*, 620–629. [CrossRef]
9. Cotîrlă, L.I. New classes of analytic and bi-univalent functions. *AIMS Math.* **2021**, *6*, 10642–10651. [CrossRef]
10. Güney, H.Ö.; Murugusundaramoorthy, G.; Sokół, J. Subclasses of bi-univalent functions related to shell-like curves connected with Fibonacci numbers. *Acta Univ. Sapient. Math.* **2018**, *10*, 70–84. [CrossRef]
11. Khan, B.; Srivastava, H.M.; Tahir, M.; Darus, M.; Ahmad, Q.Z.; Khan, N. Applications of a certain q-integral operator to the subclasses of analytic and bi-univalent functions. *AIMS Math.* **2021**, *6*, 1024–1039. [CrossRef]
12. Srivastava, H.M.; Motamednezhad, A.; Adegani, E.A. Faber polynomial coefficient estimates for bi-univalent functions defined by using differential subordination and a certain fractional derivative operator. *Mathematics* **2020**, *8*, 172. [CrossRef]
13. Wanas, A.K. Applications of (M,N)-Lucas polynomials for holomorphic and bi-univalent functions. *Filomat* **2020**, *34*, 3361–3368. [CrossRef]
14. Wanas, A.K.; Cotîrlă, L.-I. Initial coefficient estimates and Fekete–Szegö inequalities for new families of bi-univalent functions governed by $(p-q)$-Wanas operator. *Symmetry* **2021**, *13*, 2118. [CrossRef]
15. Wanas, A.K.; Cotîrlă, L.-I. Applications of $(M-N)$-Lucas polynomials on a certain family of bi-univalent functions. *Mathematics* **2022**, *10*, 595. [CrossRef]
16. Wanas, A.K.; Lupaş, A.A. Applications of Laguerre polynomials on a new family of bi-prestarlike functions. *Symmetry* **2022**, *14*, 645. [CrossRef]
17. Páll-Szabó, A.O.; Wanas, A.K. Coefficient estimates for some new classes of bi- Bazilevic functions of Ma-Minda type involving the Salagean integro-differential operator. *Quaest. Math.* **2021**, *44*, 495–502.
18. Amourah, A.; Frasin, B.A.; Murugusundaramoorthy, G.; Al-Hawary, T. Bi-Bazilevič functions of order $\vartheta + i\delta$ associated with (p,q)-Lucas polynomials. *AIMS Math.* **2021**, *6*, 4296–4305. [CrossRef]
19. Lebedev, N.N. *Special Functions and Their Applications*; Translated from the revised Russian edition (Moscow, 1963) by Richard A. Silverman; Prentice-Hall: Englewood Cliffs, NJ, USA, 1965.
20. Miller, S.S.; Mocanu, P.T. *Differential Subordinations: Theory and Applications*; Series on Monographs and Textbooks in Pure and Applied Mathematics; Marcel Dekker Inc.: New York, NY, USA, 2000; Volume 225.
21. Altınkaya, Ş.; Yalçin, S. Poisson distribution series for certain subclasses of starlike functions with negative coefficients. *Ann. Oradea Univ. Math. Fasc.* **2017**, *24*, 5–8.
22. El-Deeb, S.M.; Bulboaca, T.; Dziok, J. Pascal distribution series connected with certain subclasses of univalent functions. *Kyungpook Math. J.* **2019**, *59*, 301–314.
23. Nazeer, W.; Mehmood, Q.; Kang, S.M.; Haq, A.U. An application of Binomial distribution series on certain analytic functions. *J. Comput. Anal. Appl.* **2019**, *26*, 11–17.
24. Porwal, S. An application of a Poisson distribution series on certain analytic functions. *J. Complex Anal.* **2014**, *2014*, 984135. [CrossRef]
25. Porwal, S.; Kumar, M. A unified study on starlike and convex functions associated with Poisson distribution series. *Afr. Mat.* **2016**, *27*, 10–21. [CrossRef]
26. Wanas, A.K.; Khuttar, J.A. Applications of Borel distribution series on analytic functions. *Earthline J. Math. Sci.* **2020**, *4*, 71–82. [CrossRef]
27. Wanas, A.K.; Al-Ziadi, N.A. Applications of Beta negative binomial distribution series on holomorphic functions. *Earthline J. Math. Sci.* **2021**, *6*, 271–292. [CrossRef]
28. Keogh, F.R.; Merkes, E.P. A coefficient inequality for certain classes of analytic functions. *Proc. Am. Math. Soc.* **1969**, *20*, 8–12. [CrossRef]

Article

Geometric Study of 2D-Wave Equations in View of K-Symbol Airy Functions

Samir B. Hadid [1,2,†] and Rabha W. Ibrahim [3,*,†]

1. Department of Mathematics and Sciences, College of Humanities and Sciences, Ajman University, Ajman P.O. Box 346 00000, United Arab Emirates
2. Nonlinear Dynamics Research Center (NDRC), Ajman University, Ajman P.O. Box 346 00000, United Arab Emirates
3. Mathematics Research Center, Department of Mathematics, Near East University, Near East Boulevard, TRNC Mersin 10, Nicosia 99138, Turkey
* Correspondence: rabhawaell.ibrahim@neu.edu.tr
† These authors contributed equally to this work.

Abstract: The notion of k-symbol special functions has recently been introduced. This new concept offers many interesting geometric properties for these special functions including logarithmic convexity. The aim of the present paper is to exploit essentially two-dimensional wave propagation in the earth-ionosphere wave path using k-symbol Airy functions (KAFs) in the open unit disk. It is shown that the standard wave-mode working formula may be determined by orthogonality considerations without the use of intricate justifications of the complex plane. By taking into account the symmetry-convex depiction of the KAFs, the formula combination is derived.

Keywords: analytic function; inequalities; univalent function; open unit disk; symmetric differential operator; airy functions; normalization; complex wave equation; k-symbol calculus

MSC: 30C45; 30C15; 33C10

1. Introduction

When Diaz and Pariguan [1] were assessing Feynman integrals, they introduced and researched k-gamma functions. Because they provide a generic integral representation of the relevant functions, these integrals are fundamentally important in high-energy physics [2]. K-gamma functions have since been developed which have a variety of consequences for mathematics and applications. In light of significant applications in quantum chemistry, Karwowski and Witek [3] employed k-special functions for determining the solution of the complex Schrodinger equation for the harmonium and similar designs. In their collected papers, there is a great deal of attention to the theory of measurement and combination versions for the k-maximizing factorial numbers that are used as examples as well as to the combinatorics of the Pochhammer k-symbol.

K-gamma functions were employed for combination analysis by Lackner and Lackner [4] in light of significant applications in statistics. Applications of various k-gamma function types have eliminated the major concerns, and, as a result, multiple publications analyzing k-gamma functions have been made available. Fractional calculus plays a vital role in simulating real-world issues [5]. It is perhaps surprising that k-gamma functions and associated k-Pochhammer symbols are also used in the field of fractional calculus functions. Fractional kinetic equations, including k-Mittag–Leffler functions, have been solved by Agarwal et al. [6]. In [7], Set et al. employed the k-calculus equivalent of the Riemann–Liouville singular kernel. More in-depth discussion can be found in [8,9]. Review of the literature on k-gamma functions has led us to conclude that, on the one hand, k-gamma functions have stimulated the study of mathematical ideas using novel methods, and on

the other hand, that the application of these functions in diverse situations is fundamental. The k-symbol calculus has recently been proposed as a tool for modifying, generalizing, and analyzing classes of analytic functions, such as differential, integral, and convolution operators in the open unit disk [10–13].

Airy functions (AFs), which are the solutions of $\aleph''(\xi) - \xi\aleph(\xi) = 0$, and Legendre functions, are frequently used in place of the propagating wave functions in the approximate solution due to their asymptotic expansions. In their investigation on the optics of a raindrop, Olivier and Soares provided a thorough justification for the Airy hypothesis [14]. The theory of electromagnetic diffraction, the propagation of radio waves, the propagation of light, and physical optics are all fields in which AFs play a vital role. Additionally, they are often employed in research, as described in [15]. Applications of AFs are discussed in relation to the two characteristics of symmetry and convexity. Studies using radiation exploit the symmetry characteristic (see [16–18]). The convexity feature is used in lens research (see [19–21]).

To solve a complex k-symbol wave equation on the open unit disk, we use the characteristics of k-symbol Airy functions. We first give the k-symbol Airy functions in the normalized form in order to describe how the solution of the wave equation behaves. Investigation of the geometric characteristics is made easier by this. We establish that the normalized formula has several interesting special functions. We then locate the symmetry-convex representation of the KAFs to investigate the propagation of two-dimensional waves in a complicated domain. To acquire the univalent solution, which is crucial for solving the complex wave equation, we seek to demonstrate a set of necessary conditions. It is demonstrated that the fundamental working formula for the wave theory may be derived from orthogonality considerations without the need for a thorough explanation in the complex plane. The formula is coupled with consideration of the symmetry-convex representation of the KAFs. The approach is presented in Section 2, the findings are detailed and discussed in Section 3, and conclusions are drawn in Section 4.

2. Approaches

Different ideas that are considered in the conclusion are covered below.

2.1. Normalized Airy Function

The Airy functions are formulated by the integral structure

$$\aleph(\xi) = \int_{-\infty}^{+\infty} \exp(i[\xi t + t^3/3]) dt$$

achieving the power series

$$\aleph_1(\xi) = \left(\frac{1}{3^{2/3}\pi}\right) \sum_{n=0}^{\infty} \left(\frac{3^{n/3}\Gamma(\frac{n+1}{3})\sin\left(\frac{2(n+1)\pi}{3}\right)}{\Gamma(n+1)}\right) \xi^n$$

$$= \left(\frac{1}{3^{2/3}\pi}\right)\left(\Gamma(\frac{1}{3})\sin\left(\frac{2\pi}{3}\right)\right) + \left(\frac{1}{3^{2/3}\pi}\right)\left(3^{1/3}\Gamma(\frac{2}{3})\sin\left(\frac{4\pi}{3}\right)\right)\xi$$

$$+ \left(\frac{1}{3^{2/3}\pi}\right) \sum_{n=2}^{\infty} \left(\frac{3^{n/3}\Gamma(\frac{n+1}{3})\sin\left(\frac{2(n+1)\pi}{3}\right)}{\Gamma(n+1)}\right) \xi^n$$

$$= \frac{1}{(3^{2/3}\Gamma(2/3))} - \frac{\xi}{(3^{1/3}\Gamma(1/3))} + \frac{\xi^3}{(6 \times 3^{2/3}\Gamma(2/3))} - \frac{\xi^4}{(12(3^{1/3}\Gamma(1/3)))} + O(\xi^5)$$

and

$$\aleph_2(\xi) = \left(\frac{1}{3^{1/6}\pi}\right) \sum_{n=0}^{\infty} \left(\frac{3^{n/3}\Gamma(\frac{n+1}{3})\left|\sin\left(\frac{2(n+1)\pi}{3}\right)\right|}{\Gamma(n+1)}\right) \xi^n$$

$$= \left(\frac{1}{3^{1/6}\pi}\right)\left(\Gamma(\tfrac{1}{3})\left|\sin\left(\frac{2\pi}{3}\right)\right|\right) + \left(\frac{1}{3^{1/6}\pi}\right)\left(3^{1/3}\Gamma(\tfrac{2}{3})\left|\sin\left(\frac{4\pi}{3}\right)\right|\right)\xi$$

$$+ \left(\frac{1}{3^{1/6}\pi}\right) \sum_{n=2}^{\infty} \left(\frac{3^{n/3}\Gamma(\frac{n+1}{3})\left|\sin\left(\frac{2(n+1)\pi}{3}\right)\right|}{\Gamma(n+1)}\right) \xi^n$$

$$= \frac{1}{3^{1/6}\Gamma(2/3)} + \frac{3^{1/6}\xi}{\Gamma(1/3)} + \frac{\xi^3}{6 \times 3^{1/6}\Gamma(2/3)} + \frac{\xi^4}{4 \times 3^{5/6}\Gamma(1/3)} + O(\xi^5).$$

By setting $g(0) = 0$ and $g'(0) = 1$, we aim to normalize Airy functions. We can examine the geometrical structure of these functions using this technique. The normalized power series are as follows:

$$\mathbb{Y}_1(\xi) = \left(\frac{\aleph_1(\xi) - \left(\frac{1}{(3^{2/3}\Gamma(2/3))}\right)}{\left(-\frac{1}{(3^{1/3}\Gamma(1/3))}\right)}\right)$$

$$= \xi - \frac{\xi^3 \Gamma(1/3)}{(6(3^{1/3}\Gamma(2/3)))} + \cdots$$

$$:= \xi + \sum_{n=2}^{\infty} y_n \xi^n,$$

where

$$y_n := \left(\frac{3^{(n-1)/3}\Gamma(\frac{n+1}{3})\sin\left(\frac{2(n+1)\pi}{3}\right)}{\Gamma(\frac{2}{3})\sin\left(\frac{4\pi}{3}\right)\Gamma(n+1)}\right)$$

$$= -\frac{2 \times 3^{n-3/2} \sin(2/3\pi(n+1))\Gamma((n+1)/3)}{(\Gamma(2/3)\Gamma(n+1))};$$

and

$$\mathbb{Y}_2(\xi) = \left(\frac{\aleph_2(\xi) - \left(\frac{1}{3^{1/6}\pi}\right)\left(\Gamma(\tfrac{1}{3})\left|\sin\left(\frac{2\pi}{3}\right)\right|\right)}{\left(\frac{1}{3^{1/6}\pi}\right)\left(3^{1/3}\Gamma(\tfrac{2}{3})\left|\sin\left(\frac{4\pi}{3}\right)\right|\right)}\right)$$

$$= \xi + \sum_{n=2}^{\infty} \left(\frac{3^{(n-1)/3}\Gamma(\frac{n+1}{3})\left|\sin\left(\frac{2(n+1)\pi}{3}\right)\right|}{\Gamma(\tfrac{2}{3})\left|\sin\left(\frac{4\pi}{3}\right)\right|\Gamma(n+1)}\right) \xi^n$$

$$= \xi + \frac{\xi^3 \Gamma(1/3)}{(6 \times 3^{1/3}\Gamma(2/3))} + \cdots$$

$$= \xi + \sum_{n=2}^{\infty} |y_n| \xi^n.$$

2.2. K-Symbol Calculus

The k-symbol gamma function Γ_k, often known as the motivate gamma function, is formulated as follows [1]:

$$\Gamma_k(\xi) = \lim_{n \to \infty} \frac{n! k^n (nk)^{\frac{\xi}{k}-1}}{(\xi)_{n,k}},$$

where

$$(\xi)_{n,k} := \xi(\xi + k)(\xi + 2k) \ldots (\xi + (n-1)k)$$

and

$$(\xi)_{n,k} = \frac{\Gamma_k(\xi + nk)}{\Gamma_k(\xi)}.$$

Based on the definition of Γ_k, we present the normalized k-symbole functions as follows:

$$[\mathbb{Y}_1]_k(\xi) = \xi - \frac{\xi^3 \Gamma_k(1/3))}{(6(3^{1/3}\Gamma_k(2/3)))} + \ldots$$

$$:= \xi + \sum_{n=2}^{\infty} [y_n]_k \xi^n,$$

where

$$[y_n]_k := -\frac{2 \times 3^{n-3/2} \sin(2/3\pi(n+1))\Gamma_k((n+1)/3))}{(\Gamma_k(2/3)\Gamma_k(n+1))};$$

and

$$[\mathbb{Y}_2]_k(\xi) = \xi + \frac{\xi^3 \Gamma_k(1/3))}{(6 \times 3^{1/3}\Gamma_k(2/3))} + \ldots$$

$$= \xi + \sum_{n=2}^{\infty} |[y_n]_k| \xi^n.$$

The following outcomes demonstrate some characteristics of the k-symbol Airy functions (see Figure 1).

Proposition 1. *The following outcomes are accurate for k-special functions*

-

$$[\mathbb{Y}_1]_k(\xi) = \frac{G_k(4/3)3^{1/3}/G_k(1/3)}{G_k(5/3)3^{2/3}/G_k(2/3)}$$

$$- \frac{G_k(4/3)3^{1/3}/G_k(1/3)}{3} \left([I_{-1/3}]_k(\frac{2\xi^{3/2}}{3})(\xi^{3/2})^{1/3} - \frac{\xi[I_{1/3}]_k((2\xi^{3/2})/3))}{(\xi^{3/2})^{1/3}} \right),$$

where G_k is the k-Barnes function satisfying $G_k(n) = \frac{(\Gamma_k(n))^{n-1}}{\kappa(n)}$ (κ is the κ function) and $[I_n]_k(\xi)$ is the k-modified Bessel function.

-

$$[\mathbb{Y}_1]_k(\xi) = -\left(1/3[J_{-1/3}]_k(2/3(-\xi)^{3/2})((-\xi)^{3/2})^{1/3}\right)(G_k(4/3)3^{1/3}/G_k(1/3)$$

$$- \frac{G_k(4/3)3^{1/3}/G_k(1/3)}{G_k(5/3)3^{2/3}/G_k(2/3)} - \frac{\xi[J_{1/3}]_k(2/3(-\xi)^{3/2})(G_k(4/3)3^{1/3})/G_k(1/3)}{3((-\xi)^{3/2})^{1/3}},$$

where $[J_n]_k(\xi)$ indicates the k-Bessel function.

$$[\mathbb{Y}_2]_k(\xi) = \frac{\dfrac{\xi\,[_0F_1]_k(;4/3;\xi^3/9)3^{1/6}}{\Gamma_k(1/3)} - \dfrac{1}{\Gamma_k(2/3)3^{1/6}} + \dfrac{[_0F_1]_k(;2/3;\xi^3/9)}{\Gamma_k(2/3)3^{1/6}}}{3^{1/6}/\Gamma_k(1/3)},$$

where $[_0F_1]_k$ represents the k-hypergeometric function.

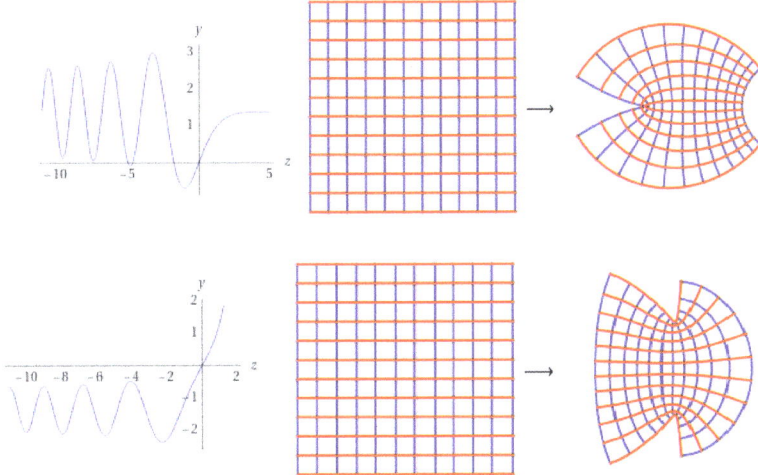

Figure 1. The graph of the normalized Airy functions $\mathbb{Y}_1$, $\mathbb{Y}_2$, respectively.

2.3. K-Airy Differential Operator

Using the normalized k-Airy functions, we then define the symmetric-convex differential operator. For an analytic function normalized in the open unit disk $\Lambda := \{\xi \in \mathbb{C} : |\xi| < 1\}$, we have the following structure:

$$v(\xi) = \xi + \sum_{n=2}^{\infty} a_n \xi^n,$$

The following power series is produced using the convoluted operator $(*)$ and the normalized Airy function $[\mathbb{Y}_1]_k(\xi)$

$$(v * [\mathbb{Y}_1])_k(\xi) = ([\mathbb{Y}_1]_k * v)(\xi) = \xi + \sum_{n=2}^{\infty} a_n [y_n]_k \xi^n, \quad \xi \in \Lambda.$$

By considering the above convoluted product, we define the following normalized k-Airy symmetric-convex differential operator (KASCO):

$$[\Omega_\beta]_k(\xi) = (1-\beta)\xi(v*[\mathbb{Y}_1]_k)'(\xi) - \beta\xi(v*[\mathbb{Y}_1]_k)'(-\xi)$$

$$= (1-\beta)\left(\xi + \sum_{n=2}^{\infty} na_n[y_n]_k \xi^n\right) - \beta\left(-\xi + \sum_{n=2}^{\infty} na_n[y_n]_k(-1)^n \xi^n\right)$$

$$= \xi + \sum_{n=2}^{\infty} na_n[y_n]_k[(1-\beta) + \beta(-1)^{n+1}]\xi^n$$

$$:= \xi + \sum_{n=2}^{\infty} na_n[y_n]_k \varpi_n(\beta)\xi^n \quad \xi \in \Lambda,$$

where
$$\omega_n(\beta) := [(1-\beta) + \beta(-1)^{n+1}].$$

The m-dimensional KASCO is illustrated as follows:

$$\begin{aligned}
[\Omega_\beta]_k^2(\zeta) &= [\Omega_\beta]_k([\Omega_\beta]_k)(\zeta) \\
&= (1-\beta)\zeta([\Omega_\beta]_k)'(\zeta) - \beta\zeta([\Omega_\beta]_k)'(-\zeta) \\
&= (1-\beta)\left(\zeta + \sum_{n=2}^\infty n^2 a_n[y_n]_k \omega_n(\beta)\zeta^n\right) - \beta\left(-\zeta + \sum_{n=2}^\infty n^2 a_n[y_n]_k \omega_n(\beta)(-1)^n\zeta^n\right) \\
&= \zeta + \sum_{n=2}^\infty n a_n[y_n]_k \omega_n(\beta)[(1-\beta) + \beta(-1)^{n+1}]\zeta^n \\
&= \zeta + \sum_{n=2}^\infty n^2 a_n[y_n]_k \omega_n^2(\beta)\zeta^n \quad \zeta \in \Lambda.
\end{aligned}$$

Generally, the m-formula is given by (see Figure 2)

$$[\Omega_\beta]_k^m(\zeta) = \zeta + \sum_{n=2}^\infty n^m a_n[y_n]_k \omega_n^m(\beta)\zeta^n \quad \zeta \in \Lambda. \tag{1}$$

Note that, under the consideration data $k=1, \beta=0$ and $[y_n]_k \approx 1$,, this implies the Salagean differential operator [22].

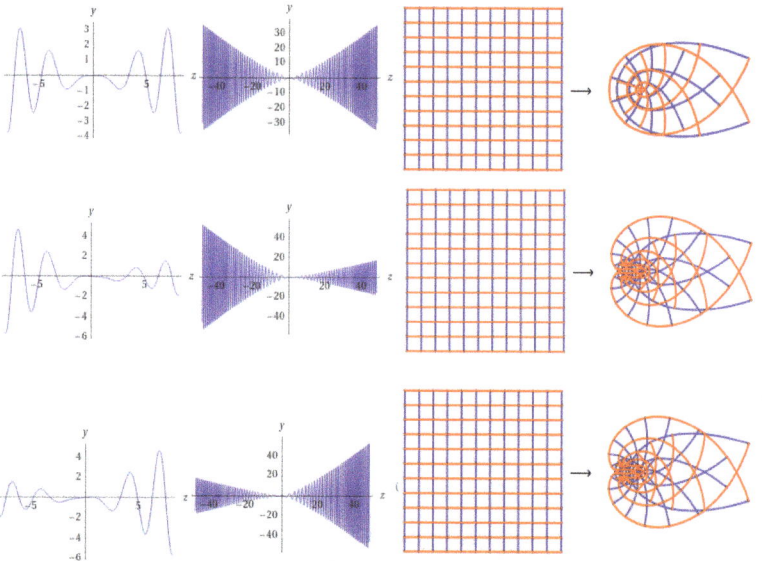

Figure 2. The graph of KASCO, when $m = k = 1, \beta = 1/2, 1/4, 3/4$ accordingly.

2.4. Univalent Solution of the k-Wave Equation

In an effort to develop the wave equation, we suggest utilizing the parametric Koebe function. The Koebe function is an extreme function that belongs to the family of convex univalent functions. The Koebe function $\sigma(\zeta) = \zeta/(1-\zeta)^2$ maps the unit disk conformally onto the complex plane $\mathbb{C}$ with a slit along the disk $|\zeta| < 1/4$. We utilize the rotate Koebe function of the structure

$$\sigma_t(\zeta) = \frac{\zeta}{(1-e^{it}\zeta)^2} = \zeta + \sum_{n=2}^\infty n e^{i(n-1)t}\zeta^n, \quad \zeta \in \Lambda.$$

The operator Ω_α^k acts on $\sigma(\xi)$, producing the following expansion

$$[\Omega_\beta]_k^m(\xi;t) = \xi + \sum_{n=2}^{\infty} n^{1+m} e^{i(n-1)t} [y_n]_k \varpi_n^m(\beta) \xi^n \quad \xi \in \Lambda. \tag{2}$$

Using the operator (2), we proceed to formulate the complex wave equation. The complex wave equation is considered in the formula

$$\left(\frac{\partial^2}{\partial t^2} + \varepsilon^2 \frac{\partial^2}{\partial \xi^2} \right) [\Omega_\beta]_k^m(\xi;t) = \Sigma(\xi), \tag{3}$$

where $[\Omega_\beta]_k^m(\xi;t)$ indicates the m-iterative wave amplitude in Λ with the convex parameter $\beta \in [0,1]$ and Σ is known as the non-linear functional of the wave under consideration owing $\Sigma(0) = 0$ and $\Sigma'(0) = 1$ (normalized function in Λ). A unique instance is examined in [23], when $\Sigma(\xi) = 0$ and $[\Omega_\beta]_k^m(\xi;t) = [\Omega_\beta]^m(\xi;t)$.

We provide a univalent outcome to the wave equation. The univalent result is significant in wave equations (see [24–27]). The wave peaks necessarily travel faster than the troughs and ultimately reach these levels since the solutions to the wave equations are known to be erroneous for infinite layers as they are not univalent functions. The primary requirement to achieve an analytic univalent solution fulfilling the inequality is covered in the next section $\Re([\Omega_\beta]_k^m(\xi;t)') > 0$ where $' = d/d\xi$). Alternatively, the answer is a complex domain Λ with a limited rotation function. In this instance, the gradients continue to increase, but eventually these effects start to occur, slowing this expansion. The precise behavior of the solution in Λ, which cannot be predicted from the wave equation, depends on the form of the dissipation components that are taken into account.

3. Results and Discussion

This section describes our findings for the univalent solution of Equation (3) for various hypotheses concerning Σ.

Proposition 2. *Consider Equation (3). If the operator $[\Omega_\beta]_k^m(\xi;t)$ fulfils the symmetrical inequality*

$$\Re\left(\frac{\xi [\Omega_\beta]_k^m(\xi;t)'}{[\Omega_\beta]_k^m(\xi;t) - [\Omega_\beta]_k^m(-\xi;t)} \right) > 0 \tag{4}$$

then $[\Omega_\beta]_k^m(\xi;t)$ is a univalent outcome for Equation (3).

Proof. The normalization formula of $[\Omega_\beta]_k^m(\xi;t)$ yields $[[\Omega_\beta]_k^m(0;t) = 0$ and $[\Omega_\beta]_k^m(0;t)' = 1$. Replacing $-\xi$ by ξ in the inequality (4), we get

$$\Re\left(\frac{\xi [\Omega_\beta]_k^m(-\xi;t)'}{[\Omega_\beta]_k^m(\xi;t) - [\Omega_\beta]_k^m(-\xi;t)} \right) > 0. \tag{5}$$

Combining inequalities (4) and (5), we receive

$$\Re\left(\frac{\xi ([\Omega_\beta]_k^m(-\xi;t)' - [\Omega_\beta]_k^m(-\xi;t)')}{[\Omega_\beta]_k^m(\xi;t) - [\Omega_\beta]_k^m(-\xi;t)} \right) > 0. \tag{6}$$

This shows that $[\Omega_\beta]_k^m(\xi;t) - [\Omega_\beta]_k^m(-\xi;t)$ is univalent in Λ. In view of the Kaplan Theorem of uni-valency [28], we obtain $[\Omega_\beta]_k^m(\xi;t)$ is a univalent outcome of Equation (3). □

Different conditions for $[\Omega_\beta]_k^m(\xi;t)$ to be univalently solvable are shown in the following outcomes.

Proposition 3. *For Equation (3), assume that the operator $[\Omega_\beta]_k^m(\xi;t)$ violates the relation*

$$\Re\big([\Omega_\beta]_k^m(\xi;t)' + \lambda(\xi)[\Omega_\beta]_k^m(\xi;t)''\big) > 0 \tag{7}$$

where $\lambda(\xi)$ is an analytic function in Λ with a non-negative real part. Then $[\Omega_\beta]_k^m(\xi;t)$ is a univalent outcome for Equation (3).

Proof. Assume that (7) is a true inequality. Formulate an admissible function $\Delta: \mathbb{C}^2 \to \mathbb{C}$, as follows:

$$\Delta(\rho,\varsigma) = \rho(\xi) + \lambda(\xi)\varsigma(\xi).$$

In view of the assumption (7), and by letting

$$\rho(\xi) := [\Omega_\beta]_k^m(\xi;t)', \quad \varsigma(\zeta) := \xi[\Omega_\beta]_k^m(\xi;t)'',$$

we have that

$$\Re\big(\Delta([\Omega_\beta]_k^m(\xi;t)', \xi[\Omega_\beta]_k^m(\xi;t)'')\big) > 0.$$

According to Theorem 5 of [29], we conclude that

$$\Re\big([\Omega_\beta]_k^m(\xi;t)'\big) > 0,$$

which leads to $[\Omega_\beta]_k^m(\xi;t)$ is a univalent solution of Equation (3). □

Extra conditions on $[\Omega_\beta]_k^m(\xi;t)$ to be univalent. The following outcome is a relation between $[\Omega_\beta]_k^m(\xi;t)$ and $\Sigma(\xi)$ in Equation (3).

Proposition 4. *Assume that Equation (3), where $\Sigma(\xi)$ is a bounded function in Λ, with*

$$\inf\left(\frac{\Sigma(\xi_1) - \Sigma(\xi_2)}{\xi_1 - \xi_2}\right) > 0, \quad \xi_1, \xi_2 \in \Lambda.$$

If

$$\left|\frac{\xi}{[\Omega_\beta]_k^m(\xi;t)} - \frac{\xi}{\Sigma(\xi)}\right| \leq \frac{2\inf\left(\frac{\Sigma(\xi_1)-\Sigma(\xi_2)}{\xi_1-\xi_2}\right)}{[\sup_{\xi\in\Lambda}(\Sigma(\xi))]^2};$$

which leads to $[\Omega_\beta]_k^m(\xi;t)$ is a univalent solution for Equation (3).

Proof. Let $[\Omega_\beta]_k^m(\xi;t) = \xi + \sum_{n=2}^\infty \vartheta_n \zeta^n$ and $\Sigma(\xi) = \xi + \sum_{n=2}^\infty \varphi_n \xi^n$. Formulate the function $F: \Lambda \to \Lambda$, as follows:

$$F(\xi) = \left[\frac{\xi}{[\Omega_\beta]_k^m(\xi;t)} - \frac{\xi}{\Sigma(\xi)}\right]''.$$

Clearly, $F(\xi)$ is analytic in Λ. Integrating both sides, we get

$$\left[\frac{\xi}{[\Omega_\beta]_k^m(\xi;t)} - \frac{\xi}{\Sigma(\xi)}\right]' = \varphi_2 - \vartheta_2 + \int_0^\xi F(\tau)d\tau.$$

Consequently, we have

$$\left[\frac{\xi}{[\Omega_\beta]_k^m(\xi;t)} - \frac{\xi}{\Sigma(\xi)}\right] = (\varphi_2 - \vartheta_2)\xi + \int_0^\xi ds \int_0^s F(\tau)d\tau.$$

Therefore, a calculation gives that

$$[\Omega_\beta]_k^m(\xi;t) = \frac{\Sigma(\xi)}{1 + (\varphi_2 - \vartheta_2)\Sigma(\xi) + \Sigma(\xi)(f(\xi)/\xi)},$$

where
$$f(\xi) = \int_0^{\xi} ds \int_0^s F(\tau) d\tau.$$

A calculation yields that
$$\left(\frac{f(\xi)}{\xi}\right)' = \frac{1}{\xi^2} \int_0^{\xi} t f''(t) dt - \frac{1}{\xi^2} \int_0^{\xi} \tau F(\tau) d\tau.$$

By virtue of the assumption, we have
$$\left| \frac{f(\xi_2)}{\xi_2} - \frac{f(\xi_1)}{\xi_1} \right| = \left| \int_{\xi_1}^{\xi_2} \left(\frac{f(\xi)}{\xi}\right)' d\xi \right|$$
$$\leq \left(\frac{2 \inf\left(\frac{\Sigma(\xi_1) - \Sigma(\xi_2)}{\xi_1 - \xi_2}\right)}{[\sup_{\xi \in \Lambda}(\Sigma(\xi))]^2} \right) \left(\frac{|\xi_2 - \xi_1|}{2} \right),$$

where $\xi_1 \neq \xi_2$. The next step is to prove that $[\Omega_\beta]_k^m(\xi_1;t) \neq [\Omega_\beta]_k^m(\xi_2;t)$ or
$$\left| [\Omega_\beta]_k^m(\xi_1;t) - [\Omega_\beta]_k^m(\xi_2;t) \right| > 0, \quad \xi_1 \neq \xi_2.$$

$$\left| [\Omega_\beta]_k^m(\xi_1;t) - [\Omega_\beta]_k^m(\xi_2;t) \right|$$
$$= \frac{\left| \Sigma(\xi_1) - \Sigma(\xi_2) + \Sigma(\xi_2)\Sigma(\xi_1)\left(\frac{f(\xi_2)}{\xi_2} - \frac{f(\xi_1)}{\xi_1}\right) \right|}{\left| 1 + (\varphi_2 - \vartheta_2)\Sigma(\xi_1) + \Sigma(\xi_1)\left(\frac{f(\xi_1)}{\xi_1}\right) \right| \left| 1 + (\varphi_2 - \vartheta_2)\Sigma(\xi_2) + \Sigma(\xi_2)\left(\frac{f(\xi_2)}{\xi_2}\right) \right|}$$
$$> \frac{|\Sigma(\xi_1) - \Sigma(\xi_2)| - \inf\left(\frac{\Sigma(\xi_1) - \Sigma(\xi_2)}{\xi_1 - \xi_2}\right)(\xi_2 - \xi_1)}{\left| 1 + (\varphi_2 - \vartheta_2)\Sigma(\xi_1) + \Sigma(\xi_1)\left(\frac{f(\xi_1)}{\xi_1}\right) \right| \left| 1 + (\varphi_2 - \vartheta_2)\Sigma(\xi_2) + \Sigma(\xi_2)\left(\frac{f(\xi_2)}{\xi_2}\right) \right|}$$
$$\geq 0.$$

Consequently, we obtain that $[\Omega_\beta]_k^m(\xi;t)$ is a univalent solution of Equation (3) in Λ. □

Some unique examples of Proposition 4 are as follows:

Corollary 1. *If*
$$\left| \left(\frac{\xi}{[\Omega_\beta]_k^m(\xi;t)}\right)'' \right| \leq 2,$$
then $[\Omega_\beta]_k^m(\xi;t)$ is a univalent solution.

Proof. By putting $\Sigma(\xi) = \xi$ in Proposition 4, we have the result. Note that this result is sharp when
$$[\Omega_\beta]_k^m(\xi;t) = \frac{\xi}{(1+\xi)^{2+\ell}},$$
where
$$\left| \left(\frac{\xi}{[\Omega_\beta]_k^m(\xi;t)}\right)'' \right| = (2+\ell)(1+\ell)(1+\xi)^\ell, \quad \ell > 0.$$

□

By Corollary 1, we have

Corollary 2. *If*
$$[\Omega_\beta]_k^m(\xi;t) = \frac{\xi}{1 + \sum_{n=1}^{\infty} b_n \xi^n},$$
where
$$\sum_{n=2}^{\infty} n(n-1)|b_n| \leq 2,$$
then $[\Omega_\beta]_k^m(\xi;t)$ *is a univalent solution.*

The concluding remarks are presented below.

Remark 1.
- *Solutions that are periodic exist because* $n-1$ *is an integer with Keobe function. Since individual modes do not necessarily have to be periodic, this restriction is not required. Instead, the value of t will be determined by the boundary conditions. Furthermore, it is asserted that* $\Re(t) > 0$ *without sacrificing generality, and special emphasis is given to solutions that behave as* $\exp(it)$. *The waves in the direction of positive t are attenuated in this way. The form of the waves traveling in the direction of negative t is the same (symmetric sense).*
- *The way in which the concept is developed here readily lends itself to many generalizations. This represents an intriguing situation when the height of the top border varies along the direction of propagation. The normalized analytic function is seen as a function of* $\xi \in \Lambda$ *to obtain the normalized univalent solution in the complex model under study.*
- *It may be anticipated that a waveguide with slowly changing characteristics will not differ greatly from a waveguide with a constant cross-section based on fundamental principles. The structure of the modes may be used to identify a normalized waveguide with a univalent function. The ideal ground conductivity is now standardized to a value that is very near to unity.*

4. Conclusions

A symmetric-convex differential formula of normalized Airy functions in the open unit disk was developed. This equation was taken into account as a differential operator working on a class of normalized analytic functions. The proposed operator (KASCO) was shown to be a solution to a wave equation in the following phase of this inquiry. We provided the necessary requirements for KASCO to be a univalent solution because we sought to analyze the geometric shape of the solution (symmetry and convexity). Based on the theory of the wave equation of a complex variable, the univalent solution is a particularly delicate property. Based on the theory of geometric functions, this characteristic leads to several geometric presentations for the solution.

Author Contributions: Conceptualization, R.W.I. and S.B.H.; methodology, R.W.I.; software, S.B.H.; validation, R.W.I. and S.B.H.; formal analysis, R.W.I.; investigation, S.B.H.; writing—original draft preparation, R.W.I. and S.B.H.; funding acquisition, S.B.H. All authors have read and agreed to the published version of the manuscript.

Funding: This research was funded by Ajman University Fund: 2022-IRG-HBS-8.

Institutional Review Board Statement: Not applicable.

Informed Consent Statement: Not applicable.

Data Availability Statement: Not applicable.

Conflicts of Interest: The authors declare no conflict of interest.

References

1. Diaz, R.; Pariguan, E. On hypergeometric functions and Pochhammer k-symbol. *Divulg. Math.* **2007**, *15*, 179–192.
2. Diaz, R.; Pariguan, E. Feynman-Jackson integrals. *J. Nonlinear Math. Phys.* **2006**, *13*, 365–376. [CrossRef]
3. Karwowski, J.; Witek, A.H. Biconfluent Heun equation in quantum chemistry: Harmonium and related systems. *Theor. Chem. Acc.* **2014**, *133*, 1494. [CrossRef]
4. Lackner, M.; Lackner, M. On the likelihood of single-peaked preferences. *Soc. Choice Welf.* **2017**, *48*, 717–745. [CrossRef] [PubMed]
5. Kilbas, A.A.; Srivastava, H.M.; Trujillo, J.J. *Theory and Applications of Fractional Differential Equations*; North-Holland Mathematical Studies; Elsevier (North-Holland) Science Publishers: Amsterdam, The Netherlands; London, UK; New York, NY, USA, 2006; Volume 204.
6. Agarwal, P.; Chand, M.; Baleanu, D.; O'Regan, D.; Shilpi, J. On the solutions of certain fractional kinetic equations involving k-Mittag-Leffler function. *Adv. Differ. Equ.* **2018**, *1*, 249. [CrossRef]
7. Set, E.; Tomar, M.; Sarikaya, M.Z. On generalized Grüss type inequalities for k-fractional integrals. *Appl. Math. Comput.* **2015**, *269*, 29–34. [CrossRef]
8. Diaz, R.; Teruel, C. q, k-generalized gamma and beta functions. *J. Nonlinear Math. Phys.* **2005**, *12*, 118–134. [CrossRef]
9. Diaz, R.; Pariguan, E. On the Gaussian q-distribution. *J. Math. Anal. Appl.* **2015**, *358*, 1–9. [CrossRef]
10. Mondal, S.R.; Mohamed, S.A. Differential equation and inequalities of the generalized k-Bessel functions. *J. Inequalities Appl.* **2018**, *2018*, 175. [CrossRef]
11. Seoudy, T.M. Some subclasses of univalent functions associated with k-Ruscheweyh derivative operator. *Ukrains' kyi Matematychnyi Zhurnal* **2022**, *74*, 122–136. [CrossRef]
12. Aktas, I. On monotonic and logarithmic concavity properties of generalized k-Bessel function. *Hacet. J. Math. Stat.* **2021**, *50*, 180–187. [CrossRef]
13. Guptaa, A.; Pariharb, C.L. Siago's K-Fractional Calculus Operators. *Malaya J. Mat.* **2017**, *5*, 494–504
14. Olivier, V.; Soares, M. *Airy Functions and Applications to Physics*; World Scientific Publishing Company: Singapore, 2010.
15. Valle'e, O. Some Integrals Involving Airy Functions and Volterra μ-Functions. *Integral Transform. Spec. Funct.* **2002**, *13*, 403–408. [CrossRef]
16. AAnikin, A.Y.; Dobrokhotov, S.Y.; Nazaikinskii, V.E.E.; Tsvetkova, A.V. Uniform asymptotic solution in the form of an Airy function for semiclassical bound states in one-dimensional and radially symmetric problems. *Theor. Math. Phys.* **2019**, *201*, 1742–1770. [CrossRef]
17. Minin, O.V.; Minin, I.V. Formation of a Photon Hook by a Symmetric Particle in a Structured Light Beam. In *The Photonic Hook*; Springer: Cham, Switzerland, 2021; pp. 23–37.
18. Chen, J.; Gao, L.; Jin, Y.; Reno, J.L.; Kumar, S. High-intensity and low-divergence THz laser with 1D autofocusing symmetric Airy beams. *Optics Express* **2019**, *27*, 22877–22889. [CrossRef]
19. Suarez, R.A.; Gesualdi, M.R. Propagation of Airy beams with ballistic trajectory passing through the Fourier transformation system. *Optik* **2020**, *207*, 163764. [CrossRef]
20. Len, M. Precise dispersive estimates for the wave equation inside cylindrical convex domains. *Proc. Am. Math. Soc.* **2022**, *150*, 12. [CrossRef]
21. Indenbom, M.V. Method for Calculation of the Interaction of Elements in a Large Convex Quasi-Periodic Phased Antenna Array. *J. Commun. Technol. Electron.* **2022**, *67*, 616–626. [CrossRef]
22. Salagean, G.S. Subclasses of univalent functions. In *Complex Analysis-Fifth Romanian-Finnish Seminar*; Springer: Berlin/Heidelberg, Germany, 1983; pp. 362–372.
23. Wait, J.R. Two-dimensional treatment of mode theory of the propagation of VLF radio waves. *Radio Sci. D* **1964**, *68*, 81–94. [CrossRef]
24. Broer, L.J.F.; Sarluy, P.H.A. On simple waves in non-linear dielectric media. *Physica* **1964**, *30*, 1421–1432. [CrossRef]
25. Ibrahim, R.W.; Meshram, C.; Hadid, S.B.; Momani, S. Analytic solutions of the generalized water wave dynamical equations based on time-space symmetric differential operator. *J. Ocean. Eng. Sci.* **2020**, *5*, 186–195. [CrossRef]
26. Ibrahim, R.W.; Baleanu, D. Symmetry breaking of a time-2D space fractional wave equation in a complex domain. *Axioms* **2021**, *10*, 141. [CrossRef]
27. Ibrahim, R.W.; Elobaid, R.M.; Obaiys, S.J. Generalized Briot-Bouquet differential equation based on new differential operator with complex connections. *Axioms* **2020**, *9*, 42. [CrossRef]
28. Kaplan, W. Close-to-convex schlicht functions. *Mich. Math. J.* **1952**, *1*, 169–185. [CrossRef]
29. Miller, S.S.; Mocanu, P.T. Second order differential inequalities in the complex plane. *J. Math. Anal. Appl.* **1978**, *65*, 289–305. [CrossRef]

Certain New Class of Analytic Functions Defined by Using a Fractional Derivative and Mittag-Leffler Functions

Mohammad Faisal Khan [1], Shahid Khan [2,*], Saqib Hussain [3], Maslina Darus [4] and Khaled Matarneh [5]

1. Department of Basic Science, College of Science and Theoretical Studies, Saudi Electronic University, Riyadh 11673, Saudi Arabia
2. Department of Mathematics, Abbottabad University of Science and Technology, Abbottabad 22500, Pakistan
3. Department of Mathematics, COMSATS University, Abbottabad Campus, Abbottabad 22060, Pakistan
4. Department of Mathematical Science, Faculty of Science and Technology, Universiti Kebangsaan Malaysia, Bangi 43600, Malaysia
5. Faculty of Computer Science, Arab Open University, Riyadh 11681, Saudi Arabia
* Correspondence: shahidmath761@gmail.com

Abstract: Fractional calculus has a number of applications in the field of science, specially in mathematics. In this paper, we discuss some applications of fractional differential operators in the field of geometric function theory. Here, we combine the fractional differential operator and the Mittag-Leffler functions to formulate and arrange a new operator of fractional calculus. We define a new class of normalized analytic functions by means of a newly defined fractional operator and discuss some of its interesting geometric properties in open unit disk.

Keywords: analytic functions; fractional derivative operator; Mittag-Leffler function; convolution

MSC: 05A30; 30C45; 11B65; 47B38

1. Introduction and Definitions

Let $\mathcal{A}$ denote the class of functions η of the form

$$\eta(z) = z + \sum_{n=2}^{\infty} a_n z^n, \tag{1}$$

which are analytic in the open unit disk

$$U = \{z \in \mathbb{C} : |z| < 1\}$$

and satisfy the normalization condition

$$\eta(0) = \eta'(0) - 1 = 0.$$

Furthermore, we denote by $\mathcal{S}$ the subclass of $\mathcal{A}$ consisting of functions of the form (1), which are also univalent in U.

For two functions $\eta, y \in \mathcal{A}$, we say that η subordinated to y, written as

$$\eta(z) \prec y(z),$$

or equivalently

$$\eta(z) = y(k(z)),$$

where, $k(z)$ is the Schwarz function in U along with the condition, (see [1])

$$k(0) = 0 \text{ and } |k(z)| < 1.$$

If y is univalent in U, then
$$\eta(z) \prec y(z) \iff \eta(0) = y(0) \text{ and } \eta(U) \subset y(U).$$
The majorization of two analytic function ($\eta \ll y$) if and only if
$$\eta(z) = k(z)y(z), \quad z \in U,$$
and also the coefficient inequality is satisfied
$$|a_n| \leq |b_n|.$$
There exists a wide formation between the subordination and majorization [2] in U for established different classes including the the class of starlike functions ($\mathcal{S}^*$):
$$\operatorname{Re}\left(\frac{z\eta'(z)}{\eta(z)}\right) > 0, \quad z \in U$$
and convex functions ($\mathcal{C}$):
$$1 + \operatorname{Re}\left(\frac{z\eta''(z)}{\eta'(z)}\right) > 0, \quad z \in U.$$
Related to classes $\mathcal{S}^*$ and $\mathcal{C}$, we define the class $\mathcal{P}$ of analytic functions $m \in \mathcal{P}$, which are normalized by
$$m(z) = 1 + \sum_{n=1}^{\infty} c_n z^n,$$
such that
$$\operatorname{Re} m(z) > 0 \text{ in } U \text{ and } m(0) = 1.$$
The convolution ($*$) of η and y, defined by
$$(\eta * y)(z) = \sum_{n=0}^{\infty} a_n b_n z^n,$$
where,
$$y(z) = \sum_{n=0}^{\infty} b_n z^n, \quad (z \in U).$$

Srivastava et al. [3] geometrically explored the class of complex fractional operators (differential and integral) and Ibrahim [4] provided the generality for a class of analytic functions into two-dimensional fractional parameters in U. Number of authors used these operators to illustrate various subclasses of analytic functions, fractional analytic functions and differential equations of complex variable [5–7].

Definition 1. *Pochhammer symbol* $(\alpha)_n$ *can be defined as:*
$$(\alpha)_n = \alpha(\alpha+1)\ldots(\alpha+n-1) \text{ if } n \neq 0$$
and
$$(\alpha)_n = 1 \text{ if } n = 0.$$

Definition 2. *The* $(\alpha)_n$ *can be expressed in terms of the Gamma function as:*
$$(\alpha)_n = \frac{\Gamma(\alpha+n)}{\Gamma(\alpha)}, \quad (n \in \mathbb{N}).$$

In [8], Mittag-Leffler introduced Mittag-Leffler functions $\mathcal{H}_\alpha(z)$ as:

$$\mathcal{H}_\alpha(z) = \sum_{n=0}^{\infty} \frac{1}{\Gamma(\alpha n + 1)} z^n, \ (\alpha \in \mathbb{C}, \ \mathrm{Re}(\alpha)) > 0,$$

and its generalization $\mathcal{H}_{\alpha,\beta}(z)$ introduced by Wiman [9] as:

$$\mathcal{H}_{\alpha,\beta}(z) = \sum_{n=0}^{\infty} \frac{1}{\Gamma(\alpha n + \beta)} z^n, \ (\alpha, \beta \in \mathbb{C}, \ \mathrm{Re}(\alpha), \mathrm{Re}(\beta)) > 0. \qquad (2)$$

Now we define the normalization of Mittag-Leffler function $\mathcal{M}_{\alpha,\beta}(z)$ as follows:

$$\mathcal{M}_{\alpha,\beta}(z) = z\Gamma(\beta)\mathcal{H}_{\alpha,\beta}(z)$$

$$\mathcal{M}_{\alpha,\beta}(z) = z + \sum_{n=2}^{\infty} \frac{\Gamma(\beta)}{\Gamma(\alpha(n-1)+\beta)} z^n, \qquad (3)$$

where, $z \in U$, $\mathrm{Re}\,\alpha > 0$, $\beta \in \mathbb{C}\setminus\{0,-1,-2,\ldots\}$).

A function $f \in \mathcal{A}$ is called bounded turning if it satisfies the condition

$$\mathrm{Re}\left(\eta'(z)\right) > 0.$$

For $0 \leq v < 1$, let $B(v)$ denote the class of functions η of the form (1), so that $\mathrm{Re}\left(\eta'\right) > v$ in U. The functions in $B(v)$ are called functions of bounded turning (c.f. [1], Vol. II). Nashiro–Warschowski Theorem (see, e.g., [1], Vol. I) stated that the functions in $B(v)$ are univalent and also close-to-convex in U. Now recall the definition of class $\mathcal{R}$ of bounded turning functions and can be defined as:

$$\mathcal{R} = \left\{\eta \in \mathcal{A} : \eta'(z) \prec \frac{1+z}{1-z}, \ z \in U\right\}.$$

In [3], Srivastava and Owa gave definitions for fractional derivative operator and fractional integral operator in the complex z-plane $\mathbb{C}$ as follows:

The fractional integral of order δ is defined for a function $\eta(z)$, by

$$I_z^\delta \eta(z) \equiv I_z^{-\delta}\eta(z) = \frac{1}{\Gamma(\delta)} \int_0^z (z-t)^{\delta-1} \eta(t) d(t), \ (\delta > 0).$$

The fractional derivative operator D_z of order δ is defined by

$$D_z^\delta \eta(z) = D_z I_z^{1-\delta} \eta(z)$$

$$= \frac{1}{\Gamma(1-\delta)} D_z \int_0^z \frac{\eta(t)}{(z-t)^\delta} d(t), \ (0 \leq \delta < 1).$$

where, the function $\eta(z)$ is analytic in the simply-connected region of the complex z-plane $\mathbb{C}$ containing the origin, and the multiplicity of $(z-t)^{-\delta}$ is removed by requiring $\log(z-t)$ to be real when $(z-t) > 0$.

Let $\delta > 0$ and m be the smallest integer, and the extended fractional derivative of $\eta(z)$ of order δ is defined as:

$$D_z^\delta \eta(z) = D_z^m I_z^{m-\delta} \eta(z), \ 0 \leq \delta, \ n > -1, \qquad (4)$$

provided that it exists. We find from (4) that is

$$D_z^\delta z^n = \frac{\Gamma(n+1)}{\Gamma(n+1-\delta)} z^{n-\delta}, \quad (0 \leq \delta < 1, n > -1)$$

and

$$I_z^\delta z^n = \frac{\Gamma(n+1)}{\Gamma(n+1-\delta)} z^{n+\delta}, \quad (0 < \delta, n > -1).$$

Owa and Srivastava [10], defined the differential integral operator $\Omega_z^\delta : \mathcal{A} \to \mathcal{A}$ in the term of series:

$$\Omega_z^\delta \eta(z) = \frac{\Gamma(2-\delta)}{\Gamma(2)} z^\delta D_z^\delta \eta(z) \tag{5}$$

$$= z + \sum_{n=2}^{\infty} \frac{\Gamma(2-\delta)\Gamma(n+1)}{\Gamma(2)\Gamma(n+1-\delta)} a_n z^n,$$

where,

$$(\delta < 2, \text{ and } z \in U).$$

Here, $D_z^\delta \eta(z)$ represents the fractional integral of $\eta(z)$ of order δ when $-\infty < \delta < 0$ and a fractional derivative of $\eta(z)$ of order δ when $0 \leq \delta < 2$.

Now, by using the definition of convolution on (3) and (5), we define fractional differential integral operator $\mathfrak{D}_z^{\delta,\alpha,\beta} : \mathcal{A} \to \mathcal{A}$, associated with normalized Mittag-Leffler function $\mathcal{M}_{\alpha,\beta}(z)$ as follows:

$$\mathfrak{D}_z^{\delta,\alpha,\beta} \eta(z) = z + \sum_{n=2}^{\infty} \left(\frac{\Gamma(2-\delta)\Gamma(n+1)}{\Gamma(2)\Gamma(n+1-\delta)} \right) \left(\frac{\Gamma(\beta)}{\Gamma(\alpha(n-1)+\beta)} \right) a_n z^n,$$

where,

$$(\delta < 2, \text{Re}\alpha > 0, \beta \in \mathbb{C} \setminus \{0, -1, -2, \ldots\}), z \in U.$$

It is noted that

$$\mathfrak{D}_z^{0,0,1} \eta(z) = \eta(z).$$

Again, by using fractional differential integral operator $\mathfrak{D}_z^{\delta,\alpha,\beta}$, we also define a linear multiplier fractional differential integral operator ${}_\beta^\alpha \Delta_\lambda^{\delta,m}$ as follows:

$${}_\beta^\alpha \Delta_\lambda^{\delta,m} \eta(z) = {}_\beta^\alpha \Delta_\lambda^{\delta,1} \left({}_\beta^\alpha \Delta_\lambda^{\delta,m-1} \eta(z) \right), \tag{6}$$

where,

$${}_\beta^\alpha \Delta_\lambda^{\delta,0} \eta(z) = \eta(z),$$

and

$${}_\beta^\alpha \Delta_\lambda^{\delta,1} \eta(z) = (1-\lambda) \mathfrak{D}_z^{\delta,\alpha,\beta} \eta(z) + \lambda z D \left(\mathfrak{D}_z^{\delta,\alpha,\beta} \eta(z) \right).$$

It is seen from $\eta(z)$ given by (1) and from (6), we have

$${}_\beta^\alpha \Delta_\lambda^{\delta,m} \eta(z) = z + \sum_{n=2}^{\infty} A(\lambda, \delta, \alpha, \beta, m, n) a_n z^n, \tag{7}$$

where,

$$A(\lambda, \delta, \alpha, \beta, m, n) = \left[\left(\frac{\Gamma(2-\delta)\Gamma(n+1)}{\Gamma(2)\Gamma(n+1-\delta)} \right) \left(\frac{\Gamma(\beta)}{\Gamma(\alpha(n-1)+\beta)} \right) (1 - \lambda + n\lambda) \right]^m$$

and

$$(\delta < 2, m \in \mathbb{N}, \lambda \geq 0, \text{Re}\alpha > 0, \beta \in \mathbb{C} \setminus \{0, -1, -2, \ldots\}), z \in U.$$

Remark 1. When, $\delta = 0$, $\alpha = 0$, and $\beta = 1$, in (7) then it is reduced to the operator given by Al-Oboudi [11].

Remark 2. For, $\delta = 0$, $\lambda = 1$, $\alpha = 0$, and $\beta = 1$ in (7) then it is reduced to the operator given by Salagean [12].

Definition 3. A function $\eta \in \mathcal{A}$, is in the class $_\alpha^\beta \mathcal{S}_\lambda^{*\delta,m}(\sigma)$ if and only if

$$_\alpha^\beta \mathcal{S}_\lambda^{*\delta,m}(\sigma) = \left\{ \eta \in \mathcal{A} : \frac{z\left(_\beta^\alpha \Delta_\lambda^{\delta,m}\eta(z)\right)'}{_\beta^\alpha \Delta_\lambda^{\delta,m}\eta(z)} \prec \sigma(z), \ \sigma(0) = 1 \right\}.$$

Definition 4. A function $\eta \in \mathcal{A}$, is in the class $_\beta^\alpha J_\lambda^{\delta,m}(L, M, b)$ if and only if

$$_\beta^\alpha J_\lambda^{\delta,m}(L, M, b) = \left\{ \eta \in \mathcal{A} : 1 + \frac{1}{b}\left(\frac{2\left(_\beta^\alpha \Delta_\lambda^{\delta,m}\eta(z)\right)}{_\beta^\alpha \Delta_\lambda^{\delta,m}\eta(z) - _\beta^\alpha \Delta_\lambda^{\delta,m}\eta(-z)} \right) \prec \frac{1+Lz}{1+Mz} \right\}.$$

The following lemmas will be use to prove our main results.

Lemma 1 ([13]). *For $\varrho \in \mathbb{C}$ and a positive integer n, the class of analytic functions is given by*

$$\mathcal{H}(\eta, n) = \left\{ \eta : \eta(z) = \varrho + \varrho_n z^n + \varrho_{n+1} z^{n+1} + \dots \right\}.$$

(i) Let $l \in \mathbb{R}$. Then

$$Re\left(\eta(z) + lz\eta'(z)\right) > 0 \longrightarrow Re(\eta(z)) > 0.$$

Moreover, $l > 0$ and $\eta \in \mathcal{H}(1, n)$, then there is constant $\delta > 0$ and $k > 0$, such that

$$k = k(l, \delta, n)$$

and

$$\eta(z) + lz\eta'(z) \prec \left(\frac{1+z}{1-z}\right)^k \longrightarrow \eta(z) \prec \left(\frac{1+z}{1-z}\right)^\delta.$$

(ii) For $\eta \in \mathcal{H}(1, n)$, and for fixed real number $l > 0$ and let $c \in [0, 1)$, so that

$$Re\left(\eta^2(z) + 2\eta(z)(zD\eta(z))\right) > c \longrightarrow Re(\eta(z)) > l.$$

(iii) Let $\eta \in \mathcal{H}(\eta, n)$, with $Re(\eta) > 0$, then

$$Re\left(\eta(z) + z\eta'(z) + z^2\eta''(z)\right) > 0,$$

or for $\mathbb{N} : U \to \mathbb{R}$, such that

$$Re\left(\eta(z) + \left(\frac{z\eta'(z)}{\eta(z)}\right)\mathbb{N}(z)\right) > 0.$$

Then

$$Re(\eta(z)) > 0.$$

2. Main Results

To make use of Lemma 1, first of all, we illustrate differential integral operator $_\beta^\alpha \Delta_\lambda^{\delta,m}\eta(z)$ is also bounded turning function.

Theorem 1. *Let $\eta \in A$, and*

(i) ${}^{\alpha}_{\beta}\Delta^{\delta,m}_{\lambda}\eta(z)$ *is of bounded turning function.*

(ii) $\left({}^{\alpha}_{\beta}\Delta^{\delta,m}_{\lambda}\eta(z)\right)' \prec \left(\dfrac{1+z}{1-z}\right)^k, \quad k > 0, \ z \in U.$

(iii) $Re\left(\left({}^{\alpha}_{\beta}\Delta^{\delta,m}_{\lambda}\eta(z)\right)'\left(\dfrac{{}^{\alpha}_{\beta}\Delta^{\delta,m}_{\lambda}\eta(z)}{z}\right)\right) > \dfrac{c}{2}, \quad c \in [0,1).$

(iv) $Re\left(z\left({}^{\alpha}_{\beta}\Delta^{\delta,m}_{\lambda}\eta(z)\right)'' - \left({}^{\alpha}_{\beta}\Delta^{\delta,m}_{\lambda}\eta(z)\right)' + 2\left(\dfrac{{}^{\alpha}_{\beta}\Delta^{\delta,m}_{\lambda}\eta(z)}{z}\right)\right) > 0.$

(v) $Re\left(\left(z\left({}^{\alpha}_{\beta}\Delta^{\delta,m}_{\lambda}\eta(z)\right)'/{}^{\alpha}_{\beta}\Delta^{\delta,m}_{\lambda}\eta(z)\right) + 2\left({}^{\alpha}_{\beta}\Delta^{\delta,m}_{\lambda}\eta(z)/z\right)\right) > 1.$

Then

$$\left(\dfrac{{}^{\alpha}_{\beta}\Delta^{\delta,m}_{\lambda}\eta(z)}{z}\right) \in \mathcal{P}(\lambda), \text{ for some } \lambda \in [0,1).$$

Proof. Define a function $m(z)$ as follows:

$$m(z) = \dfrac{{}^{\alpha}_{\beta}\Delta^{\delta,m}_{\lambda}\eta(z)}{z}, \quad z \in U. \tag{8}$$

Then computation implies that

$$zm'(z) + m(z) = \left({}^{\alpha}_{\beta}\Delta^{\delta,m}_{\lambda}\eta(z)\right)'.$$

From the first inequality (i), we have ${}^{\alpha}_{\beta}\Delta^{\delta,m}_{\lambda}\eta(z)$ is bounding turning function, and this give us

$$Re\left(zm'(z) + m(z)\right) > 0.$$

Thus, Lemma 1, part (i) implies that

$$Re(m(z)) > 0.$$

Hence (i) is proved. Accordingly, part (ii) is confirmed.

By the virtue of Lemma 1 and part (i), let $l > 0$, such that $k = k(l)$ and

$$\dfrac{{}^{\alpha}_{\beta}\Delta^{\delta,m}_{\lambda}\eta(z)}{z} \prec \left(\dfrac{1+z}{1-z}\right)^l.$$

This indicates that

$$Re\left(\dfrac{{}^{\alpha}_{\beta}\Delta^{\delta,m}_{\lambda}\eta(z)}{z}\right) > \lambda, \quad \lambda \in [0,1).$$

Suppose that

$$Re\left(m^2(z) + 2m(z).zm'(z)\right)$$

$$= 2Re\left(\dfrac{{}^{\alpha}_{\beta}\Delta^{\delta,m}_{\lambda}\eta(z)}{z}\left(\left({}^{\alpha}_{\beta}\Delta^{\delta,m}_{\lambda}\eta(z)\right)' - \dfrac{{}^{\alpha}_{\beta}\Delta^{\delta,m}_{\lambda}\eta(z)}{2z}\right)\right) > c, \quad c \in [0,1). \tag{9}$$

From the Lemma 1 and part (ii), there exists a fixed real number $l > 0$ and satisfying the condition
$$\operatorname{Re}(m(z)) > l$$
and
$$m(z) = \frac{{}_\beta^\alpha\Delta_\lambda^{\delta,m}\eta(z)}{z} \in \mathcal{P}(\lambda).$$

It follows from (9) that
$$\operatorname{Re}\left(\left({}_\beta^\alpha\Delta_\lambda^{\delta,m}\eta(z)\right)'\right) > 0.$$

Taking the derivative (8), we then obtain
$$\operatorname{Re}\left(m(z) + zm'(z) + z^2 m''(z)\right)$$
$$= \operatorname{Re}\left(z\left({}_\beta^\alpha\Delta_\lambda^{\delta,m}\eta(z)\right)'' - \left({}_\beta^\alpha\Delta_\lambda^{\delta,m}\eta(z)\right)' + 2\left(\frac{{}_\beta^\alpha\Delta_\lambda^{\delta,m}\eta(z)}{z}\right)\right) > 0.$$

Hence, Lemma 1 (ii) implies that
$$\operatorname{Re}\left(\frac{{}_\beta^\alpha\Delta_\lambda^{\delta,m}\eta(z)}{z}\right) > 0.$$

The logarithmic differentiation of (8) yields
$$\operatorname{Re}\left(m(z) + \frac{zm'(z)}{m(z)} + z^2 m''(z)\right)$$
$$= \operatorname{Re}\left(\frac{z\left({}_\beta^\alpha\Delta_\lambda^{\delta,m}\eta(z)\right)'}{{}_\beta^\alpha\Delta_{q,\lambda}^{\delta,m}\eta(z)} + 2\left(\frac{{}_\beta^\alpha\Delta_\lambda^{\delta,m}\eta(z)}{z}\right) - 1\right) > 0.$$

Hence, Lemma 1 (iii) implies, where $N(z) = 1$,
$$\operatorname{Re}\left(\frac{{}_\beta^\alpha\Delta_\lambda^{\delta,m}\eta(z)}{z}\right) > 0.$$

□

Now we find the upper bounds of the operator ${}_\beta^\alpha\Delta_\lambda^{\delta,m}\eta(z)$ by using the exponential integral in U, which provided $\eta \in \left({}_\alpha^\beta\mathcal{S}_\lambda^{*\delta,m}(\sigma)\right)$.

Theorem 2. Let $\eta \in \left({}_\alpha^\beta\mathcal{S}_\lambda^{*\delta,m}(\sigma)\right)$, where $\sigma(z)$ is convex in U. Then,

$${}_\beta^\alpha\Delta_\lambda^{\delta,m}\eta(z) \prec z\exp\int_0^z \frac{\sigma(\phi(w))-1}{w}dw, \tag{10}$$

where, $\phi(z)$ is analytic in U having condition
$$\phi(0) = 0 \text{ and } |\phi(z)| < 1.$$

Furthermore, for $|z| = \xi$, we have

$$\exp \int_0^1 \frac{\sigma(\phi(-\xi)) - 1}{w} d\xi \leq \left| \frac{{}^\alpha_\beta \Delta^{\delta,m}_\lambda \eta(z)}{z} \right| \leq \exp \int_0^1 \frac{\sigma(\phi(\xi)) - 1}{w} d\xi.$$

Proof. By the hypothesis we received the following conclusion:

$$\frac{z \left({}^\alpha_\beta \Delta^{\delta,m}_\lambda \eta(z) \right)'}{{}^\alpha_\beta \Delta^{\delta,m}_\lambda \eta(z)} \prec \sigma(z)$$

$$\frac{z \left({}^\alpha_\beta \Delta^{\delta,m}_\lambda \eta(z) \right)'}{{}^\alpha_\beta \Delta^{\delta,m}_\lambda \eta(z)} = \sigma(\phi(z)), \quad z \in U,$$

and

$$\frac{\left({}^\alpha_\beta \Delta^{\delta,m}_\lambda \eta(z) \right)'}{{}^\alpha_\beta \Delta^{\delta,m}_\lambda \eta(z)} - \frac{1}{z} = \frac{\sigma(\phi(z)) - 1}{z}. \tag{11}$$

Consequently, integrating (11), we obtain

$$\log \left(\frac{{}^\alpha_\beta \Delta^{\delta,m}_\lambda \eta(z)}{z} \right) = \int_0^z \frac{\sigma(\phi(w)) - 1}{w} dw. \tag{12}$$

By the definition of subordination we attain

$$ {}^\alpha_\beta \Delta^{\delta,m}_\lambda \eta(z) \prec z \exp \int_0^z \frac{\sigma(\Psi(w)) - 1}{w} dw.$$

Hence (10) is proved.

Note that the function $\sigma(z)$ convex and symmetric with respect to real axis. That is

$$\sigma(-\zeta|z|) \leq \text{Re}\{\sigma(\Psi(\xi z))\} \leq \sigma(\xi|z|) \quad (0 < \xi < 1, z \in U),$$

then we have the inequalities

$$\sigma(-\xi) \leq \sigma(-\xi|z|), \quad \sigma(\xi|z|) \leq \sigma(\xi).$$

Consequently, we obtain

$$\int_0^1 \frac{\sigma(\Psi(-\xi|z|)) - 1}{\xi} d\xi \leq \text{Re} \int_0^1 \frac{\sigma(\Psi(\xi)) - 1}{\xi} d\xi \leq \int_0^1 \frac{\sigma(\Psi(\xi|z|)) - 1}{\xi} d\xi.$$

In the sight of Equation (12), we obtain

$$\int_0^1 \frac{\sigma(\Psi(-\xi|z|)) - 1}{\xi} d\xi \leq \log \left| \frac{{}^\alpha_\beta \Delta^{\delta,m}_\lambda \eta(z)}{z} \right| \leq \int_0^1 \frac{\sigma(\Psi(\xi|z|)) - 1}{\xi} d\xi.$$

which implies that

$$\exp \int_0^1 \frac{\sigma(\Psi(-\xi|z|)) - 1}{\xi} d\xi \leq \left| \frac{{}^\alpha_\beta \Delta^{\delta,m}_\lambda \eta(z)}{z} \right| \leq \exp \int_0^1 \frac{\sigma(\Psi(\xi|z|)) - 1}{\xi} d\xi.$$

Hence, we have

$$\exp \int_0^1 \frac{\sigma(\Psi(-\zeta))-1}{\zeta} d\zeta \leq \left| \frac{{}_\beta^\alpha \Lambda_\lambda^{\delta,m} \eta(z)}{z} \right| \leq \exp \int_0^1 \frac{\sigma(\Psi(\zeta))-1}{\zeta} d\zeta.$$

□

Now we investigate the sufficient condition of η to be in the class ${}_\beta^\alpha \mathcal{S}_\lambda^{*,\delta,m}(\sigma)$, where σ is convex univalent satisfying $\sigma(0) = 1$.

Theorem 3. *If $\eta \in A$, satisfies the inequality*

$$\frac{z\left({}_\beta^\alpha \Delta_\lambda^{\delta,m} \eta(z)\right)'}{{}_\beta^\alpha \Delta_\lambda^{\delta,m} \eta(z)} \left(2 + \frac{z\left({}_\beta^\alpha \Delta_\lambda^{\delta,m} \eta(z)\right)''}{\left({}_\beta^\alpha \Delta_\lambda^{\delta,m} \eta(z)\right)'} \right) - \left(\frac{z\left({}_\beta^\alpha \Delta_\lambda^{\delta,m} \eta(z)\right)'}{{}_\beta^\alpha \Delta_\lambda^{\delta,m} \eta(z)} \right) \prec \sigma(z),$$

then, $\eta \in {}_\beta^\alpha \mathcal{S}_\lambda^{*,\delta,m}(\sigma)$.

Proof. Let

$$m(z) = \frac{z\left({}_\beta^\alpha \Delta_\lambda^{\delta,m} \eta(z)\right)'}{{}_\beta^\alpha \Delta_\lambda^{\delta,m} \eta(z)}$$

and $m(z) = 1$ in the inequality

$$m(z) + m(z)\left(zm'(z)\right) \prec \sigma(z),$$

then, we obtain

$$m(z) + m(z)\left(zm'(z)\right)$$
$$= \frac{z\left({}_\beta^\alpha \Delta_\lambda^{\delta,m} \eta(z)\right)'}{{}_\beta^\alpha \Delta_\lambda^{\delta,m} \eta(z)} \times \left(2 + \frac{z\left({}_\beta^\alpha \Delta_\lambda^{\delta,m} \eta(z)\right)''}{\left({}_\beta^\alpha \Delta_\lambda^{\delta,m} \eta(z)\right)'} - \left(\frac{z\left({}_\beta^\alpha \Delta_\lambda^{\delta,m} \eta(z)\right)'}{{}_\beta^\alpha \Delta_\lambda^{\delta,m} \eta(z)} \right) \right) \prec \sigma(z).$$

This implies that

$$m(z) = \frac{z\left({}_\beta^\alpha \Delta_\lambda^{\delta,m} \eta(z)\right)'}{{}_\beta^\alpha \Delta_\lambda^{\delta,m} \eta(z)} \prec \sigma(z),$$

that is

$$\eta \in \left({}_\beta^\alpha \mathcal{S}_\lambda^{*,\delta,m}(\sigma)\right).$$

□

Corollary 1. *Let the assumption of Theorem 3. Then,*

$$\frac{z\left({}_\beta^\alpha \Delta_\lambda^{\delta,m} \eta(z)\right)'}{{}_\beta^\alpha \Delta_\lambda^{\delta,m} \eta(z)} \times \left(1 + \frac{z\left({}_\beta^\alpha \Delta_\lambda^{\delta,m} \eta(z)\right)''}{\left({}_\beta^\alpha \Delta_\lambda^{\delta,m} \eta(z)\right)'} \right) - \left(\frac{z\left({}_\beta^\alpha \Delta_\lambda^{\delta,m} \eta(z)\right)'}{{}_\beta^\alpha \Delta_\lambda^{\delta,m} \eta(z)} \right) \ll \sigma'(z).$$

Proof. Let

$$m(z) = \frac{z\left({}_\beta^\alpha \Delta_\lambda^{\delta,m} \eta(z)\right)'}{{}_\beta^\alpha \Delta_\lambda^{\delta,m} \eta(z)}.$$

In the view of Theorem 3, we have

$$\frac{z\left({}^{\alpha}_{\beta}\Delta^{\delta,m}_{\lambda}\eta(z)\right)'}{{}^{\alpha}_{\beta}\Delta^{\delta,m}_{\lambda}\eta(z)} \prec \sigma(z),$$

where, $\sigma \in \mathbb{C}$. Then, by [2] (Theorem 3), we obtain

$$m'(z) \ll \sigma'(z)$$

for some $z \in U$, where

$$m'(z) = \frac{z\left({}^{\alpha}_{\beta}\Delta^{\delta,m}_{\lambda}\eta(z)\right)'}{{}^{\alpha}_{\beta}\Delta^{\delta,m}_{\lambda}\eta(z)}\left(1 + \frac{z\left({}^{\alpha}_{\beta}\Delta^{\delta,m}_{\lambda}\eta(z)\right)''}{\left({}^{\alpha}_{\beta}\Delta^{\delta,m}_{\lambda}\eta(z)\right)'} - \frac{z\left({}^{\alpha}_{\beta}\Delta^{\delta,m}_{\lambda}\eta(z)\right)'}{{}^{\alpha}_{\beta}\Delta^{\delta,m}_{\lambda}\eta(z)}\right).$$

□

It is well known that the function $\sigma(z) = e^{\theta z}$, $1 < |\theta| \leq \frac{\pi}{2}$ is not convex in U, where the domain $\sigma(U)$ is lima-bean (see [13], p. 123). Now, we can find the same result of Theorem 3 as follows:

Theorem 4. *If $\eta \in A$, it satisfies the inequality*

$$1 + \frac{z\left({}^{\alpha}_{\beta}\Delta^{\delta,m}_{\lambda}\eta(z)\right)''}{\left({}^{\alpha}_{\beta}\Delta^{\delta,m}_{\lambda}\eta(z)\right)'} \prec e^{\theta z}.$$

Then,

$$\eta \in \left({}^{\alpha}_{\beta}\mathcal{S}^{*,\delta,m}_{\lambda}(e^{\theta z})\right).$$

Proof. Let

$$m(z) = \frac{z\left({}^{\alpha}_{\beta}\Delta^{\delta,m}_{\lambda}\eta(z)\right)'}{{}^{\alpha}_{\beta}\Delta^{\delta,m}_{\lambda}\eta(z)}.$$

After some simple computation implies that

$$m(z) + \frac{zm'(z)}{m(z)}$$

$$= \left(\frac{z\left({}^{\alpha}_{\beta}\Delta^{\delta,m}_{\lambda}\eta(z)\right)'}{{}^{\alpha}_{\beta}\Delta^{\delta,m}_{\lambda}\eta(z)}\right) + \frac{\left(\frac{z\left({}^{\alpha}_{\beta}\Delta^{\delta,m}_{\lambda}\eta(z)\right)'}{{}^{\alpha}_{\beta}\Delta^{\delta,m}_{\lambda}\eta(z)}\right)\left(1 + \frac{z\left({}^{\alpha}_{\beta}\Delta^{\delta,m}_{\lambda}\eta(z)\right)''}{\left({}^{\alpha}_{\beta}\Delta^{\delta,m}_{\lambda}\eta(z)\right)'} - \frac{z\left({}^{\alpha}_{\beta}\Delta^{\delta,m}_{\lambda}\eta(z)\right)'}{{}^{\alpha}_{\beta}\Delta^{\delta,m}_{\lambda}\eta(z)}\right)}{\frac{z\left({}^{\alpha}_{\beta}\Delta^{\delta,m}_{\lambda}\eta(z)\right)'}{{}^{\alpha}_{\beta}\Delta^{\delta,m}_{\lambda}\eta(z)}}$$

$$= \left(1 + \frac{z\left({}^{\alpha}_{\beta}\Delta^{\delta,m}_{\lambda}\eta(z)\right)''}{\left({}^{\alpha}_{\beta}\Delta^{\delta,m}_{\lambda}\eta(z)\right)'}\right) \prec e^{\theta z}.$$

This implies that (see [13], p. 123)

$$m(z) = \frac{z\left({}^{\alpha}_{\beta}\Delta^{\delta,m}_{\lambda}\eta(z)\right)'}{{}^{\alpha}_{\beta}\Delta^{\delta,m}_{\lambda}\eta(z)} \prec e^{\theta z},$$

that is
$$\eta \in \left({}_{\beta}^{\alpha}S_{\lambda}^{*,\delta,m}(e^{\theta z})\right).$$

□

Theorem 5. *If* $\eta \in \left({}_{\beta}^{\alpha}J_{\lambda}^{\delta,m}(L,M,b)\right)$, *then*
$$\mathcal{M}(z) = \frac{1}{2}[\eta(z) - \eta(-z)]$$

satisfies
$$1 + \frac{1}{b}\left(\frac{z\left({}_{\beta}^{\alpha}\Delta_{\lambda}^{\delta,m}\mathcal{B}(z)\right)'}{\left({}_{\beta}^{\alpha}\Delta_{\lambda}^{\delta,m}\mathcal{B}(z)\right)}\right) \prec \frac{1+Lz}{1+Mz},$$

$$Re\left(\frac{z\mathcal{B}'(z)}{\mathcal{B}(z)}\right) \geq \frac{1-\vartheta^2}{1+\vartheta^2}, \quad |z| = \vartheta < 1.$$

Proof. Let $\eta \in \left({}_{\beta}^{\alpha}J_{\lambda}^{\delta,m}(L,M,b)\right)$, then there occurs a function $J(z)$ such that

$$b(J(z)-1) = \frac{2z\left({}_{\beta}^{\alpha}\Delta_{\lambda}^{\delta,m}\eta(z)\right)'}{{}_{\beta}^{\alpha}\Delta_{\lambda}^{\delta,m}\eta(z) - {}_{\beta}^{\alpha}\Delta_{\lambda}^{\delta,m}\eta(-z)},$$

$$b(J(-z)-1) = \frac{2z\left({}_{\beta}^{\alpha}\Delta_{\lambda}^{\delta,m}\eta(-z)\right)'}{{}_{\beta}^{\alpha}\Delta_{q,\lambda}^{\delta,m}\eta(-z) - {}_{\beta}^{\alpha}\Delta_{q,\lambda}^{\delta,m}\eta(z)}.$$

This confirm that
$$1 + \frac{1}{b}\left(\frac{z\left({}_{\beta}^{\alpha}\Delta_{\lambda}^{\delta,m}\mathcal{G}(z)\right)'}{\left({}_{\beta}^{\alpha}\Delta_{\lambda}^{\delta,m}\mathcal{G}(z)\right)} - 1\right) = \frac{J(z) + J(-z)}{2}.$$

However, J satisfies
$$J(z) \prec \frac{1+Lz}{1+Mz},$$

which is univalent, then we get
$$1 + \frac{1}{b}\left(\frac{z\left({}_{\beta}^{\alpha}\Delta_{\lambda}^{\delta,m}\mathcal{G}(z)\right)'}{{}_{\beta}^{\alpha}\Delta_{\lambda}^{\delta,m}\mathcal{G}(z)} - 1\right) \prec \frac{1+Lz}{1+Mz}.$$

Additionally, $\mathcal{G}(z)$ is starlike in z, and which implies that
$$h(z) = \frac{z\mathcal{G}(z)'}{\mathcal{G}(z)} \prec \frac{1-z^2}{1+z^2}.$$

Hence, their exist a Schwarz function $w(z)$, such that $|w(z)| \leq |z| < 1$, $k(0) = 0$, we get
$$h(z) \prec \frac{1-w(z)^2}{1+w(z)^2},$$

which leads to
$$w(\zeta)^2 = \frac{1-h(\zeta)}{1+h(\zeta)}, \quad \zeta \in z, \ |\zeta| = r < 1.$$

A simple calculation yields

$$\left|\frac{1-h(\zeta)}{1+h(\zeta)}\right| = |w(\zeta)|^2 \leq |\zeta|^2.$$

Therefore, we get the following inequalities:

$$\left|h(\zeta) - \frac{1+|\zeta|^4}{1-|\zeta|^4}\right|^2 \leq \frac{4|\zeta|^4}{\left(1-|\zeta|^4\right)^2},$$

$$\left|h(\zeta) - \frac{1+|\zeta|^4}{1-|\zeta|^4}\right| \leq \frac{2|\zeta|^2}{\left(1-|\zeta|^4\right)}.$$

Thus, we have

$$\mathrm{Re}\left(\frac{z\mathcal{G}'(z)}{\mathcal{G}(z)}\right) \geq \frac{1-\vartheta^2}{1+\vartheta^2}, \quad |\zeta| = \vartheta < 1.$$

This completes the proof of Theorem 5. □

Example 1. *Let*

$$\frac{z\eta'(z)}{\eta(z)} = \frac{z\left({}_{\beta}^{\alpha}\Delta_{\lambda}^{\delta,m}\eta(z)\right)'}{{}_{\beta}^{\alpha}\Delta_{\lambda}^{\delta,m}\eta(z)},$$

$$ {}_{\beta}^{\alpha}\Delta_{\lambda}^{\delta,m}\eta(z) = \frac{z}{(1-z)^2}, \quad \eta \in \mathcal{A}.$$

Then the solution of $\frac{z\eta'(z)}{\eta(z)} = \frac{1+z}{1-z}$ is formulated as follows:

$$ {}_{\beta}^{\alpha}\Delta_{\lambda}^{\delta,m}\eta(z) = \frac{z}{(1-z)^2}, \quad \eta \in \mathcal{A}.$$

Moreover, the solution of the equation

$$\eta(z) + \frac{z\eta'(z)}{\eta(z)} = \frac{1+z}{1-z}$$

is approximated to

$$\eta(z) = \frac{z}{1-z}.$$

3. Conclusions

Many researchers have discussed some applications of fractional differential operator in different areas of mathematics. In this paper, we combined fractional differential operator and the Mittag-Leffler functions and formulated a new operator of fractional calculus for a class of normalized functions in the open unit disk. We considered this operator on the two classes of analytic functions and investigated some of its applications in the field of geometric function theory. The suggested operator can be utilized to define some more classes of analytic functions or to generalize other types of differential operators.

Author Contributions: Conceptualization, S.K. and M.D.; data curation, K.M.; formal analysis, S.K. and K.M.; investigation, M.F.K.; methodology, M.F.K. and M.D.; supervision, S.H.; visualization, S.H.; writing—original draft, S.H.; writing—review and editing, M.D. All authors have read and agreed to the published version of the manuscript.

Funding: This study supported by UKM, under grant number: FRGS/1/2019/STG06/UKM/01/.

Data Availability Statement: No data were used to support this study.

Conflicts of Interest: The authors declare no conflict of interest.

References

1. Goodman, A.W. *Univalent Functions*; Polygonal Publishing House: Washington, NJ, USA, 1983; Volumes I–II.
2. Campbell, D.M. Majorization-subordination theorems for locally univalent functions, II. *Can. J. Math.* **1973**, *25*, 420–425. [CrossRef]
3. Srivastava, H.M.; Owa, S. (Eds.) Univalent functions, fractional calculus, and associated generalized hypergeometric functions. In *Univalent Functions, Fractional Calculus, and Their Applications*; John Wiley & Sons: New York, NY, USA, 1989.
4. Ibrahim, R.W. On generalized Srivastava-Owa fractional operators in the unit disk. *Adv. Differ. Equ.* **2011**, *2011*, 55. [CrossRef]
5. Ibrahim, R.W. Ulam stability for fractional differential equation in complex domain. *Abstr. Appl. Anal.* **2012**, *2012*, 649517. [CrossRef]
6. Ibrahim, R.W. Generalized Ulam-Hyers stability for fractional differential equations. *Int. J. Math.* **2012**, *23*, 1250056. [CrossRef]
7. Srivastava, H.M.; Darus, M.; Ibrahim, R.W. Classes of analytic functions with fractional powers defined by means of a certain linear operators. *Integral Transform. Spec. Funct.* **2011**, *22*, 17–28. [CrossRef]
8. Mittag-Leffler, G.M. Sur la nouvelle fonction $E_\alpha(x)$. *Comptes Rendus Acad. Sci. Paris* 1903, *137*, 554–558.
9. Wiman, A. Uber den fundamentalsatz in der teorie der funktionen $E(x)$. *Acta Math.* **1905**, *29*, 191–201. [CrossRef]
10. Owa, S.; Srivastava, H.M. Univalent and starlike generalized hypergeometric functions. *Can. J. Math.* **1987**, *39*, 1057–1077. [CrossRef]
11. Al-Oboudi, F.M. On univalent functions defined by a generalized Salagean operator. *Int. J. Math. Math. Sci.* **2004**, *2004*, 172525. [CrossRef]
12. Salagean, G.S. Subclasses of univalent functions. In *Complex Analysis—Fifth Romanian-Finnish Seminar, Part 1*; Lecture Notes in Mathematics; Springer: Berlin/Heidelberg, Germany, 1981; Volume 1013, pp. 362–372.
13. Miller, S.S.; Mocanu, P.T. *Differential Subordinations: Theory and Applications*; CRC Press: Boca Raton, FL, USA, 2000.

MDPI
St. Alban-Anlage 66
4052 Basel
Switzerland
Tel. +41 61 683 77 34
Fax +41 61 302 89 18
www.mdpi.com

Axioms Editorial Office
E-mail: axioms@mdpi.com
www.mdpi.com/journal/axioms

www.ingramcontent.com/pod-product-compliance
Lightning Source LLC
LaVergne TN
LVHW070717100526
838202LV00013B/1116